3/94

Authors & Artists for Young Adults

ISSN 1040-5682

Authors & Artists for Young Adults

VOLUME 12

**Kevin S. Hile,
Editor**

Gale Research Inc. • DETROIT • WASHINGTON, D.C. • LONDON

Kevin S. Hile, *Editor*

Joanna Brod, David M. Galens, Jeff Hill, Thomas F. McMahon, Terrie M. Rooney, Kenneth R. Shepherd, and Roger M. Valade III, *Associate Editors*

Hazel K. Davis, Ronie-Richele Garcia-Johnson, Joan Goldsworthy, Marian C. Gonsior, Helene Henderson, Laurie Collier Hillstrom, Anne Janette Johnson, Keith Lawrence, Tom Pendergast, Jani Prescott, Nancy E. Rampson, Marion M. Shepherd, and Laura M. Zaidman, *Sketch Contributors*

Victoria B. Cariappa, *Research Manager*
Mary Rose Bonk, *Research Supervisor*

Reginald A. Carlton, Andrew Guy Malonis, and Norma Sawaya, *Editorial Associates*

Laurel Sprague Bowden, Rachel A. Dixon, Eva Marie Felts, Shirley Gates, Doris Lewandowski, Sharon McGilvray, Dana R. Schleiffers, and Amy B. Wieczorek, *Editorial Assistants*

Margaret A. Chamberlain, *Picture Permissions Supervisor*

Pamela A. Hayes and Keith Reed, *Permissions Associates*

Susan Brohman, Arlene Johnson, and Barbara A. Wallace, *Permissions Assistants*

Mary Beth Trimper, *Production Director*
Catherine Kemp, *External Production Assistant*

Cynthia Baldwin, *Art Director*
Sherrell Hobbs and C. J. Jonik, *Desktop Publishers/Typesetters*
Willie Mathis, *Camera Operator*

The paper used in this publication meets the minimum requirements of American National Standard for Information Sciences—Permanence Paper for Printed Library Materials, ANSI Z39.48-1984.

Library of Congress Catalog Card Number 89-641100
ISBN 0-8103-8565-1
ISSN 1040-5682

10 9 8 7 6 5 4 3 2 1

Printed in the United States of America

Published simultaneously in the United Kingdom
by Gale Research International Limited
(An affiliated company of Gale Research Inc.)

The trademark **ITP** is used under license.

Authors and Artists for Young Adults
NATIONAL ADVISORY BOARD

Contents

Introduction

Authors and Artists for Young Adults is a reference series designed to serve the needs of middle school, junior high, and high school students interested in creative artists. Originally inspired by the need to bridge the gap between Gale's *Something about the Author*, created for children, and *Contemporary Authors*, intended for older students and adults, *Authors and Artists for Young Adults* has been expanded to cover not only an international scope of authors, but also a wide variety of other artists.

Although the emphasis of the series remains on the writer for young adults, we recognize that these readers have diverse interests covering a wide range of reading levels. The series therefore contains not only those creative artists who are of high interest to young adults, including cartoonists, photographers, music composers, bestselling authors of adult novels, media directors, producers, and performers, but also literary and artistic figures studied in academic curricula, such as influential novelists, playwrights, poets, and painters. The goal of *Authors and Artists for Young Adults* is to present this great diversity of creative artists in a format that is entertaining, informative, and understandable to the young adult reader.

Entry Format

Each volume of *Authors and Artists for Young Adults* will furnish in-depth coverage of about twenty to twenty-five authors and artists. The typical entry consists of:

— A detailed biographical section that includes date of birth, marriage, children, education, and addresses.

— A comprehensive bibliography or filmography including publishers, producers, and years.

— Adaptations into other media forms.

— Works in progress.

— A distinctive essay featuring comments on an artist's life, career, artistic intentions, world views, and controversies.

— References for further reading.

— Extensive illustrations, photographs, movie stills, cartoons, book covers, and other relevant visual material.

A cumulative index to featured authors and artists appears in each volume.

Compilation Methods

The editors of *Authors and Artists for Young Adults* make every effort to secure information directly from the authors and artists through personal correspondence and interviews. Sketches on living authors and artists are sent to the biographee for review prior to publication. Any sketches not personally reviewed by the biographees or their representatives are marked with an asterisk (°).

Highlights of Forthcoming Volumes

Among the authors and artists planned for future volumes are:

Ansel Adams
Isaac Asimov
Francesca Lia Block
Ben Bova
Mel Brooks
Ray Bradbury
Christopher Collier
James Lincoln Collier
Susan Cooper
Bruce Coville
Arthur Conan Doyle
M. C. Escher
James Gurney
Stephen Hawking

Will Hobbs
Mollie Hunter
Zora Neale Hurston
Hadley Irwin
Diana Wynne Jones
Jamaica Kincaid
Rudyard Kipling
Mercedes Lackey
Harper Lee
Sonia Levitin
Jack London
H. P. Lovecraft
Mad Magazine
Patricia McKillip

Stella Pevsner
Joan Phipson
Meredith Ann Pierce
Christopher Pike
Sylvia Plath
Harold Ramis
Rob Reiner
Willo Davis Roberts
Ridley Scott
Zoa Sherburne
R. L. Stine
Boris Vallejo
Jules Verne
H. G. Wells

The editors of *Authors and Artists for Young Adults* welcome any suggestions for additional biographees to be included in this series. Please write and give us your opinions and suggestions for making our series more helpful to you. Direct your comments to: Editors, *Authors and Artists for Young Adults*, Gale Research Inc., 835 Penobscot Building, Detroit, Michigan 48226-4094.

Authors & Artists for Young Adults

Margaret Atwood

■ Personal

Full name, Margaret Eleanor Atwood; born November 18, 1939, in Ottawa, Ontario, Canada; daughter of Carl Edmund (an entomologist) and Margaret Dorothy (a dietician; maiden name, Killam) Atwood; married James Polk (a writer; divorced); companion, Graeme Gibson (a writer); children: (with Gibson) Jess. *Education:* University of Toronto, B.A., 1961; Radcliffe College, A.M., 1962; Harvard University, graduate study, 1962-63, 1965-67. *Politics:* "William Morrisite." *Religion:* "Immanent Transcendentalist." *Hobbies and other interests:* Canoeing, gardening.

■ Addresses

Home—Ontario, Canada; and c/o Oxford University Press, 70 Wynford Dr., Don Mills, Ontario, Canada M3C 1J9; or c/o Jonathan Cape Ltd., 32 Bedford Square, London WC1B 3EL, England.

■ Career

Writer. University of British Columbia, Vancouver, lecturer in English literature, 1964-65; Sir George Williams University, Montreal, Quebec, lecturer in English literature, 1967-68; York University, Toronto, Ontario, assistant professor of English literature, 1971-72; House of Anansi Press, Toronto, editor and member of board of directors, 1971-73; University of Toronto, Toronto, writer-in-residence, 1972-73; University of Alabama, Tuscaloosa, writer-in-residence, 1985; New York University, New York City, Berg Visiting Professor of English, 1986; Macquarie University, North Ryde, Australia, writer-in-residence, 1987. *Member:* Amnesty International, PEN International, Writers' Union of Canada (vice-chairman, 1980-81), Royal Society of Canada (fellow), Canadian Civil Liberties Association (member of board, 1973-75), Canadian Centre, American Academy of Arts and Sciences (honorary member), Anglophone (president, 1984-85).

■ Awards, Honors

E. J. Pratt Medal, 1961, for *Double Persephone;* President's Medal, University of Western Ontario, 1965; YWCA Women of Distinction Award, 1966; Governor General's Award, 1966, for *The Circle Game,* and 1986, for *The Handmaid's Tale;* first prize in Canadian Centennial Commission Poetry Competition, 1967; Union Prize, *Poetry,* 1969; Bess Hoskins Prize, *Poetry,* 1969 and 1974; D.Litt., Trent University, 1973, Concordia University, 1980, Smith College, 1982, University of Toronto, 1983, Mount Holyoke College, 1985, University of Waterloo, 1985, and University of Guelph, 1985; LL.D., Queen's University, 1974; City of Toronto Book Award, 1977; Canadian Booksellers' Association Award, 1977; Periodical

Distributors of Canada Short Fiction Award, 1977; St. Lawrence Award for fiction, 1978; Radcliffe Medal, 1980; *Life before Man* was named a notable book of 1980 by the American Library Association; Molson Award, 1981; Guggenheim fellowship, 1981; named Companion of the Order of Canada, 1981; International Writer's Prize, Welsh Arts Council, 1982; Book of the Year Award, Periodical Distributors of Canada and the Foundation for the Advancement of Canadian Letters, 1983; Ida Nudel Humanitarian Award, 1986; Toronto Arts Award for writing and editing, 1986; *Los Angeles Times* Book Award, 1986, for *The Handmaid's Tale;* named Woman of the Year, *Ms.* magazine, 1986; Booker Prize short list, and Ritz-Paris Hemingway Prize nomination, both c. 1986, for *The Handmaid's Tale;* Arthur C. Clarke Award, 1987; Commonwealth Literature Prize, 1987; Council for the Advancement and Support of Education silver medal, 1987; Humanist of the Year award, *Humanist,* 1987; named *Chatelaine* magazine's Woman of the Year.

■ Writings

NOVELS

The Edible Woman, McClelland & Stewart, 1969, Atlantic/Little, Brown, 1970.
Surfacing, McClelland & Stewart, 1972, Simon & Schuster 1973.
Lady Oracle, Simon & Schuster, 1976.
Life before Man, McClelland & Stewart, 1979, Simon & Schuster, 1980.
Bodily Harm, McClelland & Stewart, 1981, Simon & Schuster, 1982.
The Handmaid's Tale, McClelland & Stewart, 1985, Houghton, 1986.
Cat's Eye, McClelland & Stewart, 1985, Doubleday, 1989.
The Robber Bride, Doubleday, 1993.

STORY COLLECTIONS

Dancing Girls and Other Stories, McClelland & Stewart, 1977, Simon & Schuster, 1982.
Encounters with the Element Man, Ewert (Concord, NH), 1982.
Unearthing Suite, Grand Union Press (Toronto), 1983.
Bluebeard's Egg and Other Stories, McClelland & Stewart, 1983, Fawcett, 1987.
Murder in the Dark: Short Fictions and Prose Poems, Coach House Press, 1983.
Hurricane Hazel and Other Stories, Eurographica (Helsinki), 1986.
Wilderness Tips, Doubleday, 1991.

Good Bones, Coach House Press, 1992.

POEMS

Double Persephone, Hawkshead Press, 1961.
The Circle Game (single poem), Cranbrook Academy of Art (Bloomfield Hills, MI), 1964, revised edition including more poems, Contact Press, 1966.
Kaleidoscopes Baroque: A Poem, Cranbrook Academy of Art, 1965.
Talismans for Children, Cranbrook Academy of Art, 1965.
Speeches for Doctor Frankenstein, Cranbrook Academy of Art, 1966.
Expeditions, Cranbrook Academy of Art, 1966.
The Animals in That Country, Oxford University Press (Toronto), 1968, Atlantic/Little, Brown, 1969.
What Was in the Garden, Unicorn (Santa Barbara, CA), 1969.
The Journals of Susanna Moodie, Oxford University Press, 1970.
Oratorio for Sasquatch, Man and Two Androids: Poems for Voices, Canadian Broadcasting Corp. (CBC), 1970.
Procedures for Underground, Atlantic/Little, Brown, 1970.
Power Politics, Anansi, 1971, Harper, 1973.
You Are Happy, Harper, 1974.
Selected Poems, Oxford University Press, 1976, Simon & Schuster, 1978.
Marsh Hawk, Dreadnaught, 1977.
Two-Headed Poems, Oxford University Press, 1978, Simon & Schuster, 1981.
Notes towards a Poem That Can Never Be Written, Salamander Press, 1981.
True Stories, Oxford University Press, 1981, Simon & Schuster, 1982.
Snake Poems, Salamander Press, 1983.
Interlunar, Oxford University Press, 1984.
Selected Poems II: Poems Selected and New, 1976-1986, Oxford University Press, 1986, Houghton, 1987.
Selected Poems 1966-1984, Oxford University Press, 1990.
Poems 1965-1975, Virago Press, 1991.

OTHER

The Trumpets of Summer (radio play), CBC, 1964.
Survival: A Thematic Guide to Canadian Literature, Anansi, 1972.
The Servant Girl (teleplay), CBC-TV, 1974.
Days of the Rebels, 1815-1840, Natural Science Library, 1976.

The Poetry and Voice of Margaret Atwood (recording), Caedmon, 1977.

Up in the Tree (juvenile), McClelland & Stewart, 1978.

(Author of introduction) Catherine M. Young, *To See Our World*, GLC Publishers, 1979, Morrow, 1980.

(With Joyce Barkhouse) *Anna's Pet* (juvenile), James Lorimer, 1980.

Snowbird (teleplay), CBC-TV, 1981.

Second Words: Selected Critical Prose, Anansi, 1982.

(Editor) *The New Oxford Book of Canadian Verse in English*, Oxford University Press, 1982.

(Editor with Robert Weaver) *The Oxford Book of Canadian Short Stories in English*, Oxford University Press, 1986.

(With Peter Pearson) *Heaven on Earth* (teleplay), CBC-TV, 1986.

(Editor) *The Canlit Food Book: From Pen to Palate: A Collection of Tasty Literary Fare*, Totem, 1987.

(Editor with Shannon Ravenal) *The Best American Short Stories, 1989*, Houghton, 1989.

For the Birds (juvenile), illustrated by John Bianchi, Douglas and McIntyre, 1990, Firefly Books, 1991.

(Editor) *Barbed Lyres*, Key Porter, 1990.

(Author of foreword) Allan Gould, editor, *What Did They Think of the Jews?*, Aronson, Jason, 1991.

(Author of preface) Ian Ousby, editor, *The Cambridge Guide to Literature in English*, Cambridge University Press, 1992.

(With others) *The Rushdie Letters: Freedom to Speak, Freedom to Write*, University of Nebraska Press, 1993.

Contributor to anthologies, including *Five Modern Canadian Poets*, edited by Eli Mandel, Oxford University Press, 1970, *The Canadian Imagination: Dimensions of a Literary Culture*, Harvard University Press, 1977, and *Women on Women*, 1978; contributor to periodicals, including *Atlantic, Poetry, Kayak, New Yorker, Harper's, New York Times Book Review, Saturday Night, Tamarack Review*, and *Canadian Forum*.

Atwood's books have been translated into more than twenty languages and published in over twenty-five countries; her manuscripts are kept at the University of Toronto's Fisher Library.

■ Adaptations

The Handmaid's Tale, starring Robert Duvall and Natasha Richardson, screenplay by Harold Pinter,

and directed by Volker Schloendorff, was filmed by Cinecom Entertainment Group, 1990; three other novels by Atwood have been optioned for film production. Some of Atwood's works have been recorded on audio tape.

■ Sidelights

Visiting Toronto, Ontario, in 1987 to interview author Margaret Atwood, *Ms.* contributor Lindsy Van Gelder discovered that Atwood—known as "Peggy" to her friends—is not considered to be just another writer by her fellow Canadians. "When the Canadian customs inspector at the Toronto airport discerns in the course of routine questioning that a visitor is coming to interview Atwood," Van Gelder recalls, "he literally radiates. 'Just saw Peggy on the TV yesterday,' he says in the tone most people use to talk about their immediate family. Other Canadians react similarly; the woman is clearly something of a national treasure."

This attitude toward a Canadian writer—especially a woman writer—is almost a complete reversal from how people felt during the 1950s and 1960s, when women weren't supposed to pursue literary careers. In those days, they were supposed to grow up to have jobs in teaching, nursing, home economics, or other similar occupations. Indeed, even Canadian men didn't have many opportunities to become famous authors, and the international reputation of the nation's literature was ranked below that of the United States and European countries. Today, Atwood has helped to change all that. As a poet, novelist, short story writer, critic, and essayist, she has done much to boost the credibility of Canadian literature and women writers as a whole. *Dictionary of Literary of Biography* contributor Linda Hutcheon notes that Atwood has had an "important impact on Canadian culture," adding that her books, "internationally known through translations, stand as testimony to Atwood's significant position in a contemporary literature which must deal with defining its own identity and defending its value."

Recalling her first aspirations of becoming an author in an article she wrote for *Ms.*, Atwood says that as a high school student she had a romanticized, though very gloomy, conception of what writers were like. She thought that in order to become an author of any importance she would have to give up all hope of enjoying a happy family life. She would have to become mysterious and aloof, sickly and enigmatic, living in a cold English garret and contracting tuberculosis. "I would dress in black. I would learn to smoke cigarettes, although they gave me headaches and made me cough, and drink something romantic and unusually bad for you, such as absinthe. I would live by myself in a suitably painted attic (black) and have lovers whom I would discard in appropriate ways, though I drew the line at bloodshed. (I was, after all, a nice Canadian girl.) I would never have children. This last bothered me a lot, as before this I had always intended to have some."

Many of these romantic notions were taken from Atwood's reading of Robert Grave's *The White Goddess*. After experimenting with some of these ideas, including a visit to England and some nauseating experiences with alcohol and cigarettes, Atwood decided "that maybe Robert Graves didn't have the last word on women writers." Yet to stay in Canada seemed like career suicide, since "Canadian writers, it was assumed—by my professors, my contemporaries, and myself—were a freak of Nature, like duckbill platypuses."

Overcoming the Romantic Stereotype

Still, Atwood decided—with the exception of a few years when she considered a career in home economics—to stick it out. She had begun writing at the age of six, and by the time she was sixteen she had convinced herself that a writing career was all she wanted. Inspired by "'the pre-eminent British women novelists of the 19th century' as well as two female Canadian poets, P. K. Page and Margaret Avison," according to Judy Klemesrud in a *New York Times* article, Atwood was also influenced by Northrop Frye, the renowned critic who was also one of her instructors at Victoria College. His theories about common mythical and biblical images in literature helped to determine the nature of the verses she would later compose.

Atwood's first works to be published, not counting the articles she wrote for her college newspaper, were poems. She published the verse collection *Double Persephone* the same year she graduated from the University of Toronto. The book was a success, and Atwood received the E. J. Pratt Medal for her efforts. Next, she published *The Circle Game*, which consisted entirely of a single poem. It was the revised edition of the collection to which Atwood added several more poems, however, that earned the author her country's Governor General's Award for best poetry book. Atwood was on her way up.

These early works of poetry reflect themes that Atwood would return to in later collections such as *Two-Headed Poems*. *Double Persephone* concerns "the contrast between the flux of life or nature and the fixity of man's artificial creations," as Hutcheon explains. Sherrill Grace, writing in her *Violent Duality: A Study of Margaret Atwood*, sees the central tension in all of Atwood's work as "the pull towards art on one hand and towards life on the other." Atwood "is constantly aware of opposites—self/other, subject/object, male/female, nature/man—and of the need to accept and work within them," Grace explains. "To create, Atwood chooses violent dualities, and her art re-works, probes, and dramatizes the ability to see double."

During the early 1960s, Atwood attended Harvard University off and on, studying Victorian literature and Gothic romances. When she wasn't studying, Atwood worked at jobs in—among other things—waitressing and market research, wrote book reviews and articles, and continued to write poems. She published a number of limited edition verse collections such as *Kaleidoscopes Baroque: A Poem*, *Speeches for Doctor Frankenstein*, and *What Was in the Garden*. Atwood's sense of desolation, especially evident in her early poems, and her use of frequently violent images, leads Helen Vendler to claim in the *New York Times Book Review* that Atwood has a "sense of life as mostly wounds given and received."

The 1960s and 1970s also saw a marked rise in Canadian nationalism, along with a corresponding rise in the credibility of Canadian literature. Atwood played a role in this movement as editor and member of the board of directors at the House of Anansi Press in Toronto. It was during her tenure as an editor that she published the acclaimed poetry collection, *Power Politics*. With this book, says Hutcheon, "Atwood's public visibility increased. A forceful book of verse, *Power Politics* was topical, for it is about sexual and social roles and power structures."

Growing Fame

Atwood's concern for the equal rights of women as expressed in *Power Politics* found an eager audience among the increasing ranks of feminists. Her poems, *West Coast Review* critic Gloria Onley states, concern "modern woman's anguish at finding herself isolated and exploited (although also exploiting) by the imposition of a sex role power structure." Speaking to Klemesrud, Atwood explains that her suffering characters come from real life: "My women suffer because most of the women I talk to seem to have suffered." By the early 1970s, Atwood's popularity among feminists was bringing her some unwanted fame. "Back in the days when you were supposed to pay attention to the diapers and the washing of dishes, I was a threat to other women's life positions," she tells Graeme Gibson in a 1973 interview published in *Eleven Canadian Novelists.*

In an interview with Jean W. Ross for *Contemporary Authors,* Atwood says that the first articles published about her in the newspapers during the early 1970s were strongly tainted by reporters' preconceptions: "[In] those days people tended to be frightened of or weird about young women of achievement. So a lot of that projection happened to me, which means that if you open up the papers you may find this person who has your face but the description isn't at all like what you think you are. That certainly happened a lot. It took me a while to figure out that what was coming out the other end had just as much to do with the reporter as it did with me. That's hard to keep in mind, especially when people come with their stories already written in their heads, and all they're looking for from you is something that will corroborate what they've decided in advance." Journalists would ask Atwood such silly questions as "'How do you manage to do all the housework and write too?' and 'When do you cook the lunch?' That all had to be lived through," says Atwood. "(The answers, by the way, are, 'If there's a choice the house stays dirty' and 'I try to skip big lunches.')"

Times have changed since the 1970s, however. As Atwood tells Gibson, "Now I get made into a kind of hero, which is just as unreal. It makes me just as uncomfortable. It's turning me from what I am as a writer into something I'm not." Still, there are some advantages to being a famous author. An active advocate of several political causes like protecting the arts, human rights, and the environment, Atwood does not hesitate to use her clout as an international figure to benefit the organizations she works for. She once "picked up the phone and convinced an editor at one of the country's major newspapers to do a series on the environment," reports Judith Timson in *Maclean's,* "enticing the editor on two levels. 'First I said, "Let's have lunch,"' Atwood recalled. 'Then, I offered to write something for them about the issue.'"

The author's fame—which was further increased by the success of her critical study *Survival: A Thematic Guide to Canadian Literature*—has also given her financial security. By the early 1970s,

Atwood was able to give up teaching and editing to become a full-time writer. At the same time, however, she was also going through some personal problems: her five-year marriage to American writer James Polk had ended in divorce. Atwood tells *People* contributor Cheryl McCall, "The marriage ... was not a disaster where we ended up hating each other. Neither of us is that kind of person." It was not much later that she met another writer, Graeme Gibson, the author of such novels as *Communion* and 1983's *Perpetual Motion.* Atwood was attracted to Gibson's self-confidence. "When I met Graeme," she tells Klemesrud, "he had just published two novels himself and was well enough known that he didn't feel threatened by me."

Feminism and Isolation in Atwood's Early Novels

Although most of Atwood's novels can't be considered autobiographical, they do reflect the struggle she has had to go through herself to assert her identity as a woman and an individual. Feminist concerns and personal isolation are important themes in all her novels. The first of these, *The Edible Woman,* tells the story of Marian McAlpin, a young woman who rebels against her upcoming marriage. Afraid that getting married will mean sacrificing her individuality, Marian translates her fears that her fiance is trying to consume her self-identity into an obsession with consuming food. Her preoccupation grows to the point where she rejects food completely and begins to starve herself. She is unable to eat at all, until one day when she decides to bake for her fiance a sponge cake in the shape of a woman as a symbolic gesture of his efforts to try to "assimilate" her. When he refuses to eat it and the engagement is broken, Marian is freed, both from marriage and her inability to eat.

Reaction to *The Edible Woman* was divided, with some reviewers pointing to flaws commonly found in first novels. John Stedmond of *Canadian Forum,* for example, believes that "the characters, though cleverly sketched, do not quite jell, and the narrative techniques creak a little." But other critics note successful features of Atwood's novel. Tom Marshall, writing in his *Harsh and Lovely Land: The Major Canadian Poets and the Making of a Canadian Tradition,* calls *The Edible Woman* "a largely successful comic novel, even if the mechanics are sometimes a little clumsy, the satirical accounts of consumerism a little drawn out."

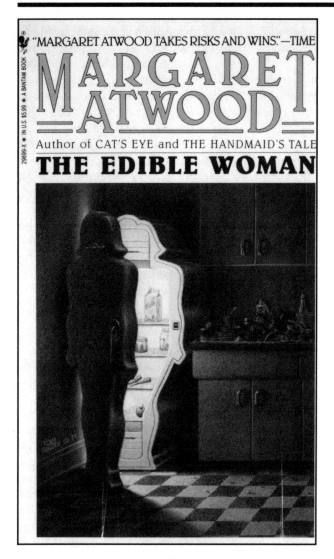

"MARGARET ATWOOD TAKES RISKS AND WINS." —TIME

MARGARET ATWOOD

Author of CAT'S EYE and THE HANDMAID'S TALE

THE EDIBLE WOMAN

A young bride-to-be rejects both food and her impending marriage in Atwood's debut novel from 1969.

Surfacing, Atwood's second novel, is "a psychological ghost story," as Marshall explains it, in which a young woman confronts and accepts her past during a visit to her rural home. She comes to realize that she has repressed disturbing events from her memory, including an abortion and her father's death. While swimming in a local lake, she has a vision of her drowned father which "drives her to a healing madness." Hutcheon states that "*Surfacing* tells of the coming to terms with the haunting, separated parts of the narrator's being . . . after surfacing from a dive, a symbolic as well as a real descent under water, where she has experienced a revealing and personally apocalyptic vision."

In *Life before Man,* Atwood dissects the relationships between three characters: Elizabeth, a married woman who mourns the recent suicide of her lover; Elizabeth's husband, Nate, who is unable to choose between his wife and his lover; and Lesje, Nate's lover, who works with Elizabeth at a museum of natural history. All three characters are isolated from one another and unable to experience their own emotions. The fossils and dinosaur bones on display at the museum are compared throughout the novel with the sterility of the characters' lives. As Laurie Stone notes in the *Village Voice, Life before Man* "is full of variations on the theme of extinction." Comparing the novel's characters to museum pieces and commenting on the analytical examination to which Atwood subjects them, Peter S. Prescott of *Newsweek* finds that "with chilly compassion and an even colder wit, Atwood exposes the interior lives of her specimens."

Praising *Life before Man, New York Times Book Review* critic Marilyn French says that Atwood "combines several talents—powerful introspection, honesty, satire and a taut, limpid style—to create a splendid, fully integrated work." The novel's title, French believes, relates to the characters' isolation from themselves, their history, and from one another. This concern is also found in Atwood's previous novels, French argues, all of which depict "the search for identity . . . a search for a better way to be—for a way of life that both satisfies the passionate, needy self and yet is decent, humane and natural."

Atwood further explores this idea in *Bodily Harm.* In this novel Rennie Wilford is a Toronto journalist who specializes in light, trivial pieces for magazines. She is, Anne Tyler explains in the *Detroit News,* "a cataloguer of current fads and fancies." Following a partial mastectomy, which causes her lover to abandon her, Rennie begins to feel dissatisfied with her life. She takes on an assignment to the Caribbean island of St. Antoine in an effort to get away from things for a while. Her planned magazine story focusing on the island's beaches, tennis courts, and restaurants is distinctly facile in comparison to the political violence she finds on St. Antoine. When Rennie is arrested and jailed, the experience causes her to find a greater meaning about her life.

Bodily Harm, Frank Davey of the *Canadian Forum* believes, follows the same pattern set in Atwood's earlier novels: "Alienation from natural order . . ., followed by descent into a more primitive but healing reality . . ., and finally some reestablishment of order." Although Davey is "troubled" by the similarities between the novels and believes that "Atwood doesn't risk much with this book," he concludes that "these reservations aside, *Bodily Harm* is still a pleasure to read." Other critics have few such reservations about the book. Tyler, for example, calls Atwood "an uncommonly skillful and perceptive writer," and goes on to state that, because of its subject matter, *Bodily Harm* "is not always easy to read. There are times when it's downright unpleasant, but it's also intelligent, provocative, and in the end—against all expectations—uplifting."

Atwood Comes of Age

Until the publication of *A Handmaid's Tale*, "a common criticism of Atwood was that she was a finer poet than she was a novelist," according to Timson. "But," the journalist later writes, "there has been little dispute about the fact that Atwood

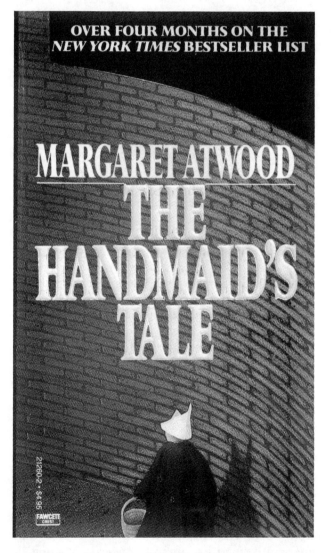

OVER FOUR MONTHS ON THE
NEW YORK TIMES BESTSELLER LIST

MARGARET ATWOOD
THE HANDMAID'S TALE

With her breakthrough 1985 book, Atwood first gained broad critical acceptance as an important novelist.

came of literary age with *The Handmaid's Tale*." In this novel Atwood turns to speculative fiction, creating the dystopia of Gilead, a future America in which Fundamentalist Christians have killed the president and members of Congress, and imposed their own dictatorial rule. In this future world, polluted by toxic chemicals and nuclear radiation, few women can bear children; the birthrate has dropped alarmingly. Those women who can bear children are forced to become "Handmaids," the official breeders for society. All other women have been reduced to servants under a repressive religious hierarchy run by men. *The Handmaid's Tale* differs from Atwood's earlier novels in several ways: it is her first novel to deal with the issue of religion, it is set in the United States rather than Canada, and the feminist theme has now become a central, rather than an incidental, part of the book.

Atwood's interest in religion did not begin with her writing of *The Handmaid's Tale*. She has been a student of the Bible from an early age. Her parents were not religious and so, as the author explains to Van Gelder, "my rebellion as a child was to go to Sunday school. I initially chose the United Church of Canada, but then as an adolescent I went out and tried *all* the religions." As an adult, she describes herself as "not unreligious, but I don't know if I'd call myself a Christian, and my interpretation of the teachings of Jesus is probably a lot more radical than a lot of the established sects are willing to go for. I would be with the people who say, 'Insomuch as you do it unto the least of these, you do it unto me.' That seems to me to be fairly central."

The repressive Christian society depicted in *The Handmaid's Tale*, however, does not follow this philosophy, and reviewers have debated as to whether the United States could ever become like Gilead. Elaine Kendall writes in the *Los Angeles Times Book Review* that Gilead is "firmly based upon actuality, beginning with events that have already taken place and extending them a bit beyond the inevitable conclusions." Yet Mary McCarthy, in her review for the *New York Times Book Review*, complains that "I just can't see the intolerance of the far right . . . as leading to a super-biblical puritanism."

Part of Atwood's unoptimistic vision of the future is the result of the story's setting. In the *Washington Post*, Mary Battiata notes that it is the first of Atwood's novels that doesn't take place "in a worried corner of contemporary Canada." "I set it in the States because I couldn't fly it in Canada," Atwood explains in an interview with Bonnie Lyons for *Shenandoah*. "In other words I tried all kinds of

Robert Duvall and Natasha Richardson starred in the 1990 movie adaptation of *The Handmaid's Tale*, a stark look at a repressive future America in which women called "Handmaids" are forced to become society's childbearers.

possibilities. Could this happen in Montreal or Toronto? And none of them felt right. Because it's not a Canadian sort of thing to do. Canadians might do it after the States did it, in some sort of watered-down version. Our television evangelists are more paltry than yours. The States are more extreme in everything. Our genius is for compromise. It's how we make our way on the French/English [Canadian language controversy] front and keep from being squashed between the two super powers."

Although Atwood's feminist concerns are clearly evident in her earlier books, *The Handmaid's Tale* is dominated by the theme. As Barbara Holliday writes in the *Detroit Free Press,* Atwood "has been concerned in her fiction with the painful psychic warfare between men and women. In *The Handmaid's Tale* ... she casts subtlety aside, exposing woman's primal fear of being used and helpless." Atwood was moved to write her story only after images and scenes from the book had been appearing to her for three years. She admits to Mervyn Rothstein of the *New York Times,* "I delayed writing it ... because I felt it was too crazy." But she eventually became convinced that her vision of

Gilead was not far from reality. Some of the anti-female measures she had imagined for the novel actually exist. "There is a sect now, a Catholic charismatic spinoff sect, which calls the women handmaids," Atwood tells Rothstein. "A law in Canada," Battiata reports, "[requires] a woman to have her husband's permission before obtaining an abortion." And Atwood, speaking to Battiata, points to repressive laws in effect as late as 1988 in the then-totalitarian state of Romania: "No abortion, no birth control, and compulsory pregnancy testing, once a month."

Prescott compares *The Handmaid's Tale* to other dystopian novels, stating that it belongs "to that breed of visionary fiction in which a metaphor is extended to elaborate a warning. ... [H. G.] Wells, [Aldous] Huxley and [George] Orwell popularized the tradition with books like 'The Time Machine,' 'Brave New World' and '1984'—yet Atwood is a better novelist than they." Christopher Lehmann-Haupt sees *The Handmaid's Tale* as a book that goes far beyond its feminist concerns. Writing in the *New York Times,* Lehmann-Haupt explains that the novel "is a political tract deploring nuclear energy, environmental waste, and antifeminist attitudes. But it [is] so much more than that—a taut thriller, a psychological study, a play on words." Van Gelder has a similar opinion. The novel, she writes, "ultimately succeeds on multiple levels: as a page-turning thriller, as a powerful political statement, and as an exquisite piece of writing." *The Handmaid's Tale* "is easily Margaret Atwood's best novel to date," Lehmann-Haupt concludes.

Atwood Gets Personal with *Cat's Eye*

In the introduction to Atwood's *Second Words,* the author says of her writing: "I began as a profoundly apolitical writer, but then I began to do what all novelists and some poets do: I began to describe the world around me." Just as Atwood became a noticeably more political writer with *The Handmaid's Tale,* she became a more personal one with *Cat's Eye.* "Much of its detail is autobiographical," states Kim Hubbard in a *People* article. "Atwood's father, like her heroine's, was a forest entomologist who spent years traipsing with his wife and children through the backwoods of northern Ontario and Quebec collecting specimens." Elaine's mother, like Atwood's, was also an unconventional woman who refused to fit herself into the mold of the 1940s housewife. "Like [*Cat's Eye* protagonist] Elaine Risley," Hubbard continues, "Margaret went to school only sporadically until she was 12, when the family finally settled in Toronto and confined their bug-seeking expeditions to summers." Other similarities include such facts as both Elaine and Atwood have brothers who are interested in science, both were married and divorced, and both rediscovered love and became mothers.

There are so many parallels between *Cat's Eye* and Atwood's real life that even some people who know the author became confused. "Her paperback publisher, Anna Porter," reports Timson, "called her after reading the book. Said Atwood: 'She told me it had left her in tears. She said to me, "But I always thought you were happy!"'" The tragedy that is at the heart of *Cat's Eye,* however, is very different from anything Atwood ever lived through. The book is a retrospective told through the eyes of Elaine, who is a successful painter. Returning to her childhood home in Toronto to appear at an exhibition of her artwork, Elaine dwells on the unhappy memories that the city evokes for her. Because she had spent the first years of her childhood with her family in the woods, Elaine had a hard time being accepted by other girls when they settled in Toronto.

Having set up this situation, Atwood explores the ways that children can be just as cruel and deceiving as adults. Elaine's main tormentor is her "best friend" Cordelia. Cordelia makes Elaine the object of numerous pranks, one of which almost ends up killing Elaine. The worst part of this is that Elaine feels helpless to defend herself and is unable to confide in her parents. As Cordelia enters her teen years, however, she becomes overweight and unhappy, and she eventually goes insane. By the book's conclusion, Elaine discovers how these events have influenced her art and her life. One point Atwood wished to make with this story is that women are not any more noble or moral than men. "There is no gene for moral wonderfulness," she points out to Timson. "To buy into that is to be back in the 19th century." Although Atwood's

Although she felt that this 1985 novel was too personal to become a bestseller, Atwood again found success with this chilling tale of one woman's traumatic childhood.

other novels have, despite their distinctive feminist leanings, also made this point, none have made it plainer than *Cat's Eye*.

Cat's Eye became a bestseller and has been praised by critics, who especially note the author's frank portrayal of the unpleasant realities of childhood that many of us share. As Philip Howard attests in the London *Times*, the "book is not just about growing up female in Toronto in the Forties: it is about life for all of us. She is," Howard concludes, "one of our finest novelists." *New York Times* reviewer Alice McDermott feels that *Cat's Eye* is "Atwood's most emotionally engaging fiction thus far." The warm reception *Cat's Eye* has received, however, surprises Atwood. "I had thought of it as a more personal, unpretentious book but it's already very big," she admits in Timson's article.

Having published popular books like *Cat's Eye, A Handmaid's Tale*, and others does not hold the same meaning for Atwood as it once would have when she was a teenager dreaming of romantic English garrets and overcoming resistance to her plans of becoming a famous author. Today, Atwood finds more comfort in family than in writing. Her life, she tells Timson, is now "pretty close to the leaves-in-the-backyard model I thought would be out-of-bounds forever. I bake (dare I admit it) chocolate-chip cookies and I find that doing the laundry with the aid of my washer-dryer is one of the more relaxing parts of my week." The author's fear of having to sacrifice motherhood for a career has also proved to be unfounded. Atwood is the happy mother of a daughter named Jess. "I love being a mother," the author says to Ross. "I'd do it some more if I weren't so elderly." As the author reflects in McCall's article, "I always wanted to have a child under the right circumstances, which for me included an interested partner and enough money. It took me a while to get both. Now my child is what I care about most, and my family as a whole. Writing is a very important part of my life, but it's not a human being. I'm pretty much aware that there is a difference between them."

■ **Works Cited**

Atwood, Margaret, interview with Graeme Gibson, in *Eleven Canadian Novelists*, Anansi, 1973.

Atwood, Margaret, *Second Words: Selected Critical Prose*, Anansi, 1982.

Atwood, Margaret, interview with Bonnie Lyons, *Shenandoah*, Volume 37, 1987.

Atwood, Margaret, "Great Unexpectations," *Ms.*, July/August, 1987, pp. 78-79, 195-196.

Atwood, Margaret, interview with Jean W. Ross for *Contemporary Authors*, Volume 24, Gale, 1988.

Battiata, Mary, review of *The Handmaid's Tale*, *Washington Post*, April 6, 1986.

Davey, Frank, "Life after Man," *Canadian Forum*, December/January, 1981-82, pp. 29-30.

French, Marilyn, "Spouses and Lovers," *New York Times Book Review*, February 3, 1980, pp. 1, 26.

Grace, Sherrill, *Violent Duality: A Study of Margaret Atwood*, Vehicule Press, 1980.

Holliday, Barbara, review of *The Handmaid's Tale*, *Detroit Free Press*, January 26, 1986.

Howard, Philip, review of *Cat's Eye*, *Times* (London), January 26, 1989.

Hubbard, Kim, "Reflected in Margaret Atwood's *Cat's Eye*, Girlhood Looms as a Time of Cruelty and Terror," *People*, March 6, 1989, pp. 205-206.

Hutcheon, Linda, "Margaret Atwood," *Dictionary of Literary Biography*, Volume 53: *Canadian Writers since 1960*, Gale, 1986, pp. 17-34.

Kendall, Elaine, review of *The Handmaid's Tale*, *Los Angeles Times Book Review*, February 9, 1986, pp. 1, 12.

Klemesrud, Judy, "High Priestess of Angst," *New York Times*, March 28, 1982.

Lehmann-Haupt, Christopher, review of *The Handmaid's Tale*, *New York Times*, January 27, 1986, p. C24.

Marshall, Tom, *Harsh and Lovely Land: The Major Canadian Poets and the Making of a Canadian Tradition*, University of British Columbia Press, 1978.

McCall, Cheryl, "Canadian Author Margaret Atwood Writes 'Life before Man' and Ponders Life after Success," *People*, May 19, 1980, pp. 69-70.

McCarthy, Mary, "Breeders, Wives and Unwomen," *New York Times Book Review*, February 9, 1986, pp. 1, 35.

McDermott, Alice, "What Little Girls Are Really Made Of," *New York Times Book Review*, February 5, 1989, pp. 1, 35.

Onley, Gloria, *West Coast Review*, January, 1973.

Prescott, Peter S., "No Balm in This Gilead," *Newsweek*, February 18, 1980, p. 70.

Rothstein, Mervyn, "No Balm in Gilead for Margaret Atwood," *New York Times*, February 17, 1986.

Stedmond, John, review of *The Edible Woman*, *Canadian Forum*, February, 1970, p. 267.

Stone, Laurie, review of *Life before Man*, *Village Voice*, January 7, 1980, p. 32.

Timson, Judith, "Atwood's Triumph," *Maclean's*, October 3, 1988, pp. 56-61.

Tyler, Anne, review of *Bodily Harm, Detroit News,* April 4, 1982.

Van Gelder, Lindsy, "Margaret Atwood," January, 1987, pp. 49-50, 90.

Vendler, Helen, "A Quarter of Poetry," *New York Times Book Review,* pp. 4-5, 29-38.

■ For More Information See

BOOKS

Contemporary Literary Criticism, Gale, Volume 2, 1974, Volume 3, 1975, Volume 4, 1975, Volume 8, 1978, Volume 13, 1980, Volume 15, 1980, Volume 25, 1983, Volume 44, 1987.

Davidson, Arnold E., and Cathy N. Davidson, editors, *The Art of Margaret Atwood: Essays in Criticism,* Anansi, 1981.

Grace, Sherrill, and Lorraine Weir, editors, *Margaret Atwood: Language, Text and System,* University of British Columbia Press, 1983.

Hancock, Geoff, *Canadian Writers at Work,* Oxford University Press, 1987.

Ingersoll, Earl G., editor, *Margaret Atwood: Conversations* (interviews), Ontario Review Press, 1990.

Lecker, Robert, and Jack David, editors, *The Annotated Bibliography of Canada's Major Authors,* ECW, 1980.

Sandler, Linda, editor, *Margaret Atwood: A Symposium,* University of British Columbia, 1977.

Twigg, Alan, *For Openers: Conversations with 24 Canadian Writers,* Harbour Publishing, 1981.

Twigg, Alan, *Strong Voices: Conversations with Fifty Canadian Authors,* Harbour Publishing, 1988.

Wilson, Sharon Rose, *Margaret Atwood's Fairy-Tale Sexual Politics,* University of Mississippi Press, 1993.

Woodcock, George, *The Canadian Novel in the Twentieth Century,* McClelland & Stewart, 1975.

PERIODICALS

American Poetry Review, November/December, 1973; March/April, 1977; September/October, 1979.

Atlantic, April, 1973.

Black Warrior Review (University of Alabama), fall, 1985, pp. 88-108.

Book Forum, Volume 4, number 1, 1978.

Books in Canada, January, 1979; June/July, 1980; March, 1981; October, 1988, pp. 11-14.

Canadian Children's Literature, Volume 65, 1992, pp. 83-85.

Canadian Forum, January, 1973; November/December, 1974; December/January, 1977-78; June/July, 1981; January, 1984.

Canadian Literature, autumn, 1971, p. 91; spring, 1972; winter, 1973; spring, 1974; spring, 1977.

Chicago Tribune, January 27, 1980; February 3, 1980; May 16, 1982; March 19, 1989.

Chicago Tribune Book World, January 26, 1986.

Christian Science Monitor, June 12, 1977.

Commonweal, July 9, 1973.

Communique, May, 1975.

Essays on Canadian Writing, spring, 1977.

Globe and Mail (Toronto), July 7, 1984; October 5, 1985; October 19, 1985; February 15, 1986; November 15, 1986; November 29, 1986; November 14, 1987; October 1, 1988.

Hudson Review, autumn, 1973; spring, 1975.

Humanist, September/October, 1986; September/October, 1987.

Inside Books, February, 1989, pp. 19, 21.

Insight, March 24, 1986.

Journal of Canadian Fiction, Volume 1, number 4, 1972.

Los Angeles Times, March 2, 1982; April 22, 1982; May 9, 1986; January 12, 1987.

Los Angeles Times Book Review, October 17, 1982; December 23, 1987.

Maclean's, January 15, 1979; October 15, 1979; March 30, 1981.

Malahat Review, January, 1977.

Manna, Number 2, 1972.

Meanjin, Volume 37, number 2, 1978.

Modern Fiction Studies, autumn, 1976.

Ms., January, 1987, pp. 49-50, 90; July/August, 1987.

New Leader, September 3, 1973.

New Orleans Review, Volume 5, number 3, 1977.

Newsweek, February 17, 1986.

New York Times, December 23, 1976; January 10, 1980; February 8, 1980; March 6, 1982; March 28, 1982; September 15, 1982; November 5, 1986; April 2, 1989.

New York Times Book Review, October 18, 1970, p. 9; March 4, 1973; April 6, 1975; September 26, 1976; May 21, 1978; October 11, 1981; February 9, 1986.

Observer, June 13, 1982.

Ontario Review, spring/summer, 1975; fall/winter, 1978.

Open Letter, summer, 1973.

Parnassus: Poetry in Review, spring/summer, 1974.

People, May 19, 1980.

Poetry, March, 1970; July, 1972; May, 1982.

Publishers Weekly, August 23, 1976.

Quill and Quire, April, 1981; September, 1984.

Room of One's Own, summer, 1975.

San Francisco Review of Books, January, 1982; summer, 1982.

Saturday Night, May, 1971; July/August, 1976; September, 1976; May, 1981.

Saturday Review, September 18, 1976; February 2, 1980.

Saturday Review of the Arts, April, 1973.

Shenandoah, Volume 37, number 2, 1987.

Studies in Canadian Literature, summer, 1977.

This Magazine Is about Schools, winter, 1973.

Time, October 11, 1976; February 25, 1980; February 6, 1989, pp. 70-71.

Times (London), March 13, 1986; June 4, 1987; June 10, 1987.

Times Literary Supplement, March 21, 1986; June 12, 1987; February 3, 1989.

University of Toronto Quarterly, summer, 1978.

Vogue, January, 1986.

Washington Post Book World, September 26, 1976; December 3, 1978; January 27, 1980; March 14, 1982; February 2, 1986.

Waves, autumn, 1975.

[Sketch reviewed by Sarah Cooper, representing Atwood at Oxford University Press, Canada]

Vera Cleaver

■ Personal

Born January 6, 1919 in Virgil, SD; died August 11, 1993, in Winter Haven, FL; daughter of Fortis Alonzo and Beryl Naiome (Reininger) Allen; married William (Bill) Joseph Cleaver (a writer), October 4, 1945 (died, 1981). *Education:* Educated at schools in Kennebeck, SD, and Perry and Tallahassee, FL. *Hobbies and other interests:* Art, music, and nature.

■ Addresses

Home—600 East Lake Elbert Dr., Winter Haven, FL 33881; and c/o Harper & Row Junior Books Group, 10 East 53rd St., New York, NY 10022.

■ Career

Writer of books for children. Free-lance accountant, 1945-54; accountant (civilian), United States Air Force, Tachikawa, Japan, 1954-56, and Chaumont, France, 1956-58.

■ Awards, Honors

Horn Book Honor List, 1967, for *Ellen Grae; Horn Book* Honor List, 1969, American Library Association (ALA) notable book, 1970, National Book Award nomination, 1970, and Newbery Honor Book, all for *Where the Lilies Bloom;* National Book Award nomination, 1971, for *Grover; New York Times* outstanding book and ALA notable book, both 1973, both for *Me Too;* National Book Award nomination, 1974, for *The Whys and Wherefores of Littabelle Lee;* Lewis Carroll Bookshelf Award and *New York Times* outstanding book citation, both 1975, and Western Writers of America's Golden Spur Award for best Western juvenile novel, 1976, all for *Dust of the Earth;* National Book Award nomination, 1979, for *Queen of Hearts;* Children's Choice Award, 1986, for *Sweetly Sings the Donkey; Belle Pruitt* was a 1988 Junior Library Guild selection.

■ Writings

FICTION FOR YOUNG READERS

Sugar Blue, illustrated by Eric Nones, Lothrop, 1984.
Sweetly Sings the Donkey, Lippincott, 1985.
Moon Lake Angel, Lothrop, 1987.
Belle Pruitt, Lippincott, 1988.

FICTION FOR YOUNG READERS; WITH HUSBAND, BILL CLEAVER

Ellen Grae (also see below), illustrated by Ellen Raskin, Lippincott, 1967.
Lady Ellen Grae (also see below), illustrated by

Raskin, Lippincott, 1968.

Where the Lilies Bloom, illustrated by Jim Spanfeller, Lippincott, 1969.

Grover, illustrated by Frederic Marvin, Lippincott, 1970.

The Mimosa Tree, Lippincott, 1970.

I Would Rather Be a Turnip, Lippincott, 1971.

The Mock Revolt, Lippincott, 1971.

Delpha Green and Company, Lippincott, 1972.

The Whys and Wherefores of Littabelle Lee, Atheneum, 1973.

Me Too, Lippincott, 1973.

Ellen Grae [and] *Lady Ellen Grae*, Hamish Hamilton, 1973.

Dust of the Earth, Lippincott, 1975.

Trial Valley, Lippincott, 1977.

Queen of Hearts, Lippincott, 1978.

A Little Destiny, Lothrop, 1979.

The Kissimmee Kid, Lothrop, 1981.

Hazel Rye, Lippincott, 1983.

OTHER

The Nurse's Dilemma (adult fiction), Avalon Books, 1966.

Contributor, with husband, of more than two hundred stories to magazines and periodicals, including *McCall's* and *Woman's Day*. Cleaver's manuscripts are included in the Kerlan Collection, University of Minnesota, Minneapolis, and also at the University of North Carolina, Chapel Hill.

■ Adaptations

Where the Lilies Bloom was filmed by United Artists, 1974.

■ Sidelights

"I would try to get them to sing or talk, do anything to raise their spirits, but they remained sullenly silent. At that hour they hated me and I hated myself, knowing how I appeared to them—a pinch-faced crone, straggle-haired, bony, ragged, too desperate for anyone with only fourteen years on them but still driven by a desperation that was unholy and ugly."

Cautious and cordial would not be good terms to use to describe the speaker of these words. Neither would these adjectives be good for describing any of the typical heroines the reader meets in a novel written by Vera Cleaver and her husband Bill. This excerpt from the Cleavers' *Where the Lilies Bloom*, spoken by Mary Call Luther, the young protagonist of that book, provides a quick glimpse at her defiant spirit. The persistent attitude displayed by

Mary Call is featured in every one of the Cleavers' novels for young people. Zena Sutherland, Dianne L. Monson, and May Hill Arbuthnot identified Mary Call in *Children and Books* as "one of the strongest characters in children's fiction," but she is one of more than a dozen strong female protagonists created by the Cleavers. A resilient, young, and usually female lead character who struggles to find the best way to meet the trials she encounters in life is one of the most notable characteristics of a Cleaver book.

In *A Sounding of Storytellers: New and Revised Essays on Contemporary Writers for Children*, John Rowe Townsend wrote, "Rereading the Cleavers' books for children ... one is struck most obviously and forcibly by their gallery of fierce, determined heroines." The world the Cleavers set their characters in is a harsh one. Their novels deal with such complex problems as divorce, suicide, and poverty, but the protagonists deal with these problems with tenacity and vigor. Unlike what the reader might tend to expect in juvenile fiction, a Cleaver novel is "rooted in an unyielding realism," noted Townsend. "No wind is tempered to the shorn lamb; no rich uncle or equivalent turns up with infusions of love and money; no dying parent recovers or absconding one returns repentant. Real life probably contains more merciful softening of harsh situations than the Cleavers ever permit themselves."

A Literary Partnership Begins

Although Vera Cleaver is said to have begun writing stories at the age of six, she is most well known for the sixteen juvenile novels produced in collaboration with her husband, Bill, which were published from 1967 to 1983. Their first joint literary efforts were hundreds of stories produced early in their marriage in the mid-1940s. These stories for adults—but dealing with children—were published first in the popular pulp magazines of the day. Later, Cleaver stories appeared in major women's periodicals such as *McCall's* and *Women's Day*. Because of Bill Cleaver's position with the U.S. Air Force, the couple spent a lot of time traveling, but once he retired they decided to devote themselves full time to the writing of children's literature.

In 1967, the Cleavers published *Ellen Grae*, their first novel for young people. Its wide critical acceptance made it a fortunate beginning for the fledgling novelists. The book ushered in a sixteen-year span of novels that ended with the publication of *Hazel Rye* in 1983. This last co-authored book had been plotted out by the couple several years earlier but was finished by Vera after the death of her husband in 1981. In general, the Cleaver books were well received by critics and readers alike: four of their books were nominated for the prestigious National Book Award, and their titles were regularly included on yearly lists of outstanding books for children. Vera Cleaver's four solo works for children have also been looked upon favorably by literary critics. Her 1985 publication, *Sweetly Sings the Donkey*, won the Children's Choice Award, while another solo effort, *Belle Pruitt,* was a Junior Library Guild selection.

Readers were introduced to the Cleaver heroine who would set the pattern for those to follow in the couple's debut novel, *Ellen Grae.* Ellen Grae Derryberry—a witty and talkative eleven-year-old—lives with the McGruders in the small, quiet town of Thicket, Florida, during the school year because her parents are divorced and there is no

Ellen Raskin illustrated Vera and Bill Cleaver's first collaborative work, 1967's *Ellen Grae,* which tells about a young girl who must live with friends of the family after her parents' divorce.

one else with whom she can stay. When the girl learns an awful secret from her friend, Ira, she is torn between loyalty to her companion and wanting to tell someone in authority. But after Ellen Grae finally reveals the startling truth to the local sheriff, her story is dismissed as a lie because of her reputation as a teller of tall tales. The girl's conscious is relieved, however, and she continues on with her life much the same as before the incident. In another theme dealt with in the book, the words and actions of Ellen Grae's divorced parents emphasize the fact that it's possible for two people to be divorced and yet still love their children.

Several critics noticed a clever mixture of seriousness and light-heartedness in *Ellen Grae* and praised its creators for their fresh approach to children's literature. "This is an unusual book," Barbara Wersba wrote in the *New York Times Book Review,* "rich in characterization and keenly observant of childhood." In *Saturday Review* Zena Sutherland commented, "Although the story has poignant moments, it is funny most of the time and perceptive all of the time." While *Horn Book* contributor Paul Heins declared the novel "a daring and honest treatment of a girl's experience with an unexpected problem"; he also called the novel a "sympathetically told story [that] reveals the irony and the tragedy that often face a child on the road to maturity." In *Publishers Weekly* a critic obviously impressed with the Cleavers' effort predicted a great future for its authors. He told his readers not to "miss *Ellen Grae.* It's an unusual story. And don't forget its authors' names; they're worth watching."

In a short time, the Cleavers' produced two more novels using characters from their first one: *Lady Ellen Grae*, published in 1967, and *Grover*, published in 1970. The first title again featured Ellen Grae. The plot revolves around her father's abrupt announcement that she will be sent to Seattle to live with her Aunt Eleanor. The purpose of the visit is to make a lady out of Ellen Grae, whose parents think she is too much of a tomboy. This sequel did not fare too well with a number of critics, who compared it unfavorably with the Cleavers' first novel. In the *New York Times Book Review,* for example, Wersba complained that "the once sparkling Ellen now seems old." In her *School Library Journal* review of the novel, Lillian N. Gerhardt maintained that "the Cleavers write well—but they either didn't realize what they created the first time or don't see how they devalued Ellen Grae in attempting to trot her out

Where the Lilies Bloom

Cleaver

Illustrated by Jim Spanfeller

This 1969 story about a family of parentless children struggling to survive in rural Appalachia was a Newbery Honor Book.

again.'' Martha Bacon, writing in the *Atlantic Monthly,* saw the book in a more positive light and confessed that she had ''enjoyed [the novel] and found it too short.'' Bacon added, ''Girls and people who have been girls, and males as well, will probably enjoy this book.''

Grover, which features Grover Ezell, a boy who appears in both *Ellen Grae* and *Lady Ellen Grae,* is one of the few novels written by the Cleavers with a male main character. Like Ellen Grae, Grover must struggle to deal with a painful situation, in this case his mother's suicide (she was suffering from cancer) and his father's grief, while at the same time dealing with the everyday problems of being a pre-adolescent. Although suicide was not a typical topic for a juvenile novel at the time, the book was published. Reviewers concluded that the Cleavers handled the subject with sensitivity, lacing the book with enough humor to counterbalance the seriousness of the situation described.

In her *Horn Book* review of *Grover,* Diane Farrell wrote, ''The language is strong and rich in imagery; the narrative is absorbing. A profoundly wise and real tale.'' In *Children's Press Review* Judith Aldridge called the book ''another successful story'' and found in it many characteristics of a typical Cleaver novel, including a ''sympathetic, realistic and unsentimental portrayal of children's concerns and conversations, their bafflement and occasional cool contempt of adult's behavior.'' The book was nominated for a National Book Award.

Popular Novels

One of the Cleavers' most widely read novels is *Where the Lilies Bloom.* Like *Grover,* it received a National Book Award nomination; it was also the authors' first Newbery Honor Book. The novel is one of several Cleaver books that explore the problem of rural poverty. In this case the setting is the Great Smokies region of the Appalachian Mountains. The heroine is fourteen-year-old Mary Call Luther, who struggles to keep her family of four children together after they are left orphans when their father dies. ''Written with flair, flavor and wry humor,'' according to a *Saturday Review* critic, the novel details how Mary Call is able to keep the children from being placed in separate foster homes by concealing their father's death from authorities. She also earns money from ''wildcrafting,'' or gathering medicinal herbs for later sale. In the *Dictionary of Literary Biography,* Jane Harper Yarbrough claimed that Mary Call is the outstanding feature of the novel. She noted that the character's ''inner strength, love of family, irrepressible dignity, pragmatic resourcefulness, indomitable will, and joy for life combine to provide readers with a vividly memorable character whose uplifting story is of one young woman's victories over the oppressive forces of nature and society.'' Novelist William Saroyan, writing in the *New York Times Book Review,* similarly found that ''most appealing in the story is the sense of earnestness and determination in the central character and narrator, Mary Call Luther.''

Trial Valley, a sequel to *Where the Lilies Bloom,* was published eight years after the original novel. According to Yarbrough, the sequel ''is as well crafted as its predecessor.'' In this continuation of Mary Call's story, she is sixteen years old and still struggling to support her family. This time she also has to deal with additional problems, including the discovery of an abandoned child and the presence of two young suitors who demand her attention. *New York Times Book Review* contributor Bryna J.

Mary Call Luther (played by Julie Gholson) and her brother and sister try to keep their father alive in this 1974 movie version of *Where the Lilies Bloom.*

Fireside called it "a coming-of-age book" and noted that "by using language that is rich and varied rather than literal and slangy, [the Cleavers] have reminded us that dignity is not just a provence of the affluent." Paul Heins also praised the Cleavers' writing ability in a *Horn Book* review of the book when he observed: "The dialogue is homespun, humorous, and natural; the simple realism of the plot is rounded out by the superb characterization." In the *Washington Post Book World,* Virginia Haviland compared the novel favorably with *Where the Lilies Bloom* and called the sequel a "gem of regional fiction."

We meet another Cleaver mountain heroine in *The Whys and Wherefores of Littabelle Lee,* also a finalist in the National Book Award competition. Littabelle Lee is sixteen and lives in the Ozark Mountains of Arkansas with her grandparents and her Aunt Sorrow, a practitioner of herbal medicine. When her aunt is injured falling off her horse and decides to leave the family household, Litta-belle is forced to take over the care of her elderly relatives. Although she manages to find a job as a "deputy schoolkeeper," she finally decides to sue an uncle and some aunts for "parent neglect" for refusing to help the struggling couple. Although Ruth Pegau in *Library Journal* referred to the novel as "another folksy nostalgia trip," other critics praised it for its depiction of rural life and found it a thoughtful addition to children's literature. "To read this book, full of truth and the natural life of the country," remarked M. H. Miller in *Children's Book Review,* "is a rewarding experience. It contains much eventful incident, and much simple, wise reflection." In the *New York Times Book Review* Jonathan Yardley noted, "The Cleavers, in this book, grant their readers the respect they deserve, using language that is forthright and honest, telling a story that touches on life's truths. *The Whys and Wherefores of Littabelle Lee* is a book children ought to read, precisely because it does not treat them as 'children.'"

The Cleavers again placed a young heroine in a rural setting in *Dust of the Earth,* a novel that earned the Western Writers of America's Golden Spur Award for best juvenile fiction. The book's fourteen-year-old protagonist, Fern Drawn, is often mentioned in lists of the authors' outstanding female personalities, along with Ellen Grae and Mary Call. Like Mary Call, Fern is determined to solve her family's emotional and financial problems all by herself. The Drawns—Fern, a sister, two brothers, and Mama and Papa—move to the small town of Chokecherry, South Dakota, in the Badlands, after Fern's mother inherits a sheep farm there. The move places added strain on the already unsteady family unity that Fern describes like this: "We were not friends—we lived as nuisances to each other, unconfiding, each forever in the way of the others, our ambitions and disappointments forever clashing. The word *love* was not spoken in our house." Fern soon determines that she must drop out of school and tend to the sheep on the farm if she wants her family to survive their first South Dakotan winter. Thanks to her efforts, the family not only survives but grows much closer together.

Although the book earned several awards, critical reception was mixed. Some reviewers like Shirley M. Wilton found the Cleavers depiction of Fern the novel's highlight. "*Earth* is rich with humor and human feeling," wrote Wilton in the *School Library Journal,* "... but it is richest in the personality of Fern herself." In the *New York Times Book Review,* Annie Gottlieb pointed out that while "the Cleavers capture excellently the half-formed, inarticulate but compelling way things come to" a fourteen-year-old, she thought the novel "an odd patchwork" filled with "earthy events and poetic emotions, but no firm dramatic ground on which the twain may meet." Other critics admired the Cleavers' description of the rugged Badlands region. A reviewer for *Books for Your Children,* for example, praised the Cleavers for their "special power of evoking a particular desolate landscape." Yarbrough declared the novel "a rare find in young adult literature" because of its "powerful comparison of environment and emotions."

Queen of Hearts, the Cleavers' fourth novel to earn a National Book Award nomination, was published in 1978. Like Littabelle in *The Whys and Wherefores of Littabelle Lee,* the protagonist of this novel must also look after an elderly relative. Twelve-year-old Wilma Omalie Lincoln is called upon to stay with Granny Lincoln until a companion/house-keeper can be found to take care of the old woman. However, as one by one the candidates for the job make a hasty departure, Wilma finds that her grandmother will only let her fill the position. The going is hard at first, noted Jean Fritz in the *New York Times Book Review,* but "Wilma learns to stand up to the cantankerous old soul, to follow her into her past, and she even finds a way to make her grandmother feel useful."

Critics found this Cleaver novel to be an insightful look at the problems of the elderly. In *Children's Book Review Service,* Leigh Dean noted, "At a time when so many elderly are being 'put away,' this novel shines forth, with another, far wiser and more loving vision. The writing sings." In her *Horn Book* review of the novel, Ethel Heins observed that the novel gave a new twist to a much discussed topic. "In the present time of proliferating isms the authors characteristically transcend a fashionable theme and produce a fine novel ...," she wrote.

The Cleavers once again explore the life of a poor mountain family—this time in the Ozark Mountains of Arkansas—in this story published in 1973.

"The incongruity of [Wilma and Granny's] relationship is seen in a devastatingly honest tragicomedy." Fritz found *Queen of Hearts* a typical Cleaver novel in that "as usual, the Cleavers face tough situations with spunk and deliver language so lively that it crackles."

A Collaboration Ends

The next two Cleaver novels, *The Kissimmee Kid* and *Hazel Rye*, would be the last the couple would work on together. Both stories take place in the central Florida region familiar to the Cleavers, who lived in the resort town of Winter Haven for many years. *The Kissimmee Kid* is a Western—complete with cowboys and cattle rustlers—but without the Western setting. Twelve-year-old Evelyn Chestnut comes to Florida to visit her older sister Reba and brother-in-law Camfield and is shocked when she accidently discovers that Cam is involved in a scheme to steal calves from his employer. With its emphasis on the conflict between loyalty to a friend and the desire to see justice done, the plot recalls Ellen Grae's similar predicament in the Cleaver's first novel.

In her *Washington Post Book World* review of *The Kissimmee Kid*, Alice Digilio wrote admiringly of the Cleavers' ability to handle "moral dilemmas without ever once being moralistic." She continued: "The issue here is honesty, specifically telling the truth when lying might protect someone you love very much. By the novel's conclusion truth has triumphed, yet so have loyalty and love." While *Horn Book* critic Ann A. Flowers called part of the novel "contrived," she too was taken by the Cleavers' skill. "The book's exposition is masterly; the language, with its light touch of Southern dialect, is just right; and the characters fairly spring forth from the page," she noted. In Jean Fritz's *New York Times Book Review* critique of the book, she also faulted the authors' for using symbolism to further the plot along, but ended the review on a positive note, commenting that the book's "fresh, witty dialogue is reason enough to enjoy it."

Hazel Rye, set in the orange-growing lands of central Florida, deals with the change that occurs in an eleven-year-old owner of an orange grove when she lets an indigent family move into a dilapidated shack on her property. As twelve-year-old Felder Poole—one of the children in the family—begins to oversee the restoration of the once flourishing grove, he and his family leave an indelible influence on Hazel Rye. From being rather disinterested and world-weary for a person

In one of their last collaborative books, the Cleavers returned to some of the themes in *Ellen Grae* in this 1981 western.

her age, she becomes fascinated with the world around her and eager to learn new things. Impatient for knowledge, she sits "at night behind her locked door, working with her pencils, her writing pads, and the dictionary" as she develops her once negligible reading skills.

As this was the last book the Cleavers would jointly produce, several critics compared Hazel Rye with other heroines created by the authors during their long career. In the *New York Times Book Review*, Carol Billman decided, "Hazel Rye is a welcome addition to the company of Ellen Grae, Mary Call and the other resourceful and sassy girls introduced in the novels of Vera and Bill Cleaver." But she also felt that *Hazel Rye* was not as well written as the Cleavers' other literary offerings. Mary M. Burns was more appreciative of the novel, writing in her *Horn Book* review that "Hazel Rye, like Ellen Grae and Mary Call Luther, is a character to be reckoned with—and not easily forgotten."

While in her *Bulletin of the Center for Children's Books* critique, Zena Sutherland found Hazel Rye "a bit too pert," she also noted that "like other Cleaver protagonists, this is, even if she's not likeable, a girl with grit."

"That children's books are richer by the Cleavers there is no doubt," wrote Ingeborg Boudreau in the *New York Times Book Review* after the pair had published only a handful of books. Patricia J. Cianciolo evaluated the richness of the Cleavers' production in a *Top of the News* feature on the authors: "One of the major objectives of this talented writing team is to get children to think, and it is an objective that has been realized. Of course, one can read the novels by Vera and Bill Cleaver for the pleasures they will bring to one. Also, their books are an excellent medium to use to inform oneself more thoroughly about diverse lifestyles and human needs." Although both these critics were addressing the Cleavers' work as a team, Vera Cleaver's novels produced after her husband's death are very similar to those the couple had produced jointly. She stuck to the tested formula—a young strong-willed female main character with a rough home life who solves a problem—that had clicked with readers and critics so many times before. For each of her solo efforts she also returned to the Florida setting she knew so well. Critics compared the four books she authored alone to those produced with her husband and, in many cases, found little difference.

Vera Cleaver's first solo novel, *Sugar Blue*, tells the story of eleven-year-old Amy Blue, who must occupy herself while both her parents work long hours for their catering business. One day Amy's four-year-old niece, Ella, comes to stay with the Blue family for a short time, and since Amy's parents are so busy, she must take care of the preschooler herself. At first, Amy resents this uncalled for intrusion in her solitary life, but soon she is won over by her little niece who adores her and calls her aunt "Sugar Blue." It seems just as the pair become inseparable friends, Ella has to rejoin her parents. Hurt when someone else replaces her in Ella's life, Amy finds a change has occurred within her, and her love of solitude has been replaced with a yearning to love. "One notes with interest that the author has retained her characteristic nonpatronizing, often cryptic style," observed Ethel Heins in *Horn Book*, "with provocative words and phrases still revealing her wisdom and sensibility."

Sweetly Sings the Donkey features Lily Snow, a fourteen-year-old who moves with her family from South Dakota to Florida. Even though the family is looking for a better life, when they get to Florida their situation deteriorates; Lily's father becomes ill and her mother runs off with one of their new neighbors. Lily finds a way to triumph over her circumstances and the book ends with the hope that the family will succeed after all. Both *Voice of Youth Advocates* contributor Andrea Davidson and *Horn Book* critic Mary M. Burns found Cleaver's portrait of Lily to be the outstanding feature of the novel. "The characters are unforgettable and strongly drawn," observed Davidson, "Lily is a plucky hero." Burns maintained that the young protagonist "demands that the reader believe in her ability to wrest something from nothing." And, Davidson continued, "It is her personality which carries the narrative and makes the plot work."

The last two additions to Vera Cleaver's family of spirited females appear in *Moon Lake Angel*, published in 1987, and *Belle Pruitt*, published the following year. Again, it seemed that critics could not help but mention the clever personalities Cleaver had created in her previous works in their reviews. "In *Moon Lake Angel* Vera Cleaver introduces another of her spunky heroines," wrote a reviewer in *Horn Book*. "She creates strangely mature children, who, blighted by some set of circumstances, all grapple with problems and come through, not just as survivors but as hands-down winners." In a critique of *Belle Pruitt* another *Horn Book* commentator noted: "One of the unique qualities of Vera Cleaver's writing is her ability to create characters who are distinctly original yet share common bonds with each other and with all of us."

Unlike many of the problems with which the young female characters in Cleaver's novels must cope, the challenges of *Moon Lake Angel* and *Belle Pruitt* are purely emotional. In *Moon Lake Angel* ten-year-old Kitty Dale must learn to somehow deal with the fact that neither of her parents have as much time for her as she would like. During the summer she spends on the shores of Moon Lake living with her Aunt Petal, Kitty plots to get revenge on her mother for neglecting her, but by the end of the novel she instead finds the ache in her heart nearly healed. *Belle Pruitt* examines how the eleven-year-old title character copes with the sudden death of her baby brother, Darwin, and with the grief that threatens to overwhelm her and her mother.

Yarbrough concluded that "the recurrent theme of meeting one's responsibilities is central to the Cleavers' work." In their books they explored the

HARPER
TROPHY

Vera Cleaver
BELLE PRUITT

$3.50 US
$4.95 CDN

After her husband's death, Vera Cleaver published
four more books, including this final 1988 work about
a girl who must face her younger brother's death.

indomitable spirit of youth and attempted to create
characters worthy of any battle. The focus of their
writing seemed to be "about growing up, about
meeting the responsibilities that are one's 'whys
and wherefores,'" as Yardley summarized the
message of their *The Whys and Wherefores of
Littabelle Lee*. Other novelists of books for young
people might have dealt their protagonists lesser
challenges, but this was unthinkable to Bill and
Vera Cleaver. Because, as Cianciolo noted, "They
firmly believe that children are capable of all
human responses. Thus their literature depicts the
gamut of human experience—just like Henry
James, long ago, said it should. They believe that
children can cope when given the opportunity."

■ Works Cited

Aldridge, Judith, review of *Grover, Children's Book
Review*, April, 1971, p. 51.

Bacon, Martha, "The Children's Trip to the
Gallows," *Atlantic Monthly*, December, 1968, p.
148.

Review of *Belle Pruitt, Horn Book*, January/
February, 1989, pp. 67-68.

Billman, Carol, review of *Hazel Rye, New York
Times Book Review*, May 15, 1983, p. 24.

Boudreau, Ingeborg, review of *Grover, New York
Times Book Review*, March 15, 1970, p. 49.

Burns, Mary M., review of *Hazel Rye, Horn Book*,
June, 1983, p. 301.

Burns, Mary M., review of *Sweetly Sings the
Donkey, Horn Book*, January/February, 1986, p.
56.

Cianciolo, Patricia J., "Vera and Bill Cleaver Know
Their Whys and Wherefores," *Top of the News*,
June, 1976, pp. 338-350.

Cleaver, Vera, and Bill Cleaver, *Where the Lilies
Bloom*, Lippincott, 1969.

Cleaver, Vera, and Bill Cleaver, *Dust of the Earth*,
Lippincott, 1975.

Cleaver, Vera, and Bill Cleaver, *Hazel Rye*,
Lippincott, 1983.

Davidson, Andrea, review of *Sweetly Sings the
Donkey, Voice of Youth Advocates*, October,
1985, p. 257.

Dean, Leigh, review of *Queen of Hearts, Children's
Book Review Service*, March, 1978, pp. 75-76.

Digilio, Alice, review of *The Kissimmee Kid,
Washington Post Book World*, June 14, 1981,
p.11.

Review of *Dust of the Earth, Books for Your
Children*, autumn, 1977, p. 11.

Review of *Ellen Grae, Publishers Weekly*, April 10,
1967, pp. 80-81.

Farrell, Diane, review of *Grover, Horn Book*, April,
1970, pp. 158-159.

Fireside, Bryna J., review of *Trial Valley, New York
Times Book Review*, June 12, 1977, p. 31.

Flowers, Ann A., review of *The Kissimmee Kid,
Horn Book*, June, 1981, p. 301.

Fritz, Jean, review of *Queen of Hearts, New York
Times Book Review*, April 30, 1978, p. 51.

Fritz, Jean, review of *The Kissimmee Kid, New York
Times Book Review*, June 21, 1981, p. 37.

Gerhardt, Lillian N., review of *Lady Ellen Grae,
School Library Journal*, October, 1968, pp. 152-
153.

Gottlieb, Annie, review of *Dust of the Earth, New
York Times Book Review*, October 19, 1975, pp.
10, 12.

Haviland, Virginia, "Magic Mountains,"
Washington Post Book World, May 1, 1977, p.
E4.

Heins, Ethel, review of *Queen of Hearts, Horn
Book*, June, 1978, p. 275.

Heins, Ethel, review of *Sugar Blue, Horn Book*,
August, 1984, p. 464.

Heins, Paul, review of *Ellen Grae, Horn Book,* February, 1968, pp. 64-65.

Heins, Paul, review of *Trial Valley, Horn Book,* June, 1977, p. 319.

Miller, M. H., review of *The Whys and Wherefores of Littabelle Lee, Children's Book Review,* summer, 1974, p.64.

Review of *Moon Lake Angel, Horn Book,* September/October, 1987, pp. 609-610.

Pegau, Ruth, review of *The Whys and Wherefores of Littabelle Lee, Library Journal,* June 15, 1973, p. 2000.

Saroyan, William, review of *Where the Lilies Bloom, New York Times Book Review,* September 28, 1969, p. 34.

Sutherland, Zena, review of *Ellen Grae, Saturday Review,* July 17, 1967, pp. 35-36.

Sutherland, Zena, review of *Hazel Rye, Bulletin of the Center for Children's Books,* May, 1983, pp. 163-164.

Sutherland, Zena, Dianne L. Monson, and May Hill Arbuthnot, *Children and Books,* 6th edition, Scott, Foresman, 1981, pp. 308-332.

Townsend, John Rowe, *A Sounding of Storytellers: New and Revised Essays on Contemporary Writers for Children,* Lippincott, 1979, pp. 30-40.

Wersba, Barbara, review of *Ellen Grae, New York Times Book Review,* May 7, 1967, p. 39.

Wersba, Barbara, review of *Lady Ellen Grae, New York Times Book Review,* September 8, 1968, p.38.

Review of *Where the Lilies Bloom, Saturday Review,* September 13, 1969, p. 37.

Wilton, Shirley M., review of *Dust of the Earth, School Library Journal,* November, 1975, pp. 87-88.

Yarbrough, Jane Harper, "Vera Cleaver and Bill Cleaver," *Dictionary of Literary of Biography,* Volume 52: *American Writers for Children since 1960: Fiction,* Gale, 1968, pp. 91-97.

Yardley, Jonathan, review of *The Whys and Wherefores of Littabelle Lee, New York Times Book Review,* March 4, 1973, pp. 6-7.

■ For More Information See

BOOKS

Children's Literature Review, Volume 6, Gale, 1984, pp. 95-114.

PERIODICALS

Horn Book, December, 1975, pp. 599-600; October, 1979, pp. 505-515.

Lion and the Unicorn, winter, 1979-80, pp. 81-95.

New York Times Book Review, November 8, 1970, p. 10; May 2, 1971, p. 4; May 28, 1972, p. 8; October 21, 1973, p. 8; January 13, 1980, p. 26; January 5, 1986, p. 21.

School Library Journal, September, 1967, pp. 116-117; April, 1971, pp. 102, 104.

Times Literary Supplement, December 11, 1970, p. 1457; July 2, 1971, p. 767; July 15, 1977, p. 865.°

—Sketch by Marian C. Gonsior

J. California Cooper

■ Personal

Born in Berkeley, CA; daughter of Joseph C. and Maxine Rosemary Cooper; children: Paris A. Williams. *Education:* Attended technical high school and various colleges. *Politics:* None. *Religion:* Christian. *Hobbies and other interests:* Writing, reading, nature, travel, painting, music, tap dancing.

■ Addresses

Home—Eastern Texas; and c/o Russell Perreault, Publicity Department, Bantam Doubleday Dell Publishing Group, 666 5th Ave., New York, NY 10103.

■ Career

Writer.

■ Awards, Honors

Black Playwright of the Year, 1978, for "Strangers"; American Book Award, 1989, for *Homemade Love;* Literary Lion Award and James Baldwin Award, both from the American Library Associa-

tion, both 1988; named Woman of the Year by the University of Massachusetts and Best Female Writer in Texas.

■ Writings

A Piece of Mine (short stories), Alice Walker, 1984.
Homemade Love (short stories), St. Martin's, 1986.
Some Soul to Keep (short stories), St. Martin's, 1987.
The Matter Is Life (short stories), Doubleday, 1991.
Family (novel), Doubleday, 1991.

Also author of seventeen plays, including "Strangers," first produced in 1978, and "Loners"; contributor to *Center Stage: An Anthology of Twenty-one Contemporary Black-American Plays*, edited by Eileen Joyce Ostrow, University of Illinois Press, 1991.

■ Work in Progress

A novel exploring the Ten Commandments, tentatively titled *In Search of Satisfaction;* a collection of short stories for children.

■ Sidelights

"I see so many fools in this world that sometimes I could just go home and cry about what people do to themselves," declares J. California Cooper in an interview with Julie Livingston of the *Bloomsbury Review.* "And so my point is to say, 'Hey, wake up, wake up, look here! Think a minute, think a minute. This is your life! You got, what, ten, twenty, thirty, forty, fifty, sixty years here, and you gonna be gone.'" It is Cooper's firm belief that people should not waste what little time they have by indulging in self-destructive behavior that forms the basis of much of her writing. She gives her works a moral center, and although she creates a wide variety of characters, both admirable and pathetic, the reader always knows how Cooper herself feels about the people she describes. "Let's say that you were God," Cooper explains to Livingston, "and you had this great big apartment complex." If your tenants "kicked out the walls and tore it up," you'd eventually come back and "put them out." Cooper's works suggest which people will be "put out" and why.

Cooper "considers herself a Bible scholar with a strong belief in God and a no-nonsense approach to life," according to *Our Texas* contributor Sharon Egiebor, so many Cooper stories are intentionally "similar to Bible stories." This does not mean, however, that Cooper writes conservative stories that avoid controversial subject matter, or even that her works always reiterate biblical morality. On the contrary, her works are ambivalent about such issues as homosexuality, and several of her stories also imply that premarital sex is not immoral when followed by marriage. Regardless of how readers' views compare with Cooper's, the author does not shy away from delivering messages about controversial subjects. For Cooper, morality is neither an option nor an afterthought—it is the main reason for her writing. As she explains to *Essence* senior editor Valerie Wilson Wesley, "My stories always have a message. That is why I write."

Another distinguishing element of Cooper's style is her straightforward and vernacular prose style. Comparing Cooper's "strong folk flavor" to that of Langston Hughes and Zora Neale Hurston, Alice Walker writes in her preface to Cooper's *A Piece of Mine* that the author's writing is "simple and direct, and the vale of tears in which some of her characters reside is never so deep that a rich chuckle at a foolish person's foolishness can't be heard." Carol Anshaw, writing in the Chicago *Tribune Books,* calls Cooper "a literary folk artist, a quilt maker arranging bright scraps of story, creating plainly told narratives with a backing woven out of the fabric of black female experience." A review of *Some Soul to Keep* in *Publishers Weekly* adds that the human relationships portrayed in Cooper's works are "illuminated in the author's sprightly vernacular prose." And in a *Library Journal* review of the same work, Elizabeth Guiney Sandvick observes that Cooper writes "in the oral folk tradition," with "touches of humor and the grotesque."

Finally, Cooper is noted for her "trademark" exclamation points. "The people in my short stories live in exclamation points," Cooper tells *Essence* contributor Stephanie Stokes Oliver. "I like to write a story that hits constantly." In her interview with Livingston, Cooper declares that it took her thirty years to read Jane Austen, largely because Austen "goes 'la daaa, la daaa.'" As for herself, says Cooper, "I like things that go 'dom, dom, dom!'"

Cooper appeals to young adult readers partly because of her uncomplicated style, partly because of her ability to tell emotionally powerful stories, and partly because of her unembarrassed willingness to confront difficult, even bizarre topics. Her fiction examines such topics as rape, abuse, incest, homosexuality, prostitution, and drug abuse. Her historical fiction explores many of these

"In its strong folk flavor, Cooper's work reminds us of Langston Hughes and Zora Neale Hurston... It is a delight to read."
—ALICE WALKER

After discovering Cooper's folksy short stories, fellow author Alice Walker published this first collection in 1984.

same issues, together with slavery, miscegenation (marriage between people of different races), and infanticide. Cooper's readers are not exclusively female, nor are they predominantly black. Rather, she counts many fans among young adults from a variety of social and ethnic backgrounds who find humor, exotic appeal, comfort, or direction in her frank yet ultimately optimistic stories. Cooper therefore sees her writing as one way to bring people from different backgrounds together. For example, she explains to Oliver that in *Family*, in which many of the characters are of mixed parentage, the message is: "I wanted to tell people that if you're white, the person you may hate could be your relative, so you should love."

Cooper's Storytelling

Although Cooper carefully probes the lives of those who populate her stories, she is very protective of her own privacy and is unwilling to reveal much about her background. She was born in Berkeley, California, admiring her home state enough to name herself after it, but she tells few people what the "J" in her name stands for. Of her youth, she reveals to Egiebor, "I went to high school, graduated and took a few courses in college. The rest of it, I chose what I needed and left. I dropped out when I got what I needed." She does not speak about her parents, former husband, or daughter to those who know her only casually.

Cooper admitted to Oliver that at age seventeen she was still playing with paper dolls, having them act out scenes, and that it was only a small step from paper doll plays to becoming a playwright. Eventually, her dramatic talents caught the attention of poet and novelist Alice Walker, who encouraged her to write fiction. When *A Piece of Mine* was completed in 1984, Walker's newly created publishing house issued it in hardback, and Walker herself wrote the book's preface. Cooper, who says she is unable to tell others exactly how she writes, prefers to be by herself when she's working on a story. She finds inspiration in nature or inanimate objects that "talk" to her. The objects can be anything from a rock to a tree to a fireplace, but the older they are the better. "New things usually don't have anything to say to me," she tells Livingston. "But if a thing has been around awhile, it talks." Cooper explains to Wesley, "Everything gives me a story. I like projecting, empathizing with things, because I believe that everything has some kind of spirit."

In 1987 Cooper moved from California to a small eastern Texas town where she can enjoy nature and be by herself when she needs to think or write. As a writer she is very conscious of her own space, of the need to move about, unencumbered and untroubled, within a private environment. She allows very few people to visit her home. This is partly to guard her privacy—and partly because, according to Egiebor, she believes her home "has balance and she doesn't like to disturb the vibrations." Cooper told Livingston that she'd like to be in love again, to have a companion or close friends, but "I can't do any of that, 'cause when I do, all my voices go away. That means I have to sit there three days and wait for them to come back."

The author's need for privacy is sometimes at ironic odds with Cooper's thematic purposes in her works: the need for friends and tight family relationships, the value of kindness and generosity of heart, and the importance of living for others. "Many . . . things, the best things, were all made at home, first," Cooper tells Wesley. And in her brief preface to *Some Soul to Keep* she writes, "Some people say, with a smile, 'You write all love stories.' Well . . . I say . . . I try to write about needs . . . and Love is our greatest need . . . after health." In a sense Cooper's works establish clear demarcations between public and private matters, between individuality and community. Ultimately, however, they are concerned with bridging the two worlds: Cooper's admirable characters transcend selfishness and egoism, clearly and deliberately engaging in saving or uplifting others. According to a *Publishers Weekly* review of *Some Soul to Keep*, Cooper's noble protagonists are invariably shown "choosing love over security, revenge or dependence."

Short Stories

"I was telling stories before I could write," Cooper says in *Essence*. The first Cooper stories to be made public—her first performed stories—were plays. That she wrote fiction at all was virtually unknown until the publication of the twelve stories collected in *A Piece of Mine*. The stories in this collection all concern the relationships between men and women. Diana Hinds further observes in *Books and Bookmen* that Cooper "writes often as the best friend, sometimes the sister of the woman whose story she tells; and we believe her." Depending on the tale, Cooper's women characters are either destroyed or rejuvenated by their relationships with men.

The stories in this 1986 book all concern people who are searching for something meaningful in their lives.

In "$100 and Nothing!," for example, a business-woman's husband is jealous of her success and constantly derides her talents and accomplishments to cover his own inadequacies. His most oft-repeated phrase to her is, "I could take $100 and nothing and have more than this in a year!" So when she contracts a fatal illness, one hundred dollars is exactly what she decides her husband will receive following her death. In a more romantic vein, "The Free and the Caged" tells how Vilma, a middle-aged widow who is "tired, tired, tired," coincidentally meets a middle-aged widower whose friendship rejuvenates her.

Library Journal reviewer Ann H. Fisher has hailed *A Piece of Mine* as "something of a literary event," declaring that Cooper's stories "sparkle with warmth, humor, and, often, revenge." Several critics have noticed a consistency in all of the stories in *A Piece of Mine*, though not all reviewers considered this a plus. One *Kirkus Reviews* contributor, for example, writes that "there's little variety

in this collection, and little shape or depth in Cooper's monologues," nevertheless concluding that "there's plenty of energy, personality, and humor." *Times Literary Supplement* critic Jeanette Winterson, however, argues that the consistent narrative voice affords *A Piece of Mine* "a continuity that improves each story and gives the whole the depth of a novel." Winterson concludes that while the themes of poverty and prejudice that run through the collection are familiar territory, the value of *A Piece of Mine* lies in Cooper's ability to restore "dignity and importance to the everyday."

In Cooper's next story collection, *Homemade Love*, the author explains in the book's preface that she wished to write about "love that is not bought, not wrapped in fancy packaging with glib lines that often lie." Besides, she says, "homemade goes a long way. Usually lasts longer than we do." The stories are unified in their concern for their characters' struggles to live and love. Many of these people do not at first realize what they really need in their lives to find happiness, but by the end of each story Cooper lets them—or at least the reader—come to a new understanding. In the humorous tale, "Living," for example, a middle-aged man leaves his wife and their rural home for the excitement of the city because he's afraid he's allowing life to pass him by. After only three days, however, he realizes how important his wife is to him and pleads for her forgiveness. In "Happiness Does Not Come in Colors" three black women learn to overcome their prejudices to happily marry the kind of men they never would have considered to be potential husbands before. These stories, and others like them in the collection, range from the comic to the tragic.

As with *A Piece of Mine*, some reviewers of *Homemade Love* have found that similarities in the stories' narrative voice and writing style detract from the freshness of the collection as a whole. One *Publishers Weekly* critic, for instance disapproves of Cooper's "aphoristic commentary and exclamation marks," as well as the "similar-sounding voices" of her narrators. *Library Journal* contributor Janet Boyarin Blundell also asserts that the "sameness of style" makes the collection "tiresome." Other reviewers, however, have much more praise for *Homemade Love*. *Writer's Digest* contributor Michael Schumacher of *Writer's Digest*, for one, calls the book "an exquisite collection." Insisting that Cooper's dialogue "runs as smooth as honey off a wooden spoon" and that her stories are "virtual performance pieces, wonderfully paced and written with an ear for the music in colloquial language,'' Schumacher believes that the magic of Cooper's style comprises a whole "from which not a word can be cut without upsetting the balance of the story."

The five stories which make up *Some Soul to Keep* are much longer than those of Cooper's earlier collections. Indeed, Cooper refers to them in her author's note for the volume as "long-short stories." Three of them, "Sisters of the Rain," "About Love and Money" and "Feeling for Life," approach the length of novellas. Once again, the central unifying quality of the work is the narrative voice, each story being told from the viewpoint of a poor, black woman who has overcome life's hardships through her perseverance and religious faith.

Although her characters often suffer because they are poor, Cooper admonishes those who are materialistic. In the opening story to *Some Soul to Keep*, "Sisters of the Rain," the author explores the maturing friendship between Superior and Glenellen, juxtaposing their morally-grounded lives with the consequences of Jewel's selfish materialism. The narrator explains the moral significance of the story in these words: "Jewel, and a lot of other people, look for the pot of gold at the end of the rainbow. They don't find it cause it just ain't there! The rainbow is a gift from God and He ain't never cared nothin for gold." Several other stories in the collection, including "About Love and Money," "Feeling for Life," and "Red-Winged Blackbirds," are concerned with the emotional consequences of sex, the latter two exploring the psyches of women who were raped when they were children.

Reviewers like Terry McMillan reiterated the usual criticism of Cooper's stories in their assessment of *Some Soul to Keep*. In the *New York Times Book Review* McMillan writes that "the narrators can be intrusive, the voice doesn't alter from one story to the next and the excessive use of exclamation points is enough to get on your nerves." Still, many critics are enamored by the immediacy of *Some Soul to Keep*. Even McMillan admits that the five stories of the collection "give you the feeling that you're sitting on the front porch with the narrator,... she's snapping beans, you're holding the bowl and she's giving you the inside scoop on everybody. You listen, pass her back the bowl and don't know whether to believe her." *Kirkus Reviews* concludes that the "sheer good nature expressed in these stories carry the reader willingly with her."

The focus of Cooper's next collection, *The Matter Is Life*, which contains seven short stories and a

novella, is just what the title implies. "Some people say it takes courage to face the matter of death," Cooper writes in the author's note at the beginning of the book, "[but] ... I believe it takes more courage to face Life. To survive the everyday matters of the mind, body and heart." Once again, readers will feel themselves in familiar Cooper territory since the themes and characters are reminiscent of earlier works.

Depending on the story, Cooper creates characters who illustrate either how to live one's life or how to waste it utterly. Some examples of the latter are "Vanity," about a beautiful woman who looks in all the wrong places for happiness and contentment, and "No Lie," which tells of a sixty-year-old man's despairing realization that his obsession with sex and other frivolous pleasures has prevented him from having a truly meaningful life. The optimistic stories in *The Matter Is Life* provide the reader with examples of characters who have a true apprecia-

Cooper begins to explore her characters and themes in more depth in this 1987 collection, which contains five lengthy "short" stories.

tion of life. "The Big Day," one of Cooper's more experimental works in its use of unusual stylistic devices such as musical notations, tells of a ninety-year-old woman who loves life so much that she protests to God and her loved ones that she isn't ready to die.

The novella in *The Matter Is Life*, entitled "The Doras," is a prime example of Cooper's vision of how one should live. It is the history of a woman named Dora and her four daughters: Lovedora, Windora, Endora, and their half sister, Splendora, who is the central character in the story. Each of the daughters lead troubled existences at first, eventually straightening themselves out to find stable work and home lives. Of the four, however, Splendora is the most self-sacrificing. Not only does she offer non-judgmental love to the misunderstood Endora, but she donates one of her kidneys to her mother (who suffers from kidney failure), a lung to Lovedora (who has tuberculosis), and an eye to Windora (who is going blind). Finally, Splendora marries the club-footed son of her mother's best friend, with the promise of a happy future ringing in the story's last words.

The clear-cut right versus wrong messages in these stories have illicited some dissatisfaction among several critics. As Anshaw points out in *Tribune Books*, Cooper's "moral vision doesn't seem to allow for nuance or shading. The thing about life that makes it both a bitch and at the same time endlessly fascinating is that good doesn't always get rewarded, wickedness and vanity often go unpunished. . . . Literature at its best—even folk literature, which is by definition naive, but not necessarily simplistic—reflects this complexity." However, Anshaw does admire Cooper as a folk artist who, in "her better moments, . . . captures the rhythms of poor and rural black speech." But *Library Journal* critic Albert E. Wilhelm is less judgmental of *The Matter Is Life*. Admitting that the plots in the collection often seem similar, Wilhelm nevertheless asserts that the stories are usually "touching without falling into sentimentality and totally honest without becoming crude."

Cooper's First Novel

With her novel *Family*, Cooper was able to develop much more fully the themes and characters she explores in her shorter fiction. A multi-generational account of black slaves and their masters in the antebellum South, *Family* also examines the posterity of central characters in the years following the Civil War. The story begins with Fammy, a black

Cooper's first novel, published in 1991, puts a twist on slave narratives by having a deceased woman's spirit tell her family's story.

woman who has borne nine children sired by her white master, and who kills him after he informs her that she will now be his young son's "nightmate," too. Fammy's daughter by a black man, Clora, is the book's narrator. Orphaned at age twelve, Clora soon becomes pregnant by the Young Master, the son of her mother's tormentor. Eventually, she bears four of his children: Always, Sun, Peach and Plum. When the Young Master's wife one day attempts to strike Plum, Clora takes up a poker, threatening the white woman. Knowing that her insubordination may cost her her life, Clora decides to commit suicide, taking her children with her in death. As it turns out, however, Clora alone dies of the poison gruel she prepares; her spirit watches and records the affairs of her children, tracing out a complex but never confusing genealogy.

Though Clora's grandchildren and great-grandchildren are ultimately happy and successful, the bulk of their tale is filled with despair and intrigue. There is a switching of white and black babies at birth; there is rape and abuse, cruelty and death; there is the Civil War and its aftermath for blacks and whites alike. By the end of the novel, "blackness" and "whiteness" are truly subjective and entirely relative terms. "Family," on the other hand, applies to everyone.

A review of *Family* in *Publishers Weekly* calls it a "beautifully textured first novel" and declares that with "power and grace, Cooper weaves the dialect, style and myths of the South into a portrait of the hell that was slavery." Sharon Dirlam, writing in the *Los Angeles Times Book Review*, declares that while many works of fiction have examined slavery, "this one is original, stirring, vividly personal and painfully intense." Writing in *Tribune Books*, Melissa Walker compares *Family* to novels by Margaret Walker, Sherley Anne Williams, and Toni Morrison. Although in the end the reviewer sees Cooper's novel as less aesthetically rich than works by the other women, she praises its "compelling voice that speaks of the past in the present with a concern for those human traits that might make possible some kind of future." On another level, Walker argues that what "most distinguishes *Family* from ... other narratives of slavery by black women writers is its persistent affirmation of the power of the human spirit to do battle with evil—and to win, even if only for a while."

Although, as Cooper has told Wesley in *Essence*, she writes to convey a message to her audience, her favorite audience is herself. "My mind is always entertaining me," she relates to Livingston. "I love myself. What I'm mainly writing for is me. I want to know what's inside of me." When asked by *AAYA* if she has a particular message for her young adult readers, Cooper responded: "Speaking to young people of any day, I know I always feel the same about life and wisdom. So may I offer you this passage from the 'Author's Note' in *The Matter is Life*?—I really do mean every word of it:

"I give a lot of thought to the matter of Life. I mean to make mine as good and easy as possible. I stay as close to God and His wisdom as possible.... Every minute is of great moment in the matter of Life. There may be no small matters. A penny piece of candy can choke you to death, like a penny piece of lover can kill your soul. A person alive at two o'clock may be dead at two ten, accidentally, from a wrong decision. A simple thing like boredom (which is really not that simple) can create havoc in a life; it has the power to destroy. All in Life there is to decide upon is important to

our living, in that it determines the quality, even the length, of our days."

■ Works Cited

Anshaw, Carol, "A Patchwork of Folklike Tales from J. California Cooper," *Tribune Books* (Chicago), July 28, 1991, p. 6.

Blundell, Janet Boyarin, review of *Homemade Love, Library Journal*, August, 1986, p. 168.

Cooper, J. California, *The Matter Is Life*, Doubleday, 1991.

Cooper, J. California, *Some Soul to Keep*, St. Martin's, 1987.

Dirlam, Sharon, review of *Family, Los Angeles Times Book Review*, January 13, 1991, p. 6.

Egiebor, Sharon, "This California States," *Our Texas*, fall, 1992, pp. 16-17.

Review of *Family, Publishers Weekly*, November 2, 1990, pp. 64-65.

Fisher, Ann H., review of *A Piece of Mine, Library Journal*, December, 1984, p. 2296.

Hinds, Diana, review of *A Piece of Mine, Books and Bookmen*, February, 1986, p. 18.

Review of *Homemade Love, Publishers Weekly*, July 11, 1986, p. 53.

Livingston, Julie, "Finding Common Human Bonds: An Interview with J. California Cooper," *Bloomsbury Review*, April/May 1991, pp. 17-19.

McMillan, Terry, "Life Goes on, and Don't You Forget It!," *New York Times Book Review*, November 8, 1987, p. 23.

Oliver, Stephanie Stokes, "J. California Cooper: From Paper Dolls to Paperbacks," *Essence*, May, 1991, p. 52.

Review of *A Piece of Mine, Kirkus Reviews*, November 15, 1984, p. 1056.

Sandvick, Elizabeth Guiney, review of *Some Soul to Keep, Library Journal*, October 15, 1987, p. 91.

Schumacher, Michael, review of *Homemade Love, Writer's Digest*, February, 1987, p. 21.

Review of *Some Soul to Keep, Kirkus Reviews*, August 15, 1987, p. 1178.

Review of *Some Soul to Keep, Publishers Weekly*, September 11, 1987, p. 79.

Walker, Alice, preface to *A Piece of Mine*, by J. California Cooper, Wild Trees Press, 1984, pp. vii-ix.

Walker, Melissa, "A Slave Woman's Ghost Observes the Lives of Her Descendants," *Tribune Books* (Chicago), February 24, 1991, p. 6.

Wesley, Valerie Wilson, interview with J. California Cooper, *Essence*, May, 1990, p. 150.

Wilhelm, Albert E., review of *The Matter is Life*, *Library Journal*, June 1, 1991, p. 188.
Winterson, Jeanette, "Lightning and Loss," *Times Literary Supplement*, August 22, 1986, p. 921.

■ For More Information See

BOOKS

Contemporary Literary Criticism, Volume 56, Gale, 1988, pp. 69-72.

PERIODICALS

Booklist, June 15, 1991, p. 1932; March 15, 1992, p. 1363.
Kirkus Reviews, July 1, 1986, p. 955.
Library Journal, December, 1990, p. 160; July 1, 1991, p. 188; September 15, 1991, p. 144.
Publishers Weekly, July 11, 1986, p. 53; May 31, 1991, p. 58.
New York Times Book Review, December 30, 1990, p. 12; January 26, 1992, p. 24.°

—*Sketch by Keith Lawrence*

Anne Frank

■ Personal

Born Annelies Marie Frank June 12, 1929, in Frankfort am Main, Germany; died in March, 1945, in the Bergen-Belsen, Germany, concentration camp of typhoid fever and malnutrition; daughter of Otto (a banker and business owner) and Edith Frank.

■ Addresses

Home—263 Prinsengracht, Amsterdam, Netherlands.

■ Writings

Het achterhuis, foreword by Annie Romein-Verschoor, Contact (Amsterdam), 1947, translated from the Dutch by B. M. Mooyaart-Doubleday as *Diary of a Young Girl,* introduction by Eleanor Roosevelt, Doubleday, 1952, published with a preface by George Stevens, Pocket Books, 1958, published as *The Diary of Anne Frank,* foreword by Storm Jameson, illustrated by Elisabeth Trimby, Heron Books, 1973, critical edition prepared by the Netherlands State Institute for War

Documentation and edited by David Barnouw and Gerrold van der Stroom published as *The Diary of Anne Frank: The Critical Edition,* introduction by Harry Paape, Gerrold van der Stroom, and David Barnouw, with a summary of the report by the State Forensic Science Laboratory of the Ministry of Justice, compiled by H. J. J. Hardy, translated by Arnold J. Pomerans and B. M. Mooyaart-Doubleday, Doubleday, 1989.

Translations of the diary are available in German, French, Italian, Spanish, Russian, Polish, and other languages.

COLLECTIONS

The Works of Anne Frank, introduction by Ann Birstein and Alfred Kazin, Doubleday, 1959.

Tales from the House Behind: Fables, Personal Reminiscences, and Short Stories (translation from original Dutch manuscript, *Verhalen rondom het Achterhuis,* by H. H. B. Mosberg and Michael Mok), illustrated by Peter Spier, World's Work, 1962.

Anne Frank's Tales from the Secret Annex (includes portions previously published in *The Works of Anne Frank* and *Tales from the House Behind* and translations from original manuscript, *Verhaaltjes en gebeurtenissen uit het Achterhuis,* by Ralph Manheim and Michel Mok), Doubleday, 1983.

■ Adaptations

Anne Frank: Diary of a Young Girl was adapted by Frances Goodrich and Albert Hackett for a two-act stage play titled *Diary of Anne Frank*, first produced in New York in 1955 and published in 1956 as *The Diary of Anne Frank Dramatized by Frances Goodrich and Albert Hackett* by Random House with a foreword by Brooks Atkinson. The diary was also adapted as *The Diary of Anne Frank*, a film released by Twentieth Century-Fox in 1959 and starring Millie Perkins in the title role. In 1980, the diary was adapted for a television movie titled *The Diary of Anne Frank* with Melissa Gilbert starring as Anne Frank. Selections of the diary have been read by Julie Harris for a recording for Spoken Arts in 1974, and by Claire Bloom for a Caedmon recording in 1977.

■ Sidelights

In 1942, an ordinary, German-born Dutch girl named Anne Frank decided to begin a diary. "It's an odd idea for someone like me to keep a diary," she wrote in the third entry of the little book. "[It] seems to me that neither I—nor for that matter anyone else—will be interested in the unbosomings of a thirteen-year-old schoolgirl." Just weeks after she began to write in her diary, Anne and her family were forced to flee from their home and seek shelter in a hidden annex; the Frank family was Jewish, and their survival depended on their ability to evade capture by the Nazis. Two years of living confined in the tiny annex with seven other people and coping with the constant fear of death transformed this "ordinary" teenager into an extraordinary young woman, and the collection of her recorded thoughts into one of the most studied testimonies of the Nazi era in existence today.

Although Anne did not live to know it, in the fifty years following the writing of her diary, more than thirteen million people all over the world have become very interested in, and even fascinated with, her "unbosomings." Anne Frank's diary has been published in over forty languages and has been adapted into plays and films. Anne's other works, including an unfinished novel, have been published in *The Works of Anne Frank, Tales From the House Behind: Fables, Personal Reminiscences, and Short Stories*, and *Anne Frank's Tales From the Secret Annex*. The Franks' hiding place in Amsterdam has been preserved by the Anne Frank Foundation, and schools in various countries, as well as a village at Wuppertal, Germany, have been named in Frank's honor. As Ann Birstein and Alfred Kazin asserted in an introduction to *The Works of Anne Frank*, "Anne Frank has become a universal legend. Out of the millions who were gassed, burned, shot, hanged, starved, tortured,

buried alive, the young girl . . . has become a prime symbol of the innocence of all those who died in the middle of the twentieth century at the hands of the most powerful state in western Europe."

Annelies Marie Frank was born in Frankfurt am Main, Germany, in 1929. Although her father was a well-to-do Jewish businessman, economic turmoil, the rise of the Nazi party, and the leadership of Adolf Hitler made life increasingly threatening for the family. In 1933, when Hitler announced that Jewish and German children would have to attend separate schools, the family realized that they had to leave Germany. They fled to Amsterdam, where Otto Frank began to direct a food import business.

In Amsterdam, Anne's life was relatively normal. Although the Germans invaded Holland in 1940 and brought their harsh anti-Jewish attitudes and laws with them, and despite the fact that Anne and Margot, her older sister, were forced to attend Jewish schools, the girls maintained the concerns and attitudes of other young women. Lies Goslar Pick, Anne's best childhood friend, discussed Anne's ambitions and behaviors in *McCall's*. According to Pick, while Margot was intent on earning honors in school and becoming a nurse, Anne was "interested mainly in dates, clothes, and parties." In contrast to Margot, who, Pick noted, "never gave her parents a moment's trouble," Anne "was a mischief-maker who annoyed the neighbors with her pranks and continually was in hot water at school for her conduct." Nicknamed "Miss Chatterbox" and "Miss Quack-Quack," Anne was repeatedly reprimanded in school for her constant chatter and sporadic joking. Anne's teacher, Pick also remembered, reported that the "compositions Anne wrote in school were just ordinary, no better than average."

Although the personality she usually displayed was vivacious, playful, and sometimes stubborn, Anne maintained a quiet discourse with herself when she was alone. She had much to contemplate—the encroaching war, the end of her childhood—and she did so with enthusiasm. But Anne felt that there was no one with whom she could confide or discuss her private thoughts, and she was lonely. "I have no . . . real friend," she would write later. "But it's the same with all my friends, just fun and joking, nothing more. We don't seem to be able to get any closer, that is the root of the whole trouble. . . . I can never bring myself to talk of anything outside the common round."

Life for Anne began innocently enough. Here she is pictured (second from the left) in Amsterdam in 1937, playing with her friends.

It was not until her parents gave her a small, clothbound book for her thirteenth birthday in June, 1942, that Anne was able to express this loneliness, as well as her contemplative and thoughtful intelligence. "I want to write," she claimed in the diary, "but more than that, I want to bring out all kinds of things that lie buried deep in my heart. . . . I don't want to set down a series of bald facts in a diary as most people do, but I want this diary itself to be my friend, and I shall call my friend Kitty."

One month after Anne received her diary, Anne's sister Margot was notified that she was required to report to the Dutch Nazi organization's Westerbork concentration camp reception center. Rather than face separation and an uncertain future, the family chose to flee again—this time to the attic of Otto Frank's warehouse. Alarmed by the increasing incarceration of Jews in concentration camps, Mr. Frank had prepared a secret hiding place in his warehouse on Prinsengracht Canal with some business partners and employees. The family would have to isolate itself and go into hiding in what Anne would later call the "Secret Annexe";

there would be no more school and no more friends for Anne. Although she had to leave her childhood behind her as she moved to this secret home, Anne did not abandon her diary: it was the first thing she packed.

The Secret Annex

While the Frank family was temporarily safe, the world outside their walls and their blackened windows became increasingly terrifying for Jews and non-Jews alike. Seeking shelter from that terror, Mr. and Mrs. Van Pelz ("Van Daan" in Anne's diary), along with their fifteen-year-old-son, Peter, and Albert Dussel, a dentist, soon joined the Frank family in the annex. Confined together, the eight crowded people depended on the efforts of Miep and Jan Gies, Jo Koophuis, Victor Kraler, and Elli Vossen to keep them alive. Risking their lives by hiding the Jews and possessing illicit ration coupons, these former employees of Otto brought those in the annex food, news, gifts, and comfort.

The inhabitants of the annex were constantly worried that they would be discovered. When they received news that Jews they knew had been captured, and when they witnessed the arrests of Jews from their windows, their tension and frustration increased. As they could not leave the annex, or make noises loud enough to be heard by anyone who might discover them, the eight people had to occupy themselves with quiet activities. This was especially difficult for Anne. She offered this note to her diary in October, 1942: "We are as quiet as mice. Who, three months ago, would ever have guessed that quicksilver Anne would have to sit still for hours—and, what's more, could?"

It was the diary that allowed Anne to keep still. More and more she turned to it, rather than her family, to amuse herself and express her thoughts and emotions. In addition to working on the educational tasks her father provided, Anne recorded entries in her diary and wrote fables, short stories, essays, and the better part of a novel, as well. She wrote constantly about life in the annex. On August 4, 1943, for example, she wrote: "Now that we have been in the 'Secret Annexe' for over a year, you know something of our lives, but some of it is quite indescribable.... To give you a closer look ..., now and again I intend to give you a description of an ordinary day. Today I'm beginning with the evening and the night...."

The tension of living so quietly and so close together wore on everyone. Not surprisingly, there were many arguments in the annex. As Antonia White reminded readers of the diary in the *New Statesman and Nation,* "In this unnatural confinement, the personal relations of two married couples, three adolescents and a peculiarly irritating elderly bachelor developed a feverish intensity. Even the continual threat of danger and the knowledge of what terrible, half-guessed fate might be awaiting them did not prevent them from bickering as fiercely, and over the same trivial things, as any two ill-assorted couples sharing a house and quarrelling as to whose turn it was to wash up."

Anne was involved in many of these arguments. She quarreled with her sister, of whom she was jealous. "Now Margot is just the prettiest, sweetest, most beautiful girl in the world," she wrote. "But all the same I feel I have some right to be taken seriously too. I have always been the dunce, the ne'er-do-well of the family." Anne found no comfort in her father, who tended to side with his elder daughter during arguments. "If he holds Margot up as an example, approves of what she

Behind a bookcase in a warehouse that is now a museum, Anne's father hid the staircase that led to the secret annex.

does, praises and caresses her, then something gnaws at me inside, because I adore Daddy. He is the one I look up to.... He doesn't notice that he treats Margot differently from me." Anne could not get along with her mother either. She wrote of her, "It is hard to speak the truth, and yet it is the truth: she herself has pushed me away, her tactless remarks and her crude jokes, which I don't find at all funny, have now made me insensitive to any love from her side." It was not until the later months of the Franks' confinement that Anne was able to live in relative peace with her family.

Anne did not reserve her quarrelsome attitude for her family, however. She argued with the Van Pelz adults and Albert Dussel as well. The only person Anne felt she could confide in, at least partially, was Peter Van Pelz; they began a relationship. According to Meyer Levin in the *New York Times Book Review,* Anne recorded this "love affair" in her diary. "All is told, from her potato-fetching devices for going up to Peter's attic lair.... And the parents worrying about the youngsters trysting up there in the dusk, sitting by the window over the canal. And her fears that her older sister is lonely and jealous." Anne even described her first kiss in her diary: "I sat pressed closely against him and felt a wave of emotion come over me, tears sprang into my eyes.... At half past eight I stood up and went to the window, where we always say good-by.... He came toward me, I flung my arms around his neck and gave him a kiss on his left cheek, and was about to kiss the other cheek, when my lips met his and we pressed them together."

Anne's infatuation with Peter did not last long, and their "affair," which never progressed much past those first kisses, ended. Pick wrote that "in Peter Anne did not find what she most longed for—'a friend for my understanding.' After the first flowering of their romance in the Secret Annex, she wrote, 'Peter hasn't enough character yet, not enough will power, too little courage and strength. He is still a child in his heart of hearts, he is no older than I am.'"

With the growing, disappointing realization that she did not love Peter came a deepening depression. Anne wrote on October 29, 1943, "The atmosphere is so oppressive, and sleepy and heavy as lead. You don't hear a single bird singing outside, and a deadly close silence hangs everywhere, catching hold of me as if it will drag me down deep into an underworld. . . . I wander from one room to another, downstairs and up again, feeling like a songbird whose wings have been clipped and who is hurling himself in utter darkness against the bars of his cage."

Despite this "darkness," Anne refused to relinquish her spirit. Her thoughts matured and her emotions intensified. Birstein and Kazin discussed this growth: "Like all young growing things, Anne, forced into a premature ripeness by the terrible intensity of events, yearned and struggled for the light." And Annie Romein-Verschoor wrote in her introduction to *Het achterhuis*, the original Dutch publication of Anne's diary that "the growth of the lively, intelligent and impressionable child Anne Frank, from girl to woman, from child to adult, occurred in a remarkably brief time."

Anne also began to imagine her future at this time, envisioning herself as a writer. She wrote on March 29, 1944, "an M.P. [Military Policeman] was speaking on the Dutch News from London, and . . . said that they ought to make a collection of diaries and letters after the war. . . . Just imagine how interesting it would be if I were to publish a romance of the 'Secret Annexe.' The title alone would be enough to make people think it was a detective story. But, seriously, it would seem quite funny ten years after the war if we Jews were to tell how we lived and what we ate and talked about here." Anne began to prepare her diary for publication after the war and wrote with renewed vigor. "I know what I want, I have a goal, an opinion, I have a religion and love," she wrote on April 6, 1944. "I know that I'm a woman, a woman with inward strength and plenty of courage. If God lets me live . . . I shall not remain insignificant, I shall work in the world and for mankind!"

Along with this faith in herself came optimism for the rest of the world. On July 15, 1944, she wrote the words which would be quoted over and over again by her readers: "in spite of everything I still believe that people are really good at heart. . . . I can feel the sufferings of millions and yet, if I look up into the heavens, I think that it will all come right, that this cruelty too will end, and that peace and tranquility will return again. . . . In the meantime, I must uphold my ideals, for perhaps the time will come when I shall be able to carry them out."

Although these words foreshadowed the influence of Anne's work on the world, Anne did not live to see it. She penned the last entry in her diary on August 1, 1944. Three days later the secret annex was raided. The Franks, the Van Peltz family, and Mr. Dussel were discovered. This time, Anne left the diary, which she had kept for twenty-six months, behind.

The Fate of Anne Frank

According Michael Small and Cathy Nolan in a *People* article, Miep Gies "can still hear the sad, slow footsteps on the stairs" as the eight people were led out of their hiding place. Sadly wandering through the annex after the arrest, the woman who had faithfully helped her friends found Anne's plaid-cloth-covered diary and her other notebooks on the floor. In their search for valuables, the secret police had overlooked these treasures. Without reading them, Miep Gies hid the books in her home under a pile of magazines.

The eight people who had lived for two years in the annex became prisoners of the Nazis just nine months before the war in Europe ended. Although the group was initially sent on a passenger train to Westerbork, they continued by cattle car to the most infamous German concentration camp of all: Auschwitz in Poland. Anne's mother died there, and the rest of the mourning group was separated. Anne and Margot were transferred to Bergen-Belsen, another concentration camp.

Those Holocaust survivors who knew Anne during her days in Bergen-Belsen remembered that she was helpful, kind, brave, and thoughtful. According to an excerpt from Ernst Schnabel's *Anne Frank: A Portrait in Courage*, "Anne was the youngest in her group, but nevertheless she was the leader of it. She also distributed the bread in the barracks, and she did it so well and fairly that there was none of the usual grumbling.... She, too, was the one who saw to the last what was going on all around us.... [We] were beyond feelings.... Something protected us, kept us from seeing. But Anne had no such protection, to the last." Two months before the Germans surrendered to the Allies in 1945, the Frank sisters, first Margot and then Anne, died of typhoid fever.

Of the eight people who had lived in the annex, only Otto Frank survived the Nazis' "final solution to the Jewish problem." When Russian troops liberated prisoners from Auschwitz, he returned to Amsterdam, hoping to find news that his daughters were alive. The day that Otto Frank received a letter notifying him of Anne and Margot's deaths, Miep Gies gave him Anne's writings. Grief stricken, Mr. Frank could not read them for days. When he finally found the strength to read them, he did so only little by little.

Otto Frank was shocked by what he read. As he later admitted to Pick, "I never realized my little Anna was so deep." With this realization came the understanding that his daughter's work was important, at least to those who had known her and her family. Mr. Frank typed a few copies to share with friends. These friends recognized the broad appeal of the work and its historical importance. They encouraged Otto Frank to edit the diary and publish it. The diary appeared in 1947 as *Het achterhuis*.

Reactions to Anne Frank's Diary

Since its publication, readers have approached the diary from various perspectives and appreciated it in diverse manners. The diary initially became famous as a historical document and description of the horrors of World War II. Later, the book became a literary classic. Many readers consider Anne Frank's diary to be the voice of the Jews who did not survive the Holocaust and believe that criticism of it is unnecessary. Others delight in the work's honesty and intimacy and dispense with literary criticism. A few criticize the diary for its frank discussions of sexuality and argue that the book is improper reading for young people. In any case, rather than discuss its aesthetic or structural elements, critics often concentrate more on the historical and sociological aspects of the diary.

One example of the historical appreciation of the diary comes from a professor of modern history, Jan Romein. Romein wrote in *A Tribute to Anne Frank,* "The Government Institute for War Docu-

Anne Frank:
The Diary of a Young Girl
with an Introduction by Eleanor Roosevelt and a new Afterword setting Anne Frank's experiences in their historical context

"A truly remarkable book... Anne Frank's diary simply bubbles with amusement, love and discovery.... It is a warm and stirring confession, to be read over and over for insight and enjoyment."   — The New York Times

One of the many editions of Anne Frank's famous diary.

mentation is in possession of about two hundred similar diaries, but it would amaze me if there was one among them as pure, as intelligent, and yet as human as this one. I read it from beginning to end without stopping.... When I finished it was evening, and I was astonished that the light was burning, that there was still bread and tea, that I heard no airplanes droning above and no soldiers' boots shuffling on the streets, so thoroughly had this diary captured me."

Romein-Verschoor provided the preface to the Dutch edition of the diary and valued it for its presentation of the triumph of the human spirit: The "most important thing about this diary is not the documentation, which so often is and will be recorded elsewhere. When people in the tropics take a young plant from the temperate mountain zone and plant it in a very hot area, it will bloom once, richly and superabundantly, only to die soon after.... In the same way, this small, plucky geranium stood and bloomed, and bloomed, behind the shuttered windows of the Annex."

John Berryman, a renowned American poet, appreciated the diary for its demonstration of the process of maturation: "I would call the subject of Anne Frank's *Diary* even more mysterious and fundamental than St. Augustine's, and describe it as: the conversion of a child into a person," Berryman judged in his *The Freedom of the Poet*, comparing Anne's personal growth to a religious conversion. Arguing that not all people become truly mature in the way that Anne Frank did, Berryman observed: "It took, I believe, a special pressure forcing the child-adult conversion, and exceptional powers of expression, to bring that strange or normal change into view. This, if I am right, is what she has done."

Others were intrigued with the intimate knowledge of Anne that the diary provides, as well as her ability to analyze her own attitudes and emotions. Henry F. Pommer represents this group in a *Judaism* article: "The chief literary merit of the diary is its permitting us to know intimately Anne's young, eager, difficult, lovable self.... Some pages read as though they had been written in the security of a Long Island suburbia; on the next page we are plunged into Nazi terror."

The fame of the diary spread. In 1952 it was published in the United States as *Diary of a Young Girl;* Former first lady Eleanor Roosevelt provided an introduction for the work. In Roosevelt's opinion, the "diary tells us much about ourselves and about our own children.... I felt how close we all are to Anne's experience, how very much involved we are in her short life and in the entire world." Roosevelt encouraged readers, "Anne's diary is an appropriate monument to her fine spirit and to the spirits of those who have worked and are working still for peace. Reading it is a rich and rewarding experience."

Millie Perkins starred in a 1959 film version of *The Diary of Anne Frank.*

By 1959, when *The Works of Anne Frank* was published, the diary was well known and its author was highly regarded around the world. It was not long before visitors to Amsterdam waited in long lines to tour the "Secret Annexe," or "the Anne Frank Huis," which was opened to the public. In the *New York Times Book Review*, Frederic Morton discussed the impact of the diary on the world: "It may well be that the single most enduring thing to be born during the entire course of the Nazi nightmare was a book a young Jewish girl wrote in the occupied Holland of the early Forties. Anne Frank's diary of the years spent in the few cubic feet of her family's hide-out has become familiar to the world as an international best seller, as a dramatization that has moved audiences in every major country, and as a motion picture."

Anne Frank's Other Works

With the publication of *The Works of Anne Frank*, the world was given access to the stories, fables, essays, and reminiscences Anne had written in addition to the entries in her diary. Notable among these pieces are "My First Article," a journalistic yet enthusiastic description of Peter Van Peltz's small room, and "Kitty," a formal composition about an imaginary friend. "The Wise Old Dwarf" is often noted for its fictional presentation of Anne's situation; the dwarf keeps two dissimilar elves confined together to teach them a lesson: "I took you here and left you together to teach you there are other things in this world beside your fun and your gloom.... Dora has become somewhat more serious, and Peldron has cheered up a bit, because you were obliged to make the best of having to live together." The fable suggests that Anne, by living in isolation with a few others, is also being forced to learn a lesson.

As Morton wrote, because the "first appearance of the diary was so great that it focused attention only on Anne the victim," rather than on "Anne the writer," the "illumination of these new pages [*The Works*] is important." While some critics agreed that these pieces demonstrate Anne's creative potential, they also decided that none of the works are as striking as the diary. In Morton's words, "none of these places, not even a charming little morality tale like 'The Wise Old Dwarf,' has the power of any single entry in the diary."

A number of critics reached the same conclusion when *Tales from the House Behind* was published in 1962. Among the works in this collection, the light fantasy piece "Dreams of Movie Stardom," the

essay "Give," "Blurry, the Explorer," a story about a wandering bear cub, and "Eve's Dream," a story in which plants are personified, are noteworthy. Also of interest is "The Sink of Iniquity," an essay in which Anne ponders the Dutch dislike of nudity. It employs frank, discursive writing to communicate an unabashed social critique and provides a useful example of Anne's talents. "Modesty and prudishness can go too far. Do you put clothes on flowers when you pick them? I don't think we're so very different from nature. Why should we be ashamed of the way nature has dressed us?"

An unfinished novel, "Cady's Life," was also included in *Tales from the House Behind.* In this work, a young woman struggles to recover from injuries sustained after she is hit by a car. She falls in love with a boy who passes by her in the woods on his way to school and ponders life with him as she writes in her diary. G. B. Stern, who wrote the introduction to the collection, asserted that "more than all the rest of this collection, Anne Frank's fragment of a novel, which she called 'Cady's Life,' corroborates all one has said about her potential powers. In it she combines a wisdom beyond her years, a sense of character and a feeling for religion, until at the very end a lapse from fiction into ... grim reality ... foreshadows what was shortly to prove the fate of her own family and herself."

In 1983, *Anne Frank's Tales from the Secret Annex*, with translations from original manuscript, was published. Containing many pieces that were previously published in *The Works of Anne Frank* and *Tales from the House Behind*, it did not create much of a stir among readers. While Stefan Kanfer, writing for *Time* magazine, claimed that "most of the 30 pieces show a heartbreaking potential," he concluded, "[there] is, of course, no way to determine what kind of writer Anne Frank might have become." A *Horn Book* reviewer, however, decided that "the value of the volume is that it draws together all known incidental pieces," and even though the writing itself is not extraordinary, its "very ordinariness reminds readers that the writer ... was an ordinary child."

Another opportunity for fans of Anne Frank to understand this "ordinariness" appeared with the publication of *The Diary of Anne Frank: The Critical Edition* in 1989. This book provides the portions of Anne's diary that her father had deleted before he published it, as well as the pieces that Anne had edited out of the version she made in preparation for publication after the war. In addition, "in response to continuing attacks on the

In April of 1945, the British liberated the Bergen-Belsen concentration camp—but it was too late for Anne and her sister Margot.

diary by extreme right-wing groups in the United States and Europe," the publisher of the book included a report from the Dutch Justice Ministry on the authenticity of the diary. According to Wendy Chapkis in *Ms.* magazine, the "diary had been attacked as 'too literate' for a teenager, 'too historical' for a girl's diary, and even, according to one critic, 'too pornographic' for a young woman to have written. But the laboratory tests of handwriting, paper, glue, and ink should silence political critics who claim the diary is not real."

Readers of this edition of the diary will find that, in addition to discussing her personal development and the trauma of the war, Anne discusses the physical and spiritual aspects of her impending womanhood. In 1944, for one example, Anne wrote, "I need my mother to be an example I can follow. I want to be able to respect her, and in most things my mother is indeed an example for me, but precisely of how I should not do it." Anne's diary entry for June 15, 1944, discusses feminism: "of

the many questions that continues to disturb me is why, in the past and often now as well, women of all cultures have been placed in a much more lowly position than men.... Soldiers and war heroes are honored and celebrated, explorers receive immortal fame, martyrs are worshipped, but how many in the whole of humanity consider women too, as soldiers?... Women are much braver, much more courageous soldiers who fight and undergo pain for the continued existence of humanity, than the many freedom fighters with their big mouths!"

The voice of Anne Frank speaks clearly in both the edited and the unedited version of her diary. According to Small and Nolan, over thirteen million people had read the diary by 1988. No one knows how many thousands of those millions wept as they read it, or found themselves inspired by it. Otto Frank could not help but notice the influence of his daughter's diary on those who had read it; many readers wrote to him to tell him how they felt about the book. In a 1967 discussion of the diary's impact on the world in *Ladies' Home Journal*, Mr. Frank quoted a letter sent to him from one young woman from Maine: "When I feel troubled, I turn to Anne's picture. I look at those beautiful dark eyes looking at us all. She was so in love with life itself. I think of all she endured and it gives me strength to go on, no matter what."

Mr. Frank also rejoiced that "Anne's wish—'I want to publish a book entitled The Secret Annexe after the war'—[was] fulfilled." Despite her untimely death, Anne's other ambitions, to "not remain insignificant" and to "work in the world and for mankind" have also been achieved. As Mr. Frank exclaimed, "How proud Anne would have been." Nevertheless, Otto Frank challenged readers of his daughter's diary in *A Tribute to Anne Frank*: "However touching and sincere the expressions of sympathy I receive may be, I always reply that it is not enough to think of Anne with pity or admiration. Her diary should be a source of inspiration toward the realization of the ideals and hopes she expressed in it."

■ Works Cited

Review of *Anne Frank's Tales from the Secret Annex*, *Horn Book*, June, 1984, p. 373.

Berryman, John, *The Freedom of the Poet*, Farrar, Straus, 1976, pp. 91-106.

Chapkis, Wendy, "The Uncensored Anne Fran," *Ms.*, October, 1986, pp.79-80.

Frank, Anne, *Diary of a Young Girl*, introduction by Eleanor Roosevelt, Doubleday, 1952.

Frank, Anne, *The Works of Anne Frank*, introduction by Anne Birstein and Alfred Kazin, Doubleday, 1959.

Frank, Anne, *Tales from the House Behind: Fables, Personal Reminiscences, and Short Stories*, introduction by G. B. Stern, Pan Books, 1965.

Frank, Anne, *Anne Frank's Tales from the Secret Annex*, Doubleday, 1983.

Frank, Anne, *The Diary of Anne Frank: The Critical Edition*, edited by David Barnouw and Gerrold van der Stroom, translated by Arnold J. Pomerans and B. M. Mooyaart-Doubleday, Doubleday, 1989.

Frank, Otto, "The Living Legacy of Anne Frank: The Memory Behind Today's Headlines," *Ladies' Home Journal*, September, 1967, pp. 87, 153-54.

Kanfer, Stefan, "Child Sacrifice," *Time*, January 30, 1984, p. 77.

Levin, Meyer, "The Child behind the Secret Door," *New York Times Book Review*, June 15, 1952, pp. 1, 22.

Morton, Frederic, "Her Literary Legacy," *New York Times Book Review*, September 20, 1959, p. 22.

Pick, Lies Goslar, "I Knew Anne Frank," *McCall's*, July, 1958, pp. 30-31, 109-11, 114-15.

Pommer, Henry F., "The Legend and Art of Anne Frank," *Judaism*, winter, 1960, pp. 37-46.

Schnabel, Ernst, *Anne Frank: A Portrait in Courage*, translated by Richard and Clara Winston, Harcourt, 1958.

Small, Michael, with Cathy Nolan, "Miep Gies, Who Hid Anne Frank, Adds a Coda to the Famous Diary," *People*, April 18, 1988, pp. 123-24.

Steenmeijer, Anna G., editor, with Otto Frank and Henri van Praag, *A Tribute to Anne Frank*, Doubleday, 1971.

White, Antonia, "From the Secret Annexe," *New Statesman and Nation*, May 17, 1952, pp. 592-93.

■ For More Information See

BOOKS

Bettelheim, Bruno, *Surviving and Other Essays*, Knopf, 1979, pp. 246-57.

Dunaway, Philip, and Evans, Melvin, editors, *Treasury of the World's Great Diaries*, Doubleday, 1957.

Ehrenburg, Ilya, *Chekhov, Stendhal, and Other Essays*, Knopf, 1963, pp. 258-64.

Fradin, Dennis B., *Remarkable Children: Twenty Who Made History*, Little, Brown, 1987.

Gies, Miep, and Alison Leslie Gold, *Anne Frank Remembered: The Story of the Woman Who Helped to Hide the Franks*, Simon & Schuster, 1987.

Her Way: Biographies of Women for Young People, American Library Association, 1976.

Tridenti, Lina, *Anne Frank*, translated by Stephen Thorne, Silver Burdett, 1985.

van de Rol, Ruud, and Rian Verhoeven, *Anne Frank: Beyond the Diary*, Viking, 1993.

PERIODICALS

Christian Century, May 6, 1959.

Commonweal, October 31, 1968.

Holiday, September 1969, pp. 16, 20-1.

Life, August 18, 1958.

Los Angeles Times, April 13, 1984.

Newsweek, June 25, 1979, pp. 14-15.

New York Times Magazine, April 21, 1957; September 15, 1957, pp. 96, 98.

People, September 16, 1984.

Saturday Review, July 19, 1952.

Seventeen, June, 1989, p. 112.
U.S. News and World Report, May 11, 1987, p. 77;
    August 1, 1989, p. 9.*

    —Sketch by Ronie-Richele Garcia-Johnson

William Gibson

"Burning Chrome"; Hugo Award from World Science Fiction Society, Philip K. Dick Memorial Award for best U.S. original paperback from Philadelphia Science Fiction Society, Nebula Award from Science Fiction Writers of America, and Porgie Award for best paperback original novel in science fiction from *West Coast Review of Books*, all 1985, and Ditmar Award from Australian National Science Fiction Convention, all for *Neuromancer;* Nebula Award nomination and Hugo Award nomination, both for *Count Zero.*

■ Personal

Full name, William Ford Gibson; born March 17, 1948, in Conway, SC; son of William Ford (a contractor) and Otey (a homemaker; maiden name, Williams) Gibson; married Deborah Jean Thompson, June, 1972; children: Graeme Ford, Claire Thompson. *Education:* University of British Columbia, B.A., 1977.

■ Addresses

Home and office—2630 West 7th Ave., Vancouver, British Columbia V6K 1Z1, Canada. *Agent*—(literary) Martha Millard Literary Agency, 204 Park Ave., Madison, NJ 07940; (film and television) Martin S. Shapiro, Shapiro-Lichtman Talent, 8827 Beverly Blvd., Los Angeles, CA 90048.

■ Career

Writer.

■ Awards, Honors

Nebula Award nomination from Science Fiction Writers of America, c. 1983, for short story

■ Writings

NOVELS

Neuromancer (first book in "Cyberspace" trilogy), Ace, 1984.
Count Zero (second book in "Cyberspace" trilogy), Arbor House, 1986.
Mona Lisa Overdrive (third book in "Cyberspace" trilogy), Bantam, 1988.
(With Bruce Sterling) *The Difference Engine,* Gollancz, 1990, Bantam, 1991.
Virtual Light, Bantam/Spectra, 1993.

OTHER

(With John Shirley, Sterling, and Michael Swanwick) *Burning Chrome* (short stories; includes "Burning Chrome," "Johnny Mnemonic," "New Rose Hotel," and one story with each coauthor), introduction by Sterling, Arbor House, 1986.
(Author of introduction) Shirley, *Heatseeker: A New Story Collection,* Scream Press, 1988.

Dream Jumbo (text to accompany performance art by Robert Longo), produced in Los Angeles, CA, at UCLA Center for the Performing Arts, 1989.

Author of a short science fiction work published on computer disk with graphics by artist Dennis Ashbaugh. Work represented in anthologies, including *Shadows 4*, Doubleday, 1981; *Universe 11*, Doubleday, 1981; *Nebula Award Stories 17*, Holt, 1983; and *Mirrorshades: The Cyberpunk Anthology*, edited with an introduction by Sterling, Arbor House, 1986. Contributor of short stories, articles, and book reviews to periodicals, including *Omni*, *Rolling Stone*, and *Science Fiction Review*.

■ Adaptations

A film version of the short story, "Johnny Mnemonic," is planned for production.

■ Work in Progress

Screenplay adaptations of his short stories "Burning Chrome" and "New Rose Hotel"; *Macrochip*, a script with John Shirley.

■ Sidelights

When science fiction author William Gibson wrote his first two novels, *Neuromancer* and *Count Zero*, on a manual typewriter, he knew almost nothing about computers. "When people started talking about them, I'd go to sleep," he told the *Missouri Review*, as quoted in the *Whole Earth Review*. "Then I went out and bought an Apple II on sale, took it home, set it up, and it started making this horrible sound like a farting toaster every time the drive would go on.... Here I'd been expecting some exotic crystalline thing ... and what I'd gotten was something with this tiny piece of a Victorian engine in it, like an old record player."

Ironically, Gibson is one of the most innovative science fiction writers to come out of the 1980s. Many critics see him as a central figure in the cyberpunk movement, a science-fiction sub-genre concerned with modern technology and embracing the attitudes that have evolved along with it. Gibson belongs to one of the first groups of science fiction writers to go beyond the limits of the genre—which were set in the 1950s by such authors as Robert A. Heinlein and Isaac Asimov— and to chart new territory, taking into account the social changes of the 1960s. As Algis Budrys, writing in the *Magazine of Fantasy & Science Fiction*, put it: "A while ago ... a slim, tall, very quiet Canadian named William Gibson published a short story called 'New Rose Hotel' and a novel called *Neuromancer,* and a new school of writing SF was born."

Cyberpunk features tough characters who inhabit a gritty world. The pace is frenetic, and the dialogue is peppered with creative and unusual slang, which Gibson credits to eavesdropping on Toronto computer hackers and dope dealers. "I listened to what hackers said, not trying to understand it but trying to groove on the poetry of it," he told Edward Zuckerman of *People* magazine. Cyberpunk differs from traditional science fiction in more than just the dialogue. As *Washington Post Book World* contributor Charles Platt wrote, "What sets [*Neuromancer*] apart from all other current science fiction is its totally modern orientation. Most writers in this field have middle-aged tastes and style; they dress, act, and write as if the 1960s never happened."

In some ways Gibson's style reflects the years before the 1950s, when so much science fiction was hitting the newsstands. He brings to cyberpunk a detached precision and deadpan quality that many find similar to the 1940s hard-boiled detective thrillers. Howard Coleman, writing in *Science Fiction Review*, saw in Gibson's short stories "the relentless pace and the can't-put-it-down style triangulated somewhere between Harlan Ellison and Raymond Chandler."

Gibson also coined the word "cyberspace," which is a form of hallucination presenting three-dimensional data drawn from all the computers on Earth. "Cyberspace ... may be Gibson's best, most original, and thus most enduring contribution to speculative fiction," commented Pat Cadigan in *Quill and Quire*. "Gibson's is an inspired variant, the answer to the question 'What does information look like?' It's a question almost no one thought of asking, let alone answering." "Cowboys," or futuristic hackers, can penetrate cyberspace with their brains, allowing them access to unlimited amounts of information. But if the computer is prepared for the invasion, it can flood the cowboy's mind with feedback and kill him or destroy part of his brain.

Early Life and Writings

Gibson was born and lived in the United States until his late teens. "I had the classic childhood of an American science-fiction writer," he told Zuckerman. "Intense, geeky isolation in a rather dull environment." Unlike his characters, who often inhabit decaying metropolitan areas, as a child, Gibson was moved by his widowed mother to

Wytheville, a small town in southwestern Virginia. Despite the fact that the library had burned down decades earlier, never to be rebuilt, Gibson managed to read a great deal, including classic science fiction literature. As he grew older, however, he discarded his science fiction interests and decided the genre was irrelevant, pursuing instead such writers as Thomas Pynchon and William Burroughs. Science fiction, he told Zuckerman, was "stodgy and geeked-out."

In order to get away from Wytheville, Gibson attended a private school in Arizona. Before he graduated, however, his mother died of a sudden stroke. He later immersed himself in the hippie culture and moved to Toronto, where he met Deborah Thompson, his art teacher's girlfriend. He and Thompson eventually married; Thompson was

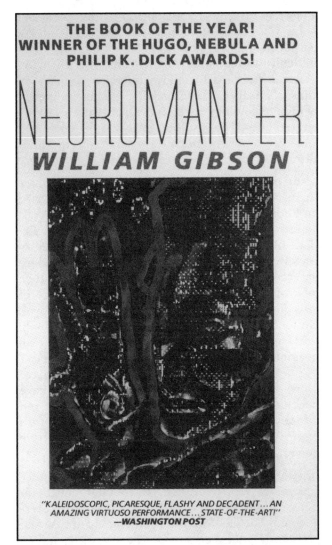

**THE BOOK OF THE YEAR!
WINNER OF THE HUGO, NEBULA AND
PHILIP K. DICK AWARDS!**

"KALEIDOSCOPIC, PICARESQUE, FLASHY AND DECADENT...AN AMAZING VIRTUOSO PERFORMANCE...STATE-OF-THE-ART!"
—WASHINGTON POST

Gibson envisions a society dehumanized by advanced technology in the first novel ever to receive the Nebula, Hugo, and Philip K. Dick Memorial Awards.

interested in finishing her education and the couple returned to Vancouver, her home town. She eventually became an instructor at the University of British Columbia, where Gibson earned his bachelor's degree at the age of twenty-nine. His first short story came about through an English teacher's challenge. Gibson took a science fiction class as an easy credit. He wasn't interested in writing the assigned term paper, so his instructor told him to write a short story instead. Although it took him an agonizing three months, the experience led him to a new career.

Gibson's first published story, "Fragments of a Hologram Rose," netted him twenty-three dollars from *Unearth* magazine in 1977. That year was also when his first child, Graeme, was born. Although Gibson had worked as a graduate assistant, he eventually settled into staying home and taking care of Graeme. "I was just kind of putzing around," Gibson said to Zuckerman. "Then I segued into being the househusband, which got me off the hook for awhile. And that was when I started writing, because it was the only thing I could do alone at the kitchen table that had any chance of getting me anywhere."

From the end of the seventies through the early eighties, Gibson focused on writing and publishing short stories. In 1981, he and John Shirley wrote "The Belonging Kind," which appeared in *Shadows 4;* "The Gernsback Continuum" was published in *Universe 11*; and "Hinterlands" was released in *Omni* magazine. "Hinterlands" and "Gernsback" are not set in Gibson's cyberspace world, but both incorporate his outlook on science and its effect on human psychology. Gibson eventually became a favorite of *Omni*'s editors. They published his stories "Johnny Mnemonic" in 1981 and "Burning Chrome" in 1982. In "Johnny," Gibson began forming his literary picture of the future and presenting some of the character types who would inhabit his novels. The title character, for instance, is a cowboy who steals data from corporate computers and stores the information on a microchip in his brain. He is marked for death by a Japanese syndicate, but is saved by Molly Millions, a bionic hitwoman whose fingernails cover implanted razor blades and whose mirrored sunglasses are surgically fused with her skin. Ultimately, the cowboy is faced with the necessity of either taking responsibility for his own life or becoming a subhuman receptacle for stolen data.

Gibson was shocked by the public's receptiveness to his writing. "I've never run into the kind of resistance I was anticipating, and that's left me

FROM THE HUGO AND NEBULA AWARD-WINNING AUTHOR OF *NEUROMANCER* AND *COUNT ZERO*

WILLIAM GIBSON

BURNING CHROME

ACE · 0-441-08934-8 · [$5.99 CANADA] · $4.99 U.S.

"SCIENCE FICTION'S HOTTEST AUTHOR."
—*ROLLING STONE*

The short stories in Gibson's 1986 collection depict futuristic battles against an all-powerful government.

totally confused," he told Mikal Gilmore in *Rolling Stone*. "I thought I was on this literary kamikaze mission—that is, I thought my work was so disturbing it would be dismissed and ignored by all but a few people." But "Burning Chrome" received a Nebula Award nomination, and Ace Books editor Terry Carr encouraged Gibson to write a novel. He did, expanding his concepts of cyberspace and the future into a more complex work. The result was *Neuromancer*, the first novel ever to sweep the Nebula, Hugo, and Philip K. Dick Memorial Awards.

The Cyberspace Trilogy

Neuromancer is a fast-moving, futuristic crime thriller, loaded with violence and eroticism. It takes place in the gritty world of the Sprawl, an enormous urban area comprising most of the Eastern United States. The world power is now Japan, but multinational corporations actually run the various governments. Budrys called the setting "a near-contemporary Earth and some of its orbital stations; a heavily industrialized world dominated by Japanese electronics and a Eurasian biotechnology.... It is not truly the future, in other words ... it is today written large." Gibson agrees that *Neuromancer* is more concerned with the present than with the future. "I really don't think of myself as a futurist," he told Victoria Hamburg in *Interview*. "I'm just trying to make sense of contemporary reality." He has compared the Sprawl—with its overcrowding and bizarre mixtures of wealth and poverty—with Los Angeles.

Neuromancer's plot involves a cowboy named Case, who plugs into the cyberspace matrix to steal data from an artificial intelligence so advanced as to be almost human. Molly reappears in the book and helps Case to avoid capture at the hands of the corporate moguls. Reviewers have found the book difficult to summarize, and its constantly changing plot can be hard to follow, but many applauded Gibson's images. "In visualizing the human impact of high technology ... he is brilliantly perceptive," wrote Platt. "The resulting society is dehumanized and even repellent, but always derived from trends that are becoming apparent today."

Many critics have compared *Neuromancer* to *Blade Runner*—Ridley Scott's science-fiction film based on Philip K. Dick's *Do Androids Dream of Electric Sheep?*—as well as other hard-edged science fiction films of the 1980s. A *Publishers Weekly* reviewer saw in the work "the computer folklore of *Tron* and *War Games;* the rundown high-tech look of *Blade Runner* and the moral ambience of '40s *film noir*." In fact, while writing the novel, Gibson went to see *Blade Runner* and left after only thirty minutes, shaken by the similarity to his own imaginings. As in the movie, in *Neuromancer* distinctions between man and machine have blurred. Humans are devalued and machines have become so complex that they possess desires and intentions of their own. Information is the culture's most valued resource: those who have it, have power.

In 1986, *Burning Chrome*, Gibson's first short story collection, was published. It contains collaborations with cyberpunk authors Shirley, Bruce Sterling, and Michael Swanwick, and included new and previously published works. The stories, including "Johnny Mnemonic," "Burning Chrome," and "New Rose Hotel," involve antiheroes battling the computer-controlling government oligarchy, and they also serve to explain some of the background in *Neuromancer*. "Although this volume was published two years after *Neuromancer,* any reader wishing to save himself a lot of time and confusion should read *Burning Chrome* first," explained J. R. Wytenbroek in *Canadian Literature.* "These stories show careful craftsmanship and a true literary edge. Gibson, like so many of his sf predecessors and colleagues, shines in the short story form."

Neuromancer's successor is *Count Zero,* the second volume of the trilogy, which, while technically not a sequel, also occurs in Gibson's cyberspace universe, taking place seven years after the events of the first novel. Although the book was only a finalist for the Nebula and Hugo awards, several critics consider it to be better written than *Neuromancer.* There are three main characters in *Count Zero*: Zero, a teenage hacker and slum resident; Turner, a mercenary; and Marly, an art dealer. Another plot line involves Chris Mitchell, a biochip researcher who attempts to defect from one multinational corporation to another. The characters find themselves caught in the machinations of the cyberspace artificial intelligence, which has separated into entities imitating voodoo gods. As Tom Easton related in *Analog Science Fiction/Science Fact,* "Behind all the intrigue and action-adventure lie the independent artificial intelligences of the net. They hide from humans most of the time, but occasionally they emerge, sometimes posing as the gods of voodoo, sometimes as Wigan's God, sometimes as ... I won't say. Gibson has knitted a masterful yarn, action-filled, suspenseful, thought-provoking."

Unlike *Neuromancer,* which has a lightening-speed plot, *Count Zero* is a slower-moving, more complex novel. "The plot-line is much easier to follow, although it revolves around three protagonists whose individual stories do not coincide until the last few chapters of the book," wrote Wytenbroek. "Most of the major characters are a little more interesting and a lot less blood-thirsty than Case and Molly. The protagonists have emotions, motivation and substance.... The world remains as brutal as ever, but that brutality is relieved a little by the characters."

Gibson next published *Mona Lisa Overdrive,* which takes place fourteen years after *Neuromancer,* completing the cyberspace trilogy. The connection between human and computer life becomes so intertwined in this tale that humans can "die" into cyberspace and still continue to influence the physical world. One of the main characters, thirteen-year-old Kumiko Yanaka, is sent from Japan to

A MAJOR NOVEL BY THE HUGO AND NEBULA AWARD-WINNING AUTHOR OF *NEUROMANCER*

COUNT ZERO

WILLIAM GIBSON

"GIBSON DISTILLS A TECHNOPUNK SENSIBILITY WITH A KICK OF WHITE LIGHTNING AND THE CLARITY OF WHITE LIGHT." —*THE VILLAGE VOICE*

This 1986 addition to the "Cyberspace" trilogy finds three characters contending with forces of artificial intelligence that assume god-like guises.

London in order to protect her from her father's business rivals. Another is Chris Mitchell's daughter Angie, a star performer on the Sense/Net media network that allows audiences to actually experience the characters' sensations. Angie's father has grafted a computer chip into her brain that gives her access to particular areas of the cybernetic "net." Still another character is an exotic dancer/prostitute named Mona, who is hired by mysterious figures and surgically altered to resemble Angie.

Some critics have called *Mona* Gibson's most absorbing story, while nevertheless observing that the plot is slowed down by too many characters. According to David Hiltbrand of *People, Mona* "has so many plot lines working that it takes most of the book for him to generate much narrative momentum." *Nation* contributor Erik Davis found the

Human and computer realms become further entwined in the 1988 sequel to *Count Zero.*

experience of following the numerous plot lines dizzying. "Chapters are short, speedy and high-res[olution], and following the various strands of the plot resembles watching four different TV programs by rapidly changing channels." Still, Cadigan felt that "readers will be left not only wanting more but imagining what it might be. That's called science fiction at the top of its form."

Beyond Cyberspace and Back Again

An abrupt turn for Gibson was his collaborative effort with Sterling on *The Difference Engine.* Here the author's focus turns to an unusual version of the nineteenth century. Gibson and Sterling imagine what would have happened to Victorian England had "sometime in the 1820's the mathematician Charles Babbage succeeded in constructing an operational Analytic Engine, a clockwork comput-

er powered not by electricity but by steam engines," according to Thomas M. Disch in the *New York Times Book Review.* The early invention gives rise to a variety of social and technological changes: Lord Byron, instead of dying in 1824, becomes a tyrannical Prime Minister, Disraeli is a Grub Street hack, and pollution worsens dramatically.

The Difference Engine offers another complex plot, featuring Sybil, a prostitute who comes into the possession of a box of mysterious punched cards. Edward Mallory, a paleontologist, meets Lord Byron's daughter Ada and accidentally becomes the next carrier of the cards. He is hounded by an assortment of villains and experiences a number of adventures, including a wild night with one of Sybil's coworkers. The final hero is detective Laurence Oliphant, who solves the mystery of the punched cards. While *Los Angeles Times Book Review* contributor John Sladek believed that "some characters, scenes and subplots seem to have no other function than to convey the pack of punched cards from one place to another," he concluded that "it's fun to follow the mixture of real and imagined history, worked up into a ripping adventure yarn." And Disch said that "working together, Mr. Gibson and Mr. Sterling have written a book that is even better than their earlier and considerable solo efforts."

Gibson's fame has taken him from his home office in Vancouver to Hollywood, where he was hired to write the script for *Aliens III.* A newcomer to the movie business, he told Maitland McDonagh in *Film Comment:* "They were awfully kind about the very first draft I turned in: they said 'This is really nice, but we priced it out and it's going to cost $70 million,' and I said, 'Is that too much?' So a few space stations and a few hundred thousand aliens were excised in the interests of economy." Unfortunately, he lost his job through a management shuffle and his script was never used. Still, he hasn't given up on Hollywood and has other projects in the works, including an adaptation of "Johnny Mnemonic." But, as Gibson revealed in an interview published in *Hailing Frequencies,* "[if] this one doesn't work out, I think I'm going to just write books. And if this one *does* work out, I think I'm just going to write books. Hollywood is an interesting world to check out, but now that I know something about how it actually works, I'm glad I don't have to make my living there."

Three years after publishing *The Difference Engine,* Gibson returned to more familiar territory with *Virtual Light.* Set in the year 2005 in California, the story revolves around the theft of a pair of special sunglasses that allow the wearer access to valuable information through a connection to the optic nerve. When Berry Rydell, a cop-for-hire, sets out to find the stolen property he becomes entangled in a nefarious plot that depends on the data stored in the sunglasses for its success. As one *Publishers Weekly* critic pointed out, however, this relatively simple storyline isn't as important as the dystopian world of superpower corporations and television-worshipping masses that Gibson portrays. Gibson "has his finger on the pulse of popular culture and social trends," the reviewer maintained; "he molds a near-future world more frighteningly possible than that of any other recent writer."

As Gibson noted in *Hailing Frequencies*, the scientific advancements that have been made since his "Cyberspace" trilogy, especially the new virtual reality technology, influenced *Virtual Light*. Virtual reality "hasn't really turned out the way I had initially envisioned it," the author said. "So [*Virtual Light*] is the future as seen from the '90s, as opposed to the future I saw from the early '80s." While some readers find his view of the future grim and oppressive, Gibson only sees it as a continuation of the present. He represents a future he himself would like to inhabit. "I'm remarkably free of utopian fantasies," he told Hamburg. "I've never really thought about what I would ideally like the future to be. I suppose I'm reactionary in this regard, but I'd like it to be as much like the present as possible. Of course, I'm sure it won't be. It'll be some inconceivable thing."

■ Works Cited

Budrys, Algis, review of *Count Zero* and *Burning Chrome*, *Magazine of Fantasy and Science Fiction*, August, 1986, pp. 64-70.

Cadigan, Pat, "Accessing Gibson's Peculiar Realm of Cyberspace," *Quill and Quire*, December, 1988, p. 20.

Coleman, Howard, "Other Voices, Other Voices," *Science Fiction Review*, winter, 1986, pp. 38-39.

"Cyberpunk Era: Interviews with William Gibson," *Whole Earth Review*, summer, 1989, pp. 78-82.

Davis, Erik, "A Cyberspace Odyssey," *Nation*, May 8, 1989, pp. 636-39.

Disch, Thomas M., review of *The Difference Engine*, *New York Times Book Review*, March 10, 1991, pp. 5-6.

Easton, Tom, review of *Count Zero*, *Analog Science Fiction/Science Fact*, December 1986, pp. 179-80.

Gilmore, Mikal, "The Rise of Cyberpunk," *Rolling Stone*, December 4, 1986, pp. 77-78, 107-08.

Hamburg, Victoria, "The King of Cyberpunk," *Interview*, January, 1989, pp. 85-86, 91.

Hiltbrand, David, review of *Mona Lisa Overdrive*, *People*, December 12, 1988, pp. 9-10.

McDonagh, Maitland, "Clive Barker and William Gibson: Future Shockers," *Film Comment*, January-February, 1990, pp. 60-63.

Review of *Neuromancer*, *Publishers Weekly*, May 25, 1984, p. 57.

Platt, Charles, review of *Neuromancer*, *Washington Post Book World*, July 29, 1984, p. 11.

Sladek, John, "A Byte Out of Time," *Los Angeles Times Book Review*, May 12, 1991, p. 9.

Review of *Virtual Light*, *Publishers Weekly*, July 12, 1993.

"William Gibson: New Futures, Just on the Horizon," *Hailing Frequencies* (Waldenbooks newsletter), Issue 8, 1993, pp. 1, 3, 5, 13.

Wytenbroek, J. R., "Cyberpunk," *Canadian Literature*, summer, 1989, pp. 162-64.

Zuckerman, Edward, "William Gibson: Teen Geek Makes Good, Redefines Sci-Fi," *People*, June 10, 1991, pp. 103-08.

■ For More Information See

BOOKS

Contemporary Literary Criticism, Gale, Volume 39, 1986, pp. 139-44; Volume 63, pp. 128-40.

PERIODICALS

Cinefantastique, December, 1987, pp. 27-31.
Rolling Stone, June 15, 1989, pp. 85-87.
Time, February 8, 1993, pp. 59-65.

—*Sketch by Jani Prescott*

Joanne Greenberg

■ Personal

Has also written under the pseudonym Hannah Green; born September 24, 1932, in Brooklyn, NY; daughter of Julius Lester and Rosalie (Bernstein) Goldenberg; married Albert Greenberg (a retired psychotherapist), September 4, 1955; children: David, Alan. *Education:* American University, B.A. *Religion:* Jewish.

■ Addresses

Home—29221 Rainbow Hill Rd., Golden, CO 80401. *Agent*—Lois Wallace, Wallace Literary Agency, 177 East 70th St., New York, NY 10021.

■ Career

Writer. Colorado School of Mines, Golden, assistant professor of anthropology and creative writing, beginning 1985. Formerly a fire fighter and certified emergency medical technician. *Member:* Authors Guild, Authors League of America, PEN, National Association of the Deaf, American Civil Liberties Union, Colorado Authors' League.

■ Awards, Honors

Harry and Ethel Daroff Memorial Award for fiction, 1963, and William and Janice Eppstein Fiction Award, 1964, both from the National Jewish Welfare Board, both for *The King's Persons;* Marcus L. Kenner Award from the New York Association of the Deaf, 1971; Christopher Book Award, 1971, for *In This Sign;* Freida Fromm-Reichmann Memorial Award from the American Academy of Psychoanalysis, 1971, for *I Never Promised You a Rose Garden;* D.H.L. from Western Maryland College, 1977, Gallaudet College, 1979, and University of Colorado, 1987; Rocky Mountain Women's Institute Award, 1983; Denver Public Library Bookplate Award, 1990; Colorado Author of the Year, 1991.

■ Writings

NOVELS; ALL PUBLISHED BY HOLT

The King's Persons, 1963.
(Under pseudonym Hannah Green) *I Never Promised You a Rose Garden,* 1964.
The Monday Voices, 1965.
In This Sign, 1970.
Founder's Praise, 1976.
A Season of Delight, 1981.
The Far Side of Victory, 1983.
Simple Gifts, 1986.
Age of Consent, 1987.
Of Such Small Differences, 1988.
No Reck'ning Made, 1993.

SHORT STORY COLLECTIONS

Summering, Holt, 1966.
Rites of Passage, Holt, 1972.
High Crimes and Misdemeanors, Holt, 1979.
With the Snow Queen, Arcade, 1991.

OTHER

Contributor of articles, reviews, and short stories to numerous periodicals, including *Hudson Review, Virginia Quarterly, Chatelaine, Saturday Review, Tikkun,* and *Shima.*

■ Adaptations

I Never Promised You a Rose Garden was filmed by New World Pictures in 1977; it starred Bibi Anderson and Kathleen Quinn. *In This Sign* was adapted for television as *Love Is Never Silent* for Hallmark Hall of Fame, 1985.

■ Sidelights

Joanne Greenberg's most popular book was, for many years, also "kind of a secret book," the author once said in *Top of the News.* Greenberg used the pseudonym Hannah Green to disguise her authorship of *I Never Promised You a Rose Garden* because the story is based on her own experiences as a teenager struggling with schizophrenia. She was afraid that people in her community would reject her and her young children if they knew that she had once been institutionalized. By asking her husband's coworkers about schizophrenia, she quickly discovered the prejudices that people foster: most of them told her they believed that the mental disease was incurable. As her children got older, Greenberg wanted to tell them the whole truth, but she didn't know exactly how to do it. For years her children only knew that she had published a book under a pseudonym, until the time came when the facts could no longer remain hidden. "One day at school a friend asked [my son] if he was going to be as crazy as his mother was," she recalled in *Top of the News.* "He came home and said to me, 'Mom, were you crazy?' And I had to tell him 'yes.'"

Greenberg's sons adjusted to the startling news about their mother and accepted her reassurances that schizophrenia is not inherited. And although her "secret book" got little attention from either the public or reviewers when it was first published, over the years it has evolved into a classic that is particularly meaningful to young adult readers. It tells the story of Deborah Blau, a sixteen-year-old girl who attempts suicide, is institutionalized, and

spends the next three years undergoing intensive treatment. Deborah is torn between getting well—which would mean coming to terms with the often troubling realities of life—and retreating to the security of Yr, a fantastic universe that exists only in her mind.

Enlightening Work on Mental Health

I Never Promised You a Rose Garden was one of the first books to tell a story about mental illness from the viewpoint of the patient, and as such it did a great deal to enlighten people. Greenberg has often been praised for her sensitivity in portraying Deborah's inner world and for showing the patient's perspective on life in an institution. A reviewer for the *Times Literary Supplement* particularly noted that the author illustrates how the mentally ill are free from the constraints of soci-

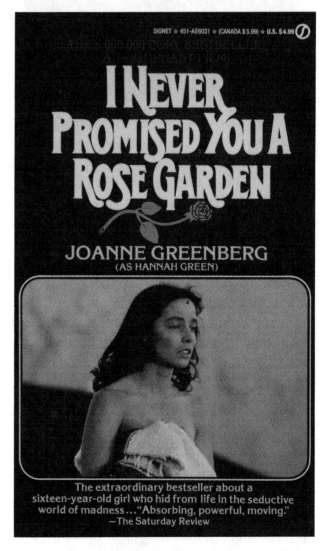

The author's struggle with schizophrenia as an adolescent inspired this classic 1964 novel.

ety's moral expectations: Greenberg "is excellent when conveying relief and delight at the freedom from the propriety, freedom from lies, and most of all the freedom to call mad mad, crazy crazy."

I Never Promised You a Rose Garden is "in many ways one of the most significant popular books of the last twenty years," according to Kary and Gary Wolfe in a 1976 issue of the *Journal of Popular Culture*. There are many reasons for this, according to the Wolfes; one of them is Greenberg's powerful imagery. "The idea of the 'secret garden'—the private respite from the world that is known only to the child—has long been popular in children's and adolescent literature," they noted. "It is not unlikely that Deborah's Kingdom of Yr is just such a garden to many readers. Though on a more intense level, it is not unlike Frances Hodgson Burnett's secret garden in her book of that title, or C. S. Lewis's Narnia.... In other words, Yr, though the myth of a psychotic mind, is still a myth, and as such bears strong attraction for the imagination.... Some of the attraction that readers feel for the novel may be akin to the attractions of [William] Blake, or Lewis, or [J. R. R.] Tolkien."

I Never Promised You a Rose Garden is based on Joanne Greenberg's own experiences, but in many of her later books, she proved that she could be just as sensitive and perceptive in portraying forms of alienation that she had not personally lived through. In *The Monday Voices*, she wrote about Ralph Oakland, a man who finds jobs for disabled people. Called "somber, disheartening, grand and gripping" by W. G. Rogers in the *New York Times Book Review*, the story takes place mostly in Oakland's office, where he meets with a stream of mentally and physically handicapped clients. He is devoted to his calling even though he must face tragedy and disappointment on an almost daily basis, and his dedication rubs off on the reader. "There could be no better plea for society's support of the lame, the halt and the blind," stated Rogers; "and when the lame, halt and blind provide us such an intense and fiery experience, they deserve all we can do for them."

Inside the Deaf World

With her fourth novel, Greenberg went inside the world of the deaf. *In This Sign* follows the course of a deaf couple over their fifty years of married life. They go deeply into debt when they are unable to hear a salesman explain the terms of payment on a car they purchase during the Great Depression; the hardships they must struggle through after that

Greenberg received a Christopher Award for her 1970 novel tracing the impact of deafness on a married couple over a fifty-year period.

drain them of their lightheartedness and also affect their daughter. *In This Sign* is an "unsettling, haunting book," wrote Ruth Nadelhaft in *Library Journal*. "The isolation and the often frenzied rage of the deaf couple are unforgettably vivid.... Reading this book is not easy; but it ends with hard-earned laughter and is worth the struggle." A *Times Literary Supplement* reviewer praised Greenberg for avoiding "the excesses of sentimentality expected of a novel about the deaf," and for finding "a way of writing conversations between deaf and hearing with inordinate skill, as well as the less usual situations between deaf and deaf."

Greenberg is well acquainted with the world of the deaf, having many friends among the deaf community who live in her area and having worked as a guide and interpreter at deaf-blind conventions. In a *Publishers Weekly* interview with Sybil Steinberg, she laughingly recalled the time she and her husband hired a tutor to teach them sign language: "We didn't know that she signed with a hillbilly accent. [Greenberg's husband] Albert was working with deaf people, and the Denver deaf community was very small and intimate, and we began to be invited to all their functions. But we didn't realize that we were half of the entertainment. Finally they told us 'You are using words out of the bushes, with a heavy Ozark accent that is really very vulgar.'"

The first time Greenberg met an individual who was both deaf and blind was at a speaking engagement at a mental hospital, where she was giving a talk on mental health services for the deaf. Ten years after writing about the deaf couple in *In This Sign*, she decided to take on the even bigger challenge of portraying the life of a man who was both deaf and blind. The resulting book, *Of Such Small Differences*, is considered by a number of critics to be one of her very best. The story begins when twenty-five-year-old John, blind since birth and deafened at the age of nine by a blow from his father, meets Leda, a sighted-hearing woman who works part time for John's handicapped workshop. Leda is an aspiring actress, but, unlike many of the people who work with the handicapped, she relates to John as a total human being rather than keeping a detached, professional distance from him. Eventually, Leda and John fall in love and move in together. Leda gains many insights from John's special sensitivities, while opening up the sighted-hearing world to him more than anyone else ever has. But the book is not a fairy tale. Communication between them remains difficult. John grows critical of sight when he perceives how often it fails and complicates matters. Leda tires of the meticulous order John must have around him in order to function, and she also wearies of the responsibility of paving the way for him.

"Greenberg has done a masterful job of portraying these two characters; of bringing you into the Deaf-Blind world," asserted Pam Spencer in the *Voice of Youth Advocates.* Spencer further lauded the author's ability to use dialogue, descriptions, and plotting to recreate in a "painfully realistic" manner John and Leda's life together. "For the entry into a different world that it offers readers," the reviewer concluded, "*Of Such Small Differences* will become one of the 'new classics.'" James Idema, a reviewer for the *Chicago Tribune*, said that the book was moving simply as a love story, as well as being an important window into the world

of the deaf and blind. *Of Such Small Differences* "is both revelation and entertainment," he wrote. "That Greenberg, a hearing and sighted writer, manages to show how the world seems to people who can neither see nor hear makes the book a wondrous *tour de force*." That the author is able to touch the reader's emotions so deeply is "all the more remarkable."

Short Stories Full of Triumph

In addition to her novels, Greenberg has also written many short stories, and these too often feature characters with physical challenges. *Rites of Passage*, one of her short story collections, includes tales of people who are deaf, epileptic, and insane. These conditions have the potential to make depressing stories, but in Greenberg's hands,

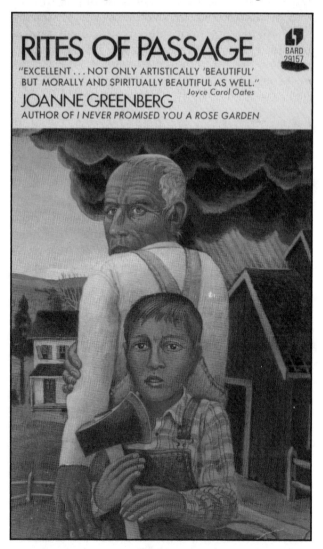

Like her popular novels, Greenberg's short stories deal with physical barriers including deafness and epilepsy.

they become tales of triumph, according to *Washington Post Book World* contributor and author Joyce Carol Oates. The twelve stories the collection contains are "not only artistically 'beautiful' but morally and spiritually beautiful as well," wrote Oates. Though "Greenberg hardly writes of people with happy problems . . . she is able through her almost miraculous sense of the complexities of the human predicament to make each person, hopeful or hopeless, demonstrate for us a way of surviving."

Not all of Greenberg's stories and novels are about the challenges of physically or mentally handicapped people. In her very first book, for example, she examined the bad feelings that existed between Jewish moneylenders and Christian barons in twelfth-century England. This historical novel, called *The King's Persons*, won much praise for its realistic characters and accurate historical detail. The action alternates between York, where the moneylenders were centered; a monastery, where the troubles of the Christian church of that time are shown; and the home of Baron Malabestia, who represents the life of the nobility. A romance springs up between a young Jewish man from a wealthy family and a poor Christian servant girl, but because of the world they live in their relationship is a frustrating one.

Over the course of the book, financial tensions between the Christian nobility and the wealthy Jewish community build until Malabestia launches a horrible attack against the Jews that ends in a bloody massacre. *The King's Persons* is "a thrilling, intelligent and disturbing book," wrote a reviewer for the *Times Literary Supplement*. A contributor to *Time* said: "With painstaking care, she has woven each of the skeins of medieval life into a vivid tapestry."

Religion is also a theme in another historical novel, *Founder's Praise*. Much of the story takes place during the so-called Dust Bowl years, when drought blighted the farmland west of the Mississippi. In the midst of this tragedy, one farmer is transformed into a man who can see the beauty of life even in the hardest circumstances. After his death, other people transform him from the simple man that he was into a religious icon, and a cult forms around his memory. Most of the novel is "devoted to the rise and dissolution of this new religion," noted James R. Frakes in the *New York Times Book Review*, especially as it affects the people who are relatives of the "Founder." "Joanne Greenberg brings unclouded vision and sureness to bear on almost everything she tou-

ches—landscapes, drought, insects, small-town insularity, family love and jealousy, the paradoxical vitality of the life-draining demands of farming."

Romance, Judaism, and Fire Fighting

Greenberg took up quite a different theme in *A Season of Delight*. This book, like many of her others, came partly from her own life experience—specifically, her eleven years of service on her local fire and rescue squad. Her adventures as a fire fighter and lifesaver provided the background for the fictional Gilboa Fire and Rescue squad. In the story, Grace Dowben is a middle-aged Jewish woman who is a member of the squad. In her personal life, Grace is disturbed by her children's rejection of their Jewish heritage. She meets and falls in love with another squad member, Ben, who is twenty years younger than she. Ben is of Jewish parentage, but he was raised in a secular household and knows nothing of the faith. Grace shares with him her delight in the old traditions. Reviewer Norma B. Williamson stated in *National Review* that while another writer might have created a stereotype in the character of Grace, thanks to Greenberg's writing, the reader sees "the unique human being beneath." Noting that the author has traditional ideas about good versus evil, the critic further praised Greenberg for demonstrating "humor and compassion in her treatment of both, making her always a joy to read."

Moral questions are again a major theme in Greenberg's *The Far Side of Victory*, a novel that some critics have compared to a classical Greek tragedy. Elaine Kendall explained in the *Los Angeles Times*: "The spare style, the inexorable progress of events and the rigid symmetry of plot all follow accepted classical principles. The characters are obedient to the capricious whims of the gods, the fundamental lesson of the book more dreadful than ordinary mortals can bear." The story begins when a young man, Eric Gordon, gets drunk and drives down a snowy highway, only to collide with another car. Of the six people in the other vehicle, only one, Helen, survives. Her husband and three children are killed in the crash.

Gordon is sentenced to nothing more than a fifteen-month probation for causing the accident. In time, he meets Helen, falls in love with her, and they are married. Years later, Helen and the children she has had with Eric are killed in another car wreck. After the accident, a growing suspicion invades Eric's thoughts, and he begins to wonder whether Helen arranged the second tragedy "in

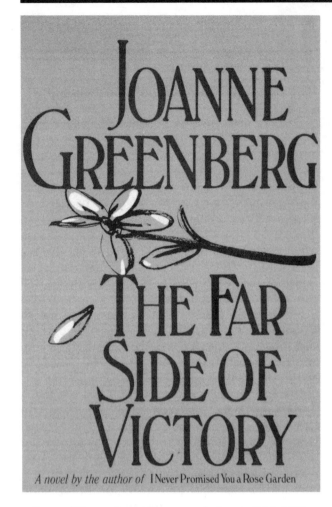

JOANNE
GREENBERG

THE FAR
SIDE OF
VICTORY

A novel by the author of I Never Promised You a Rose Garden

Issues of fate and morality are at the heart of this 1983 work.

order to satisfy her fierce sense of justice," reported Robert C. Small in *The ALAN Review. The Far Side of Victory* is "a strange and moving book that is about guilt and penitence." Susan Dooley called the book "gentle and perceptive" in her *Washington Post Book World* evaluation, noting that Greenberg "once more reaches to the hearts of her readers." And Gregory Maguire, writing in *Horn Book,* praised the book's use of "characterization and its analysis of small-town politics and society."

Joanne Greenberg encourages everyone who loves to write to do so. Although she has had great success in publishing her writing, she argued in a *Publishers Weekly* article that it is a great mistake to think that all writing should be done with the aim of publishing it. "I want all people who love words, who get pleasure and advantage from writing, to write: fiction, letters, memoirs and poetry. I think they should expend on this writing all the care and skill of which they are capable." The author later added, "Most writers I know have

a special drawer full of pieces not for sale.... Sometimes, by narrowing the purposes of our writings, we make them joyless, less than publishable and, ultimately, less than readable."

■ Works Cited

"Calling Mad Mad," *Times Literary Supplement,* August 13, 1964, p. 721.

Dooley, Susan, review of *The Far Side of Victory, Washington Post Book World,* October 2, 1983, p. 6.

"Fire and Sword," *Times Literary Supplement,* July 5, 1963, p. 497.

Frakes, James R., review of *Founder's Praise, New York Times Book Review,* October 31, 1976, pp. 28, 30.

Greenberg, Joanne, "In Praise of Unsalable Writing," *Publishers Weekly,* January 15, 1988, p. 74.

Idema, James, "A Special Novel about a Man Who Is Both Deaf and Blind," *Chicago Tribune,* October 30, 1988, section 14, p. 5.

Review of *In This Sign, Times Literary Supplement,* October 15, 1971.

Kendall, Elaine, review of *The Far Side of Victory, Los Angeles Times,* February 9, 1989.

Maguire, Gregory, review of *The Far Side of Victory, Horn Book,* December, 1983, pp. 739-741.

Nadelhaft, Ruth, review of *In This Sign, Library Journal,* November 15, 1970.

Oates, Joyce Carol, "The Need to Communicate," *Washington Post Book World,* March 19, 1972, p. 3.

"Pogrom in Yorkshire," *Time,* March 29, 1963, pp. M23-M24.

Rogers, W. G., "Broken Lives Remade," *New York Times Book Review,* July 11, 1965, pp. 38-39.

Small, Robert C., review of *The Far Side of Victory, The ALAN Review,* fall, 1983, p. 31.

Spencer, Pam, review of *Of Such Small Differences, Voice of Youth Advocates,* December, 1988, pp. 237-238.

Steinberg, Sybil, "PW Interviews Joanne Greenberg," *Publishers Weekly,* September 23, 1988, pp. 50-51.

Top of the News, April, 1972.

Williamson, Norma B., review of *A Season of Delight, National Review,* October 15, 1982, p. 1297.

Wolfe, Kary K., and Gary K. Wolfe, "Metaphors of Madness: Popular Psychological Narratives," *Journal of Popular Culture,* spring, 1976, pp. 895-907.

■ **For More Information See**

BOOKS

Contemporary Literary Criticism, Gale, Volume 7, 1977, pp. 134-135; Volume 30, 1984, pp. 160-168.

PERIODICALS

Hudson Review, winter, 1966-67.
Los Angeles Times Book Review, December 13, 1987.

New Statesman, September 3, 1971.
New York Times Book Review, October 12, 1986; December 27, 1987, p. 11; October 30, 1988.
Publishers Weekly, June 27, 1986; October 9, 1987, p. 79.
Saturday Review, September 10, 1966, pp. 63-64.
School Library Journal, September, 1986, p. 152.
Tribune Books (Chicago), November 22, 1987.
Wilson Library Bulletin, June, 1989, p. 101.

—Sketch by Joan Goldsworthy

Greg Hildebrandt

Tim Hildebrandt

Greg and Tim Hildebrandt

■ Personal

Have worked together as The Brothers Hildebrandt, and The Hildebrandts; born January 23, 1939, in Detroit, MI; twin sons of George J. (an executive) and Germaine (Lajack) Hildebrandt. *Education:* Attended Meinzinger's Art School, Detroit.

Greg Hildebrandt: Married Diana F. Stankowski, June 8, 1963; children: Mary, Laura, Gregory.

Tim Hildebrandt: Married Rita Murray, July 10, 1965; children: Charles. *Hobbies and other interests:* "I collect the old Scribner books illustrated by N. C. Wyeth, along with books illustrated by Maxfield Parrish and by Howard Pyle—the grandfather of American illustration"; classical music, collecting antiques.

■ Addresses

Greg Hildebrandt: *Home*—12 Rock Spring Rd., West Orange, NJ 07052. *Office*—90 Park Ave., Verona, NJ 07044. *Agent*—Jean L. Gruder, 90 Park Ave., Verona, NJ 07044.

Tim Hildebrandt: New Jersey.

■ Career

Free-lance illustrators and writers, 1958—. Worked for four years as artists in animation department and as film designers for Jam Handy Organization, Detroit, MI; worked for six years as heads of film department and filmmakers for

Society for the Propagation of the Faith, New York, NY.

Greg Hildebrandt: Also consultant to Columbia Pictures. *Military service:* U.S. Army, 1959-63.

Tim Hildebrandt: Also production designer for Swashbuckler Films. *Exhibitions:* Work has been exhibited in major shows in New York, Philadelphia, San Francisco, and Tokyo. *Military service:* U.S. Army, 1957-60.

■ **Awards, Honors**

Gold Medal (shared) from the Society of Illustrators, 1977, for the cover illustration of *Clive.*

Greg Hildebrandt: *The Giant Panda Book* was chosen one of the Child Study Association of America's Children's Books of the Year in 1973.

Tim Hildebrandt: Award of Merit at the Society of Illustrators Annual Show, 1987, for cover illustration of *The Children of Arabel;* Golden Eagle Award for the film *Project Hope.*

■ **Writings**

WRITTEN AND ILLUSTRATED TOGETHER

How Do You Build It?, Platt & Munk, 1974.
(With Jerry Nichols) *Urshurak* (fantasy novel), Bantam, 1979.

ILLUSTRATED TOGETHER

Gary Webster, *The Man Who Found Out Why,* Hawthorne, 1963.
Audrey and Harvey Hirsch, *A Home for Tandy,* Platt & Munk, 1971.
Watty Piper (a pseudonym), editor, *Mother Goose: A Treasury of Best-Loved Rhymes,* Platt & Munk, 1972, selections published as *My Cricket Book of Mother Goose,* Platt & Munk, 1987.
Tony Hiss, *The Giant Panda Book,* Golden Press, 1973.
Barbara Shook Hazen, *A Nose for Trouble,* Golden Press, 1973.
Aileen Fisher, *Animal Disguises,* Bowmar, 1973.
Gloria Skurzynski, *The Remarkable Journey of Gustavus Bell,* Abingdon Press, 1973.
Sarah Keyser, *The Pop-Up Action Circus Book,* Platt & Munk, 1973.
Sarah Keyser, *The Pop-Up Action Construction Book,* Platt & Munk, 1973.
Simone Zapun, *Games Animals Play,* Platt & Munk, 1974, published as *Wonderful Wild Animals,* Grosset & Dunlap, 1989.
Bill Larson, *Let's Go to Animal Town: A Book about Things That Go!,* Golden Press, 1975.

Annie Ingle, *The Big City Book,* Platt & Munk, 1975.
Winifred Rosen Casey, *The Hippopotamus Book,* Golden Press, 1975.
Kathleen N. Daly, *The Wonder of Animals,* Golden Press, 1976.
(Contributors with others) J. R. R. Tolkien, *Smith of Wootten Major and Farmer Giles of Ham,* Ballantine, 1976.
Kathleen N. Daly, *The Wonder of Animals,* Golden Press, 1976.
(As The Brothers Hildebrandt) Terry Brooks, *The Sword of Shannara,* Random House, 1977.
Ruthanna Long, *The Great Monster Contest,* Golden Press, 1977.
Kathleen N. Daly, *Hide and Defend,* Golden Press, 1977.
Kathleen N. Daly, *Today's Biggest Animals,* Golden Press, 1977.
Kathleen N. Daly, *Dinosaurs,* Golden Press, 1977.
Kathleen N. Daly, *Unusual Animals,* Golden Press, 1977.
(As The Hildebrandts) *Animals!,* Platt & Munk, 1978.
(As The Hildebrandts) *Here Come the Builders!,* Platt & Munk, 1978.
Ian Summers, *The Art of the Brothers Hildebrandt,* Ballantine, 1979.
Clement C. Moore, *The Night before Christmas,* Golden Press, 1981.

Also illustrators of calendars based on J. R. R. Tolkien's *The Lord of the Rings,* 1976, 1977, and 1978.

ILLUSTRATED BY GREG HILDEBRANDT

Charles Dickens, *A Christmas Carol,* Messner, 1983.
A Christmas Treasury, Unicorn Publishing, 1984.
Bram Stoker, *Dracula,* Unicorn Publishing, 1985.
L. Frank Baum, *The Wizard of Oz,* Unicorn Publishing, 1985.
William McGuire, *From Tolkien to Oz: The Art of Greg Hildebrandt,* Unicorn, 1985.
Bonnie Worth, *Peter Cottontail's Surprise,* Unicorn Publishing, 1985.
Carlo Collodi, *Pinocchio,* Unicorn Publishing, 1986.
Edgar Allan Poe, *Poe: Stories and Poems,* Unicorn Publishing, 1986.
J. M. Barrie, *Peter Pan,* Unicorn Publishing, 1987.
Come Play with Rutherford Raccoon, Unicorn Publishing, 1987.
Come Visit with Mr. Caterpillar, Unicorn Publishing, 1987.

Gaston Leroux, *The Phantom of the Opera*, Unicorn Publishing, 1988.

Charles E. Carryl, *Davy and the Goblin*, Unicorn Publishing, 1988.

Learning Adventures with the Wise Old Owl, Unicorn Publishing, 1988.

Jean L. Scrocco, *Reading Is Fun with Bobby Bookworm*, Unicorn Publishing, 1988.

J. Walker McSpadden, *Robin Hood*, Unicorn Publishing, 1989.

'Twas the Night before Christmas and Other Holiday Favorites, Unicorn Publishing, 1990.

Lewis Carroll, *Alice in Wonderland*, Unicorn Publishing, 1991.

Aladdin and the Magic Lamp, Unicorn Publishing, 1992.

Tad Williams and Nina Kiriki Hoffman, *Child of an Ancient City*, Atheneum, 1992.

Also illustrator of "Merlin" calendar based on Mary Stewart's novels. Illustrator of book jackets. Contributor of illustrations to *Omni* magazine.

ILLUSTRATED BY TIM HILDEBRANDT

(With wife, Rita Hildebrandt) *Who Runs the City?*, Platt & Munk, 1978.

Othello Bach, *Lilly, Willy, and the Mail-Order Witch*, Caedmon, 1983.

Othello Bach, *Hector McSnector and the Mail-Order Christmas Witch*, Caedmon, 1984.

M. S. Murdock, *Vendetta*, Warner Books, 1987.

Michael G. Coney, *Fang, the Gnome*, New American Library, 1988.

Bruce Coville, editor and compiler, *The Unicorn Treasury*, Doubleday, 1988.

Jack E. Norton, *The Fantasy Art Techniques of Tim Hildebrandt*, Paper Tiger, 1991.

Also illustrator of many jacket covers for books.

WRITTEN BY GREG HILDEBRANDT

Greg Hildebrandt's Favorite Fairy Tales, edited by Lynn Offerman, Simon & Schuster, 1984.

Treasures of Chanukah, Unicorn Publishing, 1987.

WRITTEN BY TIM HILDEBRANDT

(With Rita Hildebrandt; and illustrator) *The Rita and Tim Hildebrandt Fantasy Cookbook*, Bobbs-Merrill, 1983.

(With Rita Hildebrandt; and illustrator) *Merlin and the Dragons of Atlantis*, Bobbs-Merrill, 1983.

The Unicorn Journal II: An Illustrated Book with Space for Notes, Running Press, 1985.

Shoemaker and the Christmas Elves, Outlet Book, in press.

■ Adaptations

Animal Disguises (filmstrip with record or cassette), Bowmar/Noble, 1973.

■ Sidelights

In 1975, two almost unknown young men named Greg and Tim Hildebrandt shook the world of illustration. The beginnings of their great success as fantasy artists came through Betty and Ian Ballantine, the founders of Ballantine Books, one of the major paperback publishers in the United States. The Ballantines had published the first authorized American paperback edition of J. R. R. Tolkien's fantasy classic *The Lord of the Rings* in 1965. For the first two years following Tolkien's death in 1973, they also published very successful calendars on Middle-earth themes, using illustrations that Tolkien himself had produced. Tolkien's drawings, however, were few in number, and after two years of using the author's own illustrations, the Ballantines began searching for other artists stimulated by Tolkien's vision. In 1974 Betty Ballantine discovered the works of Tim Kirk while on a trip to Kansas City and purchased them for use in the 1975 Tolkien calendar. To attract additional contributors, Ian Summers explains in *The Art of the Brothers Hildebrandt*, the Ballantines ran a short paragraph on the back of the 1975 calendar: "We hope to find other artists who are inspired to do their own conceptions of *Middle-earth* so that we shall be able to offer calendars for future years."

"Artists," Summers relates, "were requested to send portfolios to Ballantine's art director; I had held that job for about four months when the responses and portfolios started rolling in." Summers was inundated with inquiries from amateur and professional artists, but he was searching for a particular, special quality. "The sales potential of the calendar meant big business, and I was looking for the best," Summers continues. "There were many professional artists who could paint adequate illustrations, but this had to be a project of love. The illustrators for this next calendar would have to be *obsessed*."

By February 7, 1975, time was running out for Summers and his staff. In order to produce the calendar on time, they had to have it in bookstores by August, and he still had not found any illustrators with the quality he wanted. Then his receptionist called him out of his office to meet two visitors. "Before my eyes," Summers writes, "were a pair of identical twins dressed in woolen plaid

The Hildebrandts first gained wide recognition after their artwork appeared in the popular J. R. R. Tolkien calendars.

shirts—bearded, skinny, wet, and shivering." They were carrying plastic garbage bags with "enough preliminary drawings ... to fill several Tolkien calendars." The twins were Greg and Tim Hildebrandt, and their names, writes fellow illustrator Boris Vallejo in his foreword to *Fantasy Art Techniques of Tim Hildebrandt,* "were destined to become legend in their chosen field."

An Artistic Genesis

Greg and Tim Hildebrandt were born in Detroit, Michigan, in 1939, sons of a General Motors executive and his wife. Early in life—before their second birthday, in fact—they revealed signs of the artistic interests that they would later build

into careers. "My husband sat at the dining room table with crayons and a coloring book, showing the twins how to color," their mother Germaine Hildebrandt recounts in *From Tolkien to Oz: The Art of Greg Hildebrandt.* "They instantly became involved, taking over the crayons. And wouldn't you know it, they stayed perfectly inside the lines!"

By the age of eight, the brothers had developed strong interests in comic books. *Plastic Man,* the exploits of a reformed crook whose accidental acid bath made his flesh like putty, the wartime feats of the air fighter team *Blackhawks,* the mystic powers and deeds of Alan Scott, the original *Green Lantern,* and the comic book adaptation of the adventures of radio's *Green Hornet* were favorites. Greg was particularly interested in sketching characters such as Superman, but his early efforts at drawing anatomy and working in perspective often met with disappointment. "I was drawing Superman from the cover of a comic book," Greg recalls in *From Tolkien to Oz.* "His arms were outstretched and he was crushing something in his hands. I couldn't draw the hands and the basic anatomy properly. I kept erasing and drawing, erasing and drawing until finally I screamed in frustration and stormed from the house." This incident, and others like it, taught Greg and Tim the importance of constantly trying to improve their work.

Besides the comics, the Hildebrandts found inspiration in the artwork of fine American illustrators. Hal Foster's *Prince Valiant* comic strip, set in medieval times, and Milt Caniff's *Terry and the Pirates* and *Steve Canyon* adventure strips were works that featured high-quality graphics and exciting stories, and they were readily available in daily and Sunday papers. Other important influences included traditional artists such as Howard Pyle, "one of the earliest pioneers of fantasy art,"

The Disney film *Pinocchio* served as a powerful influence on the Hildebrandts; Greg later illustrated this 1986 version of the children's classic.

according to Jack E. Norton in *Fantasy Art Techniques of Tim Hildebrandt,* whose "paintings are wonderful studies of composition, and display a unique dramatic elegance," and N. C. Wyeth, a former student of Pyle "perhaps best remembered for his fantastic illustrations of the story classics *Treasure Island, Robin Hood,* and *Mysterious Island.*" The early twentieth-century illustrator Maxfield Parrish also provided examples for Greg and Tim's personal development.

Plastic arts as well as graphic arts were a family pursuit. The budding artists constructed marionettes, hand puppets, and ventriloquist dolls modelled after famous originals from the movies and television: ventriloquist Edgar Bergen's Charlie McCarthy and Mortimer Snerd, Hope and Moray Bunin's Pinhead and Foodini, and Burr Tillstrom's Kukla and Ollie hand puppets, stars of early children's television programming. Other projects included superhero outfits and animal costumes, made with chalk, crayons, sheets, and pillowcases.

The twins also developed a great interest in science fiction. Classics such as *Frankenstein* and Robert Louis Stevenson's *Dr. Jekyll and Mr. Hyde* were favorites. The novels of Edgar Rice Burroughs were also sources of inspiration, states Summers: the Tarzan stories and the Martian series featuring John Carter, greatest swordsman of two worlds. However, Summers adds, "the *Pellucidar* novels"—stories set in a prehistoric land hidden in the center of the earth—"challenged their imaginations the most."

Moviemaker George Pal's sci-fi classics, writes Norton, "had an enormous impact" on the Hildebrandts' imaginations, especially works such as *Destination Moon, When Worlds Collide,* and *War of the Worlds.* Often the brothers tried to duplicate some of the special effects Pal had created on the screen. "Working closely with Greg," Norton explains, "Tim would spend months working on miniature sets of cities and planets. Alien ships were built, modelled closely after the tripod machines made famous in Pal's movies, and constructed so that they could be pulled on rollers down the streets of the set. Miniature explosives were placed in the buildings and under the streets, and the entire set was wired to a control box. Once everything was in place the brothers would begin filming, the tripod machines would roll down the streets, and the set would be systematically destroyed." "The time it took to get the film back was forever!," Greg declares in *From Tolkien to Oz.* "In class I wondered if the mailman had delivered that yellow Kodak box. After school, I ran home to get the film."

Perhaps the greatest influences on the young Hildebrandts, however, were the animated features of Walt Disney: *Snow White and the Seven Dwarfs, Pinocchio, Fantasia,* and *Bambi.* The powerful images of these films captured their imaginations. "Minutes into [*Pinocchio*]," writes Greg Hildebrandt in his illustrator's note to *Pinocchio,* "I was lost in the magic and mystery of not only a puppet brought to life, but also in the creation of an entire imaginary world." "I consider even the early Disney art realism," Greg declares in *From Tolkien to Oz.* "The form that it took was a cartoon but it moved and conveyed a story. It made you cry! It made you laugh! It terrified you! It inspired you!" "Minor influences go on and on—Heironymus Bosch, Bruegel, and the Impressionists among them—but the greatest still remains Disney," Tim Hildebrandt tells *Contemporary Authors (CA).* "Those works continue to give me inspiration, and I feel they are, as Peter Ustinov once said, among the wonders of the world."

Homemade Animation

The power and imagery of the Disney films inspired the brothers to try their hand at animation when they turned eleven. "Together," Norton writes, "they built a simple light box, in order to view their drawings in relation to each other. Without the benefit of animation school they painstakingly taught themselves the 'in-between' method of animation. In this procedure, the artist draws two extreme poses of a figure, then makes a series of 'in-between' drawings to fill in the motion." Working with figures taken from Disney and the *Prince Valiant* comic strip, Greg and Tim constructed their own animated films, shooting them with a small movie camera, and dreamed of future careers in animation with Disney. They also analyzed and imitated the work of Disney background artists such as Gustav Tenggrin and Claude Coates, who prepared and created the elaborate, beautifully detailed backgrounds for *Pinocchio,* and Eyvind Earle, whose stylized paintings, based on fifteenth-century designs, created the look of *Sleeping Beauty.*

High school for Tim and Greg, Summers states, "was considered . . . an interruption in their filmmaking." Nevertheless, the pair graduated from Avondale High School and joined the peacetime Army Reserve program shortly thereafter. Since Tim's contacts at the Disney studios had informed

him that all hopeful animators must have some formal art training, the two enrolled in Detroit's Meinzinger's Art School as soon as possible. They stayed there less than a year. "This brief period," states Summers, "was the extent of their formal education. The academic experience was enough to give them the positive feedback, discipline, and encouragement they needed." From Meinzinger's, Greg and Tim moved on to their first job with Jam Handy, a small company in Detroit specializing in training films and commercials for industry and the military. Both brothers applied for the job. "They arrived at the company together, showed some samples of their work, and were hired on the spot," Norton declares.

The brothers spent four years working for Jam Handy on many levels. "It was a small department," Tim continues in *CA,* "and one could be involved on all these levels. Handy's boasted having employed the great Max Fleischer, creator of all those great Popeye stories of the 1930s." However, the work made them neglect their other interests, and in 1962 they decided it was time to move on. Animation, Greg states in *From Tolkien to Oz,* "is an exciting career. But only if you are willing to pay the price. If that's what you go after, then you can't go after 50 other things. You have to work very hard at it. It has to be an obsession. It has to be the motivating factor of your existence. If it isn't, forget it! Go do something else."

After leaving Jam Handy, Tim and Greg moved to the New York City area. There Greg married Diana Stankowski and settled in Jersey City, New Jersey. "Tim moved in across the street," Summers says. "Then, in 1965, Tim met Rita Murray at choir practice and courted her for four months before they were married." The brothers worked for Bishop Fulton Sheen, making pictures for the Society for the Propagation of the Faith, an organization affiliated with the Catholic Church. "For the next six years," Norton explains, "they made documentary films depicting poverty, oppression and hunger." The work took them to locations all over the world, but it also left them no time to pursue their art.

Both Greg and Tim contributed artwork for the anti-Vietnam War movement after leaving the Society. Filmmaking had made them neglect the artistic sides of their lives, but they decided to capitalize on their abilities and find work as professional illustrators. "It dawned on me one day that I was wasting a talent," Tim declares in a more recent *CA* volume, "so I got a portfolio together and presented it to several publishers of children's

In another fortunate career move, the Hildebrandts painted the advertising poster for George Lucas's 1977 blockbuster science fiction film.

books in New York. I began to get so many assignments that I quit making documentary films and went full time into illustrating." At first, their commissions were limited largely to children's books—Tim and Greg both illustrated textbooks for Holt, Rinehart & Winston for a time—but they also "kept busy doing advertising work, and painting album covers for RCA and Victor," states Norton. "They had found their niche as freelance illustrators."

The Tolkien Calendars

Free-lance illustration, however, had its own set of drawbacks. Subject matter for advertising art—such as the Purina Cat Chow cat, which the brothers painted—was limited. Children's book illustrations tended to be highly imitative of other artists's styles. These jobs did not offer the challenges the brothers sought. Instead, they treasured the idea of illustrating great works of fantasy. This dream was finally realized in 1975, states Norton, when "Tim's wife, Rita, gave him a Tolkien calendar illustrated by fan artist Tim Kirk."

The Tolkien calendars made the Hildebrandt twins stars of the world of fantasy illustration. Labelled "The Brothers Hildebrandt" by Ballantine's marketing gurus, Greg and Tim produced artwork for three calendars in succession. "Their paintings for the 1978 Tolkien calendar," writes Norton, "sold more than one million copies, the most that any single calendar had sold before or has sold since." Their artwork enhanced Terry Brook's bestselling first novel *The Sword of Shanarra*—one of the very few adult fantasy novels to feature in-text illustrations. The brothers also attracted attention after they were chosen to create the advertising poster for George Lucas's 1978 megahit *Star Wars*—although the two were selected primarily because, as Tim states in *Fantasy Art Techniques of Tim Hildebrandt*, "the painting had to be done in 36 hours as the film was to be premiered the following week!"

"The assignment of the *Star Wars* movie poster," Norton declares, "... topp[ed] off the careers of possibly the most celebrated illustrative team in history." At the same time, however, the twins were faced with the question of what to do next. "After three years and over forty-five major paintings," Summers explains, "Tim and Greg felt that they had exhausted the Tolkien material. It was time to give someone else a chance, and they felt that the fans were entitled to other images and visions." Instead, they decided to create a calendar

that would tell a story of their own, advancing the narrative each month. They designed their own fantasy world, complete with elves, dwarfs, Amazons, wizards, and witches, using storyboards—a technique borrowed from animation—to follow the story's development. As time passed and the story evolved, however, it became too complicated to sum up in the twelve paintings a calendar required. Enlisting the help of a writer friend, Jerry Nichols, the brothers decided to turn the proposed calendar into a novel: *Urshurak*.

Urshurak is an epic fantasy, a tale of cosmic good and evil, which pits the corrupt Elfin prince Torgon, ruler of Urshurak, against Ailwon, another Elfin prince. Joined by a motley band of friends—an archer named Hugh Oxhine, the Amazon princess Zyra, twin dwarfs named Erbin and Evrawk—Ailwon presents the only barrier to Torgon's mastery of the world. Featuring 16 full-color paintings and over fifty black-and-white illustrations, *Urshurak* was a publishing event. The Quality Paperback Book Club featured it as a main selection, and the Book-of-the-Month Club chose it as an alternate. "We'd already broken down all the cultures—the Amazon culture, the dwarf culture—economics, architecture, even burial rituals," Tim tells *Publishers Weekly*'s Robert Dahlin. "We drew a city. We drew maps.... 'Urshurak,'" Tim concludes, "is the culmination of 40 years of fixation on fantasy."

The success of *Urshurak* as a book sparked hopes that it might be equally successful as a movie. "For the next two years," writes Norton, "the brothers made the rounds in Hollywood, trying to find someone to produce their story." They sunk thousands of dollars of their own money into the project, drawing on their own film experience and their background in advertising art to try to close a sale. However, "it wasn't until their finances were almost depleted," Norton explains, "that someone informed them that the bottom line was *Urshurak* would simply be too expensive to produce."

The Duo Splits

The problems Greg and Tim faced while trying to bring *Urshurak* to film put a tremendous strain on their partnership. Two years of effort had put them both out of the illustration market; they were both nearly broke, and they had families to support. In 1981 they separated to pursue individual careers, each wishing to pursue his own artistic vision. "In their search for wholeness," Vallejo declares, "the two halves of 'Hildebrandt' became two whole human beings as well as two whole artists, each one with his distinctive style and personality.''

Since their team dissolved, Greg and Tim have each sought and found niches of their own in illustration. "I was extremely nervous during those months and insecure about my art," Greg writes in *From Tolkien to Oz,* "even about my ability as an artist. The experience of working alone was so unusual that it frequently broke my concentration just enough to make me feel different in front of a sketch pad or painting. It took a while to feel just me in the art." Greg followed the example of such great illustrators as Pyle and Wyeth, illustrating classics of fantasy like L. Frank Baum's *The Wizard of Oz,* Bram Stoker's *Dracula,* and Lewis Carroll's *Alice in Wonderland.* Fantasy, Greg tells *CA,* "is now and has always been my first love. Fantasy enables people to escape into a world of pure joy and imagination. I am fortunate to have spent my entire life working with my imagination and I certainly hope I have managed to bring some joy to others through my art and writing."

After the breakup, Tim went back to calendar work for a while. He produced artwork for two calendars in TSR's *Dungeons and Dragons* series, states Norton, and then painted covers for new fantasy novels, a career move that has met with much enthusiasm. "It is one thing to describe a sinister parrot," writes Alan Dean Foster in his afterword to *Fantasy Art Techniques of Tim Hildebrandt,* "and quite another to paint its portrait, as Tim did on the cover of my novel *The Time of the Transference.*" Tim has also started working in film again, serving as executive producer for *The Return of the Aliens: The Deadly Spawn* and working on an animated short film called *The Dinosaur Rag* with special effects man John Dodds. "Whatever the subject," Norton declares, "it is certain that we will be able to enjoy Tim's work for many years to come."

One important factor that characterizes Greg and Tim's careers, both together and apart, is that their enthusiasm has consistently played a greater part in their success than has their talent. "I'm never really totally satisfied with my work. . . . I think the whole idea is to keep developing, to keep evolving up a spiral," Greg states in *From Tolkien to Oz.* "You start, and you go higher and higher, and you learn more and more, and you keep getting better and better. You never want to stop on your way up the spiral and say, 'This is it.'. . . I would say that it's a quest. It's exploration; but I never explore the territory completely." Art, Norton states, is a learned skill which can be taught, rather than a talent that must be present at birth. "It is probably

SIGNET • 451-AE5061 • (CANADA $4.50) • U.S. $3.50

SWEET SILVER BLUES
A Fantasy Novel by
Glen Cook

GARRETT INVESTIGATOR
CONFIDENTIAL AGENT

Can a hard-boiled detective find a damsel in distress in a warring land of magic, elves, and vampires?

After the brothers went their separate ways, Tim found his skills as an illustrator of book jackets—including fantasy novels like this one—in great demand.

correct to say that some people develop the necessary skills to create art at a more accelerated rate than others," he declares. "But, nonetheless, these skills are learned. If there is a gift given by God, it is the gift of determination. It is that burning desire to achieve their goals that compels people to excel, regardless of their chosen profession."

■ Works Cited

Dahlin, Robert, "Brothers Hildebrandt Create First Novel; Bantam to Publish It in September," *Publishers Weekly,* May 14, 1979, p. 96.

Hildebrandt, Greg, "Illustrator's Note," *Pinocchio,* Unicorn Publishing, 1986.

Hildebrandt, Greg, *Contemporary Authors*, Volume 104, Gale, 1982, p. 210.

Hildebrandt, Tim, *Contemporary Authors*, Volume 122, Gale, 1987, pp. 224-25.

McGuire, William, *From Tolkien to Oz: The Art of Greg Hildebrandt*, Unicorn Publishing, 1985.

Norton, Jack E., *The Fantasy Art Techniques of Tim Hildebrandt*, Paper Tiger, 1991.

Summers, Ian, *The Art of the Brothers Hildebrandt*, Ballantine, 1979, pp. 3-12.°

—Sketch by Kenneth R. Shepherd

Langston Hughes

■ Personal

Full name James Mercer Langston Hughes; born February 1, 1902, in Joplin, MO; died May 22, 1967, of a heart attack, in New York, NY; son of James Nathaniel (a businessman, lawyer, and rancher) and Carrie Mercer (a teacher; maiden name, Langston) Hughes. *Education:* Attended Columbia University, 1921-22; Lincoln University, A.B., 1929.

■ Career

Poet, short story writer, playwright, novelist, song lyricist, author of juvenile books, radio writer, translator, and lecturer. Atlanta University, Atlanta, GA, visiting professor of creative writing, 1947-48; Laboratory School of the University of Chicago, Chicago, IL, poet in residence, 1949-50. Previously employed as an English teacher in Mexico; a cabin boy on a freighter bound for Europe; and as an assistant to a film company in the Soviet Union. In his youth and during his early travels in Europe, he held a variety of odd jobs, including assistant cook, doorman, busboy, beachcomber and launderer. *Member:* National Institute of Arts and Letters, Authors Guild, Dramatists Guild, Authors League of America, PEN, American Society of Composers, Authors, and Publishers, Omega Psi Phi.

■ Awards, Honors

First prize, poetry, *Opportunity* magazine literary contest, 1925; poetry and essay prizes, Amy Spingarn Contest (*Crisis* magazine), 1925; first prize, Witter Bynner undergraduate poetry prize contest, 1926; Intercollegiate Poetry Award, *Palms* magazine, 1927; Harmon Gold Medal for Literature, 1931, for *Not without Laughter;* Rosenwald Fellowships, 1931 and 1941; Guggenheim fellowship for creative work, 1935; National Institute and American Academy of Arts and Letters Award in Literature, 1946; Anisfield-Wolfe Award for best book on racial relations, 1953, for *First Book of Africa;* Spingarn Medal, NAACP, 1960. Litt.D., Lincoln University (PA), 1943, Howard University, 1963, and Western Reserve University, 1964.

■ Writings

POETRY

The Weary Blues, Knopf, 1926.
Fine Clothes to the Jew, Knopf, 1927.
The Negro Mother and Other Dramatic Recitations, Golden Stair Press, 1931.
Dear Lovely Death, Troutbeck Press, 1931.
The Dream Keeper and Other Poems, Knopf, 1932.
Scottsboro Limited: Four Poems and a Play, Golden Stair Press, 1932.
A New Song, International Workers Order, 1938.

(With Robert Glenn) *Shakespeare in Harlem*, Knopf, 1942.

Jim Crow's Last Stand, Negro Publication Society of America, 1943.

Freedom's Plow, Musette Publishers, 1943.

Lament for Dark Peoples and Other Poems, Holland, 1944.

Fields of Wonder, Knopf, 1947.

One-Way Ticket, Knopf, 1949.

Montage of a Dream Deferred, Holt, 1951.

Ask Your Mama: 12 Moods for Jazz, Knopf, 1961.

The Panther and the Lash, Knopf, 1967.

NOVELS

Not without Laughter, Knopf, 1930.

Tambourines to Glory, John Day, 1958.

SHORT STORY COLLECTIONS

The Ways of White Folks, Knopf, 1934.

Simple Speaks His Mind, Simon & Schuster, 1950.

Laughing to Keep from Crying, Holt, 1952.

Simple Takes a Wife, Simon & Schuster, 1953.

Simple Stakes a Claim, Rinehart, 1957.

Something in Common and Other Stories, Hill & Wang, 1963.

Simple's Uncle Sam, Hill & Wang, 1965.

Thank You, Ma'am, Creative Education, 1991.

AUTOBIOGRAPHIES

The Big Sea: An Autobiography, Knopf, 1940.

I Wonder as I Wander: An Autobiographical Journey, Rinehart, 1956.

BLACK HISTORY

(With Roy de Carava) *The Sweet Flypaper of Life*, Simon & Schuster, 1955.

(With Milton Meltzer) *A Pictorial History of the Negro in America*, Crown, 1956, 5th edition published as *A Pictorial History of Blackamericans*, 1983.

Fight for Freedom: The Story of the NAACP, Norton, 1962.

(With Meltzer) *Black Magic: A Pictorial History of the Negro in American Entertainment*, Prentice-Hall, 1967, published as *Black Magic: A Pictorial History of the African American in the Performing Arts*, Da Capo, 1990.

BOOKS FOR CHILDREN AND YOUNG ADULTS

(With Arna Bontemps) *Popo and Fifina: Children of Haiti*, Macmillan, 1932.

Dream Keeper (poems), Knopf, 1932.

The First Book of Negroes, F. Watts, 1952.

The First Book of Rhythms, F. Watts, 1954.

Famous American Negroes, Dodd, 1954.

Famous Negro Music Makers, Dodd, 1955.

The First Book of Jazz, F. Watts, 1955, revised and enlarged edition published as *Jazz*, 1982.

The First Book of the West Indies, F. Watts, 1956.

Famous Negro Heroes of America, Dodd, 1958.

The First Book of Africa, F. Watts, 1960, revised edition, 1964.

Black Misery, Paul S. Eriksson, 1969.

Don't You Turn Back, edited by Lee Bennett Hopkins, Knopf, 1969.

EDITOR

Four Lincoln University Poets, Lincoln University, 1930.

(With Bontemps) *The Poetry of the Negro, 1746-1949*, Doubleday, 1949, revised edition published as *The Poetry of the Negro, 1746-1970*, 1970.

(With Waring Cuney and Bruce M. Wright) *Lincoln University Poets*, Fine Editions, 1954.

(With Bontemps) *The Book of Negro Folklore*, Dodd, 1958.

An African Treasury: Articles, Essays, Stories, Poems by Black Africans, Crown, 1960.

Poems from Black Africa, Indiana University Press, 1963.

New Negro Poets: U.S., foreword by Gwendolyn Brooks, Indiana University Press, 1964.

The Book of Negro Humor, Dodd, 1966.

The Best Short Stories by Negro Writers: An Anthology from 1899 to the Present, Little, Brown, 1967.

TRANSLATOR

(With Mercer Cook) Jacques Roumain, *Masters of Dew*, Reynal & Hitchcock, 1947, 2nd edition, Liberty Book Club, 1957.

(With Frederic Carruthers) Nicolas Guillen, *Cuba Libre*, Ward Ritchie, 1948.

Selected Poems of Gabriela Mistral, Indiana University Press, 1957.

COLLECTED EDITIONS

Selected Poems, Knopf, 1959.

The Best of Simple, Hill & Wang, 1961.

Five Plays by Langston Hughes, edited by Webster Smalley, Indiana University Press, 1963.

The Langston Hughes Reader, Braziller, 1968.

Good Morning Revolution: The Uncollected Social Protest Writing of Langston Hughes, edited by Faith Berry, Lawrence Hill, 1973, published as *Good Morning Revolution: Uncollected Writings of Social Protest by Langston Hughes*, Citadel, 1992.

Also author of *The Simple Omnibus*, Amereon.

OTHER

A Negro Looks at Soviet Central Asia, Cooperative Publishing Society of Foreign Workers in the U.S.S.R, 1934.

(With Bontemps) *Arna Bontemps-Langston Hughes Letters: 1925-1967*, edited by Charles H. Nichols, Dodd, 1980.

Also author of numerous plays, including (with Zora Neale Hurston) *Mule Bone*, 1930, *Little Ham*, 1935, *Mulatto*, 1935, *Front Porch*, 1937, *Joy to My Soul*, 1937, *Little Eva's End*, 1938, *The Sun Do Move*, 1942, *For This We Fight*, 1943, *The Barrier*, 1950, *Esther*, 1957, *Black Nativity*, 1961, and *The Prodigal Son*, 1965; author of screenplay *Way Down South*, 1942, and librettos for two operas: *The Barrier* and *Troubled Island*; author of lyrics for *Just around the Corner* and Kurt Weill's *Street Scene*. Columnist for *Chicago Defender* and *New York Post*. Contributor to periodicals and anthologies.

Some of Hughes's letters, manuscripts, lecture notes, periodical clippings, and pamphlets are included in the James Weldon Johnson Memorial Collection, Beinecke Library, Yale University. Additional materials are in the Schomburg Collection of the New York Public Library, the library of Lincoln University in Pennsylvania, and the Fisk University library.

■ Sidelights

"I didn't know the upper class Negroes well enough to write much about them," Langston Hughes said in *The Big Sea*. "I knew only the people I had grown up with, and they weren't people whose shoes were always shined, who had been to Harvard, or who had heard of Bach. But they seemed to me good people, too." Hughes's insistence on writing about common African Americans—and doing so in the idioms, cadences and rhythms of black dialects—meant that he turned a deaf ear to the complaints of black contemporaries who insisted that African Americans be portrayed as educated, culturally polished individuals in literature authored by blacks, especially literature that would be read by white audiences.

Consequently, Hughes angered many of his black contemporaries, who perceived him as the puppet of white culture and literature. White critics, while bemused by his novel style, dismissed his work as vacuous and aesthetically and thematically barren. In the words of Lindsay Patterson, who is quoted in *Black Writers*, "Serious white critics ignored him,

less serious ones compared his poetry to Cassius Clay doggerel, and most black critics only grudgingly admired him. Some, like James Baldwin, were downright malicious about his poetic achievement." What Patterson said next, however, rings truer and surer with each passing year: "But long after Baldwin and the rest of us are gone, I suspect Hughes' poetry will be blatantly around growing in stature until it is recognized for its genius."

The Formative Years

James Mercer Langston Hughes was born February 1, 1902, in Joplin, Missouri, and was the son of James Nathaniel and Carrie Langston Hughes. Hughes's mother was an educated, creative woman. She had attended college, demonstrating talents in drama and poetry. His father dreamed of becoming a lawyer, studying law through correspondence courses. Turned away from the Oklahoma Territory bar examination by members of its all-white examining board, he moved with his wife to Missouri. From there, he left for Cuba and then went on to Mexico, where he became a wealthy attorney and landowner. Hughes was seventeen before he saw his father again. He was shocked by his father's materialism and racism, by his tendency to dismiss blacks, Mexicans, and others as lazy and incompetent.

Hughes's mother had had to accept primary financial responsibility for herself and her son, moving frequently to search for work. Until he was twelve, Hughes spent most of his time with his maternal grandmother, Mary Leary Langston, the first black woman to have attended Oberlin College. She inspired in him a love of books and helped him understand how absolutely necessary it was to become educated. A proud woman of Native American and African American blood, she also helped her son sort out and accept the heritage he described in *The Big Sea*: "There are lots of different kinds of blood in our family.... I am brown. My father was a darker brown. My mother an olive-yellow. On my father's side ... both male great-grandparents were white.... On my mother's side, I had a paternal great-grandfather ... who was white and who lived in Louisa County, Virginia, before the Civil War, and who had several colored children by a colored housekeeper, who was his slave."

Hughes's grandmother was also a marvelous storyteller, narrating "long beautiful stories about people who wanted to make the Negroes free." Hughes emphasized in *The Big Sea* that "through my grandmother's stories always life moved, moved heroically toward an end. Nobody ever cried in my grandmother's stories. They worked, or schemed, or fought. But no crying." And so when his grandmother died in 1914, Hughes declared that "I didn't cry, either. Something about my grandmother's stories (without her ever having said so) taught me the uselessness of crying about anything." For the next year, Hughes was cared for by friends of his grandmother, a couple he called Auntie and Uncle Reed. "Both of them were very good and kind," he wrote, "the one who went to church and the one who didn't. And no doubt from them I learned to like both Christians and sinners equally well."

In 1915 Hughes rejoined his mother, who had just recently remarried and was living in Lincoln, Illinois. It was there that Hughes graduated from grammar school. Designated the "class poet," he read one of his verses at his school's commencement exercises. The following year, the family moved to Cleveland, where Hughes attended Central High and wrote poems for the *Belfry Owl*, the

Young Hughes with friends at Cleveland's Central High School, where the author's literary interests were initially shaped.

student magazine. During his high school years, Hughes read avidly and widely, influenced in his politics by the works of Arthur Schopenhauer, Friedrich Nietzsche, Ethel Boole Voynich, and stray copies of the *Liberator* and the *Socialist Call* passed on to him by friends. By his own admission, his early poetry was heavily influenced by "little Negro dialect poems like Paul Lawrence Dunbar's and poems without rhyme like [Carl] Sandburg's"; his literary tastes were shaped by Edna Ferber, Theodore Dreiser and Guy de Maupassant (whose works he read in French).

While on his way to visit his father in Mexico in July, 1920, Hughes drafted one of his most famous poems, "The Negro Speaks of Rivers." During the year he spent in Mexico, Hughes published poems in *Crisis* and *Brownies' Book* magazines, argued with his father about the advantages of an American versus a European education, attended bullfights, and, according to Gwendolyn Brooks in the *New York Times Book Review*, grew to hate his father for his materialistic and racial wrongheadedness. Brooks says that Hughes was convinced his father "hated Negroes," and that he "hated himself, too, for being a Negro." After returning to the States, Hughes attended Columbia University for a year beginning in 1921. Feeling stifled, he dropped out to form associations with those who, together with himself, would be responsible for the Harlem Renaissance (the post-World War I African American literary movement). He also worked as cabin boy on a ship, spent time in Africa, and continued to publish poems in *Crisis* and elsewhere. He spent most of 1923 and 1924 in Paris, where he developed a close friendship with Arna Bontemps that would last a lifetime.

The Early, Influential Works

While the period from 1925 to 1941 was not Hughes's most productive, it remains the time during which the author composed many of his most influential works: his first novel, *Not Without Laughter*; his best-known work for young readers, *The Dream Maker and Other Poems*; arguably his best collection of short stories, *The Ways of White Folks*; his most popular play, *Mulatto*; and the first volume of his autobiography, *The Big Sea*. Most importantly, the two volumes of poetry that opened Hughes's career—*The Weary Blues* and *Fine Clothes to the Jew*—have come to represent the very essence of the Harlem Renaissance. And during this period, Hughes established the Suitcase Theater in Harlem in 1938, the Negro Art Theater in Los Angeles in 1939, and the Skyloft Players in

Chicago in 1941. These companies exerted important influences on the development of black theater during the next several decades.

The publication of Hughes's first volume of poetry, *The Weary Blues,* caught the attention of critics who were quick to recognize that, in Harlem, the insistent gospel beat of showman Vachel Lindsay had been supplanted by the subtle, expressive rhythms of a poet with soul. Most of the poems in this volume employ the rhythms and nuances of blues and jazz to celebrate the heady, frenetic milieu of Harlem at night. While retaining similar meters and shadings, the rest of the verses (including "The Jester," "The Troubled Woman," "As I Grew Older," and "Mother to Son") deal with social themes: domestic tension, racial strife, and the African American sense of history and of self. *The Weary Blues* was followed about a year later by a second volume, *Fine Clothes to the Jew,* in which the poems explore the lifestyles, desires, and challenges of lower-class blacks in Harlem. Winifred Farrant Bevilacqua, writing in the *Dictionary of Literary Biography,* asserted that these two volumes, "besides projecting an intense pride in blackness and African heritage and conveying a sense of protest against prejudice and discrimination, demonstrate that the colloquial black idiom and the rhythms of blues, jazz, and spirituals could be made a part of the art of poetry." Referring indirectly to the contemporary impact and influence of these two volumes, Brooks wrote that if scholarship "wants to recognize blacks and blackness at all, it confronts the Harlem Renaissance." And, she stated emphatically, "Langston Hughes was its best-loved star."

The contemporary white press was generally receptive to both works, echoing Carl Van Vechten's words in his introduction to *The Weary Blues:* Hughes "writes caressingly of little black prostitutes in Harlem; his cabaret songs throb with the true jazz rhythm; his sea-pieces ache with a calm, melancholy lyricism; he cries bitterly from the heart of his race in 'Cross' and 'The Jester.'" The black press was less generous, more defensive. Countee Cullen, for example, reacted in *Opportunity* to *The Weary Blues* in these words: "The selections in this book ... tend to hurl this poet into the gaping pit that lies before all Negro writers, in the confines of which they become racial artists instead of artists pure and simple. There is too much emphasis here on strictly Negro themes; and this is probably an added reason for my coldness toward the jazz poems." In *The Big Sea* Hughes summarized the critical response to

Fine Clothes to the Jew: It "was well received by the literary magazines and the white press, but the Negro critics did not like it at all. The Pittsburgh *Courier* ran a big headline across the top of the page, *LANGSTON HUGHES' BOOK OF POEMS TRASH.* The headline in the New York *Amsterdam News* was *LANGSTON HUGHES—THE SEWER DWELLER.* The Chicago *Whip* characterized me as 'the poet low-rate of Harlem.' Others called the book a disgrace to the race, a return to the dialect tradition, and a parading of all our racial defects before the public." Few of Hughes's literary contemporaries, however, black or white, ignored the appearance of either volume. Later assessment of the two volumes largely follows that of Arnold Rampersad, who recognized in *Callaloo* the accomplishment of *The Weary Blues* as linguistic and structural, where "sweeter, more traditional lyr-

Hughes's first novel, the winner of the 1931 Harmon Gold Medal, is an accurate portrayal of African American life in the early twentieth century.

ics'' are preceded by ''references to the blues and poems written in dialect.'' But the critic viewed *Fine Clothes to the Jew* as marking Hughes's ''maturity as a poet after a decade of writing,'' and that it was part and parcel of ''authentic blues emotion and blues culture.''

Hughes's first novel, *Not without Laughter*, was partly autobiographical. It recounts—through the loosely-connected experiences of its protagonist, Sandy—the challenges of growing up black in Kansas. More than anything else, the novel has come to be valued as a social history, an accurate portrait of African American family and social life during the early 1900s. David Littlejohn in *Black on White* described the work as ''a gentle sequence of well-sketched social views,'' including ''the family gatherings, the colored ball, the pool hall.'' But its particular value, he said, ''lies in its completeness and truth, its control and wide humanity. It is probably the most genuine inside view of Negro life available in the fiction of the period, comparable to later works like Ann Petry's.'' Cary D. Wintz, however, complained in *Kansas Quarterly* that *Not without Laughter* is weakly plotted and that ''Sandy is never fully developed as a character, while the more interesting figures, Harriet and Aunt Hagar, remain on the periphery.'' Echoing Littlejohn's assessment, Wintz nevertheless noted that ''the characters, while not fully developed, are believable,'' and that, ''more importantly, Hughes's description of small town Negro life is unsurpassed.''

While Hughes was finishing *Not without Laughter*, he was also collaborating with Zora Neale Hurston on *Mule Bone*, which has been called the first black folk comedy by black playwrights. About this same time, Hughes began work on *Mulatto*, a serious drama about miscegenation, paternal rejection, and black oppression. The three central characters in the play are a mulatto named Bert, his black mother Cora, and his white father Norwood. In the end, Bert kills his father and then commits suicide; his mother goes insane. The play was completed in 1931; four years later, it was produced on Broadway by Martin Jones, who turned Hughes's poetic tragedy into a melodrama that pandered to the tastes of white theater-goers.

In 1931, Hughes completed *The Negro Mother*, a thin collection of poems published as a pamphlet and designed to be sold to lower-class blacks who supposedly would find its contents and price more appealing than those of Hughes's hardbound vol-

Inspired by the writings of D. H. Lawrence, the stories in this 1934 volume explore race relations from a black perspective.

umes. It nevertheless met with limited success, despite Hughes's spending part of one summer taking copies of it door-to-door. In 1932, Hughes published the first of several works intended for young readers, a short novel co-authored by Arna Bontemps called *Popo and Fifina: Children of Haiti*. It presents an idealized portrait of Haitian peasant life through a series of loosely connected sketches about Popo, Fifina, and their extended family. Encouraged by the success of the book, which went through several printings during his lifetime, Hughes selected fifty-nine poems from *The Weary Blues*, *Fine Clothes to the Jew*, and the writings of his youth, publishing them in 1932 as *The Dream Keeper and Other Poems*, a collection intended for older children and young adults.

The Attraction of Communism

The same year *Dream Keeper* was published, Hughes left with other African Americans for an unsuccessful filmmaking venture in the Soviet Union. While in Moscow, Hughes became acquainted with the short stories of D. H. Lawrence. Greatly impressed, he determined to try his own hand at short fiction. Fourteen of his early stories are collected in *The Ways of White Folks*, which one contemporary critic, E. C. Holmes, praised in *Opportunity* as a "tightly knit ... indictment against the decadence of capitalistic society." On the other hand, Leon Dennen denounced it in *Partisan Review* as utterly devoid of "the drama of the rising revolutionary consciousness of the Negro masses in America," saying it portrayed all blacks as "elemental, naive, simple and static." Later critics were less concerned about the social implications of *The Ways of White Folks* and appreciated, as David Michael Nifong stated in *Black American Literature Forum*, "the well-developed plots and the masterful character studies," and the "excellent use of point of view." The collection includes such stories as "Cora Unashamed," about a simple yet noble black woman who is mistreated and ignored by the surrounding white community; "Father and Son," which is a short story version of the play *Mulatto;* "Slave on the Block," about a handsome young black who is used and then spurned by a callous white family; and "Home," which tells how an ailing black musician is lynched after his gesture of kindness towards a white woman is misinterpreted by onlookers as a sexual advance.

With the publication of *The Big Sea: An Autobiography,* Hughes brought the first stage of his literary career to a close. A poetically structured record of his life from his birth in 1902 through the close of 1931, the book was described by R. Baxter Miller in *Black American Literature Forum* as a work of "disorganized structure, illustrating fused time" that "interweaves the themes of paradox and eternality." According to Miller, one should read the book "less for its recording of the discriminations against Blacks after World War I than for its recording of Blacks' accomplishments during the Harlem Renaissance." Miller admired Hughes's record of a world "in which Black snobbishness coexists with Black art" and where "the different tones of the Renaissance—humor, sadness, and irony"—have been preserved. Miller's primary complaint about *The Big Sea* is that "Hughes passes up two opportunities to create a distinct autobiographical self. His break with his [white] patron,

the major crisis of the book, is one.... Hughes's argument with Hurston over *Mule Bone* ... provides a second opportunity." In neither of these cases, said Miller, does Hughes "articulate [his] awareness" of his choosing "to lose many amenities of the world, but to regain his soul."

During the 1930s, Hughes became increasingly enamored of communist ideology and increasingly distressed with capitalism, which he saw as the primary instrument by which whites oppressed blacks and other minorities. Predictably, Hughes's writings reflected his increasing activism. Some critics, including Wintz, saw a deterioration in Hughes's aesthetic powers during the late 1930s. Wintz insisted that as Hughes "became angrier and more inclined toward propaganda," the "quality of his work declined."

Hughes's Productive Years

In terms of sheer output, the nineteen-year period beginning in 1942 was the most productive period of Hughes's life. As Bevilacqua asserted, Hughes's "mature work in prose, drama, and poetry"— though not necessarily his most influential work in any of these genres—followed the publication of

During the height of his productive years, Hughes appeared with his friend, Pulitzer Prize-winning poet Gwendolyn Brooks, at a Chicago public library in 1949.

The Big Sea. During these eighteen years, Hughes completed eight volumes of poetry, including *Shakespeare in Harlem, Fields of Wonder, Montage of a Dream Deferred,* and *Selected Poems;* two plays, *The Sun Do Move* and *Simply Heavenly;* librettos for the operas *The Barrier* and *Esther;* lyrics for the musicals *Street Scene* and *Just Around the Corner;* the short story collections *Simple Speaks his Mind, Laughing to Keep from Crying, Simple Takes a Wife,* and *Simple Stakes a Claim;* a novel, *Tambourines to Glory;* the second volume of his autobiography, *I Wonder as I Wander: An Autobiographical Journey;* seven books for young readers, including *The First Book of Rhythms, Famous Negro Music Makers, The First Book of Jazz,* and *Famous Negro Heroes of America;* two translations; three historical works; several anthologies; and countless newspaper and magazine columns.

Although Hughes considered himself a political activist throughout his life, his politics changed somewhat over the years. While he campaigned from first to last for African American civil rights, he became convinced during the 1940s that they could not be secured through communism. Hughes's declining sense of engagement with communist ideology was recognized by Eda Lou Walton in her review of *Shakespeare in Harlem,* which appeared in *New Masses* in 1942: "[These poems] probably had been in preparation for some time. They indicate no awareness of the changed war world, they are not even profoundly class or race-conscious.... Folk poetry is always the picture of a people. But a poet like Langston Hughes should have something more to say than is said in these strummed out 'blues songs.'" Owen Dodson, writing in *PHYLON,* was even less pleased with the volume. "Mr. Langston Shakespeare Hughes," he wrote, "is still holding his mirror up to a gold-toothed, flashy nature. It is the same mirror he has held up before but somehow the glass is cracked and his deep insight and discipline has dimmed. There is no getting away from the fact that this book, superior in format, is a careless surface job and unworthy of the author." Later critics like Patricia A. Johnson and Walter C. Farrell, Jr., writing in *MELUS,* recognized crucial similarities between *Shakespeare in Harlem* and the earlier *Fine Clothes to a Jew.* In both volumes, according to Johnson and Farrell, poems are "structurally patterned after the lyrics of the blues"; but while "at least half of the blues poems in [*Shakespeare*] focus on the economic determinants of the blues," fully "three-fourths of those in [*Clothes*] dealt exclusively with male-female relationships." Because it

The character of Simple, originally developed for the author's *Chicago Defender* column, embodied the humorous side of the black Everyman.

appeared "during the aftermath of a period of mass unemployment, *Shakespeare in Harlem* describes the social and economic conditions that continue to foster the blues among black working-class people." "No aspect of human life," Johnson and Farrell emphasized, "is void of financial implications."

Simple Stories

In 1943 Hughes created for his column in the *Chicago Defender,* a black-owned newspaper, the character of Jesse B. Semple (usually changed to "Simple"), a twentieth-century black Everyman— and Hughes's most enduring fictional creation. Simple is a rural Southerner who has moved to a large Northern city in search of employment and acceptance. Instead, he discovers new breeds of the frustration and racism he has left behind. The "Simple sketches" that Hughes wrote for his column are invariably satirical and humorous. They consist primarily of dialogues between the narrator, who does little more than ask questions and act the part of the "fall guy," and Simple, whose homey, commonsensible assessments of white "morality" greatly increased Hughes's audience and appeal. Hughes was quoted by Milton Meltzer in *Langston Hughes: A Biography* as offering this explanation for his creation of Simple and his use of humor: "If Negroes took all the white world's boorishness to heart and wept over it as profoundly as our serious writers do, we would have been dead long ago." Hughes continued, "Humor is a weapon, too, of no mean value against one's foes.... The race problem in America is serious business, I admit. But ... so many weighty volumes, cheerless novels, sad tracts, and violent books have been written on race relations that I would like to see some writers of both races write about our problems with black tongue in white cheek, or vice versa. Sometimes I try. Simple helps me." The sketches were eventually collected in four volumes: *Simple Speaks His Mind, Simple Takes a Wife, Simple Stakes a Claim,* and *Simple's Uncle Sam.* Certain of the sketches in *Simple Takes a Wife* form the basis for Hughes's 1957 play, *Simply Heavenly.*

Montage of a Dream Deferred, the opening lines of which are one of the most anthologized that Hughes ever wrote (thanks, in part, to Lorraine Hansberry's *Raisin in the Sun*), received lukewarm reviews when it first appeared. *New York Times Book Review* contributor Saunders Redding, while calling Hughes "a provocative folk singer" who, in *Montage,* has "fitted [his idiom] to the jarring dissonances and broken rhythms of be-bop" to create "a bold and frequently shocking distortion of tempo and tone," opined that Hughes has "a too great concern for perpetuating his reputation as an 'experimenter.'" Babette Deutsch, who said in the *New York Times Book Review* that the setting of *Montage* is "the particular part of the Waste Land that belongs to Harlem," argued that "the book as a whole leaves one less responsive to the poet's achievement than conscious of the limitations of folk art." John W. Parker's 1951 review, published in *PHYLON,* was more favorable, praising the volume's "popular appeal," and declaring that—unlike James Joyce—Hughes was "convinced that comprehensibility in poetic expression is a virtue, not a vice." Parker believed that the volume "betrays the inner conflict of Harlem's Brown Americans," telling the "fast-moving story of a people who, despite their own imperfections and the bitter and corroding circumstances they face from day to day, have never relinquished their dream of a [better] tomorrow"—even though

theirs is a dream "born out of a heartache, a dream much like life in dark Harlem."

Writing for Young Readers

The early and mid-1950s also saw the publication of the bulk of Hughes's writings for young people: *The First Book of Negroes, The First Book of Rhythms, Famous American Negroes, Famous Negro Music Makers, The First Book of Jazz, The First Book of the West Indies, Famous Negro Heroes of America,* and *The First Book of Africa.* Although most of these are no longer in print, well-worn library copies testify to their continued appeal to young readers. Barbara T. Rollock in *Five Owls* included a revised edition of *The First Book of Jazz,* published simply as *Jazz* (1982), and the reprinting of *The Dream Keeper* (1986) in a list of juvenile books "that will satisfy all kinds of readers all year long." Rollock also considered *A Pictorial History of Blackamericans* to be a book for young readers, primarily because of its "attractive pictures and other illustrative material." On these grounds, *A Pictorial History of the African American in the Performing Arts* could be considered a juvenile book as well—as should *The Sweet Flypaper of Life,* a photo essay for which Hughes provided a text that is, in Littlejohn's words, "as total an example

One of several popular nonfiction works for young people that Hughes penned in the 1950s.

of Langston Hughes, of his bittersweet participation in the lives of his people, as anything else he has written."

Two other works of Hughes's "middle period" have significance for mature young readers. The second volume of Hughes's autobiography, *I Wonder as I Wander: An Autobiographical Journey*, recounts his travels of the early 1930s to the California coast, Mexico, Tashkent, the Soviet Union, China, and Japan. In a review commemorating the 1986 reprint of the work, *Los Angeles Times Book Review* contributor Alex Raksin was suspicious of the "spunkiness, idealism and worldly curiosity" characterizing Hughes's writing, questioning its viability as a portrait of "the black experience in America." Yet Raksin praised Hughes's "abundance of intriguing and suspenseful yarns about [his] travels." *Tambourines to Glory*, Hughes's second novel, tells the story of Laura Reed, a con-artist of sorts who sets up a storefront church, and Buddy Lomas, a handsome womanizer. When Buddy begins paying other women more attention than what he shows her, Laura confronts him. Finally, Buddy becomes violent and Laura stabs him. When another woman is arrested for the crime, Laura atones for her past by confessing her guilt. Hughes turned the novel into a successful stage play in 1963. Of the dramatic version, *Dictionary of Literary Biography* contributor Catherine Daniels Hurst said that "the action in *Tambourines to Glory* is more fully developed than in any of Hughes's other plays."

During the "middle period" of his career, Hughes maintained an extremely busy schedule of writing, traveling, and lecturing and of immersing himself in political and cultural movements to expand the opportunities and rights of African Americans. "Most of my life from childhood on," he wrote in *I Wonder as I Wander*, "has been spent moving, traveling, changing places, knowing people in one school, in one town or in one group, or on one ship a little while, but soon never seeing most of them again."

A Growing Anger: Hughes's Last Years

Although distinctions between a "middle period" and a "later period" in Hughes's career are artificial, his biographers generally agree that while he never altogether lost hope for significant, positive changes in America's ethnic relationships, he became increasingly impatient and more cynical as his life approached its end. Sensitive readers have noted important distinctions between *Mon-*

tage of a Dream Deferred and the later *Ask Your Mama: 12 Moods for Jazz* although both are written in be-bop style and share similar themes. Simply stated, *Ask Your Mama* is angrier than *Montage*. While the latter asks to be chanted, the former demands to be shouted, its frequent refrain—"Ask your mama!"—becoming first a taunt and then an expletive. The volume, as Rampersad pointed out, "is explicitly based on the 'Hesitation Blues.'" James Presley in *Southwest Review* said that the volume, which was "written to be read to jazz accompaniment," is a "kaleidoscope of Negro names and Negro problems. Dreams follow nightmares." One poem, for example, talks about blockbusting and cold white resistance to integration; another dreams that Martin Luther King, Jr., has been made governor of Georgia and that blacks now occupy spacious mansions, pampered by their white slaves while their children are suckled by white mammies. *New York Times Book Review* contributor Dudley Fitts, reviewing *Ask Your Mama* soon after its publication, declared that its twelve jazz pieces "cannot be evaluated by any canon dealing with literary right or wrong. They are nonliterary—oral, vocal compositions to be spoken, or shouted, to the accompaniment of drum and flute and bass."

The Panther and the Lash, which Hughes dedicated to Rosa Parks, is even angrier. Donald B. Gibson, writing in *Langston Hughes, Black Genius: A Critical Evaluation*, called it "the least cheerful, the least optimistic of Hughes's volumes of poetry." Published posthumously but in press when Hughes died, the book contains seventy poems, about one third of which come from his previous volumes of poetry. The book's title refers to the rise of the Black Panther movement during the mid-1960s and the white backlash towards it. The poems of its first section, "Words on Fire," crackle with the tension of oppression and anger, sometimes erupting in militancy. These include "The Backlash Blues," "Black Panther," "Junior Addict," and a reprinting of "Dream Deferred." Other poems examine the repressive traditions of the Old South, grieve for the slowness of American social change, explore the plight of urban African Americans, and decry war, especially the one in Vietnam. All the poems in the collection, declared W. Edward Farrison in *CLA Journal*, "are indeed poems of our times, for all of them pertain directly or indirectly to the Negro's continuing struggle to achieve first-class citizenship in America."

Other important Hughes works published during the 1960s include *The Best of Simple*, which

Many critics believe Hughes will be best remembered for his poetry, a good sampling of which can be found in this 1959 collection.

contains sketches from the Simple volumes published during the 1950s; *Something in Common and Other Stories*, a collection that Robert Bone in *Down Home: Origins of the Afro-American Short Story* denounced as "a commercial rather than an imaginative venture," but which James A. Emanuel in *Freedomways* believed anthologizes some of "Hughes's best narratives"; *Five Plays by Langston Hughes*, an important volume containing *Mulatto, Soul Gone Home, Little Ham, Simply Heavenly*, and *Tambourines to Glory; Simple's Uncle Sam*, which brings together heretofore uncollected sketches from the *Chicago Defender* columns; and *The Langston Hughes Reader*, which anthologized popular as well as hard-to-find writings by Hughes, including fiction, poetry and essays. *Good Morning Revolution: The Uncollected Social Protest Writing of Langston Hughes* was published posthumously in 1973.

Hughes's later books for young adults include *Fight for Freedom: The Story of the NAACP* and two books published after Hughes's death, *Black Misery* and *Don't You Turn Back. Black Misery* is a compilation of sketches for which Hughes wrote captions shortly before his death. The captions, according to Phoebe-Lou Adams in *Atlantic Monthly*, describe "in wry single sentences" the "affronts to self-esteem suffered by all children," but most tragically by blacks. *Don't You Turn Back* is Lee Hopkins's collection of the Hughes poems especially enjoyed by young readers. Of the poems in the collection, *Saturday Review* critic Zena Sutherland wrote: "Most of them are brief, childlike in their simplicity, and timeless in their interpretations of black dreams, sea-longing, or the triumphant affirmation of faith."

During the years since Hughes's death, his appeal to American readers has matured and deepened. While admitting that Hughes's work was sometimes "uneven and much of it less than his best," James Presley nevertheless emphasized that Hughes's writings, and his poems in particular, "came from the working-class Negroes, to whom he spoke in a language they—and I—understood, a talent that poets do not always exhibit. The folks back home understood Langston Hughes because his poetry was simple and powerful. He communicated with a folk poetry that outlives the elaborate and the gorgeous. Whether it was in children's gentle verses or blues or 'protest' lines, he remained the poet of the people. This was his greatest strength."

■ Works Cited

Adams, Phoebe-Lou, review of *Black Misery*, *Atlantic Monthly*, August 1969, p. 103.

Bevilacqua, Winifred Farrant, "Langston Hughes," *Dictionary of Literary Biography*, Volume 86: *American Short Story Writers, 1910-1945, First Series*, Gale, 1989, pp. 139-150.

Black Writers, Gale, 1989.

Bone, Robert, "Langston Hughes," in his *Down Home: Origins of the Afro-American Short Story*, Columbia University Press, 1988, pp. 239-71.

Brooks, Gwendolyn, "The Darker Brother," *New York Times Book Review*, October 12, 1986, pp. 7, 9.

Cullen, Countee, "Poet on Poet," *Opportunity*, February, 1926, pp. 73-74.

Dennen, Leon, "Negroes and Whites," *Partisan Review*, November-December, 1934, pp. 50-52.

Deutsch, Babette, "Waste Land of Harlem," *New York Times Book Review*, May 6, 1951, p. 23.

Dodson, Owen, "Shakespeare in Harlem," *PHYLON: The Atlanta University Review of Race and Culture*, June, 1942, pp. 337-38.

Emanuel, James A., "The Short Fiction of Langston Hughes," *Freedomways*, spring, 1968, pp. 170-78.

Farrison, W. Edward, review of *The Panther and the Lash*, *CLA Journal*, March, 1968, pp. 259-61.

Fitts, Dudley, "A Trio of Singers in Varied Keys," *New York Times Book Review*, October 29, 1961, pp. 16-17.

Gibson, Donald B., "The Good Black Poet and the Good Gray Poet: The Poetry of Hughes and Whitman," in *Langston Hughes, Black Genius: A Critical Evaluation*, edited by Therman B. O'Daniel, Morrow, 1971, pp. 65-80.

Holmes, E. C., review of *The Ways of White Folks*, *Opportunity*, September, 1934, pp. 283-84.

Hughes, Langston, *The Big Sea: An Autobiography*, Knopf, 1940.

Hughes, Langston, *I Wonder as I Wander: An Autobiographical Journey*, Rinehart, 1956.

Hughes, Langston, *The Weary Blues*, Knopf, 1926.

Hurst, Catherine Daniels, "Langston Hughes," *Dictionary of Literary Biography*, Volume 7: *Twentieth-Century American Dramatists*, Gale, 1981, pp. 314-324.

Johnson, Patricia A., and Walter C. Farrell, Jr., "How Langston Hughes Used the Blues," *MELUS*, spring, 1979, pp. 55-63.

Littlejohn, David, *Black on White: A Critical Survey of Writing by American Negroes*, Viking, 1966.

Meltzer, Milton, *Langston Hughes: A Biography*, Crowell, 1968.

Miller, R. Baxter, "'Even After I Was Dead': 'The Big Sea'—Paradox, Preservation, and Holistic Time," *Black American Literature Forum*, winter, 1976, pp. 39-45.

Nifong, David Michael, "Narrative Technique and Theory in 'The Ways of White Folks,'" *Black American Literature Forum*, fall, 1981, pp. 93-96.

Parker, John W., "Poetry of Harlem in Transition," *PHYLON: The Atlanta University Review of Race and Culture*, June, 1951, pp. 195-97.

Presley, James, "Langston Hughes: A Personal Farewell," *Southwest Review*, winter, 1969, pp. 79-84.

Raksin, Alex, review of *I Wonder as I Wander*, *Los Angeles Times Book Review*, November 23, 1986, p. 14.

Rampersad, Arnold, "Langston Hughes's 'Fine Clothes to the Jew,'" *Callaloo*, winter, 1986, pp. 144-58.

Redding, Saunders, "Langston Hughes in an Old Vein with New Rhythms," *New York Herald Tribune Book Review*, March 11, 1951, p. 5.

Rollock, Barbara T., "The Black Experience in Children's Books," *Five Owls*, January/February, 1988, pp. 47-48.

Sutherland, Zena, review of *Don't You Turn Back*, *Saturday Review*, May 9, 1970, p. 47.

Walton, Eda Lou, "Nothing New under the Sun," *New Masses*, June 16, 1942, p. 23.

Wintz, Cary D., "Langston Hughes: A Kansas Poet in the Harlem Renaissance," *Kansas Quarterly*, June, 1975, pp. 58-71.

■ For More Information See

BOOKS

Berry, Faith, *Langston Hughes: Before and Beyond Harlem*, Lawrence Hill, 1983.

Black Literature Criticism, Volume 2, Gale, 1992.

Bloom, Howard, editor, *Langston Hughes*, Chelsea House, 1988.

Children's Literature Review, Volume 17, Gale, 1989.

Concise Dictionary of Literary Biography: The Age of Maturity, 1929-1941, Gale, 1989.

Contemporary Literary Criticism, Gale, Volume 1, 1973; Volume 5, 1976; Volume 10, 1979; Volume 15, 1980; Volume 35, 1985; Volume 44, 1987.

Dictionary of Literary Biography, Gale, Volume 4: *American Writers in Paris, 1920-1939*, 1980; Volume 48: *American Poets, 1880-1945, Second Series*, 1986; Volume 51: *Afro-American Writers from the Harlem Renaissance to 1940*, 1987.

Dunham, Montrew, *Langston Hughes: Young Black Poet*, Bobbs-Merrill, 1972.

Mikolyzk, Thomas A., *Langston Hughes: A Bio-Bibliography*, Greenwood Press, 1990.

Miller, R. Baxter, *The Art and Imagination of Langston Hughes*, University Press of Kentucky, 1989.

Poetry Criticism, Volume 1, Gale, 1991.

Rampersad, Arnold, *The Life of Langston Hughes, Volume I, 1902-1941: I, Too, Sing America*, Oxford, 1986.

Rampersad, Arnold, *The Life of Langston Hughes, Volume II, 1941-1967: I Dream A World*, Oxford, 1988.

Short Story Criticism, Volume 6, Gale, 1990.

Walker, Alice, *Langston Hughes: American Poet*, Oxford University Press, 1986.

World Literature Criticism, Gale, 1991.

PERIODICALS

Callaloo: An Afro-American and African Journal of Arts and Letters, fall, 1989, pp. 663-66.
Horn Book, November/December, 1989, p. 805.
Humanities, January 1, 1992, p. 20.

Langston Hughes Review, spring, 1992, pp. 6-13, 41-57.
New Yorker, November 9, 1963, p. 95.°

—*Sketch by Keith Lawrence*

Lynn Johnston

"For Better or for Worse" cartoon strip syndicated by Universal Press Syndicate, 1979—. President, Lynn Johnston Productions, Inc.

■ Awards, Honors

Reuben Award, National Cartoonists Society, 1986, for outstanding cartoonist of the year; named member of the Order of Canada, 1992; National Cartoonists Society Category Award for best comic strip; Quill Award, National Association of Writing Instrument Distributors; Inkpot Award, San Diego Comics Convention; EDI Award; two honorary degrees.

■ Writings

SELF-ILLUSTRATED CARTOON BOOKS

David! We're Pregnant!, Potlatch Publications, 1973, published as *David! We're Pregnant!: 101 Cartoons for Expecting Parents*, Meadowbrook, 1977, revised edition, 1992.

Hi, Mom! Hi, Dad!: The First Twelve Months of Parenthood, P.M.A. Books, 1975, revised edition, Meadowbrook, 1977.

Do They Ever Grow Up?, Meadowbrook, 1978, published as *Do They Ever Grow Up?: 101 Cartoons about the Terrible Twos and Beyond*, 1983.

"FOR BETTER OR FOR WORSE" COMIC COLLECTIONS

I've Got the One-More-Washload Blues, Andrews & McMeel, 1981.

Is This "One of Those Days," Daddy?, Andrews & McMeel, 1982.

■ Personal

Full name, Lynn Beverley Johnston; born May 28, 1947, in Collingwood, Ontario, Canada; daughter of Mervyn (a jeweler) and Ursula (an artisan; maiden name, Bainbridge) Ridgway; married first husband (a cameraman), c. 1975 (divorced); married John Roderick Johnston (a dentist and pilot), February 15, 1977; children: (first marriage) Aaron Michael; (second marriage) Katherine Elizabeth. *Education:* Attended Vancouver School of Arts, 1964-67. *Religion:* Unitarian-Universalist. *Hobbies and other interests:* Travel, doll collecting, playing the accordion, co-piloting and navigating aircraft.

■ Addresses

Home and office—North of North Bay, Ontario; and c/o Andrews & McMeel, 4900 Main St., Kansas City, MO 64122.

■ Career

McMaster University, Hamilton, Ontario, worked as a medical artist, 1968-73; free-lance commercial artist and writer, 1973—; author and illustrator of

It Must Be Nice to Be Little, Andrews & McMeel, 1983.

More Than a Month of Sundays: A for Better or for Worse Sunday Collection, Andrews & McMeel, 1983.

Our Sunday Best: A for Better or for Worse Sunday Collection, Andrews & McMeel, 1984.

Just One More Hug, Andrews & McMeel, 1984.

The Last Straw, Andrews & McMeel, 1985.

Keep the Home Fries Burning, Andrews & McMeel, 1986.

It's All Downhill from Here, Andrews & McMeel, 1987.

Pushing 40, Andrews & McMeel, 1988.

A Look Inside—For Better or for Worse: The Tenth Anniversary Collection, Andrews & McMeel, 1989.

It All Comes Out in the Wash (contains reprints from previous books), Tor Books, 1990.

If This Is a Lecture, How Long Will It Be?, Andrews & McMeel, 1990.

For Better or for Worse: Another Day, Another Lecture (contains reprints from previous books), Tor Books, 1991.

What, Me Pregnant?, Andrews & McMeel, 1991.

For Better or for Worse: You Can Play in the Barn, But You Can't Get Dirty (contains reprints from previous books), Tor Books, 1992.

For Better or for Worse: You Never Know What's around the Corner (contains reprints from previous books), Tor Books, 1992.

Things Are Looking Up, Andrews & McMeel, 1992.

For Better or for Worse: It's a Pig-Eat-Chicken World (contains reprints from previous books), Tor Books, 1993.

For Better or for Worse: Shhh—Mom's Working! (contains reprints from previous books), Tor Books, 1993.

ILLUSTRATOR

Bruce Lansky, editor, *The Best Baby Name Book in the Whole Wide World*, Meadowbrook Press, 1979.

Vicki Lansky, *The Taming of the C.A.N.D.Y. Monster*, revised edition, Book Peddlers, 1988.

Vicki Lansky, *Practical Parenting Tips for the First Five Years*, revised and enlarged edition, Meadowbrook Press, 1992.

OTHER

Has also contributed one story and a cover illustration to *Canadian Children's Annual*.

■ Sidelights

A precious, tiny baby and the family dog are sharing a moment. They are both on the floor, happily munching on the canine's food. When a parent discovers them, they look up from their feast with smiles, and dog food, on their faces. This scene of family disarray comes courtesy of Lynn Johnston, the creator of the "For Better or For Worse" comic strip, where this tableau graced the cover of her book, *Things Are Looking Up*. When it comes to chronicling the problems and phobias of the typical North American family, no one does it like Johnston. Her drawings of the fictional—but believable—Patterson family are seen in hundreds of newspapers in the United States and Canada, and "For Better or for Worse" has consistently been voted as one of the top five strips in reader polls.

"For Better or for Worse" developed out of many of Johnston's real life situations and concerns. The strip is populated by the Patterson family: two parents, two children, and a family dog. In this slice-of-life strip, there is a harried mother named Elly, and her nice and slightly bumbling husband, John. Elly was named after one of Johnston's friends, who died in high school from a tumor. Her friend Elly also wore her hair in the same way that Elly Patterson now does.

There are more similarities, too. Both the Johnstons and the Pattersons are Canadian. Johnston is married to Rod, who, like his fictional counterpart John, is a tall, affable dentist who is also a pilot. The two oldest Patterson children, Michael and Elizabeth, are near in age to the Johnston children, Aaron and Katie, whose first names have become the middle names of the cartoon characters. The Johnstons even had an English sheep dog named Farley, who has since passed away, though his boisterous spirit lives on in the comic strip. The Johnstons now own a black spaniel named Willie. Finally, Elly's brother Phil is a wayward trumpet player just like Johnston's brother, Alan Philip Ridgway.

And there are yet more subtle, more emotional similarities. Johnston herself has admitted that both she and Elly want to be rescuers. They both feel motivated to try to fix everyone and everything in their family. Rod Johnston admitted to Jeanne Malmgren in the *St. Petersburg Times Floridian* that "their insecurities are similar. They both worry about saying the wrong thing and offending somebody. Lynn also overworks like Elly. She gets exhausted, trying to please everybody all the time. And the losing weight thing. They both do that."

Johnston's emotional closeness to her characters has made them very real to her. Rod has said that "You can ask her what Elly's wearing today, and she'll tell you. If you ask about their house, she'll describe the sun room at the back and the driveway and all the junk in the garage."

The Real Characters Are ...

At a certain point, though, the parallels end. "I find that somehow the characters develop their personalities independently of me," Johnston told Janice Dineen in the *Toronto Star.* Husband Rod has also noted the differences, telling Malmgren that Lynn has more polish than her fictional character, and that she "is much more of a businessperson. And she's more in charge of our family than Elly is." Johnston's children "both look very, very different from the characters in the strip, and their lives are

very different," Johnston commented in an interview for *Authors and Artists for Young Adults* (*AAYA*). Her son once said: "'I don't want Michael to wear glasses, I want him to be as separate from me as he can be,' and so Elizabeth got the glasses, which was great for my daughter who does not wear glasses."

The recent addition of baby April also signals a departure for Johnston. While she grappled with her feelings of wanting another baby, she worked out this issue on paper instead of in reality. "I brought the baby into the strip," Johnston remarked to Dineen, "because for a while I really wanted another baby. I thought about adopting but instead, in the end, I made my baby up."

April is a very unique character in the strip, since she is the only one who is totally fictional and not based on one of Johnston's family members. "I can have a lot more fun with her and reveal a lot more about her private life because in reality she doesn't

The characters in Johnston's popular "For Better or for Worse" comic strip are based in part on herself, husband Rod, son Aaron, daughter Katie, and the family dog.

exist, so it's not as though I'm opening up a closet that no one has a right to see in," Johnston related to *AAYA*.

Better Beginnings

The suburban and slightly idyllic life of the Patterson family is somewhat removed from Johnston's own beginnings. Johnston, a self-described angry child, used drawing and art as an outlet for her emotions. "I drew lots when I was mad," she recalled in a *People* article by Ned Geeslin. "It helped me vent my anger. I was really an angry girl, even in elementary school. I wanted to be grown up. I'd fantasize and draw a picture of what I'd look like when I was old and what my husband would look like."

Sometimes this tendency for fantasizing would land her in difficulties in school, like the time where she doodled all over her math exam. "It was often hard for me to take anything seriously and even though I enjoyed school, there were times, especially during math class, when I would rather draw than take part," she told *AAYA*. But things weren't always so dire: "I remember ... getting an 'A' for the doodles and a 'D' for the exam," Johnston quipped.

The child of a watchmaker and a self-taught calligrapher and illustrator, one of Johnston's early memories was of her mother correcting her posture. "My mum was a real stickler for posture," Johnston said to Malmgren. "She made me walk around with a book on my head and stand against the wall to make sure my shoulders were back." As an adult, her rebellion against this teaching comes out in her work—Elly Patterson has an almost perpetual slouch. "So whenever I draw that slouch," she added, "it's almost a direct way of getting back at my mother."

Her parents' artistic sensibilities were to greatly influence Johnston in her later career. "My mother had tremendous talent when it came to painting and craft work. She was always making hooked rugs and all that sort of thing, but she was a calligrapher for my grandfather who had a stamp dealership." She spent a lot of time with her father, who was one of the greatest influences on her artistic talent. "My dad was a closet cartoonist. More than drawing cartoons, he appreciated cartoons. We would pour over these illustrations one at a time and he would point out the drawings and what made them funny. He just loved comics; he just loved cartoons."

Johnston's early cartoons, such as the ones collected in this 1975 book, bear a resemblance to her later "For Better or for Worse" strip.

More than simply appreciate cartoons and movies, Johnston's father would encourage her to analyze the humor in them, see how timing and setting played an important part in the humor of a piece. This was great training for the work Johnston would later do in her strip, where timing was essential. "He wouldn't just take you to a movie. He would talk about the comedy as it was timed and as it was set up and how difficult it was to set up these pratfalls. So comedy for me was not just a matter of sitting down and enjoying it, it was a matter of analyzing it as well. That went for both cartoons in the paper and cartoon behavior on live film."

For a short while, Johnston was enrolled in the Vancouver School of Art. She quit, however, and took jobs in animation and illustration. Marrying a cameraman named Doug, she moved to Ontario because of the better job opportunities. But Johnston found herself missing the mountains of British Columbia. Still, the move proved to be the right decision when she found a job in the city of Hamilton. "I got a wonderful job as a medical artist for McMaster University.... They trained me to do medical illustration. I did first year medical school and went to all the anatomy courses and did dissection and everything with the medical students," she told *AAYA*. "It was a great time of learning and a whole new career and I loved it." In 1972, her son Aaron was born. Unfortunately,

Johnston and her husband soon separated and Doug moved back to Vancouver.

After her divorce, Johnston started to do free-lance work out of her home and soon found her business booming. Oddly enough, it was her obstetrician who started a chain of events that would eventually lead to her being offered a contract for a comic strip. Knowing that she was a comic artist, he challenged her to come up with some cartoons to be put on the ceiling above his examining tables. "I was the type of person that liked a challenge, and if somebody I admired gave me a challenge, I went through that open door. That challenge was enough to make me do eighty drawings for him." With her friend's help, she found a publisher for the illustrations, eventually completing enough material for three books.

Submissions editors at Universal Press Syndicate had seen Johnston's first book, *David! We're Pregnant!,* and they were impressed with the quality and humor in her drawings. They were searching for a comic strip that could compete with the family-oriented "Blondie" and "Hi and Lois" and thought Johnston might be a shoo-in for that position. She was contacted and asked if she could produce in a four-frame format.

Comical Contracts

Johnston was both excited and nervous about the proposition. She had never written in a daily format, but was willing to give it a try. Shortly after Universal Press's offer, she sent them samples of a strip she had developed based loosely on her own family life. To her surprise, they accepted her submissions and offered her a daily, syndicated strip. She received a one-year development contract with which she was allowed to work on her strip for a year before it was published. After the year, she was offered a twenty-year contract.

"When I got the contract, I was totally blown out of the water," she told Malmgren. "It was the opportunity of a lifetime, but at the same time, it was terrifying. I never thought I would be able to come up with funny gags 200 or 300 times a year." She turned to her friend Cathy Guisewite, the creator of the very successful "Cathy" comic strip, for some friendly advice. Guisewite suggested that before doing the art she should write all the dialogue down as if she were doing script. "I had a tremendously good relationship with her on the phone," Johnston remarked to *AAYA,* "she gave me lots of hints on how she worked and then I went from there."

Over 150 papers signed on to carry "For Better or For Worse," even before the strip began to officially run. "It's hard to sell a new feature to papers, and many new cartoonists only start with about fifty papers, and maybe they never get past that," the cartoonist said. "I know now some young people who are struggling and they cannot seem to get past their fifty papers. So for me to start with 150 was quite an exciting thing. But then it was one of the first of the family strips that was not done by a man and also was done in a contemporary style. So I was breaking new ground in a way.... I was very fortunate."

Another Kind of Contract

As her comic career was developing, another story had been brewing as well. A few years before, while driving along with her young son, she happened to spot a small plane flying overhead. She loved flying and small aircraft, so on a whim she drove to the airport to see the plane land. "This nice young fellow jumped out of the plane and walked over and we had a conversation. He invited me to fly with him to the next airport for a hamburger," she told *AAYA.* Shortly afterward, the two realized that they were pretty compatible, except for one thing. He wanted to move north, and she wanted to stay in southern Canada. Overlooking this slight obstacle, she and Rod Johnston were married in 1976. He adopted her son and they had a daughter of their own shortly afterward.

Rod's graduation from dental school and their move to the north coincided with Johnston's proposal for Universal Press Syndicate. She found herself packing boxes for an income while trying to land the job with Universal. Shortly afterward, they moved to northern Manitoba, where Rod became a flying dentist.

Johnston cites some of her husband's qualities as being helpful to her career. "We [cartoonists] are very difficult people to live with," she told *AAYA.* "In order to maintain a career that's based on fantasy, you have to live with someone who is very down to earth, who is very reassuring." Rod has provided her with this stability, as well as something else equally essential. "He's also very funny. He's one of the funniest people I know."

The move to northern Canada proved to be fortuitous in many ways. First, Johnston got to have a remarkable adventure and meet new and different people. Second, it helped ease her adjustment to the fame she was getting. "It was good for me because the publicity was something that I didn't know how to handle. I'm a ham; I'm a frustrated actor as it probably shows in the work that I do. And so if I had more access to the city, I probably would have been a bigger jerk than I was. It was a very good thing that I lived in isolation for six years and I learned how to handle the publicity and not be such a ham.''

Johnston works almost every day. In the studio of the big log house Rod and she own on the edge of a lake in northern Ontario, where they moved after Manitoba, she produces her strip. "I like to sit in a corner with my feet up and a cup of coffee and a couple of pads of paper and I like to just write before I do anything." It takes her about one or two days to write the dialogue for one week of her comic strip, a task that is especially trying for her. "There's a fine line between what makes something funny and what makes something just barely amusing. I think it takes a sort of acting ability to be able to set up a scene, get the expressions and then bring it to a punch line. All in four frames. It's a knack that's taken me a long time to develop," she confided to Malmgren. Johnston feels that over the course of a week, one or two strips will be significantly funny, while the rest just build the story line.

After the writing process, she sets to work creating the art. "I waste almost no paper. I draw it in pencil, then I go over it with India ink pens, and then I put on the Lettra film, with the little dots that gives you the gray tones," she told Malmgren. "You have to be the characters as you are drawing," Johnston told Dineen. "You have to feel what the character is feeling. Even Farley the dog: as he stretches, I feel that." In this way, her feelings of being a frustrated actor have benefited her drawing. In her career, Johnston has drawn close to five thousand "For Better or for Worse" sketches. "It's like writing little sitcoms all the time and I'm playing all the roles and controlling all the camera angles," she told Dineen.

Getting Better and Braver

Johnston's early comics were very simple sketches of the Pattersons. Their two children were tiny, and they acquired a small puppy also, who was to grow into the massive Farley. They dealt with the normal grind of a family growing up together— parents and kids fighting, exhaustion and mess, etc. But as the Patterson family has grown and grown up, Johnston has tackled more complex and controversial issues in her strip.

At one point, Elly has to deal with the problem of her friend, who has give birth to a baby with six fingers on both hands. Later on, the Pattersons have to discover their own feelings on race relations as an Asian family moves into the house across the street. In a 1992 story line, Mike Patterson finds out that his friend, Gordon, is being abused by his father. Johnston admitted that the strip was taken from an incident that had happened to a friend of her daughter. She told John Przybys in the *Las Vegas Review-Journal:* "It was an experience I had and it bothered me. And, sometimes, when experiences bother you, you know how you tend to dream about them? For me, the dreaming came out on paper.''

Johnston tackled another difficult topic in a 1993 strip series. In it, family friend Lawrence Poirier admits to his family that he is gay. Unfortunately, his parents react badly, denying the news and eventually kicking him out of the house. This topic choice was partly inspired by Johnston's brother-in-law, Ralph, who is gay. Ralph revealed his feelings to the family years before, but the admission of his homosexuality changed her family forever. "What happens when you hear this news is you change," Johnston told John Tanasychuk of the *Detroit Free Press.* "You change because your point of view is shattered. You think one thing about the person and then this comes along. Then you realize that they haven't changed. It's you."

Johnston was a catalyst for family healing when this situation happened. By writing a series of strips about a gay character, the cartoonist hoped to reach her readers with this same sort of information and sharing she had discovered. However, because of the controversial topic, forty papers took alternate material and nineteen cancelled the strip outright. About this reaction, Johnston commented to Tanasychuk, "It surprises me in today's environment that people would want to [keep] something like that out of a newspaper. I think that the readers should be able to decide for themselves whether they want to read that."

Johnston received more than three thousand letters after the strips were published, two thirds of which praised her for having the courage to address the issue. However, there was also a significant amount of vicious, negative comments on the strip that could only be described as "hate mail." "What happens when something like this hits the paper," Johnston told *AAYA,* "is that the very angry people and generally very religious people unite first because they are used to crusading against something that they feel is threatening

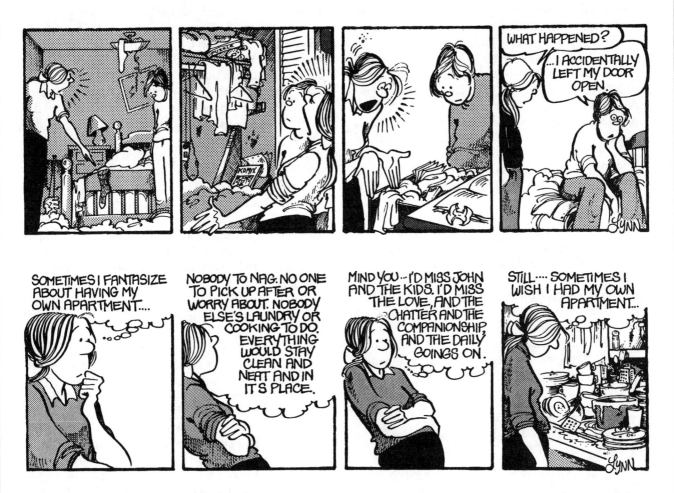

Johnston's realistic portrayal of modern family life earned her the National Cartoonists Society Reuben Award for outstanding cartoonist in 1986.

to their beliefs. The very angry, angry letters came first, the very angry response, and then, as soon as the angry response was visible, the thinking, caring people and especially people who work with families . . . started to write."

"I took a chance. I knew there would be some controversy," Johnston concluded. "And I didn't intend it to be quite as overwhelming as it was. Nonetheless it's a subject that horrifies, terrifies people. They're so afraid of it and so unwilling to learn about it, and that's why it's taking so long for acceptance and understanding to happen." Johnston has turned all the letters over to the sociology department of her local university, where they will be sorted and studied. "People were outraged that I would allow this word to enter their home. That it would be something that they would see on the comics page. . . . It was a really amazing situation. Not something I would want to engineer again." She later added, however, that a "great deal of

good was done despite the emotional roller coaster ride we all endured!"

In general, Johnston receives a lot of positive feedback from her more controversial strips. "If I do something of a serious nature, I'll get one letter against and 20 letters for," she told Przybys. "People are really comfortable reading about (serious) stuff as long as I'm careful to treat it with dignity and in a light way, because it *is* an entertainment medium and people do read comics for fun." The problem with confronting a controversial issue is that other special interest groups have sometimes requested that Johnston give equal time to their causes: A "lot of people want me to go further: 'Oh gosh, if she's willing to talk about child abuse, let's have her champion the abortion issue.' It's dangerous, when you do realistic things, turning the strip into a soapbox and people wanting you to champion their cause. You can't do that."

Asked whether she would enter into such a controversial area again, Johnston answered *AAYA:* "I often find myself writing and being surprised by the twists or the conversation that has just shown up. So I don't know what's going to happen. I certainly don't plan on shying away from controversy, but I don't intend to cause such concern for editors again. It was a difficult time for them because they were damned if they did and damned if they didn't." She feels that pretty much any topic is fair game as long as it fits her strip. "I don't think I betrayed the style of work that I do."

The cartoonist's willingness to take on just about any issue in her strip is sometimes bemoaned by her family because they realize that she will agonize for weeks until the story has run. With her children, Johnston knows that she can't use anything too personal from their lives. "I think the fact that neither of my kids reads my work is not an insult. It's a compliment in that they trust me, they know that they don't have to read it and watch over my shoulder to make sure that I'm not invading their privacy."

Johnston's 1990 collection contains both early and later scenes from the amusing day-to-day escapades of the Patterson family.

However, with her husband sometimes the issue is a little different. There was once a strip that ran where John breaks a foot by having a huge frozen turkey fall on it. Although this didn't really happen to him, he could not live it down. "I took tremendous abuse for that," he told Malmgren. "Everywhere I went, people were asking 'Where's the cast?'" On the other hand, Johnston finds that her husband is "probably my very best editor," as she related to *AAYA*. He has provided essential editing advice and suggestions on what works and what is funny. "At one point though, he was saying 'Gosh, John always ends up a bit of a buffoon and I don't like that.' I was impressed by that, and yet at the same time, he said 'But if it's funny, it's awfully hard not to let it go.'... So I try not to make John look like a twit, I try to give [John and Elly] equal twit billing."

Peers Recognize Her Talent

Johnston has won numerous awards and accolades throughout her career. In 1986, she won the prestigious Reuben Award for outstanding cartoonist of the year from the National Cartoonists Society, making her the first female and the youngest person ever to win. At the time, Johnston felt a little cowed by winning the award. "I felt at the time that it was too much, too soon. I really felt that I hadn't earned it yet," she confessed to *AAYA*. "I was afraid of the statue. It's a huge, heavy thing. I brought it home and hid it. I didn't want to look at it because I didn't feel that I could live up to it."

The award literally changed her life. "The morning after I got home from the award ceremony, I walked into my studio and everything looked different, just the whole room had a different meaning to it. It was terrifying. And the one person I knew who would understand was Charles Schultz, so I sat down and started to write him a letter. As I was sealing the letter in the envelope, the phone rang. It was [Schultz], and he said, 'Hi, when you walked into your studio this morning, did everything look different?'" That moment not only helped Johnston get over her fear, but she knew she had found a good friend in the creator of the famous "Peanuts" comic strip.

Johnston has cited the camaraderie among her fellow cartoonists as one of the benefits of her career. "There are times when you feel drained. The deadlines get you down and you can't think of anything. You feel pressured ... and it's great to call each other. We're very supportive of each other. Even though there is competition for space in magazines and on comic pages, there's a tremendous amount of camaraderie.'' She was heartened by the strong backing she received from other cartoonists when the backlash from her Lawrence story was becoming evident.

Johnston also admits she likes to visit her fellow cartoonists and peek into their studios. "The first thing you want to do is see the studio because it's sort of a shrine," she told *AAYA*. "It's one of those jobs that requires almost no equipment. I mean, most of us don't even have anything as expensive as a word processor. It's all pens and paper, which are very easy to obtain. The rest all comes from you. So there's a certain magic to that corner and that old wooden drafting table. You want to stand in that place that's so full of fantasy."

Popularity Contests

In comic strip popularity polls held by many newspapers in the early 1990s, Johnston's "For Better or for Worse" consistently placed in the top five, and, even more consistently, the top two spots. Johnston's strip was picked number one by readers of such newspapers as the *Detroit Free Press*, *The Oregonian*, the *Toronto Star*, the *L.A. Life Daily News*, the Denver *Rocky Mountain News*, the Norfolk *Virginian Pilot*, the *Cincinnati Enquirer*, and the Monterrey County, California, *Herald*.

But these statistics aren't surprising, considering the almost universal appeal of Johnston's work. She is barraged by fan mail from people who claim that the cartoonist is drawing from their experience. "I'm ... surprised by how many people read the strip then tell me, 'My daughter said that exact thing,' or 'That happened to me yesterday,'" Johnston admitted to Dineen. One woman who was confined to a body cast wrote to tell Johnston that although things were going poorly, she had laughed at one of Johnston's strips. Johnston was so touched that she sent the original of the strip to the woman.

When asked about the reasons for the popularity of her strips, Johnston told *AAYA*, "I think because people can identify with it, and I try to be very true to life. I enjoy what I do and I think it shows. The letters I get tend to tell me that people trust me and want to confide in me. They feel that I'm talking about their family and that it's the truth."

Johnston readily admits that she loves her job, telling Dineen, "I wouldn't trade it for anything. It keeps me in touch with people and their lives. I get to make people laugh." She knows that her cartooning is not only a profession, but a means of self-expression. "This is my way of communicating. Some people use music or dance or literature. I use cartooning." Her husband has mused that perhaps, with the Patterson family aging in the strip, Johnston will eventually write her way out of a job. But she disagrees, believing that there will always be a story line for her fictional family. In the final analysis, the strip is more than just work for Johnston. "I research a lot of my feelings through the strip. My personal philosophy comes out in it. The strip is what I do best."

■ Works Cited

Dineen, Janice, "Better Than Ever," *Toronto Star*, October 9, 1992.

Geeslin, Ned, "For Better or Worse, Canadian Cartoonist Lynn Johnston Draws Her Inspiration from Reality," *People*, September 15, 1986.

Johnston, Lynn, interview with Nancy E. Rampson for *Authors and Artists for Young Adults*, May 26, 1993.

Malmgren, Jeanne, "It's Getting 'Better,'" *St. Petersburg Times Floridian*, February 1, 1989.

Przybys, John, "Getting Serious," *Las Vegas Review-Journal*, May 31, 1992.

Tanasychuk, John, "Gay Teen Comes Out in For Better or for Worse," *Detroit Free Press*, March 17, 1993.

■ For More Information See

PERIODICALS

Chatelaine, February, 1987; June, 1989.

Detroit Free Press, August 8, 1993, pp. 1J, 4J.

Los Angeles Times Book Review, November 26, 1989; September 13, 1992.

Variety, January 1, 1986.

—*Sketch by Nancy E. Rampson*

Norma Johnston

■ Personal

Has also written under pseudonyms Elizabeth Bolton, Catherine E. Chambers, Kate Chambers, Pamela Dryden, Lavinia Harris, Adrian Robert, and Nicole St. John; born in Ridgewood, NJ; daughter of Eugene Chambers (an engineer) and Marjorie (a teacher; maiden name, Pierce) Johnston. *Education:* Montclair State College, B.A.; graduate studies at Montclair State College and Ithaca College. *Religion:* Reformed Church in America. *Hobbies and other interests:* Religion, psychology, mythology, youth counseling, British and American history, seventeenth-century metaphysical poetry, travel, gourmet cooking, theater, ballet, herb and flower gardening.

■ Addresses

Office—Dryden Harris St. John, Inc., Box 299, 103 Godwin Ave., Midland Park, NJ 07432. *Agent*—McIntosh & Otis, Inc., 475 5th Ave., New York, NY 10017; A. M. Heath & Co., Ltd., 40-42 William IV St., London WC2N 4DD, England.

■ Career

Writer and free-lance editor, 1961—; Glen Rock, NJ, public schools, English teacher, 1970-72. Chairman of Rutgers University Council on Children's Literature, 1988-89; president of St. John Institute of Arts and Letters, Inc., Dryden Harris St. John, Inc., and Geneva Players, Inc. (a religious drama group). Has also worked as a retailer, producer/director, actress, instructor, and businesswoman. *Member:* Authors Guild, Authors League of America, Sisters in Crime (president of mid-Atlantic chapter, 1989-91).

■ Awards, Honors

Pride of Lions: The Story of the House of Atreus was a *Horn Book* honor list book.

■ Writings

FOR YOUNG ADULTS

The Wishing Star, Funk, 1963.
The Wider Heart, Funk, 1964.
Ready or Not, Funk, 1965.
The Bridge Between, Funk, 1966.
Of Time and of Seasons, Atheneum, 1975.
Strangers Dark and Gold, Atheneum, 1976.
A Striving after Wind (sequel to *Of Time and of Seasons*), Atheneum, 1976.
If You Love Me, Let Me Go, Atheneum, 1978.
The Swallow's Song, Atheneum, 1978.
The Crucible Year, Atheneum, 1979.
Pride of Lions: The Story of the House of Atreus, Atheneum, 1979.

The Days of the Dragon's Seed, Atheneum, 1982.
Gabriel's Girl, Atheneum, 1983.
Timewarp Summer, Atheneum, 1983.
The Watcher in the Mist, Bantam, 1986.
Shadow of a Unicorn, Bantam, 1987.
The Potter's Wheel, Morrow, 1988.
Return to Morocco, Macmillan, 1988.
Whisper of the Cat, Bantam, 1988.
The Delphic Choice, Macmillan, 1989.
The Five Magpies, Macmillan, 1989.
Such Stuff as Dreams Are Made Of, Morrow, 1989.
Summer of the Citadel, Bantam, 1989.
A Small Rain, Macmillan, 1990.
Time of the Cranes, Four Winds, 1990.
The Dragon's Eye, Four Winds, 1990.
Louisa May Alcott: The Work and Worlds of Louisa May Alcott, Four Winds, 1991.

"KEEPING DAYS" SERIES; FOR YOUNG ADULTS

The Keeping Days, Atheneum, 1973.
Glory in the Flower, Atheneum, 1974.
A Mustard Seed of Magic, Atheneum, 1977.
The Sanctuary Tree, Atheneum, 1977.
A Nice Girl Like You, Atheneum, 1980.
Myself and I, Atheneum, 1981.

"CARLISLE CHRONICLES" SERIES; FOR YOUNG ADULTS

Carlisles All, Bantam, 1986.
The Carlisle's Hope, Bantam, 1986.
To Jess, with Love and Memories, Bantam, 1986.

UNDER PSEUDONYM PAMELA DRYDEN

Mask for My Heart (for young adults), New American Library, 1982.
Riding Home (for children), Bantam, 1988.

UNDER PSEUDONYM LAVINIA HARRIS; FOR YOUNG ADULTS

Dreams and Memories, Scholastic, 1982.

"COMPUTER DETECTIVES" SERIES; UNDER PSEUDONYM LAVINIA HARRIS; FOR YOUNG ADULTS

The Great Rip-Off, Scholastic, 1984.
Soaps in the Afternoon, Scholastic, 1985.
A Touch of Madness, Scholastic, 1985.
Cover Up!, Scholastic, 1986.
The Packaging of Hank and Celia, Scholastic, 1986.

"DIANA WINTHROP" SERIES; UNDER PSEUDONYM KATE CHAMBERS; FOR YOUNG ADULTS

The Case of the Dog Lover's Legacy, New American Library, 1983.
The Secret of the Singing Strings, New American Library, 1983.
Danger in the Old Fort, New American Library, 1983.

The Legacy of Lucian Van Zandt, New American Library, 1984.
The Secrets of Beacon Hill, New American Library, 1984.
The Threat of the Pirate Ship, New American Library, 1984.

"ADVENTURES IN FRONTIER AMERICA" SERIES; UNDER PSEUDONYM CATHERINE E. CHAMBERS; FOR CHILDREN

California Gold Rush: Search for Treasure, Troll, 1984.
Daniel Boone and the Wilderness Road, Troll, 1984.
Flatboats on the Ohio: Westward Bound, Troll, 1984.
Frontier Dream: Life on the Great Plains, Troll, 1984.
Frontier Farmer: Kansas Adventure, Troll, 1984.
Frontier Village: A Town Is Born, Troll, 1984.
Indiana Days: Life in a Frontier Town, Troll, 1984.
Log Cabin Home: Pioneers in the Wilderness, Troll, 1984.
Texas Roundup: Life on the Range, Troll, 1984.
Wagons West: Off to Oregon, Troll, 1984.

UNDER PSEUDONYM ELIZABETH BOLTON; FOR CHILDREN

The Case of the Wacky Cat, Troll, 1985.
Ghost in the House, Troll, 1985.
The Secret of the Ghost Piano, Troll, 1985.
The Secret of the Magic Potion, Troll, 1985.
The Tree House Detective Club, Troll, 1985.

UNDER PSEUDONYM ADRIAN ROBERT; FOR CHILDREN

The Awful Mess Mystery, Troll, 1985.
Ellen Ross, Private Detective, Troll, 1985.
My Grandma, the Witch, Troll, 1985.
The Secret of the Haunted Chimney, Troll, 1985.
The Secret of the Old Barn, Troll, 1985.

UNDER PSEUDONYM NICOLE ST. JOHN; FOR ADULTS

The Medici Ring, Random House, 1975.
Wychwood, Random House, 1976.
Guinever's Gift, Random House, 1977.

OTHER

Has also been a ghost writer of fiction, mysteries, biographies, cookbooks, reference books, religious books, and books on popular culture; author of seven unpublished manuscripts; has written columns on writing, cooking, and entertaining, including a "Keeping Days Cooking" column.

■ **Sidelights**

"There are moments when everything's so sharp and bright it almost seems I cannot bear the pain and beauty of the world. But whenever I find myself thinking that way, I cross my fingers quick and take the wish back. Because if I wasn't sensitive, I would never have stumbled onto being a writer," wrote Norma Johnston in one of her most popular books (and her own personal favorite), *The Keeping Days*. To Johnston, the idea of "keeping days" is more than a book title; it is a concept that is important to her life and to every one of her many books. She explained what she means by a "keeping day" in her *Something About the Author Autobiography Series* (*SAAS*) entry: "None of us remembers our life just as a one-after-the-other series of events. What we remember are *moments,* some enormous, some small, in which everything comes together—moments which (in our conscious or unconscious) remain with us forever. Like fleeting images in a music video, or the way sight and sound and taste and touch and smell suddenly stand out sharp and clear, for a brief instant, when we have a high fever, or are very very tired, or spaced out on medications. Those come-together, make-a-memory moments are our Keeping Days."

Author's Life Reflected in Fiction

Johnston's life has been packed with such memorable times, and her fiction books are largely drawn from her own experiences. Before becoming a full-time writer, she worked extensively in the worlds of theater and fashion, taught art and dramatics, attended debutante balls, and also endured times when she was so poor that she had to go without stockings in a snowstorm. In addition to her own rich life, she has used her family's history in her books and series, many of which take place in historical settings.

Although she was an only child, Johnston's extended family was very large, as the families she writes about tend to be. On her mother's side, she is descended from Dutch colonists who settled what is now New York and New Jersey. This branch of the family tree is fictionalized in the "Keeping Days" series. The "Carlisle Chronicles" series is based on her father's side of the family—English and Scottish settlers from the Middle Atlantic region. Family stories that were passed down through the generations are woven into these books, along with Johnston's own perceptions. "I was frequently dragged to family reunions," she remembered in *SAAS*, and for a long while these gatherings were quite dull—until "I discovered I could get my great-uncles to tell tales about each other; Uncle Elmer (Ben in 'Keeping Days') and

Uncle Joe were both newspapermen, and they and Uncle John knew how to tell good stories. My school compositions livened up after that, too. My grandmother had ten fits when I wrote about how John and Elmer once got their father drunk on year-old cider as a sort of scientific experiment, but my eighth-grade classmates liked it fine. That story got recycled . . . in 'Keeping Days,' and then my mother had the ten fits."

Creative activities were a primary focus of Johnston's life from an early age. She started ballet at the age of three, and the thrilling experience of wearing makeup, being applauded, and being handed flowers after her performance gave her a love of the stage that would stay with her for a lifetime. Art was also a great joy to her, and she wrote poetry all through her elementary school years. In the eighth grade, poor health kept her out of school for many weeks, and during that time she wrote her first full-length book. It concerned an

Beginning in 1973, Johnston followed two generations of fictional Dutch settlers in her popular—and personal favorite—"Keeping Days" series.

Abolitionist girl living in Maryland in the 1850s whose home served as a station on the Underground Railroad, and who fell in love with the son of a slave-catcher. "I never showed the book to anyone, unless maybe Mrs. Cadman, my English teacher, but I still have it," the author stated in *SAAS*. "I may do something with it yet someday."

Despite her precocity in writing, in her teens Johnston still planned to go to art school in New York and study design. When her father died unexpectedly that plan dissolved, and she realized that writing was her great love. Although she was repeatedly told that there was no future in it, she finished another book and began submitting it to contests and publishers. It was a long time and many rewrites later before it was accepted, but Johnston clung to her faith in her own talents. "That's one of the major things I want to pass on through my books: It *is* possible to make things happen. It *is* possible to make it. Especially with the encouragement and faith of friends and family, of blood or of spirit," she wrote.

One of Johnston's earliest role models in writing was Maud Hart Lovelace, author of the "Betsy-Tacy" books. She began corresponding with Mrs. Lovelace while in college and received a great deal of encouragement from her. In fact, when told by a college writing instructor that she would never, ever be a successful author, Johnston sat up all night writing a letter to Lovelace begging for advice. The older woman advised her protege to quit the professor's class immediately, to refuse advice from anyone who was not a professional in her chosen field, and to keep on writing.

First Novel Published

Several more years passed, with Johnston involved in theater groups, working in the fashion industry, and running her own dress shop, before her first book was finally published. It was a book she'd originally written at the age of sixteen—rewritten many times since then—and that was based on her memories of her church youth group and the various "crowds" she was involved with at the time. An agent sent the manuscript to the publishing company Funk and Wagnalls, which agreed to buy it if the author would cut one hundred pages from it. That was a valuable experience, for it forced Johnston to reduce *The Wishing Star* to outline form in order to see what was really necessary and what was not. Since then, she has written all her books from outlines.

Over the next several years, Johnston continued to publish about one book a year, while also working as an assistant editor at a religious publishing house and founding the Geneva Players, a theater company. The purpose of the dramatic group was to allow young actors to perform in classics and major Broadway plays as a means to helping them speak out on the issues and conflicts in their own lives. The first production put on by the group was Arthur Miller's *The Crucible*. It opened on the night of the assassination of John F. Kennedy. The events surrounding that unforgettable night became the basis of another of Johnston's books, *The Crucible Year*. In that book, the protagonist is sixteen-year-old Elizabeth Newcomb, who has recently transferred from a private to a public school. In her new environment, Elizabeth struggles with many problems, new ideas, and new people. All of life seems to be taking unpredictable, disturbing new turns, and the murder of President Kennedy greatly increases Elizabeth's sense of confusion and disillusionment with the world.

Horn Book reviewer Karen M. Kleckner praised the author's probing questions about personal values, religion, prejudice, and stereotypes. Although Kleckner felt the book was written more to "recollect and understand" a troubled time in history than to develop a story, the reviewer noted that Johnston has a "fluid style" and that the stage scenes where Elizabeth's personality blends with that of her character are "particularly effective." According to Johnston, these excerpts were taken directly from her real-life journal.

Demand for Books Increases

Several years after the events related in *The Crucible Year*, the publishing industry underwent a dramatic change when young adult books suddenly became popular, and Johnston's life changed as well. The respiratory and arthritis problems that had plagued her since her youth became much worse, limiting her activities just as the demand for her books greatly increased. Her writing increased so much that she began publishing under seven different pseudonyms: Nicole St. John, Catherine E. Chambers, Kate Chambers, Elizabeth Bolton, Lavinia Harris, Adrian Robert, and Pamela Dryden. All the names were taken from ancestors on one side of the family or another, or both. Although serious illness would usually be considered a drawback, it led Johnston to write so much that she is now able to support herself completely from her writing. She wrote philosophically about her health in *SAAS*: "If I hadn't been out of school so much

The Crucible Year
by NORMA JOHNSTON

Johnston's 1979 story of a teenage girl coping in a new school environment was influenced by the assassination of President John F. Kennedy.

when I was little, I wouldn't have read so much, I wouldn't have hung around so much with adults and had my horizons widened. I know I wouldn't have had as much empathy for others. Perhaps I wouldn't even have been a writer.... So this is something else I want to pass on through my characters—you can't control what life dishes out to you, but you can control how you react to it and what you do with it. You can use your gifts—if not one way, then another."

Johnston's strong feeling for family traditions and her positive beliefs are always reflected in her writing. The "Carlisle Chronicles" series, which includes *The Carlisles's Hope, To Jess, with Love and Memories,* and *Carlisles All,* revolves around the life of the large and loving Carlisle family. In these books, excitement and uncertainty comes from the father's job in the foreign service, which requires many moves around the world. Jess, the central character, looks for stability by clinging to

her family history. In the first book in the series, Jess's security is challenged when she learns that her father was actually adopted—the family she has so revered is not, by blood, really hers to claim after all. By the end of the book, however, Jess has learned that family means more than blood ties.

In *Carlisles All,* which Katharine Bruner called in *School Library Journal* "a smoothly written and swiftly flowing, hold-on-tight tale of adolescent adventure," the Carlisles are enjoying an idyllic Christmas holiday together when their father is sent on an emergency trip to the Middle East. Mrs. Carlisle accompanies him, leaving the children home alone. The young Carlisles are horrified when they see that the embassy where their parents were scheduled to be is the target of a bomb attack. Again, Jess is the anchor of the story. Because her father's mission was a secret one, she must put up a charade for the public, pretending that her family is intact and enjoying the holidays. Meanwhile, she waits tensely to field phone calls from overseas that will reveal if her parents are dead or alive. The young Carlisles handle "everything with remarkable dexterity," while still remaining flawed and human enough "to bond with readers," noted Bruner.

The Middle East again provides the background in the novel *The Delphic Choice.* Like so many of Johnston's books, this one carries a message about moral responsibility. A "Delphic choice" is a "choice between public and private duty," explained Linda L. Lowry in the *School Library Journal.* This is exactly what the heroine, seventeen-year-old Meredith Blake, faces in Istanbul, Turkey, where she has been acting as caretaker for her aunt's two children. Her uncle is kidnapped by terrorists, who want Meredith to deliver messages between them and the United States government. Cooperating with them might save her uncle, but could endanger many other lives. Lowry complained that some parts of the book become too "didactic," but admitted that Johnston has created a strong heroine in Meredith. She also praised the author for weaving an exciting story full of Middle Eastern color: "Teens ... will be intrigued by the excitement and mystery of the plot."

Return to Morocco combines Johnston's taste for stories of espionage and suspense with her deep feeling for family relations. In this story, Tori Clay accompanies her genteel grandmother to the Mediterranean. Once there, Tori discovers that her "Nannie" actually worked for the French Resistance as an agent in World War II. The corpses, poisonous snakes, and other physical dangers that lie in wait for Tori are nothing compared to her struggle to understand and accept her grandmother's secret past.

Not all of Johnston's mysteries are set overseas. *Shadow of a Unicorn* is a mystery, a horse story, and a romance all in one. It takes place in Kentucky bluegrass country, although the house is modelled on the beautiful New Jersey mansion the author lived in as a young girl. In the story, orphaned Sarah goes to live at Unicorn Farm, where thoroughbreds are raised and raced by her cousin Rowena. But the farm has been struck by one disaster after another, including the deaths of Rowena's parents and several horses. Rumors arise that Unicorn Farm is cursed, but Sarah and Rowena dig deep to find out the truth. A *Publishers Weekly* contributor noted that the story is "lively" and "unfolds slowly and satisfyingly," while calling Johnston "deft in evoking the Kentucky landscape."

Time of the Cranes springs from Johnston's involvement in acting, especially as it pertained to her affection for her acting teacher. In the novel, Stacy's drama teacher passes away and names Stacy her sole beneficiary, much to the girl's surprise. In investigating the woman's death, Stacy finds it to be suspicious and eventually realizes that her teacher took an intentional overdose of painkillers. She must struggle to come to terms with this death and with the death of her mother. In doing so, she reaches a breakthrough point in her own acting. Susan F. Marcus, writing in *School Library Journal*, called *Time of the Cranes* "a satisfying read for fans of fast-moving soap operas, acting enthusiasts, and mature readers who can grapple with the issue of elderly suicide."

"Keeping Days" Series Most Popular

Of all the author's writings, "The Keeping Days" series is the favorite both of readers and of Johnston herself. It includes *The Keeping Days, Glory in the Flower, A Mustard Seed of Magic, The Sanctuary Tree, A Nice Girl Like You,* and *Myself and I.* Tish Sterling is the narrator and central character in the first book, which is set in turn-of-the-century Yonkers, New York. She, like her creator, is a precocious writer with a great sense of drama who thinks of herself as "sensitive and misunderstood." *Horn Book* reviewer Mary M. Burns noted the first book's debt to *Little Women* by Louisa May Alcott, but assured potential readers that Johnston's story was "by no means a carbon copy" of Alcott's. She called *The Keeping*

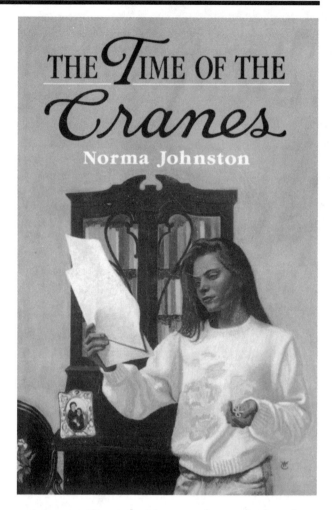

A young acting student improves her craft when she confronts the death of her teacher in this 1990 work.

Days "nostalgic but not sentimental" and a "fresh, compelling story told with perception and spontaneity" that captures the anxieties of adolescence.

The series continued into a new generation by the time it reached *A Nice Girl Like You,* set in 1917. The title character is Saranne Albright, a "nice girl" who falls in love with the neighborhood's "bad boy," Paul Hodge. Saranne's large and loving family provides her with all the comfort and warmth she could ask for, but her friends scorn her when she becomes involved with Paul. The boy has been unfairly accused of many things, and by the end of the book all have learned an important lesson about making hasty judgments. "The author is a fluent storyteller; the families are as full of vitality as ever, constantly caught up in turmoil or triumph," noted Ethel L. Heins in *Horn Book.* Saranne's romance is complicated and continued in the next book in the series, *Myself and I.*

About her "Keeping Days" books, Johnston wrote in *SAAS:* "I write of the Keeping Days that remain

In this 1980 continuation of Johnston's "Keeping Days" novels, Saranne Albright loses her friends when she falls in love with "bad boy" Paul Hodge.

in our memories forever; of the turning point in which we go from innocence to knowledge; of the abstract truths I believe to be unchanging in a changing world. And of facing change without feeling threatened by it." She readily admitted that these goals sometimes lead to what some would call "preachy" results. "I'm an author, editor, ghostwriter, entrepreneur, actress, director, designer, stylist, retailer, teacher, counselor," she concluded, "and (as some critics have said about me, and I'm proud of it) preacher."

■ Works Cited

Bruner, Katharine, review of *Carlisles All, School Library Journal,* May, 1987, p. 112.

Burns, Mary M., review of *The Keeping Days, Horn Book,* December, 1973, p. 591.

Heins, Ethel L., review of *A Nice Girl Like You, Horn Book,* June, 1980, pp. 306-307.

Johnston, Norma, *The Keeping Days,* Atheneum, 1973.

Johnston, Norma, entry in *Something about the Author Autobiography Series,* Volume 7, Gale, 1989, pp. 267-283.

Kleckner, Karen M., review of *The Crucible Year, Horn Book,* April, 1979, p. 200.

Lowry, Linda L., review of *The Delphic Choice, School Library Journal,* May, 1989, p. 126.

Marcus, Susan F., review of *Time of the Cranes, School Library Journal,* May, 1990, p. 122.

Review of *Shadow of a Unicorn, Publishers Weekly,* May 29, 1987, p. 80.

■ For More Information See

PERIODICALS

Horn Book, April, 1980; April, 1983; October, 1983.

New York Times Book Review, May 11, 1975.

School Library Journal, April 1975; November, 1975; September, 1976; September, 1977; October, 1977; May, 1978; October, 1978; March, 1979; May, 1980; November, 1981; December, 1983; March, 1988; September, 1988; December, 1990.°

—Sketch by Joan Goldsworthy

Diana Wynne Jones

Horn Book award, 1984, for *Archer's Goon; Horn Book* Honor List, 1984, for *Fire and Hemlock; Horn Book* Fanfare List, 1987, for *Howl's Moving Castle.*

■ Writings

FOR YOUNG READERS

Wilkins' Tooth, illustrated by Julia Rodber, Macmillan (London), 1973, published as *Witch's Business*, Dutton, 1974.
The Ogre Downstairs, Macmillan, 1974, Dutton, 1975.
Eight Days of Luke, Macmillan, 1974, Greenwillow, 1988.
Dogsbody, Macmillan, 1975, Greenwillow, 1977.
Power of Three, Macmillan, 1976, Greenwillow, 1977.
Who Got Rid of Angus Flint?, illustrated by John Sewell, Evans Brothers, 1978.
The Four Grannies, illustrated by Thelma Lambert, Hamish Hamilton, 1980.
The Homeward Bounders, Greenwillow, 1981.
The Time of the Ghost, Macmillan, 1981.
Warlock at the Wheel and Other Stories, Greenwillow, 1984.
Archer's Goon, Greenwillow, 1984.
Fire and Hemlock, Greenwillow, 1984.
Howl's Moving Castle, Greenwillow, 1986.
A Tale of Time City, Greenwillow, 1987.
Chair Person, illustrated by Glenys Ambrus, Hamish Hamilton, 1989.
Wild Robert, Methuen, 1989.
Castle in the Air (sequel to *Howl's Moving Castle*), Greenwillow, 1991.

■ Personal

Born August 16, 1934, in London, England; daughter of Richard Aneurin (an educator) and Marjorie (an educator; maiden name, Jackson) Jones; married John A. Burrow (a university professor), December 23, 1956; children: Richard, Michael, Colin. *Education:* St. Anne's College, Oxford, B.A., 1956.

■ Addresses

Home—9, The Polygon, Clifton, Bristol B58 4PW, England. *Agent*—Laura Cecil, 17 Alwyne Villas, London N1 2HG, England.

■ Career

Writer of books and plays for children and young adults.

■ Awards, Honors

Carnegie commendation, 1975, for *Dogsbody;* Guardian commendation, 1977, for *Power of Three;* Carnegie commendation, 1977, and Guardian Award, 1978, for *Charmed Life; Boston Globe-*

Aunt Maria, Greenwillow, 1991.

Yes, Dear, illustrated by Graham Philpot, Greenwillow Books, 1992.

Stopping for a Spell, illustrated by Joseph A. Smith, Greenwillow Books, 1993.

"CHRESTOMANCI" CYCLE; FOR YOUNG READERS

Charmed Life, Greenwillow, 1977.

The Magicians of Caprona, Greenwillow, 1980.

Witch Week, Greenwillow, 1982.

The Lives of Christopher Chant, Greenwillow, 1988.

"DALEMARK" CYCLE; FOR YOUNG READERS

Cart and Cwidder, Macmillan, 1975, Atheneum, 1977.

Drowned Ammet, Macmillan, 1977, Atheneum, 1978.

The Spellcoats, Atheneum, 1979.

The Crown of Dalemark, Methuen, 1993.

PLAYS FOR YOUNG READERS

The Batterpool Business, first produced in London at Arts Theatre, October, 1968.

The King's Things, first produced at Arts Theatre, February, 1970.

The Terrible Fisk Machine, first produced at Arts Theatre, January, 1971.

OTHER

Changeover (adult novel), Macmillan (London), 1970.

The Skiver's Guide, illustrated by Chris Winn, Knight Books, 1984.

(Editor) *Hidden Turnings: A Collection of Stories through Time and Space,* Greenwillow, 1990.

A Sudden Wild Magic (novel), Morrow, 1992.

Contributor to books, including *The Cat-Flap and the Apple Pie,* W. H. Allen, 1979, *Hecate's Cauldron,* DAW Books, 1981, *Hundreds and Hundreds,* Puffin, 1984, *Dragons and Dreams,* Harper, 1986, and *Guardian Angels,* Viking Kestrel, 1987.

■ **Work in Progress**

Hexwood, a novel for all ages.

■ **Sidelights**

Diana Wynne Jones "is a prolific novelist of enormous range who can raise hairs on the back of the neck one minute, belly laughs the next," asserts Elaine Moss in the *Times Literary Supplement.* Jones not only creates mythical worlds peopled with wizards, witches, fire demons, ghosts, djinns, genies, and moving castles, but also writes about seemingly "normal" families whose lives become complicated through the introduction of a magical element, such as the strange chemical sets in *The Ogre Downstairs.* Norse, Celtic, and Greek mythological references abound in her writings as does her reliance on a story from *The Arabian Nights* as the basis for *Castle in the Air.* As Penelope Farmer notes in the *Times Literary Supplement,* "Jones has a remarkable ability to grasp the basic elements of myth or fairy tale, twist them sharply, then fit them without undue strain into patterns of her own making." Her characters are often troubled children who are not close to the adults in their world. Parents or guardians are absent or do not want to be bothered, leaving the children to their own devices. To balance out some of the more serious problems her characters face, Jones uses humor in many of her stories.

Jones was born on August 16, 1934, in London, England. In August 1939, her father bundled five-year-old Diana and her three-year-old sister, Isobel, off to his parents' home in Wales for safety due

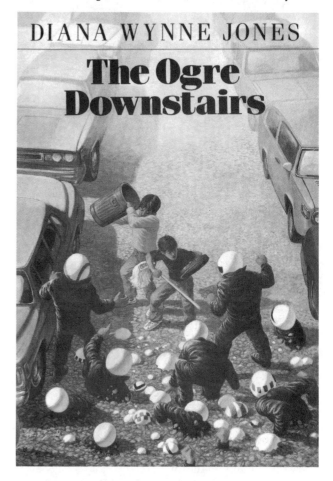

Jones's 1974 novel concerns new step-siblings who avoid their family problems by concocting magic spells with a chemistry set.

to the impending war. Although their grandparents and other relatives spoke to the girls in English, they reverted to Welsh when talking to each other, which was quite confusing for the children. Jones's grandfather was a famous Welsh preacher who tended to speak in blank verse. As the author recalls in her *Something about the Author Autobiography Series* (SAAS) essay, "[The] splendour and the rigour of it ... went into the core of my being.... I still sometimes dream in Welsh, without understanding a word. And at the bottom of my mind there is always a flow of spoken language that is not English, rolling in majestic paragraphs and resounding with splendid polysyllables. I listen to it like music when I write."

After giving birth to another daughter, Ursula, Jones's mother returned to Wales to see her other children. When she got there, however, she was upset to discover that Diana was speaking with a newly-acquired Welsh accent and Isobel was calling an aunt "Mummy." Fearing that her daughters had been away from their mother too long, Mrs. Jones decided to take the family back to London and then to Westmoreland in northern England in 1940. While in Westmoreland the family, along with other refugee families, lived in a house that belonged to a woman who had worked as a secretary for John Ruskin, the famous nineteenth-century art critic and writer. One day, the young Jones explored the off-limits attic and found a stack of high-quality drawing paper. Needing paper to write on, she diligently erased the drawings of flowers signed JR from about half of the stack before she was discovered and punished. She had unknowingly destroyed about fifty of Ruskin's famous flower drawings.

Another famous personality, children's writer Arthur Ransome, also lived nearby and did not appreciate the noise the children made. But when he came to the house to complain he "almost immediately stormed away again on finding there was nobody exactly in charge to complain to." Jones was impressed to see that the author was a real person and not just a name on a book cover, even if he did hate kids. However, she was developing the impression that writers were not fond of children, a notion that was reinforced when she came across another children's author. In *SAAS* she relates the following run-in with Beatrix Potter, the creator of the Peter Rabbit stories, who one day discovered Isobel and another child swinging on her gate. "An old woman with a sack over her shoulders stormed out of the house and hit both of them for swinging on her gate. This was Beatrix Potter. She hated

children, too. I remember the two of them running back to us, bawling with shock. Fate, I always think, seemed determined to thrust a very odd view of authorship on me."

Jones did not always get along with other children and was often involved in activities that were somewhat dangerous. She still remembers her time in the Lake district as magical. "The shape of the mountains across the lakes has, like my grandfather, become part of my dreams. Since the mountain is called the Old Man of Coniston, they sometimes seem to be the same thing." But the family did not stay there long. Living with so many people under such adverse conditions forced Mrs. Jones to find another place for them to live. In 1941, the family moved into a nunnery in York where seven-year-old Diana was placed in a class with nine-year-olds because her mother said she "was ugly, semi-delinquent, but bright." Although she tried, the work was two years above her head, and it was only during the last few weeks in York that she was put back into a lower class where she understood what she was doing.

The Uphill Struggle to Write

It was at this early age when—in 1942—she told her mother she was going to be a writer, even though most people at the time felt that girls weren't supposed to pursue such a career. Often involved in some dramatic and occasionally dangerous project or other, Jones remembers in her *SAAS* essay, "For some reason I believed it my duty to live a life of adventure and I used to worry that, for a would-be writer, I had too little imagination." Jones's parents were no help in supporting their daughter's writing ambitions: her mother told her, "You haven't got it in you," and her father just laughed at the idea.

In 1943, Jones's parents took jobs running a conference center for young adults in Thaxted in rural Essex. According to Jones, this seemingly idyllic little village had more than its share of problems and strange characters. It had the highest illegitimate birthrate in the country, cases of incest, prostitution, at least two witches, and a man who went mad when the moon was full. Her home life was anything but idyllic. The main house was used for the center while the three girls were housed alone in a two-room shack that had no heat—except what came from a paraffin stove—and no bathroom. The children remained unwashed and uncombed for six months before their mother noticed, and when she did she blamed nine-year-old Diana because she was supposed to be in charge.

The children got little attention from their parents, who were immersed in their jobs. They did not accompany their parents on vacations, but were left instead with the gardener, the minister, the matron of the orphanage, or "dumped" on Granny. Jones says she would have been lost without her grandmother. She has told various interviewers, including *Publishers Weekly* contributor Kit Alderdice, that she and her sisters were "book-hungry." Their father had bought a complete collection of Arthur Ransome's books, but only doled out one book per Christmas. The girls rode their bicycles for miles to borrow books and read all thirty Ransome selections in the public library. To supplement their sparse literary diet, Jones began to write stories which she read aloud to her sisters at night. She completed two epic tales, an exercise she now feels was good practice for her future life as a writer. "You must *know* you can finish a book," as she tells Alderdice.

Jones survived those painful childhood years of assuming more responsibility than should have been expected of her and went to St. Anne's College at Oxford. She was not happy during her years there because she had a demanding roommate, her father died of cancer during her first year there, and she then worried about her younger sisters, who did not get along well with their mother. Despite all these distractions, she managed to continue with her studies, attending lectures by C. S. Lewis and J. R. R. Tolkien, both of whom she feels influenced her writing.

Before her father's death, Jones met John Burrow. She knew when she saw him that this was the man she would marry, and she did so a few years later. During the first few months of married life, Jones had no job. She occupied herself by reading Dante, Edward Gibbon, and Norse sagas, all of which also later influenced her writings. Settling down to the life of wife and mother, she and her husband had three sons over the next few years. She wanted her children to read the kind of books she had never had a chance to read, but found that there weren't that many "good" books available. To fill this perceived gap, Jones began to write the kind of books she thought children would like to read. In a letter to *AAYA*, Jones comments, "I wrote many books over the ten years from 1963 to 1973, and all were turned down by publishers, often on strange grounds—for example, I didn't give the ages of the children in the book. After I wrote *Wilkins' Tooth* I had decided to give up writing,

because I was sure that would be turned down too."

Magical Novels

With the encouragement of her literary agent, Laura Cecil, Jones wrote *Wilkins' Tooth*, which was published in 1973 in England and a year later in the United States under the title *Witch's Business*. In this novel, young Frank and Jess set up a revenge service that backfires when the local witch becomes involved. With the help of the town bully, the witch is destroyed. In Alderdice's article, Jones calls the novel a "breakthrough" after which "there was hardly enough time to get everything written." However, Cathy S. Coyle in a *School Library Journal* review says that although the story's setting is interesting and the witch convincingly scary, "the 'Puss in Boots' plan for her destruction is too obvious so there is little suspense as the trap develops." Christopher Davis in the *New York Times Book Review* notes that no "au-

Jones received a Carnegie commendation for her 1975 story in which Sirius, the Dog Star, is banished to earth in the form of a newborn puppy.

thority but the child's own is ever recognized and adults are never appealed to." This reliance of young characters on themselves without the need for adult interference is a reflection of Jones's own childhood and is a recurring theme of her work.

Jones recalls in *SAAS* that while writing her second book, *The Ogre Downstairs*, she laughed so much "that the boys kept putting their heads round the door to ask if I was all right." In this tale, Casper, Johnny, and Gwinny's mother marries a man with two sons, and neither set of children are happy about their new situation. Douglas and Malcolm think the other children—whose mother has let them do whatever they please—are noisy and uncivilized. The stepfather, now the disciplinarian, is grumpy and would rather children be seen and not heard. To keep them occupied, he buys two chemistry sets for the children. Casper and his siblings keep the results of their experiments secret from their stepbrothers, who do the same, and they each make hilarious and frightening discoveries. Over the course of the story dust balls and toffee candy bars come alive and swarm about their rooms, the children fly, shrink, change colors, inhabit each other's bodies, and are finally attacked by a motorcycle gang they have accidentally conjured up. All five children consider their father/ stepfather to be the enemy and make two attempts to kill him, but by the end of the novel they decide he may not be so bad after all. John Fuller says in the *New Statesman* that "the last episode involving Dragon's Teeth warriors ... who mushroom up from the ground talking joke Greek ... is a fine stroke." In a *Growing Point* article, Margery Fisher thinks Jones's use of magical events as a way of revealing character is similar to E. Nesbit's writing. The critic concludes that "*The Ogre Downstairs* will be wasted if it is not accorded the widest possible readership—not that young readers won't appreciate it but their elders should not miss it either." *Bulletin of the Center for Children's Books* contributor Zena Sutherland calls the book, "A-droitly blended realism and fantasy."

Jones's first book to win recognition was *Dogsbody*, which received a Carnegie commendation. The story's canine hero was inspired by the family dog, according to Jones in her *Publishers Weekly* interview. The dog "used to groan when he saw the pad." He felt it was his duty to lie on [Jones's] feet while she wrote, "as well as on top of every paper." The title refers to the Dog Star, Sirius, who is accused of murder and the loss of a Zoi, an object of great power. As punishment, he is banished to earth to search for the Zoi. Arriving on earth in the form of a newborn puppy, the Dog Star is adopted by Kathleen, a self-reliant young lady who lives with an aunt, an uncle, and cousins who try to make her life as miserable as possible. Michelle Landsberg comments in *Reading for the Love of It: Best Books for Young Readers* that "Jones conveys a doggy nature of wagging optimism that perfectly accords with the boundless energy of an astral lord." Landsberg points out that Sirius's growth not only parallels a child's development into maturity and skill, but also the progress of the meek, Cinderella-like Kathleen toward self assertion and independence. The critic also considers *Dogsbody* one of Jones's more coherent and accessible fantasies, calling it "a sometimes rueful, sometimes lyrical journey toward self-knowledge." Margery Fisher notes in another *Growing Point* review that "this is a confident, intricate interweaving of contemporary family tensions and alliances with flashes of extra-human activity."

A hatter's apprentice finds herself in an enchanted world in this 1986 work inspired by traditional fairy tales.

Wizards and Witches

Not long after *Dogsbody* was published, Jones began her first book series: the "Chrestomanci" cycle, which includes *Charmed Life, The Magicians of Caprona, Witch Week,* and *The Lives of Christopher Chant.* In *Charmed Life,* orphaned Cat Chant and his sister Gwendolyn are transported to a mysterious castle whose owner, Chrestomanci, is in charge of all witches who are government approved and supported. Returning to her theme of how family members can make a person's life miserable, Jones tells how Gwendolyn torments Cat by using his magic (of which he is unaware) for her own evil ends. Julia Briggs in the *Times Literary Supplement* comments that *Charmed Life,* "in spite of touches of Joan Aiken and, in the final chapters, C. S. Lewis, is an outstandingly inventive and entertaining novel, which never for a moment loses its characteristic pace and verve." Like other stories by Jones, points out Margery Meek in the *School Librarian,* the Chrestomanci Cycle takes place "in a universe where magic is normal and the unexpected commonplace." Julia Eccleshare in the *New Statesman* says that it is a "brilliantly funny story" whose setting is straightforward until Gwendolyn's abuse of her powers "reveals all the characters to be part of a formidable hierarchy" led by the Enchanters.

Drawing on her childhood reading, Jones uses European fairy tales and the *Arabian Nights* for inspiration for two of her novels. In *Howl's Moving Castle,* Sophie, the oldest of three daughters, has to be apprenticed to a hatter while her younger sisters go out into the world to seek their fortunes. A wicked witch, a wizard named Howl who is said to eat the hearts of young women and whose castle moves around the countryside, a fire demon, magical clothing, invisible cloaks, seven-league boots, and a spell put on Sophie changing her from a young woman to an old crone all have roots in traditional fairy tales. "Wit and humor glint from the pages as does the author's dexterity in making a prodigious assortment of spells seem a part of everyday life," says Ethel R. Twichell in her *Horn Book* review. Margery Fisher in *Growing Point* says she "was totally captivated by this story," especially "by the special, tender, spontaneous humour which asserts positively the enduring virtues of the human spirit."

Jones turns to the *Arabian Nights* for inspiration in *Castle in the Air,* the sequel to *Howl's Moving Castle.* The castle in the sequel's title is again Howl's, who has been turned into an ill-tempered

Aunt Maria and the other women of Cranbury-on-Sea exert a mysterious power over men and children in Jones's 1991 tale.

genie in a bottle. A young carpet merchant buys a magic carpet that takes him to a perfumed garden where he meets a young princess who has never seen any man other than her father. Just as they are falling in love, a djinn steals her away and takes her to a castle in the air where other brides are waiting. The problem is how to rescue her. With the genie's help, all are finally released and the evil spell is broken. Ruth S. Vose in *School Library Journal* observes, "This is the *Arabian Nights* with a twist. Readers . . . won't put down the book until they figure out all its secrets." Although Ann Flowers in *Horn Book* feels Jones's plot "contains enough material for any number of books," she asserts that ". . . it is cleverly written, with flowing Middle-Eastern expressions and amusing, sardonic remarks." "Jones," *Publishers Weekly* contributor Sybil Steinberg concludes, "has constructed a wonderfully complicated plot, chock-full of magical mayhem."

Throughout her career, Jones has repeatedly returned to storylines mixing the ordinary with the magical. In her more recent book, *Aunt Maria*, the author also adds mystery, suspense, and physical danger, and she once again addresses the theme of children versus adults. In this case, Jones pits two young siblings against their parents, relatives, and other grownups. Mig and Chris are taken by their mother to see their Aunt Maria in Cranbury-on-Sea for the Easter holidays after their father has already disappeared during a similar visit. Once there, their aunt quickly makes the whole family her servants, and it doesn't take long before Mig and Chris realize something's terribly wrong. They notice that all the men of the town are "gray-suited zombies," the town's children live in an orphanage, and Aunt Maria and the women of the town manipulate everyone else. After Aunt Maria turns Chris into a wolf, his mother quickly forgets that Chris was ever with them and it is up to Mig to face her aunt and her horrible powers. According to Michael Cart in the *New York Times Book Review*, Jones works "out some very ancient and complex stuff about the roles of men and women, both in the natural world and in the artificial world of domestic society.... It is personal freedom, not control, that is the natural estate of men and women in Diana Wynne Jones's ideal world."

There is humor in this novel, but as Cart believes, "Here it is more jittery, somewhat uneasy, because the sense of the imminent danger and the potential for real physical harm are everywhere inside *and* out." In *Aunt Maria* there are also magic and time travel, transformation, and mystery. Steinberg writes in *Publishers Weekly*, "Wry observation about the oddities of family life, along with plenty of spine-tingling spookiness, will keep readers glued to" this story. And *School Library Journal* critic Luann Toth notes, "The intricate, multifaceted plot and rich cast of characters are deftly handled by this master storyteller."

"Jones," Cart concludes, "has joined a handful of her British contemporaries—Alan Garner and Leon Garfield come to mind—who never disappoint." After numerous books Jones is still trying not to disappoint herself or her readers. As she says in *SAAS*, "I get unhappy if I don't write. Each book is an experiment, an attempt to write the ideal book, the book my children would like, the book I *didn't* have as a child myself."

■ Works Cited

Alderdice, Kit, "Diana Wynne Jones," *Publishers Weekly*. February 22, 1991, pp. 201-202.

Briggs, Julia, review of *Charmed Life*, *Times Literary Supplement*, March 25, 1977, p. 348.

Cart, Michael, review of *Aunt Maria*, *New York Times Book Review*, April 19, 1992, p. 16.

Coyle, Cathy S., review of *Witch's Business*, *School Library Journal*, April, 1974, p. 58.

Davis, Christopher, review of *Witch's Business*, *New York Times Book Review*, May 5, 1974, pp. 22, 24, 26.

Eccleshare, Julia, review of *Charmed Life*, *New Statesman*, May 20, 1977, p. 686.

Farmer, Penelope, "Self-Examination," *Times Literary Supplement*, April 2, 1976, p. 383.

Fisher, Margery, review of *Dogsbody*, *Growing Point*, December, 1975, pp. 2771-72.

Fisher, Margery, review of *Howl's Moving Castle*, *Growing Point*, March, 1987, pp. 4772-73.

Fisher, Margery, review of *The Ogre Downstairs*, *Growing Point*, May, 1974, p. 2399.

Flowers, Ann A., review of *Castle in the Air*, *Horn Book*, March/April, 1991, p. 206.

Fuller, John, review of *The Ogre Downstairs*, *New Statesman*, May 24, 1974, pp. 738-39.

Jones, Diana Wynne, autobiographical entry in *Something about the Author Autobiography Series*, Volume 7, Gale, 1989, p. 169.

Landsberg, Michelle, "Fantasy," *Reading for the Love of It: Best Books for Young Readers*, Prentice-Hall, 1987, pp. 175-76.

Meek, Marjorie, review of *Charmed Life*, *School Librarian*, December, 1977, pp. 363-64.

Moss, Elaine, "Ghostly Forms," *Times Literary Supplement*, November 20, 1981, p. 1354.

Steinberg, Sybil, review of *Aunt Maria*, *Publishers Weekly*, August 16, 1991, p. 59.

Steinberg, Sybil, review of *Castle in the Air*, *Publishers Weekly*, February 22, 1991, p. 220.

Sutherland, Zena, review of *The Ogre Downstairs*, *Bulletin of the Center for Children's Books*, July-August, 1975, p. 179.

Toth, Luann, review of *Aunt Maria*, *School Library Journal*, October, 1991, p. 143.

Twichell, Ethel R., review of *Howl's Moving Castle*, *Horn Book*, May/June, 1986, pp. 331-32.

Vose, Ruth S., review of *Castle in the Air*, *School Library Journal*, April, 1991, p. 141.

■ For More Information See

BOOKS

Children's Literature Review, Volume 23, Gale, 1991.

Contemporary Literary Criticism. Volume 26, Gale, 1983.

PERIODICALS

Books for Keeps. January, 1985, p. 45; May, 1985, p. 19.

Booklist, March 15, 1991, p. 1503; June 15, 1991, p. 1964; October 1, 1991, p. 316; January 15, 1992, pp. 873, 932; March 15, 1992, pp. 1364, 1372; June 1, 1992, p. 1768; November 1, 1992, p. 492.

Book Report, September, 1990, pp. 54, 74; November, 1990, pp. 45, 65; January, 1991, p. 66; March, 1992, p. 39.

Bulletin of the Center for Children's Books, February, 1991, p. 143; October, 1991, p. 41.

Chicago Tribune Book World, November 4, 1982.

Children's Book Review, summer, 1974, p. 65; summer, 1975, p. 61.

Fantasy Review, January, 1985, p. 45; May, 1985, p. 19.

Globe and Mail (Toronto), July 12, 1986.

Growing Point, April, 1975, pp. 2597-2601; October, 1975, pp. 2708-09; September, 1976, p. 2936; March, 1978, p. 3279; May, 1981, pp. 3880-83; January, 1982, p. 3992; November, 1982, p. 3984; January, 1989, p. 5092; September, 1990, p. 5395; November, 1990, p. 5439; September, 1991, p. 5584.

Horn Book, June, 1977, pp. 319-20; February, 1978, pp. 47-48; December, 1979, p. 669; August, 1980, pp. 407-08; October, 1981, p. 542; July/August, 1985, pp. 453-54; January/February, 1988, p. 71; March/April, 1988, pp. 208-09; November/December, 1988, p. 789; July/August, 1990, p. 480.

Junior Bookshelf, August, 1973, pp. 270-71; October, 1977, pp. 303-04; February, 1979, p. 33; August, 1979, pp. 221-22; August, 1980, pp. 192-93; October, 1981, pp. 212-13; February, 1982, pp. 33-34; December, 1982, pp. 231-32; October, 1989, p. 227; October, 1990, p. 245; October, 1991, p. 225.

Journal of Reading, October, 1991, p. 167; November, 1991, p. 261.

Kirkus Reviews, August 1, 1977, p. 790; February 15, 1978, p. 117; September 1, 1980, p. 1163; September 15, 1991, p. 1223; February 15, 1991, p. 249; August 15, 1992, pp. 1024, 1062.

Los Angeles Times, January 31, 1987.

Magazine of Fantasy and Science Fiction, February, 1992, p. 37; April, 1992, p. 24.

Publishers Weekly, September 11, 1987, p. 99; May 13, 1988, p. 278; July 29, 1988, p. 234; December 20, 1991, p. 83; August 17, 1992, p. 500; August 31, 1992, p. 68.

School Librarian, March, 1976, p. 36; June, 1978, p. 161; December, 1982, p. 359; May, 1988, p. 64; August, 1989, p. 104; November, 1990, pp. 140, 148; November, 1991, p. 152.

School Library Journal, April, 1978, pp. 85, 94; September, 1981, p. 137; March, 1984, p. 160; October, 1984, pp. 167-68; April, 1985, pp. 97-98; August, 1986, p. 101; September, 1987, p. 196; May, 1988, p. 98; September, 1988, p. 184; August, 1990, p. 148; October, 1992, p. 89; March, 1993, p. 234.

Spectator, June 30, 1979.

Times (London), May 1, 1986.

Times Educational Supplement, November 18, 1977, p. 40; December 1, 1978, p. 24; November 30, 1979, p. 25; April 18, 1980, p. 25; November 23, 1984; November 9, 1990, p. 11; November 8, 1991, p. 38.

Times Literary Supplement, March 12, 1970; April 6, 1973, p. 387; July 5, 1974; April 1, 1975, p. 365; July 11, 1975, p. 764; April 7, 1978, p. 377; March 28, 1980; September 19, 1980, p. 1026; March 25, 1981; March 27, 1981, p. 339; July 23, 1982, p. 794; October 19, 1984; November 29, 1985, p. 1358; January 31, 1986; December 12, 1986, p. 1410; November 20, 1987, p. 1283; July 12, 1991, p. 20.

Voice of Youth Advocates, June, 1984, p. 101; June, 1985, p. 139; October, 1990, p. 229; December, 1990, pp. 297, 328; April, 1991, p. 10; April, 1992, p. 44.

Washington Post Book World, May 13, 1984, p. 18; May 11, 1986; June 14, 1987; November 8, 1987; May 12, 1991, p. 14.

Wilson Library Journal, January, 1991, p. 12; March, 1992; April, 1992.

—*Sketch by Hazel K. Davis*

Ron Koertge

■ Personal

Surname is pronounced *Kur*-chee; born Ronald Koertge, April 22, 1940, in Olney, IL; son of William Henry and Bulis Olive Koertge; married, wife's name Bianca Richards. *Education:* University of Illinois, B.A., 1962; University of Arizona, M.A., 1965.

■ Addresses

Office—Department of English, Pasadena City College, 1560 Colorado Blvd., Pasadena, CA 91106. *Agent*—William Reiss, John Hawkins and Associates, 71 West 23rd St., #1600, New York, NY 10010.

■ Career

Writer, 1962—. Pasadena City College, Pasadena, CA, professor of English, 1965—. Visiting author, Topeka (Kansas) West High School's Author Days.

■ Awards, Honors

Young Adult Author of the Year, Detroit Library System, 1990; fellowship in literature (poetry), National Endowment for the Arts, 1990; Young People's Literature Award, Friends of American Writers, c. 1990, for *The Boy in the Moon;* New York Public Library choice for Books for the Teen Age, 1992, and Maine Student Book Award Master List citation, for *Mariposa Blues;* Books for the Teen Age citation, New York Public Library, 1993, and American Library Association (ALA) notable book, for *The Harmony Arms; Where the Kissing Never Stops, The Arizona Kid, The Boy in the Moon,* and *The Harmony Arms* were all named ALA Best Books for Young Adults; "Books of the Decade" citation, *Booklist,* for *The Arizona Kid;*

■ Writings

FOR YOUNG ADULTS

Where the Kissing Never Stops, Atlantic Monthly, 1986.
The Arizona Kid, Joy Street, 1988.
The Boy in the Moon, Little, Brown, 1990.
Mariposa Blues, Little, Brown, 1991.
The Harmony Arms, Little, Brown, 1992.

POETRY FOR ADULTS

The Father-Poems, Sumac Press, 1973.
Meat: Cherry's Market-Diary, MAG Press, 1973.
The Hired Nose, MAG Press, 1974.
My Summer Vacation, Venice Poetry, 1975.
Sex Object, Country Press, 1975, revised edition, Little Caesar, 1979.
(With Charles Stetler and Gerald Locklin) *Tarzan and Shane Meet the Toad,* Haas, 1975.
Cheap Thrills, Wormwood Review, 1976.
Men under Fire, Duck Down, 1976.

12 Photographs of Yellowstone, Red Hill, 1976.

How to Live on Five Dollars a Week, Etc., Venice Poetry, 1977.

The Jockey Poems, Maelstrom, 1980.

Diary Cows, Little Caesar, 1981.

Fresh Meat, Kenmore, 1981.

Life on the Edge of the Continent: Selected Poems of Ronald Koertge, University of Arkansas Press, 1982.

(Contributor) Steve Kowit, editor, *The Maverick Poets: An Anthology,* Gorilla Press, 1988.

High School Dirty Poems, Red Wind, 1991.

OTHER

The Boogeyman (novel for adults), Norton, 1980.

100 Things to Write About (college textbook), Holt, 1990.

■ Work in Progress

Tiger, Tiger, Burning Bright, a young adult novel to be published by Orchard Books.

■ Sidelights

It is dawn at the local racetrack. While the rest of the world is still asleep, the track's backstretch bustles with activity: grooms walk proud, high-strung horses; trainers examine hooves and legs that are soaking in ice buckets; energetic helpers shovel dirty straw out of stalls. Occasionally a horse whinnies, paws the ground, or kicks with surprising force. This is a place where horses and humans work hard together. The stakes are high and the tasks are dangerous, but the rewards can be lasting as bonds of friendship form. Author Ron Koertge has drawn inspiration from this rich milieu for some of his best-known novels.

Koertge has not forgotten what it feels like to be young. The heroes of his stories for young adults suffer anxieties over acne pimples or being too short. They ponder their futures and quarrel with eccentric or domineering parents. Most of all, they learn how to manage their sexual longings and their romantic impulses as they become seriously involved with girls they care about. As Jane Hoogestraat puts it in the *Dictionary of Literary Biography,* Koertge has made a name for himself with books that are "remarkable for the realism with which they present tough and not-so-tough teenage characters coming of age in a world of AIDS and widespread divorce, but often in a world in which tenderness and love are not absent."

The racetrack is just one of several settings Koertge uses to propel his stories about dawning

independence. For Koertge's characters, love, friendship, and honest labor help to quell insecurities and build happiness. A *Horn Book* reviewer noted that the author of *The Arizona Kid, Where the Kissing Never Stops,* and other works has a rare gift "for taking adolescent worries seriously while presenting them with large doses of humor."

A Midwestern Childhood

Ron Koertge was born April 22, 1940, in Olney, Illinois. Both of his parents had grown up on working farms, and when he was born they were employed at a large dairy farm. World War II caught up with the family, and Koertge's father went into the army for two years. An only child, Koertge lived with his mother and received extra attention from two childless aunts. He told *AAYA* that so much loving care "gave me a sense that I was special. That feeling got knocked flat as early as first grade, but it was already a part of some microcircuitry that could never be completely dismantled."

While Koertge was still a youngster, his parents moved to Collinsville, Illinois, and opened an ice cream business. It flourished until the town's first supermarket opened, and then—like so many other specialty stores—it could not keep abreast of the new competition. Koertge's father became a janitor in the public school system while his mother stayed at home. They were comfortable financially and, as the author told *AAYA,* "fairly happy."

"As a poet and a fiction writer I have worked and reworked my childhood to such an extent that a reality shortage set in long ago," Koertge related. "I would much rather have an interesting childhood than a so-called true one, anyway." Echoes of the author's youth in the Midwest find their way into all of his stories: his heroes either hail from the region or live there. They are self-conscious about their origins when they relocate, but they are usually quietly comfortable with—and stand up for—their grass-roots lifestyles. In *Where the Kissing Never Stops,* for instance, seventeen-year-old Walker begins to farm a piece of land he has inherited and ultimately decides not to sell the parcel to a developer who wants to build a shopping mall.

Koertge said that he was "a pretty normal kid" who enjoyed sports and school. As a teenager he discovered a special talent—he had a "way with words," so to speak. He could express himself well, and beyond that, he found himself open to the vast

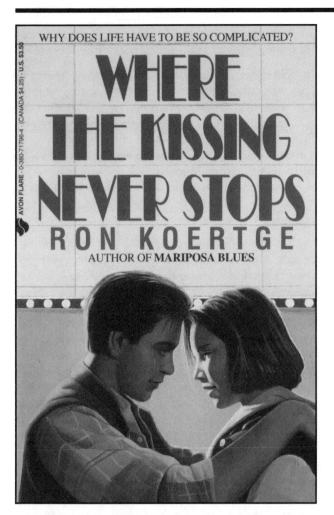

WHY DOES LIFE HAVE TO BE SO COMPLICATED?

WHERE THE KISSING NEVER STOPS

RON KOERTGE

AUTHOR OF **MARIPOSA BLUES**

In Koertge's first young adult work, published in 1986, troubled Walker falls in love with both sophisticated Rachel and a plot of land inherited from his father.

possibilities words offered as a means to communicate feelings. "I ... discovered I was more glib than most of my friends," he told *AAYA*, "but I also somehow sensed that my gift wouldn't be really valuable until I was older. Very early on, words seemed to have lives of their own.... Still today, the way the words fit together and the way they lie on the music they generate is more interesting to me than the so-called arc of the story." In this way, Koertge was laying the groundwork for a career as a poet and novelist.

He also loved attention and had a flair for drama. Though not the "class clown," he enjoyed saying and doing outrageous things. "I would say out loud things that other kids seemed reluctant to say," he recalled. "... I liked to shock people—to leave them lurching, not laughing." His sense of life's quirks was heightened by a serious bout of rheumatic fever when he was a young teen. The illness, which had the potential to debilitate him with a weakened heart for the rest of his life, or even kill him, left Koertge with a "sense of the insubstantiality of my body and made me alternately tentative and foolishly bold," he told *AAYA*.

A Writer Comes of Age

Koertge began writing in high school. "It was certainly something I was drawn to partly because it was something I could do," he remembered. His interest in the field led him to the University of Illinois, where he earned his bachelor's degree in 1962, and then on to the University of Arizona, where he received a master's degree in 1965. He began writing poetry during graduate school and soon became confident enough to seek publication for his work. "I didn't so much plan to be a writer," he said. "Mostly I wrote a lot. Then people started to call me a writer."

Teaching and writing often go hand-in-hand. In Koertge's case, he took a position as a professor of English at Pasadena City College in 1965 and has remained on the faculty there ever since. He began publishing poems in magazines as early as 1970 and a few years after that released the first of many chapbooks of verse. In 1980 he completed his only novel for adults, *The Boogeyman.* But as Koertge told *AAYA*, he is more deeply committed to the music of words and language than he is to any particular theme or story. "There are painters who love the paint more than the painting," he said. "I understand that completely. When books are valued for their message or moral, then they aren't valued for their art or even their craft. Any pinhead can be popular or politically correct, but not everybody can write a graceful sentence."

By 1984 Koertge had reached a crossroads in his career. He was still producing poetry, but his writings for adults seemed dull and derivative to him. A friend suggested he try writing a young adult novel. In an essay for the *Los Angeles Times Book Review*, the author recalled his first experience with writing for teens: "I trudged to the nearest library and checked out two or three [novels]. Had they been clothes, all could have hung in the closet of any Assistant Manager for Sears—they were drip-dry, wrinkle-free, sky blue. Worse, they struck me as bogus resumes of what it was like to be sixteen." Koertge thought he could produce better books than that. He remembered what it was like to be sixteen, and he could empathize with the particular problems teens face today. In 1985 he wrote and published his first work for teens, *Where the Kissing Never Stops.*

Where the Kissing Never Stops offers a glimpse into the life of a seventeen-year-old Midwesterner named Walker. Walker is plagued with problems. His cravings for junk food run unchecked, his girlfriend has left town, and, worst of all, his mother has taken a job as a stripper in a nearby burlesque parlor. At his lowest ebb he meets Rachel, a mall-loving, cosmopolitan girl who has just arrived in town. Different as they are, Walker and Rachel begin a romance and ultimately learn to trust one another. *School Library Journal* contributor Marjorie Lewis wrote, "Walker's attempts to keep his mother's occupation a secret and make his romance with Rachel a rich, fulfilling one is believable and engrossing." *Where the Kissing Never Stops* was awarded a "best book for young

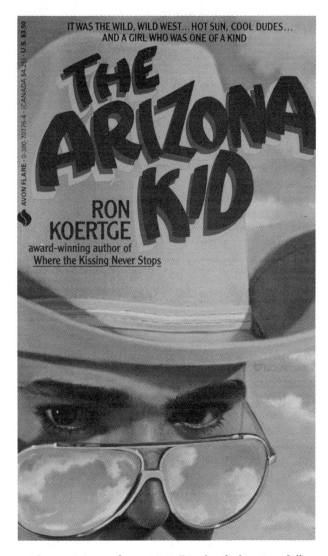

IT WAS THE WILD, WILD WEST... HOT SUN, COOL DUDES... AND A GIRL WHO WAS ONE OF A KIND

THE ARIZONA KID

RON KOERTGE

award-winning author of Where the Kissing Never Stops

The recipient of an ALA "Book of the Decade" citation, Koertge's 1988 story of horses and romance is set at a Tucson racetrack where a teenage boy works for the summer.

adults" citation by the American Library Association.

In *Where the Kissing Never Stops,* Walker learns to love not only Rachel, but also the tract of land he has inherited from his father. In Koertge's next young adult novel, *The Arizona Kid,* Billy Kennedy finds romance and a possible future career at a Tucson racetrack where he works for the summer. Billy travels from Missouri to Tucson, where he lives with his gay uncle and works with a horse trainer. He falls in love with volatile Cara Mae, a girl who exercises the spirited thoroughbreds.

Both books offer humorous and touching coming-of-age stories. Both also ignited controversy for their frank and realistic depiction of sexual encounters and alternative lifestyles. "It might have been naive of me to think that straight talk about sex would be universally welcomed in the secret garden of children's books or that a gay character in a YA would be treated like any other character," Koertge admitted in the *Los Angeles Times Book Review.* "But I was simply looking for something interesting to write.... I remind everyone that novels aren't the same as pamphlets for Hygiene II or leftover tracts from a personal growth weekend in the mountains. They're at least objects of craftsmanship and at best works of art." Critics notwithstanding, the American Library Association awarded *The Arizona Kid* a "best books for young adults" citation, and *Booklist* magazine named the work among its YA "books of the decade."

Koertge has continued his frank exploration of teenage sexuality in his other novels. In *The Boy in the Moon,* a shy young man finds the courage to begin a romance with his best friend. In *Mariposa Blues,* thirteen-year-old Graham confronts new and not necessarily welcome attractions to his friend Leslie. In *The Harmony Arms,* Gabriel McKay discovers not only love but also a host of adults with eccentric personalities. *Booklist* reviewer Stephanie Zvirin suggests that Koertge's work is popular for its wealth of feelings—and its hearty optimism. "Offbeat though they are, Koertge's characters are both real and compassionate," declared Zvirin. "They respect and care for one another.... And Koertge's right on the mark when it comes to that first passionate kiss."

Koertge told the *Los Angeles Times Book Review* that he thoroughly enjoys writing for young adults. The months he spends creating a novel are pleasant ones, a chance to recall happy times, a chance to craft witty phrases, and a chance to breathe life into fascinating characters both young and old. The

Gabriel McKay finds love amid a host of unusual characters in this 1992 novel, which was named an ALA notable book.

books even offer him an opportunity to write about horse racing, a hobby he has enjoyed for years. His advice to would-be writers is simple: "maybe read less and *do* more, so they have something to write about," he told *AAYA*. Koertge added: "I'd also suggest one other thing: Learn some simple technique of meditation (nearly any book on the subject would do) and cultivate the role of Witness. Most of us make up the stories of our lives and then get caught up on the melodrama. Learning to step outside ourselves and observe the tumult is an invaluable skill, especially for a writer."

■ Works Cited

Hoogestraat, Jane, "Ronald Koertge," *Dictionary of Literary Biography*, Volume 105: *American Poets since World War II*, Gale, 1992, pp. 137-142.

Horn Book Magazine, July-August 1990, p. 462.

Koertge, Ron, "Sex and the Single Kid," *Los Angeles Times Book Review*, March 21, 1993.

Lewis, Marjorie, review of *Where the Kissing Never Stops, School Library Journal*, December, 1986, p. 119.

Zvirin, Stephanie, "The Harmony Arms," *Booklist*, October 15, 1992, p. 418.

■ For More Information See

PERIODICALS

Horn Book, July-August, 1991; November-December, 1992.

New York Times Book Review, August 21, 1988, p. 25.

Publishers Weekly, May 10, 1991; September 14, 1992.

School Library Journal, May, 1990; May, 1991; August, 1992.

Wilson Library Bulletin, April, 1989.

—Sketch by Anne Janette Johnson

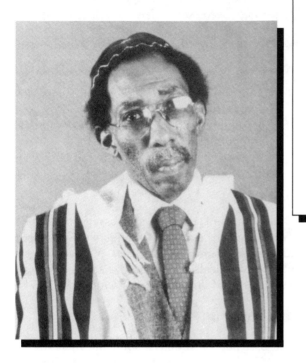

Julius Lester

herst, professor of African American Studies, 1971-88, professor of Judaic Studies, 1979—, acting director and associate director of Institute for Advanced Studies in Humanities, 1982-84. Lecturer, New School for Social Research, New York City, 1968-70; writer in residence, Vanderbilt University, 1985.

■ Personal

Born January 27, 1939, in St. Louis, MO; son of W. D. (a minister) and Julia (Smith) Lester; married Joan Stenau, 1962 (divorced, 1970); married Alida Carolyn Fechner, 1979 (divorced, 1993); children: (first marriage) Jody Simone, Malcolm Coltrane; (second marriage) Elena Milad (stepdaughter), David Julius. *Education:* Fisk University, B.A., 1960. *Religion:* Jewish. *Hobbies and other interests:* Stamp collecting, computers, astrology.

■ Addresses

c/o P.O. Box 9634, North Amherst, MA 01059-9634. *Office*—University of Massachusetts, Amherst, MA 01003.

■ Career

During the 1960s, worked as a professional musician and singer recording for Vanguard Records; Newport Folk Festival, Newport, RI, director, 1966-68; WBAI-FM, New York City, producer and host of live radio show, 1968-75; *Free Time* (live television program), WNET-TV, New York City, host, 1971-73; University of Massachusetts—Am-

■ Awards, Honors

Newbery Award nomination, American Library Association (ALA) Notable Children's Book, *School Library Journal* Best Book of the Year, *Horn Book* Fanfare Honor List, *New York Times* Outstanding Book of the Year, and Lewis Carroll Shelf Award, all 1969, for *To Be a Slave;* Lewis Carroll Shelf Award, 1972, and National Book Award finalist, 1973, both for *Long Journey Home: Stories from Black History;* Lewis Carroll Shelf Award, 1973, for *The Knee-High Man and Other Tales;* Honorable Mention, Coretta Scott King Award, 1983, for *This Strange New Feeling,* and 1988, for *The Tales of Uncle Remus: The Adventures of Brer Rabbit;* Jewish Book Award finalist for *Lovesong: Becoming a Jew,* 1989; ALA Notable Children's Book for *How Many Spots Does a Leopard Have?: And Other Tales.*

Distinguished Teacher's Award, 1983-84; Faculty Fellowship Award, 1985, for distinguished research and scholarship; National Professor of the Year Silver Medal Award, Council for Advancement and Support of Education, 1985; Massachusetts State Professor of the Year and Gold Medal Award for National Professor of the Year, Council for Advancement and Support of Education, 1986; Distinguished Faculty Lecturer, 1986-87.

■ Writings

FICTION

Long Journey Home: Stories from Black History (young adult), Dial, 1972.

Two Love Stories (novellas; young adult), Dial, 1972.

This Strange New Feeling (short stories; young adult), Dial, 1982, published as *A Taste of Freedom: Three Stories from Black History*, Longman, 1983.

Do Lord Remember Me, Holt, 1984.

FOLKLORE FOR YOUNG ADULTS

(Editor with Mary Varela) *Our Folk Tales: High John, The Conqueror, and Other Afro-American Tales*, illustrated by Jennifer Lawson, privately printed, 1967.

Black Folktales, illustrated by Tom Feelings, Baron, 1969, published with new introduction by Lester, Grove, 1991.

The Knee-High Man and Other Tales, illustrated by Ralph Pinto, Dial, 1972.

The Tales of Uncle Remus: The Adventures of Brer Rabbit, illustrated by Jerry Pinkney, Dial, 1987.

More Tales of Uncle Remus: Further Adventures of Brer Rabbit, His Friends, Enemies, and Others, illustrated by Pinkney, Dial, 1988.

How Many Spots Does a Leopard Have?: And Other Tales, illustrated by David Shannon, Scholastic, 1989.

Further Tales of Uncle Remus: The Misadventures of Brer Rabbit, Brer Fox, Brer Wolf, the Doodang, and Other Creatures, illustrated by Pinkney, Dial, 1990.

NONFICTION

(With Pete Seeger) *The 12-String Guitar as Played by Leadbelly: An Instructional Manual*, Oak, 1965.

(Editor with Varela) Fanny Lou Hamer, *To Praise Our Bridges: An Autobiography*, KIPCO, 1967.

Look Out, Whitey! Black Power's Gon' Get Your Mama! Dial, 1968.

(Author of commentary and editor) *To Be a Slave* (collection of slave narratives; young adult), illustrated by Feelings, Dial, 1968.

Search for the New Land: History as Subjective Experience, Dial, 1969.

Revolutionary Notes, Baron, 1969.

(Editor with Rae Pace Alexander) *Young and Black in America* (young adult), Random, 1971.

(Editor and author of introduction) *The Seventh Son: The Thought and Writings of W. E. B. DuBois*, two volumes, Random, 1971.

All Is Well (autobiography), Morrow, 1976.

Lovesong: Becoming a Jew (autobiography), Holt, 1988.

Falling Pieces of the Broken Sky, Arcade, 1990.

POETRY

The Mud of Vietnam: Photographs and Poems, Folklore Press, 1967.

(Editor) Stanley Couch, *Ain't No Ambulances for No Nigguhs Tonight*, Baron, 1969.

Who I Am (young adult), photographs by David Gahr, Dial, 1974.

OTHER

Contributor of reviews and essays to *New York Times Book Review*, *National Review*, *New Republic*, *Reform Judaism*, *Commonweal*, *Village Voice*, and other periodicals. Contributing editor to *Sing Out*, 1964-70, and *Broadside of New York*, 1964-70.

■ Work in Progress

The Last Tales of Uncle Remus, the final volume of the "Uncle Remus" series; two picture books, *The Man Who Knew Too Much* and *John Henry*.

■ Sidelights

In 1968—the same year riots exploded after the assassination of Martin Luther King, Jr.—Julius Lester interviewed a black history teacher from a predominantly black school in Brooklyn. To make listeners aware of some blacks' anti-Semitic rage in the midst of a bitter teachers' strike, Lester convinced the teacher to read the following poem by a fourteen-year-old black student. Barry List's interview with Lester in *Publishers Weekly* quotes the youth's "inflammatory words": "'Hey, Jewboy, with that yarmulke on your head / You pale-faced Jew boy—I wish you were dead.'" Although Lester thought his audience should hear this student's hostility aroused by the striking, predominantly Jewish teachers, some accused Lester of anti-Semitism, a charge he angrily denies. This radio program brought Lester notoriety and marked his emergence as a controversial figure.

Ever since his 1960s political activism, Lester, himself a converted Jew, has continued to talk and write about black-Jewish relations in America, past and present. He has taught the course "Blacks and Jews: A Comparative Study of Oppression" at the University of Massachusetts since 1980, and he has spoken at many synagogues and college and university campuses. In his 1989 essay, "The Simple Truth About Blacks and Jews" in *Reform Judaism,* he acknowledges that American Jews have been subjected to anti-Semitism, but he refuses to equate this experience to American blacks' legacy of two hundred years of slavery. Some American Jews borrow their "victim" identity from identifying with the Holocaust, he says. American blacks, however, have been victims themselves with. a history of physical, economic, and social oppression. Lester asserts, "The simple truth is that Jews are among the 'haves' of American society; blacks comprise a significant portion of the 'have-nots.'" Accepting this stark reality about Jews and blacks will permit the creation of "new possibilities for black-Jewish relations," Lester concludes, for it would allow American Jews to understand that "beneath the angry words is a deep and excruciating agony which comes when it is felt that no one cares, the loneliness experienced when no one seems to be listening."

Becoming a Jew

Lester's conversion to Judaism in 1982 gives him the insight to comment on the relationship between Jews and blacks in his writing; his young adult and adult books focus primarily on the black experience in America. His writing has also been influenced by his many different careers: civil rights activist, radio and television personality, folksinger, and university professor. Lester encourages teenagers to be proud of where they came from and to know who they are, communicating his ideas in many different forms of storytelling, including autobiography, poetry, nonfiction, fiction, and folklore.

A professor of Judaic studies—and former professor of African-American studies—at the University of Massachusetts, Lester has written about the many influences in his life, particularly his conversion to Judaism. According to List, the author wrote his autobiographical *Lovesong: Becoming a Jew* to "tell the story of how someone born the son of a minister could become a Jew." Born on January 27, 1939, in St. Louis, Lester lived in various states, including Arkansas, Kansas, and Tennessee, where his father led Methodist congregations. Lester describes in *Lovesong* how as a nine-year-old, curious about his maternal grandmother's maiden name, Altschul, he found out that his great-grandfather was a German Jew named Adolph Altschul, who had emigrated to the South in the late 1800s and married a former slave,

Maggie Carson. One of the man's descendants owned a store in Pine Bluff, Arkansas, but his father warned him, "'They're your blood relatives. But don't you go marching in the store and call them cousin. They'd pretend like they don't know what you were talking about.'" After Lester converted to Judaism, he tried to contact Altschul's descendants in Pine Bluff, only to discovered that all of them had converted to Christianity.

The above anecdote is one of many in *Lovesong,* which *New York Times Book Review* contributor Joel Oppenheimer calls "a moving memoir." He believes Lester's skill in "mixing past and present, the self and the real world" offers insights into the public figure and family man, as well as various relationships with blacks and whites, Christians and Jews. Douglas Stone comments in the *Christian Century* that this is an "unusual spiritual journey" providing "insight into what it means to be both black and Jewish in America." *Lovesong* is Lester's spiritual odyssey, moving from nominal Protestantism through an investigation of Catholicism and American Indian faiths to conversion to Judaism. This "introspective memoir of a black man confronting his identity in a white environment" is "beautifully written," states Stone. Lester's other autobiographical work, *All Is Well,* also portrays his private and public life. Kathryn Robinson in *School Library Journal* recommends *All Is Well* to mature young adults who "will find much to ponder" from Lester's journal, books, articles, and radio shows.

Lester the poet explores identity in America in *Who I Am.* The title comes from an African-American spiritual ("'If anybody ask you who I am / Tell 'em I'm a child of God,'"). Through Lester's verses and David Gahr's photographs, the book celebrates simple scenes in New York City like "smiles of joy and contentment," whereas "tourists see only litter, weariness, and winos," as one *Horn Book* reviewer notes. These photopoems "surge with new vitality, and the sensitivity of both photographer and poet comes through strongly," Deborah H. Williams writes in *Library Journal.* She observes that the poems and pictures enhance each other, making "a unified, strong statement." *Interracial Books for Children Bulletin* critic Barbara Walker praises the book's "beauty, pain, humor, tenderness ... [urging] the reader to share in the powerful emotional panorama of life as it is lived by people of different racial backgrounds, ages and sexes."

To Be a Slave

Lester has portrayed America's racial diversity from the beginning of his career as a young adult writer in the late 1960s, writing about African Americans' heritage and experiences as slaves. He has received much acclaim for the young adult nonfiction work *To Be a Slave,* which was named a 1969 Newbery Honor Book. This collection of slave narratives interspersed with commentary is "one of the most powerful documents to appear in children's literature" and "a moving chronicle," according to a *Library Journal* review quoted in *Publishers Weekly.* Lester dedicates the book to the memory of his great-grandparents and countless unknown slaves. "I never knew them," writes Lester, "but I am proud to be one of their

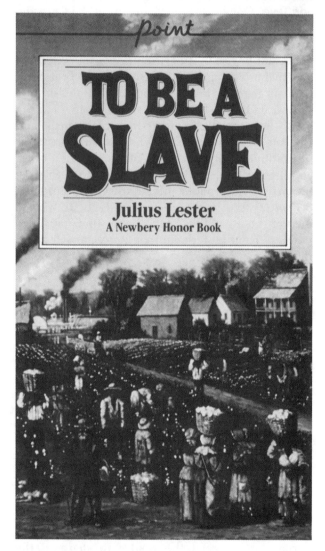

Weaving together nineteenth-century slave narratives with his own commentary, Lester created this 1968 nonfiction work, which garnered a Newbery Award nomination.

descendants. I hope that I may be worthy of them, their strength, and their courage."

The book is a mixture of nineteenth-century ex-slave narratives recorded by abolitionist groups and 1930s narratives collected by the Federal Writers' Project, all interspersed with commentaries by Lester. A *New York Times Book Review* contributor notes that the "many voices and specific incidents make the experience of slavery vivid." The title for the book comes from the following passage: "To be a slave. To be owned by another person, as a car, house, or table is owned. To live as a piece of property that could be sold—a child sold from its mother, a wife from her husband. To be considered not human, but a 'thing' that plowed the fields, cut the wood, cooked the food, nursed another's child; a 'thing' whose sole function was determined by the one who owned you." In another excerpt, an ex-slave vividly describes what caused the whip's crack and the slaves' shrieking when they were stripped and made to lie upon the ground, face downwards, to receive punishment for their offenses: "Twenty-five [lashes] are deemed a mere brush, inflicted, for instance, when a dry leaf or a piece of boll is found in the cotton, or when a branch is broken in the field. Fifty is ordinary penalty.... One hundred is called severe; it is the punishment inflicted for the serious offense of standing idle in the field."

Writing in the *New York Times Book Review,* John Howard Griffin observes that these "tremendously moving documents" explain both the intense suffering of blacks from slavery's far-reaching cruelties and the depth of their current resentments. Griffin states that blacks "find parallels in their own present life or near past, and realize that the same fundamental myths have kept them enslaved without the actual trappings of slavery." In her review for the *Bulletin of the Center for Children's Books,* Zena Sutherland calls *To Be a Slave* "a moving and explicit" documentation of slavery from "capture to auction, from servitude to freedom." Evelyn Geller, writing in *School Library Journal,* believes that *To Be a Slave* "quietly lays bare the shame of American history while making slavery, suffering, and resistance part of [a] black child's heritage. Its manner of revealing dignity in humiliation, expressing the haunting ever-present sense of the slave experience in the racial memory, is reminiscent of the Jews' ritual celebration of their history of persecution."

Lester's several collections of adult nonfiction contain a wide range of subjects that relate to the above topics of the black experience in America.

He raised black and white consciousnesses during the turbulent sixties with several nonfiction works, including *Look Out, Whitey! Black Power's Gon' Get Your Mama!*; *Search for the New Land: History as Subjective Experience*; and *Revolutionary Notes*. His more recent essay anthology, *Falling Pieces of the Broken Sky*, reflects his concerns for young people as well as his black and Jewish heritage. A *Publishers Weekly* review praises Lester's "forthrightness and independence" in handling topics such as teenage suicide, video games, safe sex, the Jewish holiday Rosh Hashanah, and writing to reach out to people. According to the critic, Lester's "aversion to anti-Semitism" becomes apparent in his assessments of James Baldwin, Louis Farrakhan, and Jesse Jackson; his "sensitivity" is clear in essays on Aldous Huxley and Thomas Merton. The article cites Lester's reason for disassociating himself from the 1960s black power movement: he saw that the "'black collective cared only for itself,'" and it might have destroyed "that singular and unique identity" he knew as himself.

In the 1970s and 1980s, Lester published young adult works reflecting his interests in black history. His historical tales come from documented source material. *Long Journey Home: Stories from Black History*, named by the *New York Times Book Review* as one of the year's outstanding books for ages twelve to sixteen, contains six stories about common people. According to Lester's introductory note, these footnotes of black history tell about those "whose individual deeds are seldom recorded and who are never known outside their own small circles of friends and acquaintances." Rosalind K. Goddard says in the *New York Times Book Review* that Lester captures "the essence of a human experience" by "powerfully recalling the era of slavery and its effects on black men and women." She cites the following example of these stories' exciting human drama: "You feel the suspense as a 17-year-old slave runs away and travels the Underground Railroad; you sicken at the holocaust as slaves in the shiphold die in their own waste; you empathize with the enraged woman who mixes sputum and ground glass into her master's food; and finally you learn the roots of the Blues and how they kept a man spiritually free." Besides offering a stimulating, informative experience, these authentic tales allow young blacks to find their roots and realize their identities, concludes Goddard. Also, a *Publishers Weekly* reviewer recommends *Long Journey Home* for its "emotional, chilling, colorful, painful, unsentimental, totally compelling stories of slaves and ex-slaves."

The stories in this 1982 collection, derived from historical documents, earned praise for their realistic portrayal of slave life.

The contributor adds, "Even if you have heard or sensed that interest in 'black books' is on the wane, don't overlook this one. It is exceptionally good reading."

Lester's story collection, *This Strange New Feeling*, provides three more factual stories documented from black history. A *Horn Book* reviewer considers the story "Where the Sun Lives" "moving, sensitive, and elegantly fashioned" for its portrayal of the spirited Maria who comes close to liberation until her husband, a free black, is accidentally killed and she is sold to pay off his debts. Hazel Rochman in *School Library Journal* notes that when Maria faces being stripped and fondled at the slave auction, she resolutely promises to herself, "'I won't cry.... Won't many of them want to buy me, and whichever one does will wish he hadn't.'" The

Lester uses fresh, contemporary language to breathe new life into classic folktales in this 1969 collection.

stories reflect women's reluctance to bear children into slavery and the constant threat of being separated from loved ones. In "This Strange New Feeling," Ras, a betrayed fugitive slave, outwits a brutal master and escapes with his beloved Sally. "A Christmas Love Story," completing the trio, depicts William and Ellen Craft in their successful flight from Georgia to Philadelphia. Rochman concludes that these stories are "less tautly written" than *Long Journey Home*, yet "memorable for their graphic details of day-to-day life under slavery and emancipation."

From Contemporary Fiction to Folklore

Two Love Stories offers two views of love in the modern world. The first, "Basketball Game," tells about Allen and Rebecca. Fourteen-year-old Allen is the son of a black minister. His family moves to an all-white Nashville neighborhood, next door to Rebecca Van, who is white, about Allen's age, and also the daughter of a minister. The teenagers play

basketball and talk, vowing eternal friendship before she moves away. Months later, Allen sees her in a department store with another white girl and, in the words of *New York Times* critic Anatole Broyard, Rebecca "cuts him dead—whereupon he goes home, pulls down the basketball hoop and cries on the shoulder of his I-told-you-so father." In the second story, "Catskill Morning," white teenagers Emily and Mark meet and, following a brief period of ecstasy, go their separate ways. Although Broyard is not too impressed with the book, remarking that even "in their time and place, these pictures, these sentiments can hardly have been vivid or moving," a *Publishers Weekly* critic asserts that "Lester writes beautifully, lyrically, strongly" and that the "fresh, moving and very human stories herald a haunting and mature talent."

Just as Lester's historical and contemporary fiction explains human nature, his folklore explains animal nature in a way strangely reminiscent of human nature. Bringing to life imaginary characters such as Uncle Remus's Brer Rabbit and Brer Fox, Lester draws predominantly upon African-American tales; yet he does add two Jewish folktales to *How Many Spots Does a Leopard Have?: And Other Tales.*

Black Folktales, Lester's first book of folk stories, has been praised by a *New York Times Book Review* critic for its "fresh, street-talk language." The reviewer also feels that Lester "breathes new life" into the dozen stories, including the classic "Stagolee." The reviewer points to Lester's characterization, such as "the God who oversees most of the humans and animals that romp through these pages. His God [is] ... a black, cigar-smoking, extremely fallible God who is sometimes wise, but often not; he makes mistakes, admits them and tries to rectify them." Characters such as God and Mrs. God, taken from African folklore and American slave tales, prove that "black resistance to white oppression is as old as the confrontation between the two groups." According to *Publishers Weekly*, Lester's contemporary language captures the essence of black people: "So immediate is the force of their telling, you almost hear his voice." However, *Bulletin of the Center for Children's Books* critic Zena Sutherland calls this collection "a vehicle for hostility" against whites: "There is no story that concerns white people in which they are not pictured as venal or stupid or both."

Lester's next folklore anthology, *The Knee-High Man and Other Tales,* collects six short animal tales from American slave lore, such as the Mr. Rabbit and Mr. Bear stories. *Horn Book* praises Lester's "pleasantly colloquial style" that is easy to read. Ethel Richard, writing in the *New York Times Book Review*, comments that these tales contain subtleties of the black experience reflecting the fun of folk wit, yet "powerfully important lessons ride the humor." For example, the title story shows the follies of failing to think things through and of trying to obtain frivolous possessions. Richard observes that these stories appeal to a wide range of readers: elementary school readers can enjoy the rich illustrations complementing the text, and older readers can use Lester's "rapping on black" for its storytelling. A *Publishers Weekly* reviewer also recommends this book with tales explaining why dogs chase cats and why waves have white-caps, for the "stories are well told and skillfully edited."

Lester's Uncle Remus tales, all illustrated by Jerry Pinkney, continue to build the author's reputation as a black folklorist. *The Tales of Uncle Remus: The Adventures of Brer Rabbit* focuses on forty-eight Joel Chandler Harris stories, such as "Why Brer Bear Has No Tail" and "How Brer Fox and Brer

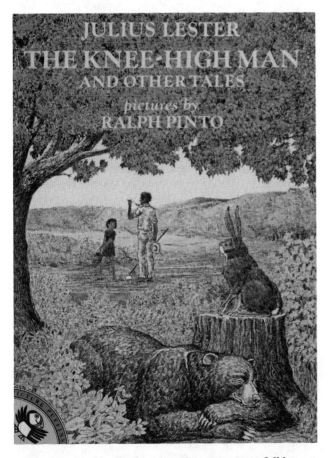

The six animal tales found in this witty 1972 folklore anthology are designed to both amuse readers and teach powerful lessons.

Dog Became Enemies." *Horn Book* critic Mary M. Burns recommends this book because Harris's "almost impenetrable phonetic transcription of the dialect" has been made more accessible through Lester's translations into standard English. Moreover, the tales no longer suffer from the stereotyped image of Uncle Remus, which confirmed black inferiority. Burns points to the "wonderful imagery, remarkable sense of sound, [and] unique turn of phrase."

The *Publishers Weekly* critic appreciates Lester's retelling of Harris's tales from their difficult Gullah dialect to standard English, although Lester's shift from formal language to dialect is also seen as distracting. "For many purists . . . it will not replace the original stories," the critic holds. Other reviewers, however, feel that Lester's translations make the stories more accessible to readers not used to black dialects. Kay McPherson, for example, remarks in *School Library Journal* that Lester's version "gives new life to an American classic," and adds that he uses the sharp, witty Uncle Remus narrator—not the servile character from the opening and closing segments whom many found offensive.

More Tales of Uncle Remus: Further Adventures of Brer Rabbit, His Friends, Enemies, and Others, the second volume in the series, also receives McPherson's endorsement as an outstanding choice for storytellers of all ages. She regards these thirty-seven additional folktales as "striking in their faithfulness to the spirit of the originals but without their drawbacks of heavy dialect and stereotypical narrator." Third in the series, *Further Tales of Uncle Remus: The Misadventures of Brer Rabbit, Brer Fox, Brer Wolf, the Doodang, and Other Creatures* offers the less familiar antics of Brer Fox, Brer Wolf, and Brer Bear—with Brer Rabbit reduced to a minor character. McPherson, in another *School Library Journal*, commends Lester's "spirited and witty" retellings, describing Uncle Remus as "forceful and audacious," and the animals as "a lively crowd" trying to outfox each other. *Horn Book*'s Elizabeth S. Watson comments that storytellers will be especially happy to find "Taily-po" in this "engaging and accessible" book.

How Many Spots Does a Leopard Have?: And Other Tales provides still another resource for storytelling to appeal to modern audiences. A *New York Times Book Review* article quotes Lester as commenting: "Although I am of African and Jewish ancestry, I am also an American. . . . I have fitted the story to my mouth and tongue." In *School Library Journal*, McPherson observes that the

Jewish tale "The Wonderful Healing Leaves" and the African "Why the Sun and the Moon Live in the Sky" represent Lester's best adaptations which fit together "like a well-made watch." *Publishers Weekly*'s reviewer recommends this "eclectic collection" for its combination of two cultures and for its "beguiling and graceful" language attuned to each story's nuances. The collected stories come from the *pourquoi* ("Why?") stories that answer questions about the nature of life like the one posed in the book's title. Pamela A. Todd, a *Booktalker* critic, likes these "crafty animals and cruel monsters, quick-witted, brave heroes and dastardly cowards." Lester's relaxed conversational style flows with the easy informality of a true storyteller, observes *Horn Book*'s reviewer, who quotes the description of the Elephant in "Tug-of-War": "His trunk was ten years long, his ears were as big as a thunderstorm and his feet were bigger than a broken heart."

Whether telling about his own life, folktales, or courageous acts by ordinary people, real and imaginary, Lester demonstrates the need for balance, wholeness, and humanity in our lives. But why does he write young adult books? List quotes Lester's answer to that question: "Children's literature is the one place where you can tell a story . . . and have it received as narrative without any literary garbage. I've done a fair amount of historically based fiction that would be derided as adult literature because it's not 'sophisticated.' I'm just telling a story about people's lives. In children's literature, I can do that."

■ Works Cited

Review of *Black Folktales, New York Times Book Review*, November 9, 1969, pp. 10, 12.

Review of *Black Folktales, Publishers Weekly*, October 20, 1969, p. 60.

Broyard, Anatole, review of *Two Love Stories, New York Times*, October 11, 1972, p. 41.

Burns, Mary M., review of *The Tales of Uncle Remus, Publishers Weekly*, March 20, 1987, p. 80.

Burns, Mary M., review of *The Tales of Uncle Remus, Horn Book*, July/August, 1987, pp. 477-478.

Review of *Falling Pieces of the Broken Sky, Publishers Weekly*, September 14, 1990, p. 115.

Geller, Evelyn, "Julius Lester: Newbery Runner-Up," *School Library Journal*, May, 1969.

Goddard, Rosalind K., review of *Long Journey Home, New York Times Book Review*, July 23, 1972, p. 8.

Griffin, John Howard, review of *To Be a Slave, New York Times Book Review*, November 3, 1968, p. 7.

Review of *How Many Spots Does a Leopard Have? Horn Book*, January/February, 1990, p. 79.

Review of *How Many Spots Does a Leopard Have? New York Times Book Review*, January 14, 1990, p. 17.

Review of *How Many Spots Does a Leopard Have? Publishers Weekly*, October 27, 1989, p. 68.

Review of *The Knee-High Man and Other Tales, Horn Book*, October, 1972, p. 463.

Review of *The Knee-High Man and Other Tales, Publishers Weekly*, August 7, 1972, p. 50.

Lester, Julius, *Long Journey Home: Stories from Black History*, Dial, 1972.

Lester, Julius, "The Simple Truth About Blacks and Jews," *Reform Judaism*, summer, 1989, pp. 8-9.

Lester, Julius, *To Be a Slave*, Dial, 1968, p. 72.

List, Barry, "PW Interviews: Julius Lester." *Publishers Weekly*, February 12, 1988, pp. 67-68.

Review of *Long Journey Home, Publishers Weekly*, June 5, 1972, p. 140.

McPherson, Kay, review of *Further Tales of Uncle Remus: The Misadventures of Brer Rabbit, Brer Fox, Brer Wolf, the Doodang, and Other Creatures, School Library Journal*, May, 1990, p. 99.

McPherson, Kay, review of *How Many Spots Does a Leopard Have? School Library Journal*, November, 1989, p. 99.

McPherson, Kay, review of *More Tales of Uncle Remus: Further Adventures of Brer Rabbit, His Friends, Enemies, and Others, School Library Journal*, June-July, 1988, p. 92.

McPherson, Kay, review of *The Tales of Uncle Remus, School Library Journal*, April, 1987, p. 99.

Oppenheimer, Joel, "The Soul That Wanders," *New York Times Book Review*, January 31, 1988, p. 12.

Richard, Ethel, review of *The Knee-High Man and Other Tales, New York Times Book Review*, February 4, 1973, p. 8.

Robinson, Kathryn, review of *All Is Well, School Library Journal*, September, 1976, p. 146.

Rochman, Hazel, review of *This Strange New Feeling, School Library Journal*, April, 1982, p. 83.

Stone, Douglas, review of *Lovesong, Christian Century*, July 20, 1988, p. 682.

Sutherland, Zena, review of *Black Folktales*, *Bulletin of the Center for Children's Books*, February, 1970, p. 101.

Sutherland, Zena, review of *To Be a Slave*, *Bulletin of the Center for Children's Books*, April, 1969, pp. 129-130.

Review of *This Strange New Feeling*, *Horn Book*, August, 1982, pp. 414-415.

Review of *To Be a Slave*, *New York Times Book Review*, February 9, 1986, p. 32.

Review of *To Be a Slave*, *Publishers Weekly*, January 19, 1970, p. 83.

Todd, Pamela A., review of *How Many Spots Does a Leopard Have?*, *Booktalker*, September, 1990, p. 5.

Review of *Two Love Stories*, *Publishers Weekly*, August 28, 1972, p. 259.

Walker, Barbara, review of *Who I Am*, *Interracial Books for Children Bulletin*, Volume 5, numbers 7 and 8, 1975, p. 18.

Watson, Elizabeth S., review of *Further Tales of Uncle Remus: The Misadventures of Brer Rabbit, Brer Fox, Brer Wolf, the Doodang, and Other Creatures*, *Horn Book*, July/August, 1990, p. 478.

Review of *Who I Am*, *Horn Book*, June, 1975, p. 198.

Williams, Deborah H., review of *Who I Am*, *Library Journal*, January 1, 1975, p. 54.

■ For More Information See

BOOKS

Chevalier, Tracy, editor, *Twentieth-Century Children's Writers*, 3rd edition, St. James Press, 1989, pp. 575-576.

Children's Literature Review, Volume 2, Gale, 1976.

Krim, Seymour, *You and Me*, Holt, 1972.

PERIODICALS

Commonweal, March 25, 1988, pp. 167-169.

Horn Book, April, 1973, p. 146.

Junior Bookshelf, December, 1973, p. 409; February, 1975.

Kirkus Reviews, June 1, 1972, p. 629; August 15, 1972, p. 941.

Nation, June 22, 1970.

New York Review of Books, April 20, 1972, pp. 41-42.

New York Times Book Review, October 13, 1968, p. 16; November 3, 1968; November 2, 1969, pp. 3, 38; November 9, 1969; July 12, 1970, pp. 5, 32; June 4, 1972, p. 28; July 23, 1972; November 5, 1972, p. 26; February 4, 1973; August 22, 1976, p. 2; September 5, 1982; February 17, 1985, p. 9; May 25, 1986, p. 24.

Publishers Weekly, May 13, 1968, p. 55; March 24, 1969, p. 57; May 12, 1969, p. 54; August 18, 1969, p. 69; April 20, 1970, p. 64; September 14, 1970, p. 71; June 5, 1972, p. 140; April 26, 1976, p. 55; November 2, 1984, p. 66; April 4, 1986; December 4, 1987, p. 59; September 14, 1990, p. 115.

School Library Journal, September, 1970, p. 173; September, 1972, p. 143; February, 1975, p. 15; September, 1976, p. 146; January, 1984, p. 42; January, 1991, p. 118.

Times Literary Supplement, December 11, 1970, p. 1456; September 20, 1974, p. 1003; April 3, 1987.

Washington Post, March 12, 1985.

Washington Post Book World, September 3, 1972, p. 9.

—*Sketch by Laura M. Zaidman*

Sharon Bell Mathis

Charles Hart Junior High School, Washington, DC, special education teacher, 1966-73; Stuart Junior High School, Washington, DC, special education teacher, 1973-74; Benning Elementary School, Washington, DC, librarian, 1975-76; Friendship Educational Center (now Patricia Roberts Harris Educational Center), Washington, DC, library media specialist, 1976—. Black Writers Workshop, Washington, DC, writer in charge of children's literature division, 1970-73; Howard University, Washington, DC, writer-in-residence, 1972-74. Lawyers Committee of District of Columbia Commission on the Arts, member of board of advisors, 1972-73; Black Women's Community Development Foundation, member, 1973-74.

■ Personal

Born February 26, 1937, in Atlantic City, NJ; daughter of John Willie (a longshoreman) and Alice Mary (a seamstress, welder, and clerk; maiden name, Frazier) Bell; married Leroy Franklin Mathis, July 11, 1957 (divorced, 1979); children: Sherie, Stacy, Stephanie. *Education:* Morgan State College (now Morgan State University), B.A. (magna cum laude), 1958; Catholic University of America, M.L.S., 1975; also attended D.C. Teachers College. *Religion:* Roman Catholic.

■ Addresses

Home—P.O. Box 44714, Fort Washington, MD 20744. *Agent*—Marilyn Marlow, Curtis Brown Ltd., 10 Astor Place, New York, NY 10003.

■ Career

Writer of books for children and young adults. Children's Hospital of District of Columbia, Washington, DC, interviewer, 1958-59; Holy Redeemer Elementary School, Washington, DC, teacher, 1959-65; Bertie Backus Junior High School, Washington, DC, special education teacher, 1965-66;

■ Awards, Honors

Award for a children's book manuscript, Council on Interracial Books for Children, 1969, for *Sidewalk Story;* Fellow, Bread Loaf Writers Conference, 1970; Children's Book of the Year, Child Study Association of America, 1971, for *Sidewalk Story; Teacup Full of Roses* was chosen one of Child Study Association of America's Children's Books of the Year, one of *New York Times'* Best Books of the Year, and one of the American Library Association's (ALA) Best Young Adult Books, all 1972, and Coretta Scott King Award, runner-up, 1973; Coretta Scott King Award, 1974, for *Ray Charles;* ALA Best Young Adult Book, 1974, for *Listen for the Fig Tree; Boston Globe-Horn Book* Honor Book for Text, 1975, for *The Hundred Penny Box;* Children's Book of the Year, Child Study Association of America, 1975, for *The Hundred Penny Box;* Notable Children's Trade Book in the Field of Social Studies, National Council of Social Studies and the Children's Book Council, 1975, for *The Hundred Penny Box;* *New York Times'* Outstanding Book, 1975, for *The Hundred Penny Box;* Arts and Humanities Award, Club Twenty, 1975; Newbery Honor Book, 1976, for *The Hundred Penny Box;* District of Columbia Association of School Libraries award, 1976; Arts and Humanities Award, Archdiocese of Washington, DC, 1978; Wallace Johnson Memorial Award, 1984, for "Outstanding Contributions to the Literary Arts"; Arts and Letters Award, Boys and Girls Clubs of Greater Washington, 1984; Arts and Letters Award, Delta Sigma Theta Sorority, 1985; Outstanding Writer Award, Writing-to-Read Program, DC Public Schools, 1986; Bank Street College "Outstanding Book of the Year" for *Red Dog/Blue Fly: Football Poems; The Hundred Penny Box* was an ALA Notable Book; *The Hundred Penny Box, Teacup Full of Roses,* and *Listen for the Fig Tree* were all named on the *Horn Book* honor list.

■ Writings

FOR CHILDREN

Sidewalk Story, illustrated by Leo Carty, Viking, 1971.
Ray Charles (nonfiction), illustrated by George Ford, Crowell, 1973.
The Hundred Penny Box, illustrated by Leo and Diane Dillon, Viking, 1975.
Red Dog, Blue Fly: Football Poems, Viking, 1991.

FOR YOUNG ADULTS

Brooklyn Story, illustrated by Charles Bible, Hill & Wang, 1970.
Teacup Full of Roses, Viking, 1972.
Listen for the Fig Tree, Viking, 1974.
Cartwheels, Scholastic, 1977.

OTHER

Also contributor to poetry anthology *Night Comes Softly: Anthology of Black Female Voices,* edited by Nikki Giovanni, 1970; contributor of stories, reviews, and articles to periodicals, including *Washington Post, Negro History Bulletin, Black America, Essence, Encore, Black World, Black Books Bulletin, Acorn,* and *Horn Book.* Author of "Ebony Juniors Speak!," a monthly column in *Ebony, Jr.!,* 1972-85, and "Society and Youth," a bi-weekly column in *Liteside: D.C. Buyers Guide.*

■ Work in Progress

Harcourt, Brace (Browndeer Books) is considering a manuscript, "Ebonee Rose: Running Girl," inspired by and dedicated to Mathis's granddaughter, Stacia; *Seagrass and Wooden Biscuits,* in which "the inspiration for the grandfather" character is Mathis's brother, John.

■ Adaptations

Teacup Full of Roses (record; cassette), Live Oak Media, 1977; *The Hundred Penny Box* (cassette; record; filmstrip), Random House.

■ Sidelights

"I don't remember when I actually realized how very special was this private playground/haven/sanctuary of mine.... Everything was possible while I sat and imagined on my fire escape," reflects Sharon Bell Mathis in her *Something about the Author Autobiography Series (SAAS)* entry. On that fire escape of a Brooklyn apartment, Mathis found a place where her imagination reigned as she wrote her first stories and poems. In her fiction for children and young people, Mathis today plants hope, strength, and possibility into her uncompromising portrayals of urban life and the difficulties encountered by her African-American protagonists.

Mathis was born in Atlantic City, New Jersey. She was the first of four children—three girls and a boy—born to Alice Frazier and John Willie Bell. Her brother John—known as "Bubba"—is a retired New York City detective, who is now a county deputy sheriff in Maryland; she has two sisters: Patrellis (Pat), who died tragically of lung cancer, and Marcia, a CAT scan technologist. When Mathis was a year old, her parents were able to move from her maternal grandparents' home to a house of their own, where her brother was born. Shortly after her third sibling, Pat, was born, Mathis's father found a better job at the Brooklyn Navy Yard, and he was eventually able to move the family to the Bedford-Stuyvesant section of Brooklyn. However, when Mathis was five years old her parents separated, and her mother moved the children to an apartment on Bainbridge Street. It was there, in the apartment with the fire escape, that Mathis discovered her sanctuary of the imagination.

Mathis's talents were encouraged by her mother, her teachers, and other family members and friends. Her mother—with whom she retained a very close relationship until her death—read often, wrote poetry, and sketched, all in addition to working two jobs. In her *SAAS* entry, Mathis shares an image from her childhood of her mother "curled up in a comfy chair, usually near a window—natural light flooding her lovely hair, the book, and the room." As she grew up, Mathis's favorite books included *Black Boy* by Richard Wright, *A Tree Grows in Brooklyn* by Betty Smith, and *Knock On Any Door* by Willard Motley. She also read works by Langston Hughes, Frank Yerby, Zora Neale Hurston, Countee Cullen, Gwendolyn Brooks, Paul Laurence Dunbar, James Michener, and many others.

While attending Catholic school, Mathis's teachers "provided an early showcase" for her writing. But that was just the beginning of the recognition she would earn. After graduating from St. Michael's Academy in 1954, Mathis went on to Morgan State College—now Morgan State University—in Baltimore, Maryland, where she fortunately found refuge from the racism that was erupting across the United States as a result of the desegregation law passed that year. The U.S. Supreme Court had found that school segregation on the basis of race was illegal, and some white Americans protested violently. Many African-American children went to school each morning in fear, "armed," as Mathis remembers, "only with courage."

While at college, Mathis learned to play violin, performing in the college orchestra, and she matured politically. She remembers, for example, how Morgan students organized a sit-in at a drugstore near campus that banned African Americans from its lunch counter. Such protests made her more aware that civil rights still had a long way to go. It was also while at Morgan that Mathis met the man with whom she would elope during her senior year: Leroy Franklin Mathis, a psychiatric forensic technician. After an eventful four years, the author graduated magna cum laude in 1958 and still cherishes the memory of hearing the commencement speaker, Dr. Martin Luther King, Jr.

In her *SAAS* essay, Mathis not only vividly recalls the events and people from her own childhood and adolescence, but also remembers all the tales told to her by her family and friends. It was these stories that helped inspire her to spend more and more of her time writing. The lives of children and young people gradually took center stage in her work: "I began to notice that my stories for, and about, children began to develop more frequent-

This 1970 novel, set against the backdrop of the Martin Luther King, Jr., assassination, describes the efforts of a brother and sister to make peace with their long-absent mother.

ly," Mathis remembers. "The characterization of children was superior to my depiction of adults." Her continued efforts eventually resulted in Mathis's first novel for young adults, *Brooklyn Story*. Published in 1970 as "a high-interest, low-vocabulary novel for teenagers with reading deficiencies," *Brooklyn Story* was included in Hill & Wang's Challenger book series, intended largely for young African-American and Spanish-speaking audiences. At the time she wrote the book, Mathis was a special education teacher at the junior high level for Washington, DC, Public Schools. Her close continuous contact with the students there nourished her talent for creating stories for teenage audiences.

Storytelling That Inspires, Entertains

One of the hallmarks of Mathis's writing is her ability to confront and strive to remedy the often ugly realities of life, transforming unfortunate events into memories from which positive meanings can be gleaned. This approach to writing is a reflection of her own childhood experiences. In her *SAAS* entry, for example, she recalls that the young aunt baby-sitting her one day accidently burned her with a lid while boiling cabbage. Rather than bemoan the scar that remains on her otherwise blemish-free skin, Mathis relates that it "serves nicely as a make-your-own birthmark." The issues she confronts in her books—racism, economic injustice, violence, drugs—address more challenging themes, however.

Mathis sets her stories in contemporary, realistic contexts. *Brooklyn Story*, published in 1970, reflects the time in which it was written, an era when many people—particularly African Americans—remained disconsolate over the assassination of Martin Luther King, Jr. The tragedy serves not merely as a backdrop to the story, but as an integral part of the protagonists' lives. Vi and Eddie Keeler are suddenly faced with a visit by their mother, Della, who has been absent. Vi looks forward to seeing her mother, while Eddie is filled with resentment at her apparently cruel abandonment of them. Once Della has arrived, however, Vi must cope with her mother's absorption with Eddie. The novel reaches a crisis point when Eddie is accidently shot in the melee resulting from Dr. King's death.

Frances Smith Foster, writing in the *Dictionary of Literary Biography*, notes that, as a consequence, "each member of the family must plumb the depths of personal and communal grief to learn the power of their love." She continues that *Brooklyn Story* "explores the familial responsibilities and relationships, and it affirms the healing power of love. At the same time the historical moment and its effect on the ... family and their community make *Brooklyn Story* a larger, very positive statement."

The author's next book, *Sidewalk Story*, launched Mathis's career as an award-winning writer. Written for a younger audience, the manuscript was selected for the annual Council on Interracial Books award for 1970. *Sidewalk Story* is about nine-year-old Lilly Etta Allen, who defies her mother in order to prevent her best friend's family from being evicted. Despite the awards *Sidewalk Story* earned, the book received some mixed reviews. Ethel L. Heins characterizes Mathis's prose in a *Horn Book* review as "reportorial" and opines that the events "fail to leave their mark" emotionally. But Toni Morrison, reviewing the work in the *New York Times Book Review*, found it neither naively sentimental nor despairing: "warm but not sticky, serious but not relentlessly grim."

A Family Confronts Drug Abuse

Teacup Full of Roses, Mathis's next novel for young adults, received numerous awards and distinctions. According to Mathis in her *SAAS* entry, the novel is "another salute to Black kids." It portrays strength, courage, faith, and commitment toward a better life in the face of adversities that confront the inner-city children in the story. The title comes from the image that seventeen-year-old Joe, the second of three sons, uses to picture his dream of a trouble-free future. With an older brother who's

TEACUP FULL OF ROSES

Sharon Bell Mathis

In this award-winning 1972 work, seventeen-year-old Joe must deal with the problems created by a drug-addicted brother, an ill father, and a neglectful mother.

addicted to drugs, a younger brother who's far more academically talented than street smart, a mother obsessed with her oldest son, and a chronically ill father, Joe struggles with more than his share of problems.

As Joe prepares for his own high school graduation and plans for the future, he tries to care for his younger brother, Davey, since his mother is preoccupied with her son Paul, a gifted artist who nonetheless is letting his life disintegrate. In one scene, Joe pleads to his mother, "Davey is as great as Paul . . . a 'gift,' as you say. Besides being smart, he's a natural athlete. And just a good, clean chump—and I love him. Like I love Paul. But Paul's not coming through because for some reason he's given up. So, Davey's the one." Because his mother does not take action on behalf of Davey, Joe does. He withdraws his savings for his own college education, enlists in the Navy, and gives the money to Davey along with an encouraging

The seven principles of the African holiday Kwanza help a blind teenager overcome a series of tragedies in this 1974 novel.

letter. After Paul steals the money, Joe, a former gang leader, feels fairly confident about retrieving it from Warwick, Paul's dealer. But his efforts end in horrible results.

In her review of *Teacup Full of Roses* for the *New York Times Book Review,* Janet Harris writes that Mathis "weaves her plots with sure authority," adding that while the book is "'another salute to Black kids,' . . . it has a lot to say to white ones, too." Lois Belfield Watt, however, objects to the narrative devices used. In *Childhood Education,* the reviewer points out two "doubtful elements": that Joe did not open an account in Davey's name and that he would leave money in a house in which a known addict was staying. These two parts in the story combined with "the contrived ending," Watt concludes, "weakens the whole." On the other hand, *Negro History Bulletin* contributor Eloise Greenfield asserts that in "addition to being an excellent choice for young people, this book should be put on the *must* reading list of every black filmmaker." Mathis's portrayal of the mother, Mrs. Mattie Brooks, especially provoked mixed reactions. Watt finds her a "stereotyped black matriarch," while Mary M. Burns notes in *Horn Book* the "superb" depiction of "a purposeful, devoted woman caught in a bewildering and difficult situation."

For her next writing project, Mathis shifted her focus entirely. She wrote a biography of the "Genius of Soul," Ray Charles, for young children. Mathis holds in *SAAS* that "the triumphs of Ray Charles are the triumphs of all black people—a story of great will, of great strength, and a profound sense of survival." The biography was warmly received by reviewers like Betty Lanier Jenkins, who in *School Library Journal* calls Mathis's account "inspiring."

Celebrating Kwanza

The research Mathis performed in order to write about the blind musician also served her well in her next fictional endeavor. *Listen for the Fig Tree,* another award-winning novel, is Mathis's third book written for young adults. In this story, sixteen-year-old Muffin Johnson has been blind since the age of ten as a result of glaucoma. As the novel begins, Christmas and Kwanza, an annual African-American celebration, are days away. But for Muffin and her mother Leola the holidays this year bring grief. The season reminds them of how Muffin's father, Marvin, had been murdered by thieves while driving his cab on Christmas night

Wearing a smock she sewed herself, Mathis entertains smiling schoolchildren during a classroom visit to promote reading.

the year before. Over the past year, her mother has developed a serious drinking problem and is filled with anger toward the murderers and the police, who did not phone an ambulance in time to save her husband's life.

Though Muffin also mourns the loss of her father, she takes on many of the household responsibilities and still manages to look forward to Christmas and Kwanza. In addition to the normal emotional upheavals characteristic of her age, Muffin must deal with a mother whose grip on reality loosens with each passing day. The worst, however, is yet to come. Two days before Christmas, Muffin is almost raped by a man in the hallway of her apartment building. But the loving support of friends and neighbors, including her boyfriend Ernie, her upstairs neighbor and special confidant Mr. Dale, and Reverend Willie Williams, help to heal her spirits. With their aid, she is able to attend the Kwanza festival on Christmas night, which becomes a poignant and recuperative experience

for her. After listening to the preacher and the gatherers ceremoniously pronounce the seven principles of Kwanza—unity, self-determination, collective work and responsibility, cooperative economics, purpose, creativity, and faith—Muffin senses a change in herself. A passage from the book concludes that "she felt something delicate emerge within her and get stronger and spread. And she knew what it was. . . . What she felt was strength."

As Foster points out, Mathis illustrates the principles of Kwanza by weaving them into events and relationships in *Listen for the Fig Tree,* "from the black salesperson who refuses to exploit the mentally incompetent Leola to the mute, elderly Mr. Thomas who is savagely beaten as he fends off Muffin's would-be rapist." Rochelle Cortez, writing in *Black Books Bulletin,* also praises the narrative function Kwanza serves, adding that Muffin's "knowledge about her Afrikan identity," which her father instilled in her, "is being constantly heightened by those around her." In a *New York*

Times Book Review article, however, Dale Carlson believes that toward the end of the book the plot strays too far away from Muffin in order to become a tribute to Africa. Despite this problem, Carlson judges that Mathis's "ability to describe delicate relationships" and her skill at characterization in general make *Listen to the Fig Tree* a powerful story.

Relationships, Young and Old

In *The Hundred Penny Box* Mathis again explores the importance of family relationships. The book sketches some moments in the bond between young Michael and his one-hundred-year-old great-great aunt, Dew. Aunt Dew's prized possession is a box containing a penny for each year of her life. Michael loves to hear her tell stories that the pennies evoke for her. But the box of pennies has become a point of contention within a larger conflict: Aunt Dew has just come to live with Michael and his parents, and Michael's mother is having an especially difficult time adjusting to her husband's great aunt's presence in the household. *New York Times Book Review* critic Annie Gottlieb calls *The Hundred Penny Box* "a quiet work of art" that deals with old age and extended family living situations without being "kind, condescending, nervous." As Gottlieb reminisces about her own grandfather, she remarks that this is a book that offers much to older readers as well.

But relationships don't have to cross generation gaps in order to be important. In Mathis's young adult novel, *Cartwheels*, the author explores how three girls competing in a gymnastics contest affect each others' lives. The story is told from the point of view of Zettie, who wants to use the prize money to return to her family in South Carolina. But she must compete with Thomasina, who has bullied her in the past, and Fawn, the self-centered niece of her mother's friend. Foster notes that although "only one girl wins the fifty dollars, each wins respect for herself and for her place in the community."

A New Direction

Mathis dedicated *Red Dog, Blue Fly: Football Poems* to her grandson, Tommy, and her nephew, John, and she credits both of them for assisting her with its writing. Published in 1991, the collection of verse represents a new creative direction for Mathis. She was inspired by watching her grandson's football team become county-wide champions in their division. John Peters, in a *School Library Journal* review of *Red Dog, Blue Fly*, observes that her "fluid, rhythmic poems evoke the tensions, triumphs, and risks of football for young players and readers."

Although Mathis has begun to explore new areas of writing, African-American children remain both her inspiration and purpose in writing. Mathis voices her hope in *SAAS* that "Black children will leave my books with a feeling that I know they *live*." With a profound sense of generational respect and commitment to family and community, the author dedicates her books to family members and friends who have helped her grow as well as to those whom she herself nurtures. And the epigraphs she has chosen for her books from such luminaries as Nikki Giovanni, June Jordan, and Leopold Sedar Senghor reinforce this impression. They are voices outside her immediate family but within the larger circle of Africans and the African-American community in the largest sense.

■ Works Cited

Burns, Mary M., review of *Teacup Full of Roses*, *Horn Book*, February, 1973, pp. 58-59.

Carlson, Dale, review of *Listen for the Fig Tree*, *New York Times Book Review*, April 7, 1974, p. 8.

Cortez, Rochelle, review of *Listen for the Fig Tree*, *Black Books Bulletin*, spring, 1974, pp. 39-40.

Foster, Frances Smith, "Sharon Bell Mathis," *Dictionary of Literary Biography*, Volume 33: *Afro-American Fiction Writers after 1955*, Gale, 1984, pp. 170-173.

Gottlieb, Annie, review of *The Hundred Penny Box*, *New York Times Book Review*, May 4, 1975, p. 20.

Greenfield, Eloise, review of *Teacup Full of Roses*, *Negro History Bulletin*, March, 1973, p. 69.

Harris, Janet, review of *Teacup Full of Roses*, *New York Times Book Review*, September 10, 1972, p. 8.

Heins, Ethel L., review of *Sidewalk Story*, *Horn Book*, August, 1971, p. 385.

Jenkins, Betty Lanier, review of *Ray Charles*, *School Library Journal*, May, 1974, p. 56.

Mathis, Sharon Bell, *Teacup Full of Roses*, Viking, 1972.

Mathis, Sharon Bell, *Listen for the Fig Tree*, Viking, 1974.

Mathis, Sharon Bell, in her essay in *Something about the Author Autobiography Series*, Volume 3, Gale, 1987.

Morrison, Toni, review of *Sidewalk Story*, *New York Times Book Review*, May 2, 1971, p. 43.

Peters, John, review of *Red Dog, Blue Fly: Football Poems, School Library Journal*, February 1992, p. 103.
Watt, Lois Belfield, review of *Teacup Full of Roses, Childhood Education*, May, 1973, p. 422.

■ For More Information See

BOOKS

Children's Literature Review, Volume 3, Gale, 1978.

Nilsen, Alleen Pace, and Kenneth L. Donelson, *Literature for Today's Young Adults*, 2nd edition, Scott, Foresman, 1985.

PERIODICALS

Horn Book, August, 1976.
New York Times, March 27, 1970, p. 22.
Parent and Child, January/February, 1992, p. 11.
Redbook, August, 1972.
Washington Post, March 21, 1971.

—Sketch by Helene Henderson

Lorne Michaels

■ Personal

Born Lorne David Lipowitz, November 17, 1944, in Forest Hill, Toronto, Canada; emigrated to the United States; naturalized U.S. citizen, April 1, 1987; son of Abraham (a furrier) and Florence (Becker) Lipowitz; married Rosie Schuster (a comedy writer), November, 1967 (divorced, 1980); married Susan Forristal (an actress and art gallery owner), September 13, 1981 (divorced); married Alice Barry, April, 1991; children: One. *Education:* Graduated from University of Toronto, 1966.

■ Addresses

Office—Broadway Video, 1619 Broadway, New York, NY 10019; National Broadcasting Company, 30 Rockefeller Plaza, 9th Floor, New York, NY 10020.

■ Career

Worked for Film Canada, c. 1967; writer and performer, with Hart Pomerantz, for Canadian television, until 1968; producer and performer, with Pomerantz, of comedy specials for Canadian Broadcasting Corporation (CBC), 1969-73; pro-

ducer of television specials, various networks, 1973—; creator and producer of *Saturday Night Live,* National Broadcasting Company (NBC), 1975-80, executive producer, 1985—; chair of Broadway Video, 1979—; producer of motion pictures, including *Mr. Mike's Mondo Video, Wayne's World,* and *The Coneheads,* 1979—; creator and producer of *The New Show,* NBC, 1984; creator and executive producer of *Michelob Presents Sunday Night,* NBC, 1987-89; executive producer of *The Kids in the Hall,* CBC and Home Box Office (HBO), 1988-92; executive producer of *Late Night with Conan O'Brien,* NBC, 1993—. *Member:* American Federation of Television and Radio Artists, Writers Guild of America (board member), Astoria Foundation.

■ Awards, Honors

Emmy Award, best writing in comedy-variety special, 1973, for *Lily;* Writers Guild of America award, best variety, 1975, and Emmy Award, best writing in a comedy-variety special, 1976, both for *The Lily Tomlin Special;* Emmy Awards, outstanding producer of a comedy-variety series, 1976, outstanding writing in a comedy-variety series, 1977 and 1989, all for *Saturday Night Live;* San Francisco Film Award, 1976; Emmy Award, outstanding writing in a comedy-variety special, 1978, for *The Paul Simon Special;* The Charlie Local and National Comedy Awards, named best in the comedy business, 1988; received Peabody Award for *Saturday Night Live;* numerous other awards.

■ Writings

TELEVISION SERIES

(With Hart Pomerantz and others) *The Beautiful Phyllis Diller Show,* NBC, 1968.

(With Pomerantz and others) *Rowan and Martin's Laugh-In,* NBC, 1968.

(With others; and producer) *The Burns and Schreiber Comedy Hour,* ABC, 1973.

(With others) *Saturday Night Live,* NBC, 1975-81, 1985—.

(With others) *The New Show,* NBC, 1984.

TELEVISION SPECIALS

(With others) *Lily,* CBS, 1973.

(With Bob Wells and Johnny Bradford) *The Perry Como Winter Show,* CBS, 1973.

(With others; and producer) *Flip Wilson ... Of Course,* NBC, 1974.

(With others; and producer, with Jane Wagner) *Lily,* ABC, 1975.

(With others; and producer, with Wagner) *The Lily Tomlin Special,* ABC, 1975.

(With Alan Zweibel, Dan Ackroyd, and John Belushi; and producer) *The Beach Boys Special,* NBC, 1976.

(With others; and producer) *The Paul Simon Special,* NBC, 1977.

Also producer and writer, with Pomerantz, of triannual comedy specials for the Canadian Broadcasting Corporation, including *The Hart and Lorne Terrific Hour* and *Today Makes Me Nervous,* 1969-71.

OTHER

(With others; and producer and director) *Gilda Live from New York* (stage performance), produced at the Winter Garden Theatre, New York City, 1979, released as a motion picture, Warner Brothers, 1980.

(With Steve Martin and Randy Newman; and producer) *The Three Amigos* (motion picture), Orion, 1987.

Joke writer for Woody Allen, New York City, 1968.

■ Work in Progress

Working on plans for more movie spin-offs featuring characters from *Saturday Night Live.*

■ Sidelights

David Rensin described film and television producer Lorne Michaels in a *Playboy* article as "the

unofficial godfather of modern comedy." Known primarily for creating, producing, and writing the late night program *Saturday Night Live* (or as it is commonly referred to, *SNL*), Michaels is credited with pioneering a style of television comedy that was revolutionary when the show debuted in 1975. With its political, social, and often confrontational content, *SNL* took viewers by surprise and established a loyal audience for more than eighteen years. As the show grew in popularity, Michaels branched out and began work on other projects, including writing and producing numerous television programs and acting as producer for a variety of films, including the immensely popular *Wayne's World.* In 1993, Michaels was chosen by the National Broadcasting Company (NBC) to create and produce a new late night show to replace the celebrated *Late Night with David Letterman.* His work has permeated popular culture to the point where lines of dialogue from his shows and films are used by millions of people worldwide as catchphrases in regular conversation. David Marc appraised Michaels's career in the *Voice,* stating that "his mastery of television history and gesture, and his willingness to take chances with both pen and camera put late-night TV satire on the cultural map."

Lorne David Michaels entered the world on November 17, 1944, in Toronto, Canada. Growing up in the affluent suburb of Forest Hill, Michaels was raised in the burgeoning age of visual media. "I watched everything," he told Michael Winship in *Television.* "I remember television sort of being a miracle." As Michaels matured, so too did television, evolving from the sparse staging of live shows like *The Honeymooners* (a favorite of Michaels's that would greatly influence his career) to more sophisticated, prerecorded material. Initially, however, Michaels did not consider television as his future career. As the son of a successful furrier, he was expected to follow the traditional path of college and career. As a result, Michaels found himself enrolled in the English program at the University of Toronto, heading toward a profession in law or teaching.

Gets the Show Biz Bug

While attending college, Michaels became involved with a theatre group and began acting, writing, and directing. Most of the projects he was involved with were satirical revues, shows that featured sketch comedy and humorous musical numbers. Those productions increased his interest in show business, and their popularity proved to

Michaels that his brand of humor was appealing to others. Despite this, a career in television was not the foremost thing in his mind. As Michaels told Winship, "I think I was headed more toward theater or to film. I was from the what-I-really-want-to-do-is-direct generation." He paired with Hart Pomerantz, whom he had met while producing a revue, and the duo began writing and performing a comedy act. In the course of presenting their material, Michaels and Pomerantz attracted the attention of some influential people. "Through a series of happy accidents," Michaels told Winship, "we got to write for some good comedians, and that material got shown to other people. We were sent out to California to do a television series, and that led to another television series."

The "good comedians" that Michaels mentioned to Winship included Woody Allen, who would later go on to make such films as *Sleeper* and *Annie Hall*. The television series that he and Pomerantz wrote for were *The Beautiful Phyllis Diller Show* and *Rowan and Martin's Laugh-In*. While Diller's show lasted only one season, when the team began work on *Laugh-In* in 1968 the show was one of television comedy's most popular. Michaels and Pomerantz were contracted to write opening monologues for the show's hosts, Dan Rowan and Dick Martin. As junior writers on the program, however, the duo was subjected to the whims and tastes of the senior writing staff. As a result, much of the material they wrote was extensively rewritten—sometimes to an unrecognizable degree. Disillusioned with the process of television writing, the pair returned to Canada. They eventually came to the conclusion that if they were to continue working in television, they would have to produce their own shows. As Michaels told Timothy White in *Rolling Stone*: "I became a producer to protect my writing, which was being [ruined] by producers."

Michaels and Pomerantz made an agreement with the Canadian Broadcasting Corporation (CBC) to write, produce, and star in a series of specials. Over the course of three years, beginning in 1969, they created three specials a year with titles such as *The Hart and Lorne Terrific Hour* and *Today Makes Me Nervous*. The format of these specials, which would later provide loose blueprints for *SNL*, had Hart and Lorne hosting a program of sketch comedy with musical guests like Cat Stevens and James Taylor. While the shows were moderately popular and made Michaels and Pomerantz well-known among younger viewers, they also served in an instructional capacity for Mi-

chaels. He related in Winship's *Television:* "I learned how to do television mostly because the CBC was this tremendous training ground. If you were prepared to work from midnight to eight, you could edit all you wanted. I began to feel very comfortable in a television studio.... I was able to learn an enormous amount in a very short time." Michaels became so interested in the processes behind the cameras that he eventually lost interest in performing. He and Pomerantz severed their partnership on these grounds, with Hart continuing to perform and Michaels going on to produce several programs for the CBC. While Michaels was indebted to Canadian television for his technical knowledge, he realized that the real media opportunities—the real test of his talent—lay in the much larger American market. So in 1971, confident of his ability, he returned to California and American network television.

Upon his return to America, Michaels landed a job producing and writing a show built around the comedy team of Burns and Schreiber. The show was unsuccessful and Michaels moved on to other projects. In 1973 he was introduced to comedian Lily Tomlin, who was enjoying a wave of success following her role as a regular performer on *Laugh-In*. In their first meeting, Tomlin and Michaels talked for nearly seven hours. After that first impression, Tomlin hired Michaels as a writer on her second television special for the Columbia Broadcasting System (CBS), which she was just starting to produce. Titled *Lily*, the show proved a turning point for Michaels. While he and Tomlin clashed over certain issues, neither could deny that their work together created great comedy. When Tomlin signed on with the American Broadcasting Company (ABC) for two more specials, she named Michaels as a chief writer and coproducer. "Tomlin's specials were daring," wrote Doug Hill and Jeff Weingrad in their book *Saturday Night: A Backstage History of Saturday Night Live*, "they seemed to have *experimental* written all over them." The shows contained pieces that were surreal for the television standards of the 1970s, and they often dealt strongly with such taboo topics as drugs and politics—issues that had plagued and later scuttled the popular *Smothers Brothers Show*. While her material found a significant audience with young urban viewers, Tomlin and her creative team's renegade approach incensed executives at both CBS and ABC. Her specials were not expanded into series form, as she and Michaels had hoped. As Tomlin went on to star in such films as Robert Altman's *Nashville*, Mi-

Michaels shares a laugh with members of the original Not Ready for Prime Time Players, including Gilda Radner, Chevy Chase, and John Belushi.

chaels halfheartedly worked on several TV specials for entertainers such as Perry Como and Flip Wilson. He quit after producing one of four specials for Wilson, once again disillusioned with television.

When Michaels first returned to the United States, his agent arranged a meeting with executives at NBC. The purpose of the meeting was for Michaels to pitch his idea for a new show to the network. Having long been a fan of the television series produced by the comedy troupe Monty Python, Michaels wanted to do a show in America that reflected the off-kilter, anarchic spirit of the English group. Armed with videotape of choice Python bits and excerpts from the Hart and Lorne shows, he pitched his idea to the men in charge of America's viewing habits. They laughed heartily at the material they were shown, but at the end of the meeting the executives told Michaels that no one in America would appreciate that type of humor. By 1975, about the time that Michaels was contemp-

lating a permanent separation from television work, executives at NBC were trying to develop a new show that would air at 11:30 on Saturday nights, replacing the reruns of the *Tonight Show* that the network had been airing. The problem was that they couldn't find a producer with a concept that appealed to them. Michaels was approached by an NBC vice president, Dick Ebersol, with the prospect of pitching a show. He was told to meet two of NBC's top decision-makers in the Polo Lounge of the Beverly Hill Hotel. That meeting would change late night television history.

Setting the Stage

The show that Michaels pitched to the NBC executives that morning in the Polo Lounge was a radical departure from current television standards—and yet its foundation lay in practices from TV's early years. Michaels described the show as such: as its backbone, it would have a regular, troupe-style cast performing in various sketch pieces; it would be hosted by a different celebrity each week; a different musical guest would also be featured each week; it would highlight the work of unique artists such as filmmaker Albert Brooks and puppeteer Jim Henson; and, to the discomfort of the executives, the show would be produced live. Despite their reservations, the NBC executives liked Michaels's ideas enough to give him a chance at producing the show.

They decided to call the show *Saturday Night* (it would not be until 1977 that the word "live" was officially added to the title). The fact that live television had given way to prerecording and that live telecasts were basically limited to sporting events and news programs did little to faze Michaels. To the contrary, the prospect of a show in which mistakes could not be corrected and anything could happen excited the producer. As he told Lillian Ross in *Interview*, "I wanted to be able to combine television technique with theater technique. . . . The [television] technology meshing with the live comedy is a miracle." Further addressing his reasons for producing the show live, Michaels later told Rensin, "I believe *The Tonight Show* lost its soul when it moved out of New York and stopped being live. I liked it, when I was a kid, that they *were up* at eleven-thirty. People are different when they're up at eleven-thirty."

Saturday Night would be produced in New York City and broadcast from studio 8H in the network's facility at 30 Rockefeller Plaza. Once it was committed to a debut, Michaels set about building the team that would create the show. He assembled a group of writers and production staff based on people whose work he knew—or was at least familiar with. Among this group were the writing and performing team of Al Franken and Tom Davis, dark comedy specialist Michael O'Donoghue, and Michaels's wife at the time, Rosie Schuster. To make the show really work, however, the producer needed to put together a cast that could write as well as perform, that had little or no preconceptions regarding the limits of television, and, most importantly, that reflected his own comic sensibilities. In preparing the first show, Michaels explained to Winship, "I just did a show that I would watch if I were the audience. Everyone else I assembled in the first year really had just sprung from the audience. With one or two exceptions, they weren't people with very long resumes." For his seven cast members, to be dubbed the Not Ready for Prime Time Players (the name was later dropped in the early 1980s), Michaels chose a varied group of performers. Dan

Ackroyd was a writer and comedian with whom Michaels had worked when he and Pomerantz were producing their specials for the CBC. Ackroyd had previously worked with the Canadian version of the comedy troupe Second City. From a similar source, the National Lampoon comedy group, Michaels chose John Belushi, Chevy Chase, and Gilda Radner. To round the cast out he selected Laraine Newman, Jane Curtin, and Garrett Morris. The key players were in place, Michaels had the production staff he needed, now all that was required was getting America's late night television audiences to watch.

Live from New York . . . It's *Saturday Night!!*

Saturday Night's first show aired on October 11, 1975, with popular comedian George Carlin hosting. In homes across America, people tuned into a program that took chances, spoke frankly, and was a fresh departure from the usual television crop of sitcoms, police dramas, and variety shows hosted by egotistical celebrities. As *Playboy* described it, "The humor was hip, the music contemporary, and young urban adults responded enthusiastically." The second show featured a reunion of the legendary music duo (Paul) Simon and (Art) Garfunkel, who had disbanded in the early 1970s. Michaels's creation was up and running. As the first season progressed, several of the performers distinguished themselves with energetic and inspired performances, establishing several popular and recurring characters. A noteworthy performer on *SNL*'s maiden voyage was Chase, who captured viewers' attention with his dry, off-the-cuff delivery and his slapstick pratfalls, which he often performed in the show's prologue segment. It was these prologues, a traditional sequence preceding the show's theme music and opening credits, that ended with the now legendary line "Live, from New York, it's Saturday Night!," a signal to the audience that the show's festivities were under way.

As *SNL* grew in popularity, so too did the attention lavished on Chase. At the end of the first season, Chase announced that he would be leaving the show to pursue a career in the movies. The performer's departure was a harbinger of things to come for Michaels, as future years would see the defection of other cast members, lured by the stardom and financial rewards that Hollywood offered. To replace Chase, Michaels chose Bill Murray, a young comedian who had distinguished himself in his work with the Chicago chapter of Second City as well as the National Lampoon troupe. With the addition of Murray, the Not

Ready for Prime Time Players recovered from Chase's absence and began producing the shows that are considered definitive of *SNL*'s heyday.

Throughout the latter half of the 1970s, *Saturday Night Live* became the event of Saturday night television, with each of the Not Ready for Prime Time Players proving themselves key comedic players. Curtin assumed the reins of Chase's mock news segment, "Weekend Update" (which has, throughout the show's history, been a staple), and also created the role of Prymaat in the popular "Coneheads" skits. Newman specialized in parodies of the more outrageous personalities found in 1970s society, including spaced-out hippies, bubble-headed talk show hostesses, and jaded partygoers. And Morris not only proved himself a capable comedian but a gifted singer. Despite the strong work of these three performers, many critics consider the work done by Ackroyd, Belushi, Murray, and Radner during this time to be among the best ever presented on *SNL*. Ackroyd not only distinguished himself with a host of characters, including Beldar Conehead, sleazy cable-TV host

E. Buzz Miller, and ex-presidents Richard Nixon and Jimmy Carter, but as a linchpin on the show's writing staff. Belushi's kinetic energy was translated into such lasting performances as the Samurai warrior, a satiric Captain James T. Kirk (in a sketch spoof of the popular show *Star Trek*), and the proprietor of a Greek diner that offered a limited menu of cheeseburgers and cola ("No Coke ... Pepsi!"). Radner created such beloved characters as prissy "Weekend Update" commentator Emily Littella, crass "Update" commentator Rosanne Rosanna Danna, and the nerdish, runny-nosed Lisa Lupner. Playing a spastic Romeo to Lisa Lupner's bespectacled Juliet was the equally nerdy, sexually and scatologically obsessed Todd DeLamucca, created by Murray. Murray also came forth with a greasy, no-talent lounge singer and a variety of shallow egomaniacal game show hosts.

With the establishment of the Not Ready for Prime Time Players as recognizable stars, *SNL* reached its greatest popularity. The show was a top-rated success that audiences repeatedly watched. Michaels related to White in *Rolling Stone* that he felt

The success of characters like the Blues Brothers, played by Dan Ackroyd and John Belushi, spawned film and theater careers for several *Saturday Night Live* cast members and drained the show of much of its talent, hastening Michaels's decision to leave in 1980.

the show's success boiled down to the audience identifying with what *SNL* presented. As Michaels stated, "I always felt that the show at its best was a record of what had gone on that week in the country, the world, and in the lives of the people doing the show." Writing in *Interview*, Ross commented that the show was able to both challenge and entertain its audience using intellect and irreverence: "From the start, *Saturday Night Live* under Michaels, has been pitched ... to a higher level of sophistication than any other comedy on American network television. It was obvious that Michaels did not worry about whether his show was too sophisticated or not." Michaels responded in the same *Interview* article, "What we did, and what I was incredibly serious about doing, was to establish that in comedy it was and still is perfectly proper to question the official version of everything. We have always played to a *movie* and a *book* audience and not to the audience of television."

The combination of *SNL*'s success and the youth of the writers and cast fostered an era of camaraderie and fertile creativity; from the years 1975 to 1978, the show flourished. Michaels described these early years to Winship as a "state of grace." As time progressed, however, the environment of *SNL* began to change. Michaels told Winship: "I don't know how long groups can stay together in a kind of innocence. I think there's a point at which the age of experience takes over, and people view each other and themselves differently. They become conscious of 'Is this the best sketch for me to be doing?' The *work* ceases to be the guiding thing and this other word—*career*—begins to take over." Several of the cast members had embarked on outside projects during *SNL*'s summer vacations. Radner had parlayed many of her *SNL* characters into a hit stage show, *Gilda Live*—which Michaels cowrote, produced, and directed—and Radner, Curtin, and Newman had starred in a special, *Bob and Ray, Jane, Laraine, and Gilda*, with legendary radio comedians Bob Elliot and Ray Goulding. Following Chase's lead into movies, John Belushi took a role in the college fraternity comedy *National Lampoon's Animal House*. The movie became a large commercial success and Belushi became a viable movie star. Belushi and Ackroyd then teamed to make a movie adaption of their popular *SNL* characters the Blues Brothers. The taste of Hollywood success proved too alluring for Ackroyd and Belushi, and they announced that they would be leaving *SNL* at the end of the 1978 season.

Out with the Old, in with the New

The remainder of the cast, Curtin, Morris, Murray, Newman, and Radner returned for the 1979 season, joined by supporting players Harry Shearer, Don Novello (known primarily for his Father Guido Sarducci character), and the team of Franken and Davis. To many critics and viewers, however, it was clear that the *SNL* spark was fading. Michaels was upset by the departure of Belushi and Ackroyd, and he was also distressed by the current perception of the show. As he told Rensin in *Playboy*, "Everything we did was now popular. If we could do an old thing, we did. Worse, *Saturday Night Live* began to be perceived as a step, not an end. It changed the attitude of the people who worked there. I was trying to hold the show together.... It gave me all I needed, used all my talent, all my energy. But for others, it was time to move on." With the remaining cast members growing restless and his own attitude toward the show becoming jaded, Michaels announced his departure in 1980, at the end of *SNL*'s fifth season. The entire cast and crew of the show also left at the end of that season, marking the end of *SNL*'s first chapter.

With the old cast now pursuing careers in films, Michaels decided to distance himself from television for a while. As a result he lent his talents to producing occasional television specials and concert events, including Simon and Garfunkel's reunion concert in New York City's Central Park. He also built up his production company, Broadway Video, and produced a film, *Nothing Lasts Forever*, that was written and directed by former *SNL* writer Tom Schiller. By 1984, however, he was ready to commit himself to regular television work once again. NBC asked him to develop a new comedy show that would air at ten o'clock on Friday nights.

Assembling many of the writers from *SNL*, Michaels created a show that bore a format similar to his old show. Unlike *SNL*, however, Michaels's new show, titled *The New Show*, would not have a guest host. Rather, it would feature three guests—usually actors or comedians—per week who would join the regular cast in sketches. The show would also feature a special musical guest. Michaels assembled a small regular cast to work with each week's guests: well-known comedy writer and performer Buck Henry, *SCTV* (a Canadian comedy show similar to *SNL*) alumnus Dave Thomas, and comedian Valri Bromfield, whom Michaels had unsuccessfully recruited for the original cast of *SNL*. The show debuted in January of 1984 to a less than enthusiastic response from the network. Despite the fact that virtually the same creative team that had driven *SNL* to its zenith was working on it, *The New Show* could not quickly establish the viewer loyalty that its predecessor had enjoyed, and NBC was unwilling to give the show a lengthy chance to build an audience. *The New Show* was cancelled in March, three months after its debut.

While *The New Show* failed, its quick demise could not be compared to the troubles plaguing *Saturday Night Live* in the years after Michaels left the show. The season following Michaels's departure, NBC hired Jean Doumanian as the producer and charged her with putting together a new creative staff. Doumanian's new *Saturday Night Live* was greeted with brutal reviews, receiving negative publicity from a majority of the critics and viewers who watched it. Amid several behind the scenes conflicts, Doumanian, her entire production staff, and all but two of the cast members were fired. Dick Ebersol, the man who was instrumental in securing Michaels's position as creator and producer of *SNL* in 1975, assumed the role of producer in 1981. Ebersol produced one show before a writer's strike shut down production. After the strike, Ebersol managed to somewhat revitalize the show and simultaneously launch the careers of cast members Joe Piscopo and Eddie Murphy. But the show's budget had gone up and its ratings were not justifying the money. By the end of the 1985 season, Ebersol had left the show over a budget dispute and NBC began looking for a new producer.

Saturday Night Lorne ... Again

NBC contacted Michaels about returning to *SNL* in the spring of 1985. He accepted the network's offer and agreed to put together a new staff, work with a reduced budget, and deliver the first new show by November of that year. "When I was asked to return," Michaels told Susan Orlean in *Rolling Stone*, "everyone advised me against doing it. But it's what I do, so I decided to come back." Rather than resume his role as active producer, Michaels decided to let the Franken and Davis team handle that job. He would act as executive producer, contributing writing and advice and overseeing the entire production. Despite putting together a cast that featured some promising newcomers, Michaels's return season was plagued by a number of troubles. Foremost was the short amount of time that he had to put his first show together. Cast members and writers were hired in a rush and many of them had no experience

working in television. Several well-known actors, Anthony Michael Hall, Randy Quaid, and Robert Downey, Jr., were hired to improve the appeal of the all new cast. As the season got underway, however, many critics complained that these film actors were out of place in *SNL*'s live comedy arena and were actually a detriment to the show. It also didn't help the show that, after ten seasons, it was no longer seen as a novel concept. By the end of the season, NBC laid out plans to cancel *Saturday Night Live*.

Michaels managed to save *SNL* from cancellation by appealing to NBC entertainment president Brandon Tartikoff. He promised Tartikoff a significant change in the cast and writing staff and also guaranteed the executive better ratings. Retaining only two performers, Nora Dunn and Dennis Miller, from the 1985 season, Michaels set about recruiting a new cast. This time he used the ethic that had guided him in selecting the first *SNL* cast in 1975. He went for virtual unknowns, people who were hungry and were fighting for territory in the comedy landscape. Joining Dunn and Miller for the 1986 season were Jon Lovitz, Victoria Jackson,

Returning to *SNL* in 1985, Michaels revitalized the ailing show with new, recurring characters like the androgynous Pat (Julia Sweeney, center), some of whom became the subjects of successful movie spinoffs.

Phil Hartman, Dana Carvey, Jan Hooks, and supporting player Kevin Nealon. Reviews for the new ensemble were enthusiastic and viewers once again began watching. Bolstered by the cast and a revitalized staff of writers, Michaels's *SNL* once again bloomed into a popular show.

As they had in the show's first incarnation, recurring characters began appearing on *SNL* and gaining popularity among viewers. There was Lovitz's Tommy Flanagan, a pathological liar whose catchphrase was "Yeah, that's the ticket!" Hooks and Dunn created the Sweeney Sisters, a terrible singing duo whose roots could be traced back to Bill Murray's lounge singer. And Carvey brought forth a host of characters and impersonations, including Andy Rooney, Jimmy Stewart, and U.S. president George Bush. Carvey also contributed the Church Lady, a holier-than-thou TV evangelist who is fond of sarcastically proclaiming "Isn't that special?!?" when guests on her show display prideful behavior. As *SNL* progressed through the late 1980s, its popularity grew. In an interview with Bob Guccione, Jr. in *Spin*, Michaels attributed the show's rebirth to some troubleshooting he did at the end of the 1985 season: "By the end of '85, I was able to see: Wait a minute, we need ... we don't have enough of this. So I tried bringing in two or three key performers who could balance what I already had, a couple of writers who were better writers for them." Michaels also began featuring players who would earn their stripes in supporting roles and eventually become full cast members. Nealon was added to the cast in this manner, as were Mike Myers, Chris Rock, and Chris Farley. By maintaining a steady influx of new talent, Michaels was able to weather the defections of key cast members like Miller, Hooks, and Carvey without having the whole show fall apart in the process. His formula worked so well that by the early 1990s, *SNL* was enjoying its highest ratings ever—this despite personnel changes.

Branches out from *SNL*

As Michaels made his return to *SNL* in 1985, he was also expanding his influence in other areas. During his years away from the show he had developed his company Broadway Video, which, in addition to creating new programs, administered the syndication of *SNL* reruns. He also returned to the business of making movies, a venture he had unsuccessfully attempted in the late 1970s with *Nothing Lasts Forever* and *SNL* writer O'Donoghue's *Mr. Mike's Mondo Video*. This time teaming with comedian and frequent *SNL* host

Steve Martin and singer/songwriter Randy Newman, Michaels wrote the script for a film called *The Three Amigos*, which he also produced. The film stars Martin along with former *SNL* cast members Chevy Chase and Martin Short, who appeared on the show during Dick Ebersol's reign as producer.

Chase, Martin, and Short star as Dusty Bottoms, Lucky Day, and Ned Nederlander, silent movie stars who are known collectively as the Three Amigos. Dressed in sombreros and Mexican-style costumes, the Amigos are a colorful crime-fighting team patrolling the western frontier in Hollywood films. Bottoms, Day, and Nederlander feel that their Amigo characters are popular American icons who deserve more respect—in the form of money. So the three confront the head of the studio that produces the Three Amigo films and demand more money. The studio boss laughs in their faces and throws them out on their collective behinds.

Things appear dark for the Amigos until a telegram arrives from Mexico. A young woman named Carmen has requested a performance by the Three Amigos in her village, and she has promised to pay the actors handsomely for their services. The three immediately agree to appear. Unknown to the Amigos, however, Carmen's communique was poorly translated. Having seen newsreel footage of the Amigos rescuing a town and then refusing reward money, Carmen believes that the three men are real heroes carrying out egalitarian crusades against evil. She has asked them to come—free of charge—and rescue her poor village from the terrors of the outlaw El Guapo. The Amigos arrive in town with the belief that they will be playacting a gun battle, but instead come face-to-face with the deadly serious El Guapo. In the climax, the three actors must live up to their screen personas and actually rescue the town.

Critical reaction to *The Three Amigos* was mixed, with most reviewers agreeing upon the film's lightheartedness. *Washington Post* contributor Rita Kempley had the least patience for the film, calling it "the cinematic equivalent of Montezuma's revenge [diarrhea]." Writing in the *New York Times*, Janet Maslin complained of the film's excessive indulgence in sets and bad jokes, but she did praise the film as "likable" with "a strain of subtle wit," proclaiming that *The Three Amigos'* "best gags reflect an enjoyable sophistication." Finding the film very entertaining, Patrick Goldstein wrote in the *Los Angeles Times*: "There's hardly a moment in 'Three Amigos' that isn't silly—make that incredibly, outrageously and breathtakingly silly. Maybe that's why this tale ... is such a goofy

Michaels served as executive producer for a Canadian television show starring The Kids in the Hall, a comedy troupe he discovered while on a talent search in Toronto.

delight." Goldstein went on to praise the film as "one of the daffiest comedies of the year."

In addition to making *The Three Amigos,* Michaels also became involved in a number of other television projects. He served as executive producer for the program *Michelob Presents Sunday Night,* which was hosted by jazz musician David Sanborn and featured musicians from a variety of backgrounds getting together and jamming. When he was faced with the possibility of NBC cancelling *SNL,* Michaels went in search of new talent. While in Toronto, Canada, he came across a comedy troupe called The Kids in the Hall (the moniker is taken from the nickname comedian Jack Benny bestowed upon his writing staff). Michaels was

interested in recruiting fresh talent for the beleaguered *SNL,* but as he told Guccione in *Spin,* "I've always had a sort of taboo in my mind about breaking up comedy groups. I just know how hard it is for an ensemble to get together." Despite seeing potential *SNL* cast members among the Kids, Michaels admired their comedy too much to risk breaking up the group. Instead, he became the troupe's executive producer and arranged a deal for them with the Home Box Office (HBO) cable channel. The Kids in the Hall proved so popular on HBO that CBS offered them a late night network spot. The group amicably separated with Michaels when they signed with CBS in 1992. Despite the comparisons made between *The Kids in the Hall* and *SNL*, Michaels told Guccione that he doesn't view the show as a rival: "I think they do something different than what we do here and I think that they're brilliant."

Wayne's World! Party Time, It's Excellent!

With the re-emergence of *Saturday Night Live* as a powerful comedic voice, Michaels's talents as a creator became an in-demand commodity. In the early 1990s, he signed a production deal with Paramount Pictures, agreeing to create and produce a series of motion picture comedies for the studio. For his first film Michaels went to familiar territory. Approached by *SNL* cast member Mike Myers about making a film, Michaels suggested expanding the popular "Wayne's World" sketch into a feature. Like the sketch, the resulting movie is titled *Wayne's World* and, in a loose narrative, follows the exploits of teenagers Wayne Campbell, played by Myers, and his faithful sidekick Garth Algar, played by *SNL* regular Dana Carvey.

Wayne's World the movie opens much the same way that "Wayne's World" the sketch opens on *SNL*. Wayne and Garth are seated on the couch in Wayne's basement. Wayne is tunelessly chainsawing chords on his electric guitar to the accompaniment of Garth's drumsticks as they meatily collide with his thighs. It is the opening sequence to the duo's cable access show, titled, oddly enough, "Wayne's World." As Wayne and Garth go through their usual program of aesthetic appreciation (ogling a poster of model Claudia Schiffer), consumer product reviews (the Suck Cut, a new invention that sucks hair as it cuts), and witty verbal sparring ("No Way!" "Way!" "No Way!" "Way!!"), the scene shifts to a young couple watching the show. As fate would have it, the man is a television producer on a quest for a new television program to lure in big advertising dollars. Thirty seconds of Wayne and Garth's adolescent banter and party-on attitude convince him that "Wayne's World" is the show that he is seeking.

The producer meets with Wayne and Garth, and, innocently believing in the producer's goodwill, they soon sign a Faustian deal. As the show goes into production, Wayne and Garth are horrified to learn that the set for "Wayne's World" has been moved from Wayne's basement to a monstrous studio that has been made up to look like Wayne's basement—only cleaner. They are further unsettled to find that all of the dialogue for the new "Wayne's World" has been written out for them

on cue cards. The final straw is when the duo are informed by the producer that they must conduct an on-air interview with the show's greasy sponsor. Wayne goes along with this, but while he conducts the interview as it has been written, he holds up cue cards that only the audience can see. To the chagrin of the producer, Wayne is displaying cards that indicate that the sponsor is a "sphincter boy" who engages in sexual acts with farm animals. When the producer threatens to fire Wayne and Garth and replace them, the two tell him that's fine, they'll just go back to doing "Wayne's World" from Wayne's basement. Unfortunately, the boys did not read the fine print on their contract. The producer owns the rights to the show. To add insult to injury, the producer is attempting to steal Wayne's girlfriend, the sultry rock singer Cassandra, away from Wayne. The film climaxes with Wayne and Garth battling the producer to regain their beloved show.

While *Wayne's World* has a loose plot, most of the attention the film received focused on the characters of Wayne and Garth; the storyline is a backdrop for Myers and Carvey to display their comedic talents. The film went on to tremendous success, becoming the number one money-maker of 1992. *Wayne's World* appealed to young adults, who incorporated such Wayne and Garth phrases as "Yeah, and monkeys might fly out my butt!!" (a dismissal of a patently absurd statement), "Schwing!" (an admission of sexual arousal), and the immensely popular "Not!" (which is a sarcastic tag that follows a falsely sincere statement) into their everyday speech. While many adults (mostly parents of the kids mimicking Wayne and Garth) found the film ridiculous beyond compare, several critics were quick to notice *Wayne's World*'s lightheaded appeal. As Anne Billson wrote in the *New Statesman and Society*, "the jokes come thick and fast. Some *are* just thick, but the best are howlingly clever." *New York* contributor David Denby stated that the film "is funny in a nagging sort of way." "*Wayne's World* is a goofy, good-natured comedy," affirmed Brian D. Johnson in *Maclean's*, "a movie so wilfully sophomoric that no matter how inane it gets, it never loses its charm."

Invasion of *The Coneheads*

"In a world of recycled entertainment in which movies end up being pilots for television shows . . . and old television shows turn out to be previews for movies . . . it makes perfect sense to take . . . characters whose natural comedic life span is about five minutes and extend it by a factor of twenty."

This sentiment stated by Emily Yoffe in *Rolling Stone* regarding the justification of making a movie out of the "Wayne's World" skit was echoed by Michaels. The success of the *Wayne's World* film proved to him that, done properly, characters from short pieces could be sustained throughout longer formats. So, in 1993, Michaels again parlayed an *SNL* sketch into a full-length motion picture. Going back to the show's "golden" era, Michaels met with former cast member Ackroyd to formulate a movie idea based on one of *SNL*'s most popular and enduring sketches, "The Coneheads." The movie that Michaels ended up producing is titled simply *The Coneheads* and was released in the summer of 1993. It tells the story of the familiar Conehead family, Beldar, his wife Prymaat (played, respectively, by Ackroyd and Curtin in a reprisal of the roles they originated on *SNL*), and their daughter Connie, natives of the planet Remulak.

As the movie opens, the Conehead family has crash-landed their spaceship on the planet Earth—specifically, the state of New Jersey. Deciding to assimilate into the native culture and learn as much as they can about the human race, the aliens pose as a normal American family. The problem is they are not normal. As their name indicates, they have enormous, pointed heads. In addition, they employ an odd vocabulary—delivered in clipped, mechanical tones—that sets them apart from humans. And then there is their eating habits. The Coneheads have voracious appetites for "mass quantities" of food and beer, which they "consume" by simultaneously opening all of the cans in a six pack and pouring all seventy-two ounces down their throats in one powerful swallow. Despite these abnormalities, the Coneheads are accepted by their neighbors as a nice normal family who have just moved to New Jersey from Remulak, which, the neighbors are led to believe, is a little-known town in France. Problems arise when an agent for the United States Immigration and Naturalization Service begins to track the Coneheads. The agent believes that the Coneheads are illegal aliens from France and he wants to deport them. Further conflicts arise when the family is summoned back to Remulak to answer to their leaders. The Remulakians wish to colonize Earth, and the Coneheads must decide where their allegiance lies: with their native planet or their newly adopted home.

In Praise of Lorne

Despite his success with movies, however, Michaels is still most often associated with his television work. "Michaels revolutionized late-night television with a live show that defied network censors," Johnson wrote of the series in another *Maclean's* article. *Saturday Night Live* and Lorne Michaels are often mentioned in the same breath, and to many he is the personification of the show. Critics such as Johnson have pointed to Michaels's work on the show as defining modern comedy on television. As Elizabeth Kolbert wrote in the *Detroit Free Press,* "By now *SNL* has been on the air so long it has shaped the comic sensibilities of an entire generation."

For all of the praise directed toward *SNL* and its creator, Michaels is modest about the work that he and his numerous cohorts have produced since 1975. In his discussion with Rensin, Michaels explained his *SNL* career by way of Stanley Myron Handelman's variation on the monkey/typewriter theory: if a group of monkeys are placed in a room with typewriters, they will eventually write the entire works of Shakespeare. As Michaels related to Rensin: "He [Handelman] left the monkeys in the room, and a couple of weeks later, he looked in on them, and he said, 'You know something? They were just fooling around.'" Michaels continued, "I always loved that joke because for me it represented what we were doing at the show: We were just fooling around." When Rensin later asked him if he agreed that *SNL* was his life's work, Michaels responded: "To a large extent. Being with the show has been like meeting somebody and falling in love when you're young, and it ends up that it's the person you're with for your entire life—and you think you must have made some mistake."

Although Michaels jokes about his role as a comedy innovator, others are quick to appraise his worth and the reasons for his successes. Ross wrote in *Interview* that "Michaels is attracted to talented people, and talented people are attracted to him." This holds true in Michaels's friendships as well as his business relationships. He has many close friends in the artistic community, a few of whom summarized Michaels for Ross. Singer/songwriter Paul Simon said of Michaels: "His intelligence is exhibited in the context of his wit. People are attracted to Lorne because they feel safe with his comedic sensibility. All this makes him the perfect producer." Writer/director Mike Nichols (*Catch-22, Silkwood*) also described his friend to Ross: "The main thing about Lorne is his generosity. He sees people in the most positive way, and then they become their best selves. As an artist and as a friend, Lorne demonstrates more loyalty and love through his acts than anyone else I know. As his humor is unsentimental in the extreme, I think it is the tension and the contradiction between his heartless humor and the great heart with which he lives that distinguishes him from others in his field. He's also very cute, and that's why the girls like him.''

■ Works Cited

Billson, Anne, ''Screen Dreamers,'' *New Statesman and Society,* May 22, 1992, p. 36.

Denby, David, ''Saturday Night Dumb,'' *New York,* February 24, 1992, p. 118.

Goldstein, Patrick, ''Rib-Tickling Corn in 'Three Amigos,''' *Los Angeles Times,* December 12, 1986.

Guccione, Bob, Jr., *Spin,* February, 1993, pp. 65-69, 90-93.

Hill, Doug, and Jeff Weingrad, *Saturday Night: A Backstage History of Saturday Night Live,* Morrow, 1987, pp. 32-41, 480-505.

Johnson, Brian D., ''From Gags to Riches,'' *Maclean's,* June 9, 1986, pp. 38-41.

Johnson, Brian D., ''Heavy-Metal Hilarity,'' *Maclean's,* February 24, 1992, p. 58.

Kempley, Rita, ''Adios, Amigos,'' *Washington Post,* December 12, 1986.

Kolbert, Elizabeth, ''Michaels to 'Grow up' in Post-midnight Slot,'' *Detroit Free Press,* March 22, 1993, p. 7D.

Marc, David, *Voice,* November 19, 1985, p. 33.

Maslin, Janet, *New York Times,* December 12, 1986.

Myers, Mike, Bonnie Turner, and Terry Turner, *Wayne's World* (film script), Paramount, 1992.

Orlean, Susan, '''Saturday Night' Alive!,'' *Rolling Stone,* June 19, 1986, pp. 33-34, 96.

Rensin, David, *Playboy,* March, 1992, pp. 51-64.

Ross, Lillian, ''Saturday Night Lorne,'' *Interview,* June, 1988, pp. 53-61, 113-15.

White, Timothy, ''Saturday Night Quarterback,'' *Rolling Stone,* December 27, 1979.

Winship, Michael, *Television,* Random House, 1988, pp. 196-203.

Yoffe, Emily, *Rolling Stone,* March 19, 1992, pp. 34-40.

■ For More Information See

PERIODICALS

Details, March, 1993, pp. 103-08.

Films in Review, February, 1987, pp. 97-98.

Metro Times (Detroit), July 28/August 3, 1993, p. 29.

Newsweek, December 18, 1986, p. 83; April 13, 1987, p. 70.

New York, January 9, 1984, pp. 41-43.

New York Times, October 1, 1989, pp. 31, 40.

Rolling Stone, November 20, 1986, pp. 45-46.

Time, December 29, 1986, p. 71.°

—Sketch by David M. Galens

L. M. Montgomery

Personal

Full name, Lucy Maud Montgomery; born November 30, 1874, in Clifton (now New London), Prince Edward Island, Canada; died April 24, 1942, in Toronto, Ontario, Canada; buried in Cavendish Cemetery, Cavendish, Prince Edward Island; daughter of Hugh John (a merchant) and Clara Woolner (Macneill) Montgomery; married Ewan Macdonald (a Presbyterian minister), July 5, 1911; children: Chester Cameron, Hugh Alexander, Ewan Stuart. *Education:* Prince of Wales College, Charlottetown, Prince Edward Island, second-class teacher's certificate, 1894, first-class teacher's license, 1895; attended Dalhousie College (now Dalhousie University), Halifax, Nova Scotia, 1895-96. *Hobbies and other interests:* Knitting, crocheting, astronomy, sewing, designing needlepoint lace, books, photography, the outdoors.

Addresses

Home—Toronto, Ontario, Canada.

Career

Novelist and author for children. Schoolteacher in Bideford, Prince Edward Island, 1894-95 and 1896-97, and Belmont Lot 16 and Lower Bedeque, Prince Edward Island, 1897-98; assistant postmistress, Cavendish, Prince Edward Island, 1898-1911; staff member, Halifax *Daily Echo,* 1901-02. *Member:* Royal Society of Arts and Letters, Canadian Authors Association, Canadian Women's Press Association, Toronto Woman's Press.

Awards, Honors

Royal Society of Arts fellow, 1923; Officer, Order of the British Empire, 1935; a Canadian stamp has been issued commemorating Montgomery and *Anne of Green Gables;* various museums on Prince Edward Island have been dedicated to Montgomery; *Anne of Green Gables* has appeared on several children's "favorites" lists in North America and Eastern Europe.

Writings

"ANNE" SERIES

Anne of Green Gables (also see below), illustrated by M. A. and W. A. J. Claus, Page, 1908.
Anne of Avonlea (also see below), illustrated by George Gibbs, Page, 1909.
Chronicles of Avonlea: In Which Anne Shirley of Green Gables and Avonlea Plays Some Part (short stories), illustrated by Gibbs, Page, 1912.
Anne of the Island, illustrated by H. Weston Taylor, Page, 1915.

Anne's House of Dreams (also see below), Stokes, 1917.

Rainbow Valley, Stokes, 1919.

Further Chronicles of Avonlea: Which Have to Do with Many Personalities and Events in and about Avonlea (short stories), illustrated by John Goss, Page, 1920.

Rilla of Ingleside, Stokes, 1921.

Anne of Windy Poplars, Stokes, 1936, published as *Anne of Windy Willows*, McClelland & Stewart, 1936.

Anne of Ingleside, Stokes, 1939.

Anne of Green Gables has appeared in several editions with different illustrators and has been translated into sixty languages; the "Anne" series has been translated into more than thirty-five languages.

OTHER NOVELS

Kilmeny of the Orchard (also see below), illustrated by George Gibbs, Page, 1910.

The Story Girl (also see below), illustrated by Gibbs, Page, 1911.

The Golden Road (sequel to *The Story Girl;* also see below), illustrated by Gibbs, Page, 1913.

Emily of New Moon, Stokes, 1923.

Emily Climbs, McClelland & Stewart, 1924, Stokes, 1925.

The Blue Castle, Stokes, 1926.

Emily's Quest, Stokes, 1927.

Magic for Marigold, McClelland & Stewart, 1927, Stokes, 1929.

A Tangled Web, Stokes, 1931, published as *Aunt Becky Began It*, Hodder & Stoughton, c. 1931.

Pat of Silver Bush, Stokes, 1933.

Mistress Pat: A Novel of Silver Bush, Stokes, 1935.

Jane of Lantern Hill, Stokes, 1937.

POSTHUMOUSLY PUBLISHED COLLECTIONS

The Green Gables Letters, from L. M. Montgomery to Ephraim Weber, 1905-1909, edited by Wilfrid Eggleston, Ryerson, 1960.

The Alpine Path: The Story of My Career (autobiographical articles originally published as a series in the Toronto magazine *Everywoman's World*, 1917), Fitzhenry & Whiteside, 1974.

The Road to Yesterday (short stories), McGraw/Ryerson, 1974.

The Doctor's Sweetheart and Other Stories, selected and introduced by Catherine McLay, McGraw/Ryerson, 1979.

My Dear Mr. M.: Letters to G. B. MacMillan from L. M. Montgomery, edited by Francis W. P. Bolger and Elizabeth R. Epperly, McGraw/Ryerson, 1980.

Spirit of Place: Lucy Maud Montgomery and Prince Edward Island, selected and edited by Bolger, photography by Wayne Barrett and Anne MacKay, Oxford University Press, 1982.

The Selected Journals of L. M. Montgomery, Volume 1: *1889-1910*, Volume 2: *1910-1921*, Volume 3: *1921-1929*, edited by Mary Rubio and Elizabeth Waterston, Oxford University Press, 1985-93.

Anne of Green Gables: Three Volumes in One (includes *Anne of Green Gables*, *Anne of Avonlea*, and *Anne's House of Dreams*), Avenel Books, 1986.

The Poetry of Lucy Maud Montgomery, selected and introduced by John Ferns and Kevin McCabe, Fitzhenry & Whiteside, 1987.

Akin to Anne: Tales of Other Orphans (short stories), edited by Rea Wilmhurst, McClelland, 1988.

Along the Shore: Tales by the Sea, edited by Wilmhurst, McClelland, 1989.

Among the Shadows: Tales from the Darker Side, edited by Wilmhurst, McClelland, 1990.

Days of Dreams and Laughter: The Story Girl and Other Tales (includes *The Story Girl*, *The Golden Road*, and *Kilmeny of the Orchard*), Avenel, 1990.

OTHER

The Watchman, and Other Poems, McClelland & Stewart, 1916, Stokes, 1917.

(With Mary E. MacGregor under pseudonym Marian Keith, and Mabel Burns McKinley) *Courageous Women* (biography), McClelland & Stewart, 1934.

Excerpts from Montgomery's writings appear in *The Years before "Anne": The Early Career of Lucy Maud Montgomery*, by Francis W. P. Bolger, Prince Edward Island Heritage Foundation, 1974. Contributor of articles, verses, and short stories to magazines and newspapers.

■ **Adaptations**

Anne of Green Gables has been adapted into motion pictures, released by Realart Pictures, 1919, and RKO Radio Pictures, 1934; a stage production by Wilbur Braun, published by Samuel French, 1937; a filmstrip released by the National Film Board of Canada, 1953; a musical by Donald Harron and Norman Campbell, presented yearly at the Charlottetown Summer Festival, Prince Edward Island, 1965—, published by Samuel French, 1972; a television play by Julia Jones, BBC-1, 1972, and a televised sequel based on *Anne of Avonlea* and *Anne of the Island*, 1975; a television play by Kevin Sullivan and Joe Wiesenfeld, *WonderWorks*, PBS, c. 1986, and a sequel, *Anne of Avonlea: The Continuing Story of Anne of Green Gables* (also see below), by Sullivan, The Disney Channel, 1987; other television productions based on *Green Gables* have aired on CBC. *Green Gables* has also been adapted into several children's editions, including *A Child's Anne: Adapted from Lucy Maud Montgomery's Anne of Green Gables*, by Deirdre Kessler, illustrated by Floyd Trainor, Ragweed Press, 1983. And *Anne of Green Gables: The Sequel* was adapted by Fiona McHugh as a companion volume to the TV production, *Anne of Avonlea: The Continuing Story of Anne of Green Gables*, Firefly Books, 1987.

Anne of Windy Poplars has been adapted into a motion picture, released by RKO Radio Pictures, 1940; and *Jane of Lantern Hill* has been adapted into an audiocassette, narrated by Marion Bennett, released by Bantam Audio, 1989, and a television play, co-written by Sullivan, The Disney Channel, 1990. A television feature, based in part on Montgomery's diaries, aired on CBC, 1974.

■ Sidelights

"'The five-thirty train has been in and gone half an hour ago,' answered that brisk official. 'But there was a passenger dropped off for you—a little girl. She's sitting out there on the shingles. I asked her to go into the ladies' waiting room, but she informed me gravely that she preferred to stay outside. "There was more scope for the imagination," she said. She's a case, I should say.'

"'I'm not expecting a girl,' said Matthew blankly. 'It's a boy I've come for. He should be here. Mrs. Alexander Spencer was to bring him over from Nova Scotia for me.'

"The stationmaster whistled.

"'Guess there's some mistake,' he said."

Thus begins Anne Shirley's new life in Prince Edward Island, with her adoptive guardian finding out at the train station that the orphanage sent a girl, instead of the boy that was requested. This red-headed, imaginative heroine of L. M. Montgomery's *Anne of Green Gables* is a memorable character who has appealed to many readers, especially young adults, since the novel's first publication in 1908. According to *Canadian Children's Literature* contributor T. D. MacLulich, Mark Twain once called Anne "the dearest, and most lovable child in fiction since the immortal Alice." Canadian author Montgomery is best known for her popular "Anne" series, which follows the life of an orphan from adoption through marriage, family, and old age, beginning with *Anne of Green Gables*. Montgomery also wrote many other novels, including several other series, poetry, and short stories, while her letters and journals have been separately collected and published posthumously. Montgomery had many titles in her life—including wife, mother, and teacher—but above all, she was a writer.

Montgomery's Life

Born on Prince Edward Island, Canada, Montgomery was raised on the Island by her maternal grandparents after the death of her mother when Montgomery was two years old. Christened Lucy Maud, she insisted on being called Maud as she grew up. Her grandparents, a pair of strict Presbyterians, raised Montgomery in their Cavendish farmhouse in a religious environment and isolated her from much social involvement with other children. "I had no companionship except that of books and solitary rambles in wood and fields," wrote Montgomery in one of her many journals, as quoted by Mollie Gillen in *The Wheel of Things: A Biography of L. M. Montgomery, Author of "Anne of Green Gables."* "This drove me in on myself and early forced me to construct for myself a world of fancy and imagination very different indeed from the world in which I lived." Her natural surroundings gave her a "passport to fairyland" as she used her imagination to escape the day to day life on the farm.

Montgomery also recalled in her journals that childish pranks were met with commands to kneel and pray to God for forgiveness, even while the flame of rebellion still smoldered. "The enforced confessions and prayers left Montgomery with a feeling of profound humiliation and a confused sense that religion was, like sex, necessary but shameful," noted Francis Frazer in the *Dictionary of Literary Biography*. While Montgomery's grandparents fulfilled the material side of her childhood needs, they were unable to supply the additional emotional and mental support she required. As a sensitive child, she was especially vulnerable, and when her grandmother harshly reminded her of such things as her father's abandonment of Maud, she recoiled into her own world.

Hugh John Montgomery, L. M. Montgomery's father, eventually settled in Saskatchewan in 1887, remarried, and later sent for his daughter. Unfortunately, his attempts to reunite his family were

The first novel in the series that has delighted millions of young readers.

The most beloved, beguiling and timeless heroine in all of fiction

Anne of Green Gables

by L. M. Montgomery

The exploits of orphaned Anne Shirley, one of the most beloved heroines in children's literature, are chronicled in this 1908 work.

unsuccessful because his bride and his daughter could not get along. When fifteen-year-old Montgomery had to stay out of school to help with her half-brother and half-sister, this only caused further unhappiness. Gillen excerpted from the diaries: "I am ready to cut my throat in despair. Oh I *couldn't* live another year in this place if I were paid a thousand dollars an hour." In 1891, Montgomery returned to live with her grandparents.

The next few years saw Montgomery in school, on both sides of the teacher's desk. In 1894, she earned her teaching certificate at Prince of Wales College in Charlottetown, and in 1895, she received her first class license to teach. She taught at schools throughout the Island until her grandfather's death in 1898. At that time she left the teaching profession in order to return home to

Cavendish to help her grandmother, who had been appointed postmistress of the town. Except for a brief period from the fall of 1901 to June of 1902, when she moved to Halifax to work for the *Daily Echo*, Montgomery stayed with, worked for, and nursed her grandmother until the woman's death in March of 1911.

On July 5, 1911, Montgomery married the Reverend Ewan Macdonald. They had secretly been engaged since 1906. While a youthful infatuation with a local farmer had shown Montgomery glimpses of what she termed the "flame divine," she felt that a marriage based on mutual affection, close ages, and common interests and social positions had an excellent chance for happiness. "After all, this is a practical world and marriage must share in its practicalities," as she wrote in a letter to George Boyd MacMillan quoted by Gillen. The newly married couple moved to a parish in Leaskdale, Ontario, a farming community near Toronto. In 1925, they moved to another parish in Norval, Ontario. Montgomery gave birth to three sons, one of whom was still born, in the early years of her marriage. These years were to become her most productive as a writer. Unfortunately, they were also very trying mentally, emotionally, and physically.

As a minister's wife, Montgomery was a public figure in the community. Her husband was prone to long-lasting episodes of deep depression, and Montgomery felt it was her duty to shield his disorder from his congregation. In a letter written in 1941 quoted by Gillen, Montgomery noted: "My husband is very miserable. I have tried to keep the secret of his melancholic attacks for twenty years, as people do not want a minister who is known to be such." In 1919, Macdonald was diagnosed with nervous prostration, and in 1935 he had a complete breakdown that forced him into retirement.

Among her difficulties, Montgomery was also involved with a lengthy lawsuit against her first publisher, L. C. Page. Initiated in 1919, the suit concerned royalties and a collection of stories Page published that Montgomery thought had been destroyed. After nine years of suit and counter suit, she won the case, but the stress only added to her other problems. Along with the strain of coping with her husband's mental disorder, Montgomery had health problems of her own, especially towards the end of her life. The years of covering for her husband took their toll, as did worries about her law suit, the two world wars, and her own concerns. In 1938, she suffered a physical and nervous breakdown, and another in 1940. She never completely recovered and died on April 24, 1942.

The Young Writer

As a child, Montgomery began keeping journals. In a quote from one of them, selected for use in the introduction to *The Selected Journals of L. M. Montgomery* edited by Mary Rubio and Elizabeth Waterston, Montgomery wrote, "Temperaments such as mine *must* have some outlet, else they become poisoned and morbid by 'consuming their own smoke.' And the only safe outlet is in some record such as this." Montgomery kept a record her entire life. At first, it was more of a game, a way to express her love of wordplay and to foster her dream of becoming a writer. "I wrote about all the little incidents of my existence," she commented in *The Alpine Path: The Story of My Career*. "I wrote descriptions of my favourite haunts, biographies of my many cats, histories of visits, and school affairs, and even critical reviews of the books I had read."

Later, as Montgomery grew up and became more introspective, the journals were a method of keeping herself in control and a place to express her thoughts. As a minister's wife, especially, she had to be circumspect, and her inner life kept private. Gradually, she forged what she termed a "life document." The journals from her childhood also served as a source for her later writings, a chance to recapture the innocence and wonder of a child. Rubio and Waterston commented, "An unhappily married woman [of the time] had no dignified course but to bear her pain in silence—unless, of course, she was a skilful writer who could sublimate her tensions by creating fiction and express her personal feelings in a journal. Unlike the average woman of her time, Montgomery managed to find a voice. In her fiction it was indirect. . . . But in her journals she gave vent to her feelings, believing that she herself, and those discussed, would be in their graves before her words were heard."

From childhood, writing was Montgomery's dream. In *Writers for Children* she was quoted by Jon C. Stott as saying: "I cannot remember the time when I was not writing, or when I did not mean to be an author. To write has always been my central purpose toward which every effort and hope and ambition of my life has grouped itself." To that end, Montgomery wrote something every day. In her childhood stories, as she explained in *The Alpine Path*, "battle, murder and sudden death

were the order of the day." In 1890, at the age of sixteen, her poem, *On Cape Le Force*, was published in Charlottetown's newspaper. "It was the first sweet bubble on the cup of success and of course it intoxicated me," declared Montgomery in her journals, as quoted by Gillen. Shortly after, she started publishing articles, essays, short stories, and verse in other newspapers. But it wasn't until 1895 that she started receiving financial payment for her work with the publication of the poem, *Our Charivari*, in a Philadelphia magazine. "I am frankly in literature to make my living out of it," Montgomery wrote in a letter cited by Gillen. "My prose sells and so I write it, although I prefer writing verse. I know that I can never be a really great writer. My aspiration is limited to this—I want to be a good *workman* in my chosen profession. I cannot be one of the masters but I hope to attain to a recognized position among the everyday workers of my time."

Montgomery's works have established her as a notable author of books for young adults. Her first novel, *Anne of Green Gables*, inspired by the title character, spawned a series of eight books and two slightly connected story collections. Other successful series include one focusing on Emily Byrd Starr, a childhood writer who grows up in the space of three books, beginning with *Emily of New Moon*, and becomes a professional writer by the series' conclusion. Montgomery's most popular and successful books have been about children, from young adults to those adults who never completely grew up. As Frazer describes the author's work, "Montgomery's childhood was crucial to the nature of her writing, for all of her successfully realized characters *are* children, in spirit if not in years."

All about Anne

"In the end, I never deliberately sat down and said . . . 'write a book.' It really all just 'happened,'" explained Montgomery in *The Alpine Path*, describing the beginnings of *Anne of Green Gables*. While looking for story ideas in one of her notebooks, she came across an old entry, "Elderly couple apply to orphan asylum for a boy. By mistake a girl is sent them." She thought this would make a nice story for the serial she wanted to write. "I began to block out the chapters, devise, and select incidents and 'brood up' my heroine. Anne . . . began to expand in such a fashion that she soon seemed very real to me and took possession of me to an unusual extent. She appealed to me, and I thought it rather a shame to waste her on an ephemeral little serial.

Then the thought came, 'Write a book. You have the central idea. All you need do is to spread it out over enough chapters to amount to a book.'"

Anne of Green Gables became that book, the one for which Montgomery is most widely recognized. The novel took shape in the evenings between the spring of 1904 and the fall of 1905. But when Montgomery sent the finished volume off to several publishers, she received only rejection slips. She then put the book away for two years before revising and submitting it to the Boston publishing company L. C. Page. On April 8, 1907, Montgomery received an acceptance letter, and in slightly more than a year, *Anne of Green Gables* was published. Montgomery cited a journal entry in *The Alpine Path*, written on the day of her first book's publication: "My book came today.... I

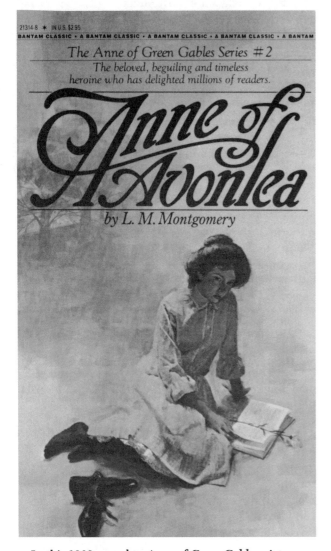

In this 1909 sequel to *Anne of Green Gables*, sixteen-year-old Anne finds adventure, begins a teaching career, and falls in love.

candidly confess that it was to me a proud and wonderful and thrilling moment. There, in my hand, lay material realization of all the dreams and hopes and ambitions of my whole conscious existence—my first book. Not a great book, but mine, mine, mine, something which I had created."

Anne of Green Gables was extremely popular and went through several printings the first year. Intended mainly for a young female audience, readers of all ages and both sexes have read and enjoyed the book. The story involves an orphan girl, sent by mistake to a farmer and his sister who had requested a boy from a far-off orphanage. Eleven-year-old Anne Shirley is the orphan, and she transforms the lives of those around her. An imaginative waif with red hair that she dreams is a handsome shade of auburn, freckles, and a willowy build, she talks of "kindred spirits," renames a road lined with flowering trees the "White Way of Delight," and dubs a pond the "Lake of Shining Waters." Anne takes the ordinary and captures it in a new light, with a word or phrase or an explanation. To the Cuthberts, who adopt Anne, and to the other inhabitants of the village, she is unlike anything they have ever experienced.

Anne is orphaned while still a baby, and from that point on she is sent to live with families who only need her to look after their own children once she is able. They never love or care about her. She spends four months at the orphan asylum in Nova Scotia before she arrives at Green Gables, the house the Cuthberts share. In a life of drudgery and loneliness, Anne escapes into her imagination, echoing Montgomery's own technique while growing up with her restrictive grandparents. Intelligent, good natured, but quick-tempered, Anne also possesses an imaginative outlook on life and love which shows a romantic tendency. In one incident, she recites Tennyson's "The Lady of Shalott" while floating down a river near Green Gables in an old row boat, reclined and draped in shawls for effect. Unfortunately, the boat has a hole, and Anne is rescued by her arch-enemy, Gilbert Blythe, the boy who once pulled her braids and called her "carrot-top" at school. Quick to anger, she brakes her slate over his head and still hasn't forgiven him by the end of the book. Another such temperamental encounter with Marilla's friend Rachel Lynde, and the vocally elaborate apology that ensues, also illustrates the complex, human character of Anne Shirley.

Anne displays a love of life and an endless hope for happiness that in Montgomery's tales turns her detractors into friends, while among readers her

Montgomery's works have been adapted for the stage and the screen, as with this 1987 television play, *Anne of Avonlea: The Continuing Story of Anne of Green Gables.*

qualities likewise contribute to her enduring popularity as a character. Criticism of the novel, however, has been mixed. "*Anne of Green Gables* just misses the kind of success which convinces the critic while it captivates the unreflecting general reader," noted Archibald MacMechan as quoted by Gillen. Based on the novel's popularity, MacMechan ultimately concluded that the "great reading public ... has ... a great indifference toward the rulings of the critics." Lesley Willis, writing in the *Dalhousie Review,* remarked that "*Anne of Green Gables* is unquestionably one of the best-known examples of Canadian children's fiction. But much of the book's appeal consists in its catering to a desire for wish-fulfillment and, on the part of the older reader, nostalgia for a sentimentally-envisioned past." "The author undoubtedly meant her to be queer, but she is altogether too queer," judged a reviewer in the *New York Times Book Review,* citing Anne's extraordinary literacy and vocabulary after having been raised by illiterate families and having had almost no formal educa-

tion. The reviewer, however, also declared that Anne "is one of the most extraordinary girls that ever came out of an ink pot."

Anne "may be a pretentious little girl who has read too much without digesting it, but as such she represents a type of precocious adolescent who is familiar and realistic," wrote Mary Rubio in *L. M. Montgomery: An Assessment.* "Anne's overripe diction is clearly intended to be comic, not only because it is inappropriate speech for a girl her age, but also because it is very trite and hackneyed." Rubio made the point that a professional writer such as Montgomery was not only aware of the difference between fresh and stale, overused expressions, but "is clearly satirizing the popular literary taste for sentimental cliches." Rubio concluded that Anne "presents herself as an interesting and impulsive child, one the Cuthberts need because she can furnish them with the psychological, emotional, and imaginative dimensions which are lacking in their own lives. And she does the same for us, the readers."

Willis, on the other hand, found Anne's imaginative leaps and expressions to be contrived. "The habit of attributing human qualities to inanimate nature—often very appealing both to the sentimental adult and to the pre-adolescent child—is central to L. M. Montgomery's concept of the imagination and colours Anne's observations of nature. This can be extremely tiresome." At age eleven, Anne names the cherry tree outside her bedroom window the "Snow Queen." But as Anne ages, she retains her conceit of naming flowers and equating them with angels or souls, or imagining them as a comforting presence to those in Heaven. She is seventeen when Matthew dies, and she hopes the souls of all the white roses he favored each summer are there to greet him in Heaven. "Once Montgomery has got hold of a good thing, she does not relinquish it easily," wrote Willis. "What L. M. Montgomery really wants is to engage for Anne the same kind of sympathy which might be given to a fairy-tale heroine, but without making her undergo the same trials; and, thanks largely to affective transference on the part of many readers, she succeeds to a quite remarkable degree." Yet the very things Willis disparaged are the elements that have made *Anne of Green Gables* continuously popular since its first publication. As a 1908 reviewer in the *Outlook* proclaimed: "*Anne of Green Gables* is one of the best books for girls we have seen for a long time. It is cheerful, amusing, and happy."

In the sequel, *Anne of Avonlea,* sixteen-year-old Anne becomes a teacher in the school she had attended after arriving at Green Gables. "The next few years of Anne's life is a story of crystal clearness, of tenderness, humor, and fancy," described a reviewer in the *Nation*. Anne gives up a scholarship in order to remain at Green Gables with Marilla, whose eyesight is failing. New friends, along with the old, fill her life with adventure, love, and social events. Her friendship with Gilbert Blythe is restored and by the end of the novel they are romantically interested in one another. Stepping into adulthood, Anne loses some of her childish ways. But "childhood still pervades the pages, for Anne has her schoolful of youngsters, and Marilla adopts twins," noted Margaret Merwin in the *Bookman*. "The book is as simple as a daisy, and if not quite as bewitching as the first we were given, the fault is doubtless with ourselves rather than the little flower." "*Anne of Avonlea* is a little more sentimental than the earlier 'Anne,' but

it is jolly and friendly. . . . The story will surely be read," declared a critic in the *Outlook*.

"The 'Anne' series of the Montgomery novels has as its main interest the development of this scrawny, sensitive orphan into a toughened and enlightened mother," explained Ephraim Weber in the *Dalhousie Review*. Montgomery continued to write about Anne and her children until 1939, with the publication of the final novel in the series, *Anne of Ingleside*. Now married to Gilbert Blythe and a mother of six, Anne is more concerned with motherhood than with the elements of childhood. Less a children's book than was the original *Anne of Green Gables*, *Anne of Ingleside* centers on rearing children, not on being a child. Anne has the responsibilities and emotions of a married woman, and not the relatively carefree life she lived after coming to Green Gables. "Mark Twain, had he been alive, would have approved of the later Anne," wrote Jane Spence Southron in the *New York Times Book Review*. "She has worn well; or rather, there is no sign of wear about her. Natural wit, a fine constitution and a zest for living nothing could dampen, plus the inherent capacity for doing the decent thing in a crisis (as when she gave up ambition for the sake of the aging woman who had mothered her), have kept her sweet as a sound-cored apple with a good sharp bite to it."

The Story Girl

Montgomery was a prolific author, and Anne Shirley was not her only heroine. In 1911 she published *The Story Girl*. "It was the last book I wrote in my old home by the gable window. . . . It is my own favourite among my books, the one that gave me the greatest pleasure to write, the one whose characters and landscape seem to me the most real," Montgomery wrote in *The Alpine Path*. The novel is about a group of children living on Prince Edward Island. "The children are of all sorts, except very bad," noted a reviewer in the *Nation*. "Inevitably one of them must be dowered with a fantastic soul, and this one is the Story Girl who has the gift of remembering, inventing, and, above all, of telling." Sara Stanley, the Story Girl, tells tales of legends, fairy tales, and family stories as the others gather around. Motherless, she is being raised by an aunt and uncle while her father is abroad.

The Story Girl is a novel of childhood, and Montgomery describes childish adventures, play, work, school, and summer vacation, interspersed with the tales of Sara Stanley. "The thread on which the story is strung is a frail one," Gillen claimed, noting that, unlike Anne Shirley, no extreme passions of love and hate run through these children. She also remarked that there is little action to motivate the story or promote continued interest in the characters. It is only the "gentle pleasure in the mood and setting" that keeps the reader going. A reviewer in the *Outlook*, however, called *The Story Girl* "capital reading. Like its predecessors, this story is clean, wholesome, and unsensational, but alive with character and rich in amusement."

Sara Stanley again leads the same group of children in Montgomery's sequel to *The Story Girl, The Golden Road*. Published in 1913, *The Golden Road* revolves around the children, especially Sara telling her stories, as daily life on Prince Edward Island continues. A reviewer in the *Outlook* judged the book to have the same "wholesome and natural fun" as its predecessors, and the stories within to possess "quaintness" and "imagination." A *Literary Digest* contributor described the spontaneity of the children as charming, and declared: "Fun and pathos alternate in these interesting pages, and a glimpse of romance is not lacking."

A professional writer of short stories, Montgomery published several collections, including *Chronicles of Avonlea: In Which Anne Shirley of Green Gables and Avonlea Plays Some Part* in 1912. Packaged as part of the "Anne" series, Anne Shirley only appears briefly in a few of the dozen stories. Tales of love lost and regained predominate the collection, as middle aged couples rekindle their past romances. In these stories, the pride or misunderstanding that ended the earlier attraction is cleared away. "Montgomery has written a series of short stories full of pathos and humor," wrote a critic in *Catholic World*. "Quaint, clean sparkling humor" shines forth in such stories as "Aunt Olivia's Beau" and "The Courting of Prissy Strong." A reviewer in the *Outlook* called the stories both "gently sentimental and enjoyably humorous." "Montgomery has certainly the story-teller's instinct, genuine humor, and a sentiment altogether clear of sentimentality—when she chooses to keep it so," judged a reviewer in the *Nation*.

The Emily Books

For the next ten years after *The Golden Road* was published, Montgomery devoted her writing skills mainly to the "Anne" series, producing four more novels. Although during this same period she became involved in a lawsuit when L. C. Page published a collection of short stories without her permission, Montgomery managed to begin a new series of books in addition to her "Anne" tales. In 1923 she published *Emily of New Moon*, the beginning of what was to become a trilogy, including *Emily Climbs* and *Emily's Quest*. The "Emily" series is the most autobiographical of all Montgomery's work. Focusing on the heroine, Emily Byrd Starr, from pre-teen child to adulthood and probable marriage, Montgomery reveals a little of her own struggle to become a published author. For both Montgomery and her heroine, an imaginative childhood fosters the dream of publication. Emily is an orphan, like other Montgomery protagonists, facing a childhood of being raised by unsympathetic relatives. But, like Anne, Emily has an unquenchable spirit and love of life.

This 1924 work, the second in a trilogy about orphan Emily Byrd Starr, focuses on her tempestuous relationship with her adoptive aunts.

"Emily Starr is brought face to face with her mother's family for the first time after her father's death. Eleven years old, she had little education except for what her father gave her, but she can read. With her imagination she peoples the woods, pastures, and spruce barrens of Prince Edward Island with fanciful beings," related Norma R. Fryatt in *Horn Book*. Reminiscent of Anne, Emily can turn her unhappy circumstances into a beautiful, imaginative world. But in comparison to the "Anne" series, "Emily's story offers a sharper picture of a child fighting for her identity in a world of adult values," commented Margery Fisher in *Growing Point*.

Emily Starr's life with her strict Aunt Elizabeth and loving Aunt Laura at New Moon farm is far different from the one she had shared with her beloved father. Cruel schoolmates and relations, an unsympathetic teacher, and new rules of daily life all conspire to make Emily miserable. But she can write, and that helps her deal with the loss of her father and the adjustments she must make at New Moon. Letters Emily writes to her late father keep him close to her and serve as both a journal and as a way to express her feelings. "Writing out all the painful episodes helps her to gain courage and to hope that one day she will be a writer," explained Fryatt.

But when Aunt Elizabeth finds and reads these letters, Emily is furious and hurt as her secret thoughts and emotions are revealed. "All of Emily's most striking assertions of her individuality revolve around her determined pursuit of her literary ambitions," wrote MacLulich. "When Emily insists that she simply must write—the need to express herself is part of her very being—she is defending herself against those who view her as little more than another piece of family property." In reading the letters, Aunt Elizabeth realizes both the way in which Emily views her and how she had trespassed on Emily's thoughts as an individual. She comes to the knowledge that Emily is not just a child relation, but a person. Eventually, the two grow to trust and love one another through acceptance and understanding.

"Both as a study of the early life of a very precocious child and for its original setting in Prince Edward Island, this story makes a considerable appeal," judged a reviewer in the *Times Literary Supplement*. Montgomery's "greatest charm lies in a real understanding and sympathy

Visitors tour the Green Gables home on Prince Edward Island, the setting for Montgomery's popular series about her imaginative heroine.

for children, a sympathy which, even though it may degenerate at times into the sentimental, nevertheless has a certain appealing quality and a depth of sincerity that is disarming," noted a *New York Times Book Review* critic. In describing *Emily of New Moon,* Fisher concluded, "As well as creating a heroine brimful of life, believable and entertaining, L. M. Montgomery has created a world for her to inhabit which for the reflective reader could become at once real and magical."

In *Emily Climbs* and *Emily's Quest,* Montgomery continues the story of Emily Starr. In these later books in which narrative tales alternate with journal extracts and letters, Emily moves through high school and into the world of work and romance. As an adult, she pursues her dreams of writing professionally and is always writing something, even submitting stories for publication. Her childhood companions mature along with her, and many remain merely friends while others turn into romantic interests. Dean Priest and Teddy Kent are two old friends who not only share her deepest thoughts, but fall in love with her. Ultimately, she chooses Teddy over Dean because Teddy is the one who believes in her and her writing ability. At the end of *Emily's Quest,* after a serious misunderstanding, Teddy and Emily are reunited and become a couple with marriage on their minds. "These are romantic novels, speaking directly to adolescents, and the particular form they take gives them a direct, intimate air," wrote a reviewer in *Growing Point,* discussing *Emily Climbs* and *Emily's Quest.* The critic also judged that the novels' "graceful mixture of humor and sharp perception will have a wide appeal."

An Abundance of Young Girls

Young heroines, including Pat, Jane, and Marigold, are featured in Montgomery's other books. All young girls, their surroundings on Prince Edward Island color their whole outlook toward life. Pat of *Pat of Silver Bush* is seven at the start of her story. Naive and imaginative, she believes the tales told to her by her family's Irish servant, including the story that her little sister was found in the parsley bed. Jane of *Jane of Lantern Hill,* on the other hand, is an only child living with her mother in Toronto. Discovering that her father is alive and not dead as she had been led to believe, she spends the summer with him on Prince Edward Island. As she grows to love him, she forms a plan to reunite her parents. "Jane's story is a good, solid, old fashioned one, complete with the mandatory happy

ending," declared Helene H. Levene in the *School Library Journal.*

Magic for Marigold revolves around Marigold, a lonely child living on the Island, surrounded by older relatives. The "magic" in the title refers to elements of childhood, the "magic" of being young, innocent, and able to create imaginary playmates. Marigold is much like Montgomery's other heroines—imaginative and sensitive. *In Review: Canadian Books for Children* contributor John McGrath noted that "seldom has the delicate, precious relationship between the very young and the very old been so sympathetically treated" as when Marigold and her great-grandmother spend the last night of the older woman's life together. McGrath also commented in general that Montgomery's "work was founded on a solid bedrock of belief in the power of love and goodness; of the importance of tradition and wholesome family pride."

"Many women *have* lived 'fabulous' lives," explained Elizabeth Waterston in *The Clear Spirit: Twenty Canadian Women and Their Times,* "But in L. M. Montgomery's case the real miracle is that she could exploit her experience in an enduring art-form. She universalized her story; she recreated it against vivid regional settings; she structured it into mythical patterns. She retold the legends she had lived, in haunting and memorable style."

"Overall, Montgomery's work is marked by a succession of unforgettable heroines seen against the backdrop of the beautiful Prince Edward Island landscape," judged John Robert Sorfleet in *Twentieth-Century Children's Writers.* "Within them their isolated selves struggle to flourish against a set of outside pressures that urge conformity and denial of selfhood as the price of social acceptance. Yet they do not submit, and eventually their struggles are rewarded by their acceptance as them*selves,* not as mere specious semblances." Montgomery was able to recall her childhood with such detail and emotion that her young adult heroines such as Anne and Emily capture the essence of a child's life for generations of readers. As Frazer explained: "Montgomery remained a child at heart, with an exhaustive, unforgiving memory of what a thinskinned, imaginative child can suffer and an unquenchable delight in children's pleasures."

■ Works Cited

Review of *Anne of Avonlea, Nation,* September 2, 1909, p. 212.

Review of *Anne of Avonlea, Outlook,* October 2, 1909, p. 276.

Review of *Anne of Green Gables, Outlook,* August 22, 1908, pp. 956-57.

Review of *Chronicles of Avonlea: In Which Anne Shirley of Green Gables and Avonlea Plays Some Part, Catholic World,* October, 1912, p. 103.

Review of *Chronicles of Avonlea: In Which Anne Shirley of Green Gables and Avonlea Plays Some Part, Nation,* August 22, 1912, p. 171.

Review of *Chronicles of Avonlea: In Which Anne Shirley of Green Gables and Avonlea Plays Some Part, Outlook,* June 29, 1912, p. 500.

Review of *Emily Climbs* and *Emily's Quest, Growing Point,* January, 1980.

Review of *Emily of New Moon, New York Times Book Review,* August 26, 1923, pp. 24, 26.

Review of *Emily of New Moon, Times Literary Supplement,* September 13, 1923, p. 105.

Fisher, Margery, review of *Emily of New Moon, Growing Point,* January, 1978, pp. 3244-45.

Frazer, Frances, "Lucy Maud Montgomery," *Dictionary of Literary Biography,* Volume 92: *Canadian Writers, 1890-1920,* Gale, 1990, pp. 246-53.

Fryatt, Norma R., "A Second Look: *Emily of New Moon,*" *Horn Book,* March/April, 1986, pp. 174-75.

Gillen, Mollie, editor, *The Wheel of Things: A Biography of L. M. Montgomery, Author of "Anne of Green Gables,"* Fitzhenry & Whiteside, 1975.

Review of *The Golden Road, Literary Digest,* October 18, 1913, p. 692.

Review of *The Golden Road, Outlook,* October 4, 1913, p. 280.

"A Heroine from an Asylum," *New York Times Book Review,* July 18, 1908, p. 404.

Levene, Helen, H., review of *Jane of Lantern Hill, School Library Journal,* May, 1990, p. 73.

MacLulich, T. D., "L. M. Montgomery and the Literary Heroine: Jo, Rebecca, Anne, and Emily," *Canadian Children's Literature,* Number 37, 1985, pp. 5-16.

McGrath, John, review of *Magic for Marigold, In Review: Canadian Books for Children,* summer, 1977, pp. 42-43.

Merwin, Margaret, "L. M. Montgomery's *Anne of Avonlea,*" *Bookman,* October, 1909, p. 152.

Montgomery, L. M., *The Alpine Path: The Story of My Career,* Fitzhenry & Whiteside, 1974.

Montgomery, L. M., *Anne of Green Gables,* Bantam, 1976.

Rubio, Mary, "Satire, Realism & Imagination in *Anne of Green Gables,*" *L. M. Montgomery: An Assessment,* edited by John Robert Sorfleet, Canadian Children's Press, 1976, pp. 27-36.

Rubio, Mary, and Elizabeth Waterston, editors, *The Selected Journals of L. M. Montgomery,* Volume 2: *1910-1921,* Oxford University Press, 1987.

Sorfleet, John Robert, essay in *Twentieth-Century Children's Writers,* 3rd edition, edited by Tracy Chevalier, St. James Press, 1989, pp. 690-91.

Southron, Jane Spence, "After Green Gables," *New York Times Book Review,* July 30, 1939, p. 7.

Review of *The Story Girl, Nation,* August 10, 1911, p. 122.

Review of *The Story Girl, Outlook,* September 2, 1911, pp. 46-47.

Stott, Jon C., "L. M. Montgomery," *Writers for Children,* edited by Jane M. Bingham, Scribner, 1988.

Waterston, Elizabeth, "Lucy Maud Montgomery," *The Clear Spirit: Twenty Canadian Women and Their Times,* edited by Mary Quayle Innis, University of Toronto Press, 1966, pp. 198-220.

Weber, Ephraim, "L. M. Montgomery's 'Anne,'" *Dalhousie Review,* April, 1944, pp. 64-73.

Willis, Lesley, "The Bogus Ugly Duckling: Anne Shirley Unmasked," *Dalhousie Review,* summer, 1976, pp. 247-51.

■ For More Information See

BOOKS

Children's Literature Review, Volume 8, Gale, 1985, pp. 107-40.

Egoff, Sheila, *The Republic of Childhood: A Critical Guide to Canadian Children's Literature in English,* 2nd edition, Oxford University Press, 1975, pp. 292-309.

Fisher, Margery, *Who's Who in Children's Books: A Treasury of the Familiar Characters of Childhood,* Holt, 1975, p. 23.

L. M. Montgomery: An Assessment, edited by John Robert Sorfleet, Canadian Children's Press, 1976.

Phelphs, Arthur L., *Canadian Writers,* McClelland & Stewart, 1951, pp. 85-93.

Reimer, Mavis, editor, *Such a Simple Little Tale: Critical Responses to L. M. Montgomery's Anne of Green Gables,* Scarecrow, 1992.

Ridley, Hilda M., *The Story of L. M. Montgomery,* Ryerson, 1956.

Twentieth-Century Romance and Historical Writers, 2nd edition, edited by Lesley Henderson, St. James Press, 1990, pp. 469-70.

PERIODICALS

Canadian Children's Literature, autumn, 1975; Number 1, 1977, pp. 4-81; Number 30, 1983, pp. 5-20; Number 37, 1985, pp. 40-46, 47-52; Number 38, 1985, pp. 68-80; Number 42, 1986, pp. 29-40; Number 52, 1988, pp. 67-68; Number 53, 1989, pp. 46-47; Number 55, 1989, pp. 8-17.

Children's Literature in Education, Volume 20, number 3, 1989, pp. 165-73.
Horn Book, September/October, 1988, pp. 663-66.
Maclean's, December 7, 1987, p. 50.
Nature Canada, winter, 1987, pp. 30-35.
New York Times, April 25, 1942, p. 13.
New York Times Book Review, September 21, 1919, p. 484; September 11, 1921, p. 23.
Publishers Weekly, September 18, 1915, p. 790; August 16, 1919, pp. 484-85.
Saturday Night, November, 1987, pp. 52-58.°

—Sketch by Terrie M. Rooney

Joan Lowery Nixon

thors Guild, Authors League of America, Society of Children's Book Writers (charter member and former member of board of directors), Mystery Writers of America (regional vice-president, Southwest chapter), Western Writers of America, Kappa Delta Alumnae Association.

■ Awards, Honors

Steck-Vaughn Award, Texas Institute of Letters, 1975, for *The Alligator under the Bed*; Edgar Allan Poe Award nomination, Mystery Writers of America, 1975, for *The Mysterious Red Tape Gang*, 1985, for *The Ghosts of Now*, and 1992, for *The Weekend Was Murder*; Outstanding Science Trade Book for children, National Science Teachers Association and Children's Book Council Joint Committee, 1979, for *Volcanoes: Nature's Fireworks*, 1980, for *Glaciers: Nature's Frozen Rivers*, and 1981, for *Earthquakes: Nature in Motion*; Edgar Allan Poe Award for best juvenile mystery, Mystery Writers of America, 1980, for *The Kidnapping of Christina Lattimore*, 1981, for *The Seance*, and 1987, for *The Other Side of Dark*; Crabbery Award, Oxon Hill branch of Prince George's County (MD) Library, 1984, for *Magnolia's Mixed-Up Magic*; Golden Spur, Western Writers of America, 1988, for *A Family Apart*, and 1989, for *In the Face of Danger*; Young Hoosier Award, 1988, for *A Deadly Game of Magic*, and 1989, for *The Dark and Deadly Pool*; Colorado Blue Spruce Young Adult Award, 1988, Virginia Young Adult Silver Cup, 1989, Oklahoma Sequoyah Young Adult Book Award, 1989, Iowa Teen Award, 1989, California Young Readers Medal, 1990, and Utah Young Adult Award, 1991,

■ Personal

Has also written under pseudonym Jaye Ellen; born February 3, 1927, in Los Angeles, CA; daughter of Joseph Michael (an accountant) and Margaret (Meyer) Lowery; married Hershell H. Nixon (a petroleum geologist), August 6, 1949; children: Kathleen Nixon Brush, Maureen Nixon Quinlan, Joseph Michael, Eileen Marie. *Education:* University of Southern California, B.A., 1947; California State College, certificate in elementary education, 1949. *Religion:* Roman Catholic.

■ Addresses

Home—10215 Cedar Creek Dr., Houston, TX 77042. *Agent*—Amy Berkower, Writers House Inc., 21 West 26th St., New York, NY 10010.

■ Career

Writer. Elementary school teacher in Los Angeles, CA, 1947-50; Midland College, Midland, TX, instructor in creative writing, 1971-73; University of Houston, Houston, TX, instructor in creative writing, 1974-78; has taught creative writing in numerous publics schools in Texas. *Member:* Au-

all for *The Other Side of Dark;* California Young Readers Medal, 1990, for *The Stalker; The Secret Box Mystery, Danger in Dinosaur Valley, Muffie Mouse and the Busy Birthday,* and *Beats Me, Claude* are all Junior Literary Guild selections.

■ Writings

FICTION; FOR YOUNG PEOPLE

The Mystery of Hurricane Castle, illustrated by Velma Ilsley, Criterion, 1964.

The Mystery of the Grinning Idol, illustrated by Alvin Smith, Criterion, 1965.

The Mystery of the Hidden Cockatoo, illustrated by Richard Lewis, Criterion, 1966.

The Mystery of the Haunted Woods (sequel to *The Mystery of Hurricane Castle*), illustrated by Theresa Brudi, Criterion, 1967.

The Mystery of the Secret Stowaway, illustrated by Joan Drescher, Criterion, 1968.

Delbert, the Plainclothes Detective, illustrated by Philip Smith, Criterion, 1971.

The Alligator under the Bed, illustrated by Jan Hughes, Putnam, 1974.

The Mysterious Red Tape Gang, illustrated by Joan Sandin, Putnam, 1974, published in paperback as *The Adventures of the Red Tape Gang,* illustrations by Steven H. Stroud, Scholastic, 1983.

The Secret Box Mystery, illustrated by Leigh Grant, Putnam, 1974.

The Mysterious Prowler, illustrated by Berthe Amoss, Harcourt, 1976.

The Boy Who Could Find Anything, illustrated by Syd Hoff, Harcourt, 1978.

Danger in Dinosaur Valley, illustrated by Marc Simont, Putnam, 1978.

Muffie Mouse and the Busy Birthday, illustrated by Geoffrey Hayes, Seabury, 1978, also published as *Muffy and the Birthday Party,* Scholastic, 1979.

Bigfoot Makes a Movie, illustrated by Hoff, Putnam, 1979.

The Kidnapping of Christina Lattimore, Harcourt, 1979.

Gloria Chipmunk, Star!, illustrated by Diane Dawson, Houghton, 1980, published in paperback with illustrations by Hayes, Scholastic, 1980.

Casey and the Great Idea, illustrated by Amy Rowen, Dutton, 1980.

The Seance, Harcourt, 1980.

The Spotlight Gang and the Backstage Ghost, Harlequin, 1981.

The Specter, Delacorte, 1982, published in England as *The Spectre,* Granada, 1983.

(Under pseudonym Jaye Ellen) *The Trouble with Charlie,* Bantam, 1982.

Days of Fear, photographs by Joan Menschenfreund, Dutton, 1983.

The Gift, illustrated by Andrew Glass, Macmillan, 1983.

A Deadly Game of Magic, Harcourt, 1983.

Magnolia's Mixed-Up Magic, illustrated by Linda Bucholtz-Ross, Putnam, 1983.

The Ghosts of Now, Delacorte, 1984.

The House on Hackman's Hill, Scholastic, 1985.

The Stalker, Delacorte, 1985.

The Other Side of Dark, Delacorte, 1986.

Haunted Island, Scholastic, 1987.

Secret, Silent Screams, Delacorte, 1988.

If You Were a Writer (picture book), illustrated by Bruce Degen, Four Winds Press, 1988.

The Island of Dangerous Dreams, Dell, 1989.

Whispers from the Dead, Delacorte, 1989.

A Candidate for Murder, Delacorte, 1991.

High Trail to Danger, Bantam, 1991.

Honeycutt Street Celebrities, Dell, 1991.

Mystery Box, Dell, 1991.

Watch Out for Dinosaurs, Dell, 1991.

The Haunted House on Honeycutt Street, Dell, 1991.

A Deadly Promise (sequel to *High Trail to Danger*), Bantam, 1992.

The Name of the Game Was Murder, Delacorte, 1993.

Will You Give Me a Dream? (picture book), illustrated by Degen, Four Winds Press, 1994.

When I Am Eight (picture book), illustrated by Dick Gackenbach, Dial, 1994.

Shadowmaker (mystery), Delacorte, 1994.

"FIRST READ-ALONE MYSTERIES" SERIES; ILLUSTRATED BY JIM CUMMINS

The New Year's Mystery, Albert Whitman, 1979.

The Halloween Mystery, Albert Whitman, 1979.

The Valentine Mystery, Albert Whitman, 1979.

The Happy Birthday Mystery, Albert Whitman, 1979.

The Thanksgiving Mystery, Albert Whitman, 1980.

The April Fool Mystery, Albert Whitman, 1980.

The Easter Mystery, Albert Whitman, 1981.

The Christmas Eve Mystery, Albert Whitman, 1981.

"CLAUDE AND SHIRLEY" SERIES

If You Say So, Claude, illustrated by Lorinda Bryan Cauley, Warne, 1980.

Beats Me, Claude, illustrated by Tracey Campbell Pearson, Viking, 1986.

Fat Chance, Claude, illustrated by Pearson, Viking Kestrel, 1987.

You Bet Your Britches, Claude, illustrated by Pearson, Viking, 1989.

That's the Spirit, Claude, Viking, 1990.

"KLEEP: SPACE DETECTIVE" SERIES; ILLUSTRATED BY PAUL FRAME

Kidnapped on Astarr, Garrard, 1981.

Mysterious Queen of Magic, Garrard, 1981.

Mystery Dolls from Planet Urd, Garrard, 1981.

"MAGGIE" SERIES; YOUNG ADULT NOVELS

Maggie, Too, illustrations by Darrel Millsap, Harcourt, 1985.

And Maggie Makes Three, Harcourt, 1986.

Maggie Forevermore, Harcourt, 1987.

"ORPHAN TRAIN" QUARTET; YOUNG ADULT NOVELS

A Family Apart, Bantam, 1987.

Caught in the Act, Bantam, 1988.

In the Face of Danger, Bantam, 1988.

A Place to Belong, Bantam, 1989.

"HOLLYWOOD DAUGHTERS" TRILOGY; YOUNG ADULT NOVELS

Star Baby, Bantam, 1989.

Overnight Sensation, Bantam, 1990.

Encore, Bantam, 1990.

"MARY ELIZABETH" SERIES; YOUNG ADULT NOVELS

The Dark and Deadly Pool, Delacorte, 1987.

The Weekend Was Murder!, Delacorte, 1992.

"LAND OF HOPE" SERIES

Land of Hope, Bantam, 1992.

Land of Promise, Bantam, 1993.

Land of Dreams, Bantam, 1994.

NONFICTION; WITH HUSBAND, HERSHELL H. NIXON

Oil and Gas: From Fossils to Fuels, illustrated by Jean Day Zallinger, Harcourt, 1977.

Volcanoes: Nature's Fireworks, Dodd, 1978.

Glaciers: Nature's Frozen Rivers, Dodd, 1980.

Earthquakes: Nature in Motion, Dodd, 1981.

Land under the Sea, Dodd, 1985.

OTHER

(With others) *This I Can Be* (textbook), Benefic, 1975.

(With others) *People and Me* (textbook), Benefic, 1975.

Five Loaves and Two Fishes: Feeding of Five Thousand for Beginning Readers; John 6:1-15 for Children, illustrated by Aline Cunningham, Concordia, 1976.

Who Is My Neighbor?: The Good Samaritan for Beginning Readers; Luke 10:29-37 for Children, illustrated by Cunningham, Concordia, 1976.

The Son Who Came Home Again: The Prodigal Son for Beginning Readers; Luke 15:11-32 for Children, illustrated by Cunningham, Concordia, 1977.

Writing Mysteries for Young People (for adults), The Writer, 1977.

When God Listens, illustrated by James McIlrath, Our Sunday Visitor, 1978.

When God Speaks, illustrated by McIlrath, Our Sunday Visitor, 1978.

The Grandmother's Book (for adults), Abingdon Press, 1979.

The Butterfly Tree, illustrated by McIlrath, Our Sunday Visitor, 1979.

Before You Were Born, illustrated by McIlrath, Our Sunday Visitor, 1980.

(Author of introduction) Cynthia Manson, editor, *Tales from Ellery Queen's Mystery Magazine: Short Stories for Young Adults,* Harcourt, 1986.

Also contributor to magazines, including *West Coast Review of Books, The Writer, American Home, Parents, Woman's Day,* and *Ms.* Humor columnist for the *Houston Post.*

■ **Sidelights**

"Writing is hard," writes Joan Lowery Nixon in her entry for the *Something about the Author Autobiography Series (SAAS).* "It's not easy. But it's such a fulfilling, enjoyable occupation that it's worth all the effort. There are days in which ideas flow and I can hardly type fast enough as I try to get every word down on paper, but there are other days during which I feel as though I'm painfully removing every word from my brain with a pair of pliers." Whether flowing freely or pried with pliers, Nixon's words have already won her the Mystery Writers of America's coveted Edgar Award for best juvenile mystery three times—the first writer to do so—and three of her other works have been nominated for that honor, including her 1992 novel *The Weekend Was Murder.* "In the field of young adult mystery writers, a field crowded with authors," states Melissa Fletcher Stoeltje in the *Houston Chronicle,* "she is by all accounts the grande dame."

Nixon was born in Los Angeles, California. She lived with her parents, grandparents, and two younger sisters in a large double house. The two halves of the house were separated by a playroom, which Nixon remembers fondly: "Mother, who had been a kindergarten teacher before she married, equipped the room with an upright piano, paints and an easel, and a worktable on which we could create with clay, colored construction paper, crayons, glue, and scissors. There were cupboards containing puzzles, paper dolls, and games, a doll house, and playhouse furniture. With my two younger sisters, Marilyn and Pat, I spent many enjoyable hours in that playroom.''

Nixon recalls that at a very young age she wanted to be a writer. When she was three, she began teaching herself to read by memorizing the words in her favorite books. She also followed her mother around, saying, "Write this down. I have a poem." She created verses for every holiday or family celebration, writing in *SAAS* that "from the time I discovered mysteries I was in love with them." Her first published work, a poem, appeared in *Children's Playmate* magazine when she was ten years old.

One of the items in the playroom that stimulated her imagination was a puppet theater for which the young Nixon composed and performed plays. "My younger sisters and some of the kids who lived in the neighborhood would often come to me and say, 'Make us a show, Joan,'" the author recalls in *SAAS*. "So I'd sit on the floor in front of the doll house, my audience seated around me, and use the small, glass, doll-house dolls to create a play." "Under my mother's direction," she continues in *Something about the Author (SATA)*, "we wrote our scripts, based on some of the classic fairy tales, such as 'Peter Rabbit' and the traditional 'Punch and Judy,' and took our shows—on a volunteer basis—to children's hospitals and orphanages and schools for many years. One moment I shall always remember: when we put on our puppet show for a group of very young Japanese children, none of whom spoke English. I realized that day the power of 'story telling' and laughter and friendship, as these little ones, unable to understand the dialogue, still responded to the puppets with as much enthusiasm as any audience we had ever met."

Hollywood

Nixon attended first Seventy-Fourth Street elementary school in Los Angeles only two blocks from her home, and then Horace Mann Junior High, which was just as close but in the other direction. She liked school and was a good student, but she was not at all athletic, always being among the last to be chosen in any team sport. However, she received a good education, earning A's in everything but physical education. Part of her problem, she explains in *SAAS*, was her need for eyeglasses: "Because of the Depression many parents couldn't afford to have their children's eyesight tested. Those who wore glasses, as I did, were often called 'Four eyes!' usually by some boy who was doing his best to be obnoxious."

When Nixon was twelve, her grandfather died and the family moved to a large stucco house in East Hollywood. From her bedroom, which she shared with her grandmother, Nixon could see the lights from the Hollywood theaters. "We had some famous neighbors," she recalls in *SAAS*: "the producer-director, Cecil B. DeMille; the comedian, W. C. Fields; and the champion prizefighter, Jack Dempsey. I liked Mr. DeMille because he always tipped his hat to me if he drove by while I was on the road; but I didn't like W. C. Fields at

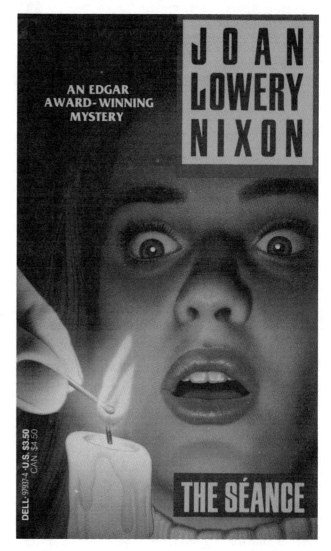

This 1980 work won an Edgar Allan Poe Award for best juvenile mystery.

all. He didn't like children? Well, who cared? I didn't like him at all." At one point when she and a friend stopped for ice cream, Nixon remembers in a more recent volume of *SATA*, "Shirley Temple came in . . . and sat down at the table next to us. Well, we refused to acknowledge that she was there at all. We didn't want anyone to think us so uncouth as to stare at a movie star."

After entering ninth grade at Le Conte Junior High in Hollywood, Nixon became interested in journalism and almost at once became editor of the school newspaper. This was in 1941, the year of the attack on Pearl Harbor. Nixon tried to volunteer as a writer of propaganda for the Red Cross, but her offer was ignored. Instead, the next year when she entered Hollywood High School, she wrote letters to lonely servicemen and helped serve breakfast to them in the school cafeteria. The entire family also entertained servicemen at their home: "My mother's theory," the author writes in *SAAS*, "was that any boy away from home who went to church was probably a good boy, so she and my father would linger after Mass was over to invite to dinner any servicemen who had been attending Mass."

It was also at Hollywood High that Nixon met her favorite teacher, Miss Bertha Standfast. During the next three years, she enrolled in every English class taught by this lady, seeking her support in her writing. "I treasured the direction and encouragement Miss Standfast gave to me," she declares. "'You have talent,' she'd tell me. 'You're going to be a writer.' It was she who insisted that I major in journalism when I went to college." At the age of seventeen, Nixon wrote her first article for a magazine, selling it to *Ford Times*.

One week after her high school graduation, Nixon entered the University of Southern California as a journalism student. "My training in journalism taught me discipline," she remembers in *SATA*. "For one thing, I learned to create at the typewriter. We took our exams on the typewriter. Journalism taught me to focus because I had to sit down and *write*, whether I felt like it or not—no waiting for inspiration. I learned the skill of finding the important facts in a story, and how to isolate them from all of the unnecessary details." She also joined a service club and a sorority, wrote skits and programs for college functions, and worked for the Red Cross, mostly doing mending of servicemen's uniforms. Later she worked as a staff writer for a movie magazine and took a class on writing for radio. "I was interested in writing for dramatic radio programs," she explains in *SAAS*, "but I wasn't satisfied with the class I'd taken at USC.

Mother heard of one being taught at night school at Hollywood High, and I decided to sign up for it. She didn't want me to travel alone on the Hollywood streetcar at night, and she thought she might enjoy taking the class, too, so she signed up with me." Nixon eventually lost interest in script-writing, but, she continues, "Mother, whose creativity found a wonderful outlet, went on to write scripts and sell them to many of the top dramatic programs on the radio network."

Nixon's degree in journalism did not lead to a job in that field, partly because of competition from returning war correspondents. But the Los Angeles School District was in need of teachers, so she found work as a substitute for kindergarten through third grade classes. Soon she received an assignment to teach kindergarten at Ramona Elementary School, taking night school education courses at the nearby Los Angeles City College campus.

While at USC, Nixon also met her future husband, Hershell "Nick" Nixon, who was a student majoring in naval science. Two weeks after their first date they became engaged, but, as she states in *SAAS*, "Nick still had over a year left to serve on his six-year hitch, so off he went to China for ten months. He was back for a few weeks, then off again to Hawaii for a few months." Their marriage was postponed until after he finished his stint in the Navy, but the couple was finally united on August 6, 1947. During the three years Nixon taught at Ramona, their first daughter, Kathleen Mary, was born.

In 1952 Nick graduated from USC, having changed his major to geology. His first job, which was with the Shell Oil Company, sent the young family to Billings, Montana. It would be the first of many moves in the following years. "We lived in Billings for three years," Nixon remembers, "and after a stint in Palmdale, California, Nick went to work for Tidewater (later called Getty Oil), and was sent to Ventura, Los Angeles, San Francisco, back to Los Angeles, and to Corpus Christi, Texas." By the time they moved to Corpus Christi, Kathy had been joined by Maureen, Joe, and the youngest, Eileen. "I shed many tears over that move to Texas," Nixon recalls. "All I knew about the state was that it was full of cattle and cactus, and I didn't want to leave my family, my friends, and my beautiful state of California."

Inspiration

The move to Texas, however, marked an important event in Nixon's life. When she read an announcement of the upcoming Southwest Writers Conference only a little while after her arrival, she became enthusiastic about writing for children. "I had children, I had taught children, and I have the vivid kind of memory which enables me to remember all the details I saw and the emotions I felt when I was a child," she recalls. "I made a mental note to myself. Maybe I'd try writing something for children." Kathy and Maureen discussed this development and, states the author, announced to their mother, "We've decided. If you're going to write for children, you have to write a book, and it has to be a mystery, and you have to put us in it." Nixon worked every Wednesday from nine a.m to three p.m. "All week I wrote in my mind, dialogue and scenes coming together, demanding to be written as I shoved them back. 'Not yet!' I'd say with a groan. 'Wait until I can get to my typewriter.'" Each day after school, Nixon read the material she had completed that day to her children. Often she used their suggestions (such as Kathy's "Put something funny in it.") Nixon even joined the Byliners, a local group of writers who read and criticized each other's manuscripts. Despite all this input, *The Mystery of Hurricane Castle* was rejected twelve times by different publishers before Criterion finally accepted it.

The Mystery of Hurricane Castle tells the story of two girls—the Nickson sisters, Kathy and Maureen—and their younger brother, Danny, who are left behind during an evacuation of the Gulf of Texas area just before a hurricane. The book follows them as they seek shelter in a house that, according to local legend, is haunted. Nixon declares in *The Writer* that the plot of the book came from a family experience: "When we moved to Corpus Christi, Texas, we found ourselves in the middle of a hurricane. The eye of the storm missed our city, but the force of the rain, wind, and waves caused tremendous damage." "The area had been evacuated," Nixon continues, "but I wondered what someone would have done who couldn't leave—who, for some reason, had been left behind in the confusion. The beach houses could not withstand the force of the storm, or stay intact, but what if high on the hill there stood a stone 'castle,' strong enough to survive the storm and to shelter its occupants? And what if this castle were known to have as its only occupant a ghost?" As it turns out, Kathy's interest in painting helps the children to unmask the "ghost."

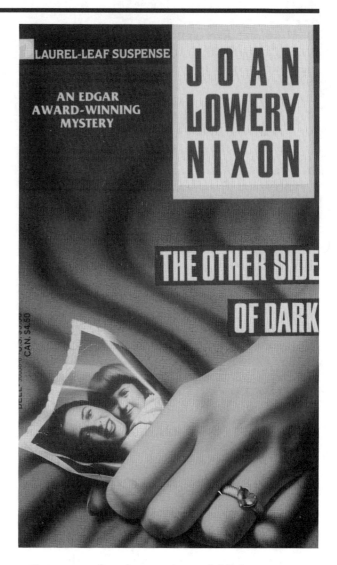

Four years after she was shot and fell into a coma, seventeen-year-old Stacy awakens and must identify her assailant, who also killed her mother, in this 1986 thriller.

That first book persuaded Nixon to continue writing. After *Hurricane Castle*, she wrote *The Mystery of the Grinning Idol*, a story about smuggling Mexican artifacts (which starred her youngest child, Eileen), and *The Mystery of the Hidden Cockatoo*, about a jewelled pin lost in a house in the French Quarter of New Orleans, before bringing the Nicksons back in *The Mystery of the Haunted Woods*. Son Joe finally got a starring role in *The Mystery of the Secret Stowaway*. Nixon soon found herself busy writing children's books, teaching creative classes at local children's schools, libraries, and colleges, and writing a humor column for the *Houston Post*. Nixon says in *SAAS* that it "soon became apparent that I would have to make a decision about the direction of my career," for "... the careful time I spent on the work from the students in my writing classes subtracted from the time I had for my own writing. It was a difficult decision, but I gave up teaching." This decision allowed her to devote every morning to writing, a hard task, she says in her autobiographical sketch, "but it's such a fulfilling, enjoyable occupation that it's worth all the effort."

Writing for Young Adults

Nixon's earliest work was for young readers—it was not until later in her career that she began writing for young adults. This is how she first started writing for teens: in 1975, Nixon and her daughter Kathy attended the first International Crime Writers Congress in London, England, where a speaker's comment encouraged her to try writing a mystery for young adults. This book became *The Kidnapping of Christina Lattimore*, which was awarded the Edgar for best juvenile mystery by the Mystery Writers of America in 1980. *The Kidnapping of Christina Lattimore* tells in the title character's own words her ordeal of being kidnapped, held for ransom, and then suspected of having engineered the whole project to get money from her grandmother for a school trip. When she is rescued, she dedicates herself to bringing the criminals to justice and proving that she did not try to defraud her grandmother. *New York Times Book Review* contributor Paxton Davis finds this part of the novel particularly intriguing, writing that "Christina's inability to persuade the authorities or her family that she was not an accomplice in the crime makes for good narrative." Other critics have also reviewed Nixon's first teen novel favorably. Linda E. Morrall, for one, asserts in the *School Library Journal* that it is "an above-average addition to young adult collections."

One year after *The Kidnapping of Christina Lattimore* won the Edgar, Nixon repeated the accomplishment with *The Seance*, and in 1987 *The Other Side of Dark* made her a three-time recipient of the prize. The latter book presents quite a different type of problem to the reader. Seventeen-year-old Stacy wakes up to find that she has lost four years of her life in a coma after an intruder shot her and killed her mother. Not only does she have to adapt to a new lifestyle and catch up on the missing years, but she also has to identify the killer before she becomes his next victim. "Stacy is a vivid character," David Gale writes in *School Library Journal*, "whose need to be brought up to date provides some comic moments." Also praising the story, *Voice of Youth Advocates* reviewer Mary L. Adams finds "believable characters, suspense, mys-

tery, a little romance" in the book, which she thinks will "make its readers want to read Nixon's other books."

From Mystery to History and Beyond

Besides her acclaimed mysteries, Nixon has won awards for her historical fiction. Two volumes of her "Orphan Train" quartet, *A Family Apart* and *In the Face of Danger*, won the Golden Spur Award—the Western Writers of America's equivalent of the Edgar. The idea, she told *AAYA*, came from a publisher who asked her if she had ever heard of the "Orphan Train children." The historical Children's Aid Society, an organization of social activists, operated between 1854 and 1929 to place more than 100,000 children with foster families in the West. The children—not necessarily orphans—were usually from immigrant families living in slums in New York City.

Such was the case with Nixon's fictional Kelly family, first generation immigrants living in New York shortly before the Civil War. In *A Family Apart*, Nixon tells how, after the oldest boy is arrested for petty robbery, the widowed Mrs. Kelly realizes that she can no longer provide for her six children. She accepts the offer of Mr. Charles Loring Brace, a social activist, to have them placed with other families in the West. When the Kellys reach St. Louis, Missouri, however, they find to their dismay that they will be adopted by different people and must split up. *A Family Apart* goes on to show how Frances Mary, the oldest girl, and Petey, the youngest boy, are adopted by the Swensons, an abolitionist couple living in Kansas who help escaping slaves flee north. Megan, the second-oldest girl, is chosen by prairie farmers Ben and Emma Browder, and in *In the Face of Danger* she learns to overcome her grief about her family's disintegration and her lack of self-esteem. Ten year old Danny and his little sister Peg also end up with a family named Swenson in *A Place to Belong*, while Mike—the would-be thief whose activities precipitated the family's exodus—finds a home with a German family named Friedrich in *Caught in the Act*.

Nixon's popular "Claude and Shirley" series for younger readers is also set in the West. In a series of adventures ranging from *If You Say So, Claude*, in which the pioneer couple leave their noisy mining town for the peace of the Texas frontier, to *You Bet Your Britches, Claude*, in which the couple adopts a little boy and girl, Nixon displays a sense of humor that echoes the West's traditional "tall tales.'' A reviewer for *Publishers Weekly* appreciates the humor in the book, calling it a ''rib-tickling yarn,'' while Betsy Hearne, writing in the *Bulletin of the Center for Children's Books*, further adds that it contains ''endearing characters, adroit writing, and an action-packed feminist pioneer.''

''The West to me is a state of mind,'' Nixon declares in *The Writer*. ''While immersed in stories set west of the Mississippi in the last half of the eighteen-hundreds, modern readers are discovering concepts like *sacrifice* and *self-denial* and *unwavering commitment to an ideal*—concepts that are not too common in today's very different world.'' ''Writing western historical novels for young adults is immensely satisfying,'' she concludes. ''It gives me the opportunity to show that

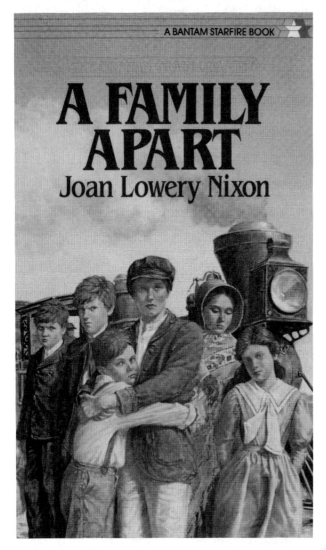

A BANTAM STARFIRE BOOK

A FAMILY APART
Joan Lowery Nixon

Set in pre-Civil War America, this 1987 novel chronicles the lives of two children who are raised by Kansas abolitionists after their mother is no longer able to care for them.

history isn't simply a collection of dates and wars and kings and presidents, but that *children* have always helped make history, that *children* are not only important to the past but are helping to shape history being made today.''

Nixon also draws on her own past for inspiration. Her ''Hollywood Daughters'' series, she related to *AAYA*, was based on ''some of the kids I knew at Hollywood High during the 1940s—kids who had been stars as children but who were 'has-beens' by the time they were teenagers.'' The first volume, *Star Baby*, is set in 1942 and tells the story of seventeen-year-old former child star Abby Baynes. Dominated by her bossy mother, Abby slowly breaks out of the children's roles her mother keeps forcing on her and becomes a successful comedienne. *Overnight Sensation*, the second volume, is the story of Abby's daughter, Cassie Martin, who is faced with the difficulty of growing up in the late 1960s and dealing with parents whose lifestyles leave little time for their daughter. Cassie finally achieves her dream of becoming a successful photographer. *Encore*, the third volume, is the story of Cassie's daughter, Erin Jenkins. Although she is the star of a TV sitcom, Erin's home life seems empty—her parents' closeness, she feels, shuts her out. When the sitcom is cancelled, Erin loses the support of her TV family, but she finds an ally in her grandmother Abby and comes up with a movie plot that will let her continue her career.

Nixon's ''Maggie'' stories deal with the problems of growing up in an unstable environment, too. Young Maggie lost her mother in an accident several years before the opening chapters of *Maggie, Too*, and she has little contact with her filmmaker father. Maggie becomes openly resentful when her father announces his plans to remarry (to a twenty-one-year-old starlet) and packs her off to spend the summer with her librarian grandmother (also named Maggie) in Texas. Over the course of the book and its two sequels, *And Maggie Makes Three* and *Maggie Forevermore*, Maggie learns to love her grandmother, to lose her resentment toward her father and his new wife, and to appreciate her own life. ''Generation to generation, emotions don't change,'' Nixon states in *The Writer*. ''Loneliness, fear, joy, sorrow, embarrassment. . . . External situations may differ greatly, but the emotions they cause are always the same. Our basic needs—such as the need to be loved, to be comforted, and to be secure—remain constant.''

In *The Writer* Nixon also tells of ways to be successful when writing mysteries for young adults. She reminds the would-be author that, for this age group, the opening must catch their attention with intrigue, action or suspense; but the main character must be interesting enough to keep that attention. The dialogue must be true to life— not dated, but using the words that readers would use. And she ends by saying about teenagers, "Appreciating them, really liking them—this, too, I think, is an essential part of the answer." Nixon writes in *SAAS* that "even imaginary characters can have wills of their own," and relates that she sees her characters in her dreams and hears them talking about the story. She feels that the beginning is important to capture young readers' interest, and if she knows how it will end, she is sure she will finish it. She writes on an IBM computer, and every morning rewrites the previous day's text. Her favorite book is "the one on which I'm working!" Her bulletin board is her "idea bank" where she tacks up ideas as they occur to her, then does a lot of research to be sure that everything is accurate. She always has two levels in her books,

This 1992 work, which examines the history of Ellis Island, is part of Nixon's more recent "Land of Hope" series.

"a problem to solve, and a mystery to solve," she states. "Later the characters can weave them together." Her message to young people, she declares, is: "For those of you who have hopes of becoming writers, it's important to know that you'll need that determination and persistence and the courage to continue, no matter what might happen.... [If] you want to be successful, published writers, you'll have to be able to take editorial direction."

After more than three decades and ninety books, Nixon's popularity shows no signs of flagging. Why is her work so popular with young people? "It's because her writing gives them a feeling of hope," Nick Nixon tells Stoeltje. "Through her heroines, she tells children that anything is possible for them. 'Be strong, be confident. You can do things.'" And she remains constantly inventive. Even a trip in a hot-air balloon doesn't stop her imagination: while admiring the desert scenery around Sedona, Arizona, "I glanced down and a man just happened to be in his driveway, putting something in the trunk of his car," she tells Stoeltje. "I said to Nick, 'Suppose he had just committed a crime and was stuffing the body bags in the trunk?' And Nick sort of gave this exasperated sigh and said, 'Can't you just enjoy this lovely scenery and forget about mysteries for a while?'"

■ **Works Cited**

Adams, Mary L., review of *The Other Side of Dark*, *Voice of Youth Advocates*, December, 1986, p. 221.

Davis, Paxton, review of *The Kidnapping of Christina Lattimore*, *New York Times Book Review*, May 13, 1979, p. 27.

Review of *Fat Chance, Claude*, *Publishers Weekly*, September 25, 1987, p. 107.

Gale, David, review of *The Other Side of Dark*, *School Library Journal*, September, 1986, pp. 145-46.

Hearne, Betsy, review of *Fat Chance, Claude*, *Bulletin of the Center for Children's Books*, September, 1987, p. 15.

Morrell, Linda E., review of *The Kidnapping of Christina Lattimore*, *School Library Journal*, September, 1979, p. 160.

Nixon, Joan Lowery, "Clues to the Juvenile Mystery," *The Writer*, February, 1977, pp. 23-26.

Nixon, Joan Lowery, autobiographical sketch in *Something about the Author Autobiography Series*, Volume 9, Gale, 1990, pp. 267-84.

Nixon, Joan Lowery, "Writing Mysteries Young Adults Want to Read," *The Writer,* July, 1991, pp. 18-20.

Nixon, Joan Lowery, "Writing the Western Novel for Young Adults," *The Writer,* June, 1992, pp. 21-23.

Something about the Author, Volume 8, Gale, 1976, pp. 143-44.

Something about the Author, Volume 44, Gale, 1986, pp. 131-39.

Stoeltje, Melissa Fletcher, "Murder for Gentle Readers," *Houston Chronicle Magazine,* June 20, 1993, pp. 8-11.

■ **For More Information See**

BOOKS

Children's Literature Review, Volume 24, Gale, 1991.

Twentieth-Century Children's Writers, 3rd edition, St. James, 1989, pp. 723-24.

Ward, Martha E., *Authors of Books for Young People,* 3rd edition, Scarecrow Press, 1990.

PERIODICALS

Horn Book, November, 1986, p. 748.

Los Angeles Times Book Review, November 23, 1986, p. 12.

New York Times Book Review, February 27, 1983, p. 37; October 9, 1988.

Publishers Weekly, February 22, 1980, p. 108; December 5, 1980, p. 52; April 1, 1983, p. 103; April 22, 1983, p. 104; October 5, 1984, p. 91; May 30, 1986, p. 67; November 28, 1986, p. 77; October 9, 1987, p. 89; October 23, 1987, p. 73; December 11, 1987, p. 66; August 12, 1988, p. 462; September 9, 1988, pp. 133-34; September 8, 1989, p. 67; October 13, 1989, p. 55; November 10, 1989, p. 62; March 15, 1991, p. 59; June 14, 1991, p. 58.

School Library Journal, April, 1976, p. 58; January, 1979, p. 45; December, 1979, p. 97; May, 1980, p. 85; September, 1980, p. 62; November, 1980, p. 66; October, 1981, p. 157; December, 1981, p. 82; December, 1982, p. 81; May, 1983, p. 74; October, 1983, p. 152; December, 1984, p. 102; May, 1985, p. 111; September, 1985, pp. 137-38; September, 1986, p. 138; January, 1987; March, 1987, p. 164; May, 1987, p. 102; December, 1987, p. 75; February, 1988, p. 85-86; August, 1988, p. 97; November, 1988, p. 94; September, 1989, pp. 275-76; November, 1989, p. 128; January, 1990, p. 87; May, 1990, p. 126; March, 1991, pp. 194, 216; July, 1991, p. 88; March, 1992, pp. 240, 259; March, 1993, p. 222.

School Library Media Quarterly, fall, 1982.

Voice of Youth Advocates, October, 1987, p. 204; December, 1987, p. 236; August, 1988, p. 134; December, 1988, pp. 240-41; February, 1989, p. 288; August, 1989, p. 160; October, 1989, p. 215; June, 1990, p. 108; December, 1990, p. 287; February, 1991, p. 355; August, 1991, p. 174; April, 1992, pp. 18, 34; June, 1993, p. 93.

The Writer, September, 1972.

Susan Beth Pfeffer

■ Personal

Born February 17, 1948, in New York, NY; daughter of Leo (a lawyer and professor) and Freda (a secretary; maiden name, Plotkin) Pfeffer. *Education:* New York University, B.A., 1969. *Hobbies and other interests:* Old movies, baseball, used book shopping, and Friends of the Library.

■ Addresses

Home—14 South Railroad Ave., Middletown, NY, 10940. *Agent*—Marilyn E. Marlow, Curtis Brown Agency, 10 Astor Place, New York, NY, 10003.

■ Career

Writer.

■ Awards, Honors

Dorothy Canfield Fisher Award and Sequoya Book Award, both for *Kid Power*; South Carolina Young Adult Book Award for *About David* and for *The Year without Michael*.

■ Writings

YOUNG ADULT NOVELS

Just Morgan, Walck, 1970.
Better Than All Right, Doubleday, 1972.
Rainbows and Fireworks, Walck, 1973.
The Beauty Queen, Doubleday, 1974.
Whatever Words You Want to Hear, Walck, 1974.
Marly the Kid, Doubleday, 1975.
Kid Power, illustrated by Leigh Grant, F. Watts, 1977.
Starring Peter and Leigh, Delacorte, 1978.
Awful Evelina, illustrated by Diane Dawson, A. Whitman, 1979.
Just Between Us, illustrated by Lorna Tomei, Delacorte, 1980.
About David, Delacorte, 1980.
What Do You Do When Your Mouth Won't Open?, illustrated by Tomei, Delacorte, 1981.
A Matter of Principle, Delacorte, 1982.
Starting with Melodie, Four Winds, 1982.
Courage, Dana, illustrated by Jenny Rutherford, Delacorte, 1983.
Truth or Dare, Four Winds, 1984.
Fantasy Summer, Pacer, 1984.
Kid Power Strikes Back, F. Watts, 1984.
Paperdolls, Dell, 1984.
The Friendship Pact, Scholastic, 1986.
Getting Even, Pacer, 1986.
The Year without Michael, Bantam, 1987.
Rewind to Yesterday, illustrated by Andrew Glass, Delacorte, 1988.
Turning Thirteen, Scholastic, 1988.
Future Forward, illustrated by Glass, Delacorte, 1989.

Head of the Class, Bantam, 1989.

(And illustrator) *Dear Dad, Love Laurie,* Scholastic, 1989.

Darcy Downstairs, Holt, 1990.

April Upstairs, Holt, 1990.

Most Precious Blood, Bantam, 1991.

Twin Surprises, illustrated by Abby Carter, Holt, 1991.

Twin Troubles, illustrated by Carter, Holt, 1992.

Family of Strangers, Bantam, 1992.

The Ring of Truth, Bantam, 1993.

Make Believe, Holt, 1993.

The Riddle Streak, Holt, 1993.

"MAKE ME A STAR" SERIES

Prime Time, Berkley Publishing, 1985.

Take Two and Rolling, Putnam, 1985.

Wanting It All, Berkley Publishing, 1985.

On the Move, Berkley Publishing, 1985.

Love Scenes, Berkley Publishing, 1986.

Hard Times High, Berkley Publishing, 1986.

"SEBASTIAN SISTERS" SERIES

Evvie at Sixteen, Bantam, 1988.

Thea at Sixteen, Bantam, 1988.

Claire at Sixteen, Bantam, 1989.

Sybil at Sixteen, Bantam, 1989.

Meg at Sixteen, Bantam, 1990.

OTHER

Contributor of short stories to *Sixteen, Visions,* and *Connections;* contributor of one-act play to *Center Stage,* edited by Donald R. Gallo; contributor of an essay to *Vital Signs 1,* edited by James L. Collins.

■ Sidelights

"Being a writer is really easy," author Susan Beth Pfeffer told *AAYA* as her fat cat Louisa purred on her lap. "I wrote my first book during my final semester at New York University. I was twenty years old, taking seventeen credits and nearly flunking one class, having extensive dental work done, and pursuing the normal social life of anyone living in New York City in 1968. With all that I found time to write a book in one semester. I wrote five pages a day five days a week. I worked with the refrigerator behind me and reached back without knowing what I was grabbing just so I could keep working. I ate a lot of hot dogs. One of the real advantages of hating school was that I got real self-disciplined." Ever since that hectic year when she wrote *Just Morgan,* Pfeffer has published at least one book for young teenagers each year. She insists that she never considered being anything but a writer.

Pfeffer was born on February 17, 1948, in New York City. Her family soon moved out into the suburbs of the city—first to Queens and then to Long Island. "I had the best of all environmental childhoods," she told *AAYA.* Her mother, Freda Pfeffer, who worked as a secretary, took her and her older brother Alan into New York City regularly. "We visited the planetarium, the Metropolitan Museum of Art, and did a lot of used book shopping, which was a special treat because then we would go to the Horn and Hardart Automat for lunch." Her father, Leo Pfeffer, was a constitutional lawyer who had tried cases before the Supreme Court before becoming a law professor at Long Island University. The family spent summers at their country house in Livingston Manor, a small town in the Catskill mountains of New York. "The house was totally isolated, the only house on the hill, and it was wonderful," Pfeffer remembered. "We got the benefits of living near the city for part of the year and in the country for the rest."

During one of those country summers, Leo Pfeffer sat down to write what became a six-hundred page book on constitutional law. His six-year-old daughter has "vague memories of his writing the book," she recalled, "but I was thrilled to read the title page with the word 'Pfeffer,' and the dedication, which had my name on it. I knew right then that I wanted to be a writer. And growing up in a household where people wrote books I didn't have the sense that only special people wrote books, that you had to do well in school to write books. It was just one more career choice." That same year, Pfeffer began her writing career with the story of a love affair between an Oreo cookie and a pair of scissors. Though her mother loved it, "Dookie the Cookie" remains unpublished.

Growing Up in Suburbia

Growing up in New York City's wealthy suburbs was made easier, Pfeffer claimed, because she "had the comfortable position of the outsider." Her family's lack of wealth helped Pfeffer maintain her distance from the center of the suburban social scene. They lived in what she described as a "middle-class house on a middle-class block in a very wealthy town. Because my parents weren't part of the social world of the town I never had to know who was sleeping with whose Mom, and there was no golf or bridge." Furthermore, she had gone to private school until seventh grade and didn't know many of the students when she entered the public schools.

Being an outsider didn't keep Pfeffer from having friends or having fun. She was an avid movie watcher and had her own circle of companions. As she got older, Pfeffer often travelled into New York City on her own, just like some of the characters in her books. "My mom had no problem with my taking the Long Island Railroad into the city and running around and doing whatever I wanted to do," she told *AAYA*. "I was supposed to take a cab from the train station to my home, which was five blocks away and in the suburbs. Five blocks terrified my mom, but I used to lie to her and walk. There was a very relaxed sense in the late 1950s and early 1960s. A young girl could do that kind of thing back then."

"High school was very interesting," Pfeffer recalled with a laugh. "The school had a real academic caste system. After all when you get 350 Jewish kids and only 70 non-Jewish kids you are not going to be known for your football, though our tennis and golf teams were very good." While her older brother excelled in school, graduating second in his class, Pfeffer's grades "floundered in many different directions. I was an underachiever in everybody's estimation and that was fine by me. But I hated school! It was just one of those things I had to endure to become an adult." Despite her ambivalence about school, Pfeffer went on to New York University, which accepted her, she claimed, because they had the strange quirk of liking underachievers.

Pfeffer rented her first apartment in New York City when she was nineteen. "Being in New York City in the late 1960s forced you to grow up," she remembered. "All those choices: which rock concert to go to, which protest to attend, which movie to see." Even though she still wanted to be a writer, Pfeffer decided to major in television, motion pictures, and radio. She had loved to watch old movies when she was younger, and decided that she would direct documentaries. "But I found out early on that I stunk!," she laughed. "I had no visual gift whatsoever—I couldn't hold the camera steady, couldn't read a light meter, couldn't direct people. Heck, I even stank at screenwriting. I should have been a history major." There were bright points—Martin Scorcese, now a well-known Hollywood movie director, was her teaching assistant, and everybody had a crush on him—but school was mostly a chore and Pfeffer worked hard to graduate early. During that last term, she sent out the manuscript for *Just Morgan,* and four months later it was accepted for publication. Fresh out of college, Susan Beth Pfeffer was a professional writer.

Pfeffer's first book earned her a 750 dollar advance—not enough to live on even in the 1960s—so her parents supported her financially while she got to work on her next book, which took two years to sell. "I floundered around a great deal in those early years, offering my manuscripts to everybody, and finally I had two books accepted at two different publishing houses." Though she envies people who have the security of staying with one publisher, Pfeffer said that she tends to be loyal to editors instead. Despite her early struggles as an author, she insisted that "writing has never really been sweat labor. The words always just pour out of me, but sometimes what comes out is not very good. After several years of having editors and agents tell me to think before I write, the words still pour out but now I do a lot of preparatory work and it comes out pretty clean."

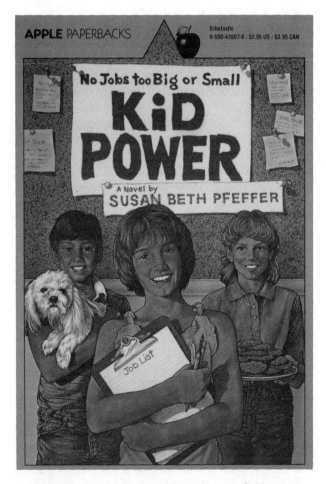

This 1977 novel received the Dorothy Canfield Fisher Award and the Sequoya Book Award, the first awards Pfeffer won for her work.

Pfeffer's World

Although Pfeffer has written over forty books, her characters all come from a common world: the world of suburban, middle-class American adolescence. From her first book, *Just Morgan*, to her five-volume *Sebastian Sisters* series, Pfeffer has written about teenage girls who struggle with problems as small as how to throw a party for a group of friends and as big as how to cope with the fact that a best friend just shot his parents and then turned the gun on himself. Her subject matter has been frivolous and quite serious, but it always reflects the interests of teenagers. Several reviewers think that Pfeffer has been at her best when dealing with the bigger issues, as she does in *About David, The Year without Michael*, and *Family of Strangers*. But she has also garnered praise for the *Sebastian Sisters* series, which a *Publishers Weekly* reviewer lauded as a "thoughtful exploration of family ties [that] fairly sparkles with romance."

About David, Pfeffer's most controversial work, opens as seventeen-year-old Lynn returns home to find her friend David's house surrounded by police and emergency medical vehicles. She soon learns from her father that David has killed his parents and then committed suicide, and he has left a mysterious note that the police refuse to discuss. We read Lynn's notebook as she describes her attempts to understand David's motivations, and as her grief and anger disrupt her relationships with her friends. Lynn's record "carries the half-numb sensation of emerging from anesthesia," wrote *Best Sellers* reviewer John Lansingh Bennett. Lynn seeks help from her sympathetic parents, but they too are distraught: David's parents were their best friends. As the novel progresses Lynn slowly emerges from her shock with the help of a psychologist and a very patient boyfriend. By the book's end she is ready to engage in social life again, but Pfeffer makes it clear that one doesn't just forget such a traumatic incident. Lynn is scarred but she has also grown.

New York Times Book Review contributor Joyce Milton complained that Pfeffer left the conditions within David's family too vague, but Pfeffer claimed that she made David's problems with his family intentionally blurry. "I didn't want anyone to kill their parents as a result of what I put in this book, so I made it very hazy as to what his parents did that was so awful. *About David* is not just a suicide book, it is a murder-suicide book, which is very different." According to Patty Campbell, writing in the *Wilson Library Bulletin*, Pfeffer

In this 1980 work, Lynn must cope with feelings of sadness and shock after learning of a murder-suicide committed by her friend David.

presents David's act as "a psychopathology that harms the lives of all those around the self-destroyer." Although Lynn loved David, she recognizes that he was a very disturbed person and that his act was unpardonable.

Despite the book's generally positive critical reception and the fact that some schools use the book in suicide prevention programs, parent groups in Panama City, Florida, wanted the book removed from their school system, according to *Washington Post Magazine* reporter Peter Carlson. Protesting the use of profanity, blasphemy, and the violent subject matter, the parents removed *About David*, as well as other award-winning books for young people, including Robert Cormier's *I Am the Cheese*. But Pfeffer insisted in her *AAYA* interview that "censorship affects me very minimally. I try to avoid obscenity, but sometimes young people use obscenity and I put it in for very specific effects. I wrote *About David* because I wanted to portray an unimaginable disaster that was peculiarly teenage and I wanted to concentrate on the reactions of the survivors. One way people react is to get angry and swear and to question the existence of God. But these censorship incidents happen in the strangest ways in school systems that you can not predict in any way. It's just not something I can worry about."

"I Don't Know What Happened to Michael"

In *The Year without Michael,* Pfeffer again deals with a difficult social issue: the problem of missing or runaway children. As the book opens, thirteen-year-old Michael Chapman disappears, and the story recounts the struggles that Michael's already troubled family go through as they deal with this crisis. *New York Times Book Review* contributor Elinor Lenz noted that "the Chapmans' unhappiness is all too familiar. The strained marriage, the constant tension in the air, the infighting that pits

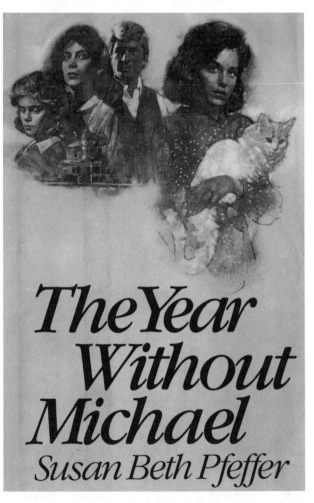

After her younger brother Michael disappears, sixteen-year-old Jody struggles to keep her troubled family together in this 1987 novel.

parents against children and children against one another . . . reflect[s] more or less faithfully family life in the United States in these ebbing years of the century." Sixteen-year-old Jody tries to keep the family together despite these difficulties, and though there is hope that her parents' marriage will survive, by the end of a year there is still no sign of Michael. Lenz called the book "a sensitive and probing view of a contemporary family in agony." A *Horn Book* reviewer wrote that the fact that the book "creates so wrenching an effect on the reader speaks to the author's considerable talent in bringing a sense of intimacy and immediacy to her writing." *Publishers Weekly* simply called *The Year without Michael* "heart-breaking."

"I got a letter from someone who said they read *Michael* and it helped them to decide not to run away," Pfeffer told *AAYA,* "but most kids said that the ending drove them crazy. They wanted Michael to return. I have to explain to kids that it would have been cheating to have Michael come back." Pfeffer and her editor have discussed a sequel to the book, but she said that it would be difficult to write because she doesn't know what happened to Michael. "I don't know if he ran away or was killed or what happened to him. Nobody told me and there is nothing in the text that says what happened." Pfeffer told *AAYA,* "I didn't want to know more than the characters in the story did because I thought that would be a handicap. My theory is that Michael hitched a ride and was killed, but I didn't come up with that until after I finished the book and I'm still not sure that it's true."

Pfeffer enjoys withholding the typical happy ending to her stories. In *What to Do When Your Mouth Won't Open,* a young girl struggles to overcome her phobia of public speaking and finally reads an essay aloud in front of four hundred people. "So she reads the essay, and she even improvises," Pfeffer recounted with obvious relish, "and she doesn't win the contest. It drives kids crazy! There is a certain kind of happy ending that they expect, whether they get it from TV or what, I don't know, but they really think that everything should work out alright. It gives me a certain amount of perverse pleasure not to do that, because in life you don't always win the essay contest and lost children don't always come home."

Killing Off Nicky

Unexpected endings don't always come easy for the author, however. Pfeffer said that one of her most difficult writing experiences was when she had to "kill off" Nicky, the father in the *Sebastian Sisters* series. The five-book series tells the story of the tumultuous Sebastian family—the parents, Nicky and Megs, and the four daughters, Evvie, Thea, Claire, and Sybil. The Sebastian parents are hardly typical: Nicky keeps the family moving from town to town as he concocts various get-rich-quick schemes that never quite work out. But Nicky and Megs share a joyful, exuberant love for each other and for their four unique daughters that gets them through the toughest times—until they get to the fourth book, *Sybil at Sixteen.* "When I was halfway through the first book," Pfeffer told *AAYA*, "I realized that I was going to have to kill Nicky off in the fourth book, but I was fond of him and didn't want to do it."

With the family in deep financial trouble, Nicky kills himself so that his family will get a life insurance payoff. Pfeffer described the agony of killing one of her favorite characters: "There was at least one night when I lay in bed and said to myself, 'Do I have to kill him? Can't I please just let him live?' But then I said, 'No, no, no. You have to kill him, you just have to.' Now remember, I write fast, so by the end of the book there are two funerals and a wedding in approximately four chapters. It was incredibly draining to write this and—I know this sounds phoney but it is true—I couldn't make Nicky's funeral arrangements." Pfeffer laughed as she remembered her solution: "I said, 'I know, I'll let Claire do it because she is smarter than me.' Claire is the only character I have ever created that is smarter than me so I just figured out what she would have done to arrange the funeral rather than what I would do."

Pfeffer ranks the *Sebastian Sisters* series as one of her finest accomplishments. "I'm in the fast and sloppy school of writing," she mused. "I don't take a lot of pride in characterization, I don't really care about finding just the right word of phrase, and I don't do description. I find description incredibly boring and I just won't do it. I get my biggest joy out of mixing a bunch of stuff together and creating people or families that you know really well. And I like being funny." The *Sebastian Sisters* allowed her to do both. The first four books deal with each of the daughters during the year they turn sixteen, and the last book, *Meg at Sixteen,* follows the mother back in time to the summer she fell in love with the dashing young Nicky. Pfeffer shows that turning sixteen can be romantic, frightening, and fun. *School Library Journal* reviewer Merilyn S. Burrington called the Sebastians "some of the most

complicated, intriguing people in contemporary [young adult] literature."

Another of Pfeffer's personal favorites is *Family of Strangers,* Abby Talbott's story of her dysfunctional family. Abby is the youngest of three sisters, and she is in the unenviable position of knowing that her demanding parents wanted her to replace a son who had died as an infant. Her sisters compound the pressure on her: one is a drug-addicted dropout while the other is a brilliant overachiever. Abby responds to a family crisis by attempting suicide, and as she goes through a process of slow recovery she provides the letters, journal entries, and imaginary dialogues that make up the text of the book. "I like juggling all the different kinds of information that make up the story," says Pfeffer, "and I was particularly proud of the psychiatrist who helps Abby recover."

Psychiatrists and psychologists are regular characters in Pfeffer's fiction, where they often help

This 1988 novel, part of the "Sebastian Sisters" series, follows the tumultuous family life of Evvie Sebastian, her scheming father Nicky, and the rest of the Sebastian clan.

young characters understand their actions and their feelings. "I was in therapy for a year-and-a-half when I was in college," remembers Pfeffer, "and it was a very helpful, very fine step. I recommend it for anyone eighteen or nineteen years old. It's probably not coincidental that the day after I finished therapy I started my first book." At one time, Pfeffer considered becoming a therapist herself, but she claims "I wouldn't have been a good one. I would have been too meddlesome and interfering and not open enough to listen to what the person was saying." As a writer, she can be meddlesome and solve her characters' problems, which she did by modelling the psychiatrist in *Family of Strangers* after herself.

Troubled Families

"It's odd that so many of the families in my books are troubled," noted Pfeffer, "because my own family was so stable." But when happy families appear in her books, as they often do, she says they are usually modelled after her own. Many of the fathers are lawyers, and the main character is usually a younger sibling, just like Pfeffer. "The older brother in *About David* is modelled after my own older brother, Alan, who is very supportive and very caring. He denies it but it's true. But when I write a book where there is a very mean older brother or sister, that's my brother too." If Pfeffer's female protagonists are often precocious and resourceful, it is because the author was that way when she was a girl, travelling alone in New York City and exploring museums and book shops.

Although her books for older teens have attracted a great deal of attention, Pfeffer also writes books for slightly younger readers. *Twin Surprises, April Upstairs, Darcy Downstairs, The Friendship Pact, Turning Thirteen,* and *Dear Dad, Love Laurie* all deal with trademark Pfeffer themes—the problems of getting along with family and friends—but tend to avoid the traumatic experiences that make *About David* and *The Year without Michael* such challenging books. Carole B. Kirkpatrick, in a *School Library Journal* review, called *Twin Surprises* "a gem of a story," and *Horn Book* praised *Turning Thirteen* as "lively, believable, humorous, and intriguing." Pfeffer declared that it is the subject matter that dictates the age level of the book. "Can you imagine writing *About David* or *The Year without Michael* for a ten year old?," she asked *AAYA*.

Pfeffer never really imagined being anything but a writer, and she swore that her job is incredibly easy. "I think everybody has a creative mind, and it's just a question of which muscles you use and which muscles are allowed to atrophy," she told *AAYA*. In fact, the prolific author claimed that she can teach anyone to write a book for kids. Her formula is simple: "I tell people to start with a situation that appeals to them, and they can get that anywhere—from their favorite novel or TV show or fairy tale or just something that has been eating away at them for a long time. Then you ask, 'Who would be in this situation, what would their ages be, how did they get in this situation,' and so on. That leads into the plot, what is going to happen. Then I teach people how to outline, which is remarkably easy. Finally I teach people how to find the time, and everyone has an hour a day that they can call their own." Pfeffer is so enthusiastic about her job that she vowed she will give her writing seminars to people on the street if they ask.

Pfeffer writes from her home in Middletown, New York, an industrial town near the same Catskill Mountains where she vacationed with her parents as a child. She measures Middletown's distance from New York City by the time it takes to get to her favorite places: ninety minutes from the Lincoln Center for the Performing Arts and ninety minutes from Yankee Stadium. Her office windows look downhill onto spreading hardwoods, and her two cats—"one very fat and very old, and one a little less fat and a little less old"—find their way amidst her file cabinet, computer, and bookcases. Pfeffer professes to be quite content as a writer, though she still dreams that she might have been Queen of England. "I would have done a better job," she joked. "Let's face it, I have a better sense of humor."

■ Works Cited

Bennett, John Lansingh, review of *About David, Best Sellers,* November, 1980, p. 303.

Burrington, Merilyn S., review of *Sybil at Sixteen, School Library Journal,* September, 1989, p. 276.

Campbell, Patty, review of *About David, Wilson Library Bulletin,* December, 1980, p. 292.

Carlson, Peter, "A Chilling Case of Censorship," *Washington Post Magazine,* January 4, 1987, p. 10.

Review of *Evvie at Sixteen, Publishers Weekly,* May 20, 1988, p. 93.

Kirkpatrick, Carole B., review of *Twin Surprises, School Library Journal,* November, 1991, p. 106.

Lenz, Elinor, review of *The Year without Michael, New York Times Book Review,* November 8, 1987, p. 38.

Milton, Joyce, review of *About David, New York Times Book Review,* February 1, 1981, p. 28.

Pfeffer, Susan Beth, in an interview with Tom Pendergast for *Authors and Artists for Young Adults,* March 24, 1993.

Review of *Turning Thirteen, Horn Book,* March-April, 1989, p. 211.

Review of *The Year without Michael, Horn Book,* March-April, 1988, p. 205.

Review of *The Year without Michael, Publishers Weekly,* June 26, 1987, p. 74.

■ For More Information See

BOOKS

Children's Literature Review, Volume 11, Gale, 1986.

PERIODICALS

Horn Book, May-June, 1992.

Publishers Weekly, December 23, 1988; November 9, 1990; July 5, 1991; February 10, 1992; April 12, 1993, p. 64.

School Library Journal, September, 1986; October, 1986; November, 1986; November, 1987; October, 1988; November, 1988; June, 1989; August, 1990; September, 1991; April, 1993, p. 143.

Voice of Youth Advocates, June, 1993, p. 93.

—Sketch by Tom Pendergast

Richard and Wendy Pini

Science Fiction Artists, Science Fiction Writers of America.

Wendy Pini: Free-lance illustrator, 1974—; WaRP Graphics, Poughkeepsie, NY, vice-president and art director, 1977—. *Exhibitions:* "Women in Comics," Museum of Cartoon Art, Port Chester, NY, 1984; "Broad Humor," Cartoon Museum, San Francisco, CA, 1992. *Member:* Cartoonists Guild, Association of Science Fiction Artists.

■ Personal

Richard Pini: Born July 19, 1950, in New Haven, CT; son of Adolf and Grace Pini; married Wendy Fletcher (an artist and illustrator), June 17, 1972. *Education:* Massachusetts Institute of Technology, B.S. in astronomy, 1972.

Wendy Pini: Born June 4, 1951, in Gilroy, CA; daughter of Stuart and Elizabeth (Talcott) Fletcher; married Richard Alan Pini (a writer, editor, and publisher), June 17, 1972. *Education:* Attended Pitzer College, 1970-72.

■ Addresses

Office—WaRP Graphics, 5 Reno Rd., Poughkeepsie, NY 12603.

■ Career

Richard Pini: Hayden Planetarium, Boston Museum of Science, Boston, MA, writer and speaker, 1972-75; Taunton High School, Taunton, MA, planetarium director, 1975-79; WaRP Graphics, Poughkeepsie, NY, president, licensing manager, editor, and writer, 1977—. *Member:* Association of

■ Awards, Honors

Ed Aprill Award from the New York Comics Convention, 1979; Alley Award, 1979, 1980; Inkpot Award, San Diego Comics Convention, 1980; Small Press and Writers Association Award for best artist, best comic, 1983, for *Elfquest;* New Yorkers Distinguished Service Award from the New York State Jaycees, 1984; Balrog Award for best artist from the Sword and Shield Corp. (Denver, CO), 1985, for *Elfquest;* Golden Pen Award, Young Adult Advisory Committee (Spokane, WA), 1989.

■ Writings

"ELFQUEST" SERIES

Elfquest (twenty-episode comic series), WaRP Graphics, 1978-84.
Elfquest (four-volume comic collection), Donning/Starblaze, 1981-84.
Elfquest Gatherum, Fantagraphics, 1981.
Elfquest Novel: Journey to Sorrow's End, Berkley, 1982.

Elfquest (thirty-two issue comic series), Marvel Comics, 1985-88.

Elfquest: Siege at Blue Mountain (eight-issue comic series), WaRP Graphics, 1986-88.

Elfquest Gatherum: Volume Two, Father Tree Press, 1988.

Elfquest: The Hidden Years, WaRP Graphics, 1993.

"ELFQUEST" GRAPHIC NOVEL SERIES

Elfquest: Fire and Flight, WaRP Graphics, 1988.

Elfquest: The Forbidden Grove, WaRP Graphics, 1988.

Elfquest: Captives of Blue Mountain, WaRP Graphics, 1988.

Elfquest: Quest's End, WaRP Graphics, 1988.

Elfquest: Siege at Blue Mountain, WaRP Graphics, 1988.

Elfquest: The Secret of Two-Edge, WaRP Graphics, 1988.

Elfquest: The Cry from Beyond, WaRP Graphics, 1990.

Elfquest: Kings of the Broken Wheel, WaRP Graphics, 1992.

Elfquest: The Hidden Years, WaRP Graphics, 1992.

"ELFQUEST"-RELATED ANTHOLOGIES

Elfquest: The Blood of Ten Chiefs, Tor Books, 1986.

Elfquest: Wolfsong, Tor Books, 1988.

Elfquest: Winds of Change, Tor Books, 1989.

Elfquest: Against the Wind, Tor Books, 1990.

Elfquest: Dark Hours, Tor Books, 1993.

OTHER

Law and Chaos: The Stormbringer Art of Wendy Pini, Father Tree Press, 1987.

Beauty and the Beast: Portrait of Love, First Publishing, 1989.

Beauty and the Beast: Night of Beauty, First Publishing, 1990.

■ Adaptations

Perrin, Steve, *Elfquest: The Complete Roleplaying Game*, Chaosium Inc., 1989; a board game from Mayfair Games; an album of Elfquest-inspired music.

■ Work in Progress

Jink, an Elfquest-related saga of the future; prose story anthologies and novelizations; an illustrated series of children's books; animation for both television and motion pictures; licensing of the Elfquest properties and characters.

■ Sidelights

In 1969, as an eighteen-year-old high school senior in California, Wendy Pini wrote a letter that was published in the *Silver Surfer* comic book series. Soon she began "receiving letters from all over the country, from boys who were interested in meeting a *girl* who read comics," she explained to John Weber in an interview for *The Elfquest Gatherum, Volume 2.* One of her admirers was Richard Pini, then a nineteen-year-old freshman at the Massachusetts Institute of Technology. After corresponding by mail and telephone for several months, Richard recalled for Weber: "I got into a little Renault and, sixty hours later, I was getting out of the car in Los Angeles." This marked the beginning of one of the most successful partnerships in independent comics—and the celebrated *Elfquest* series.

The Pinis maintained their long-distance relationship until 1972, when Wendy moved east and the couple were married. After working for several years, they began combining their mutual interest in fantasy and comics to form the foundation for *Elfquest.* They developed a unique working partnership in which they outlined the story lines and

The first of the Elfquest graphic novels, this 1988 story traces the adventures of the Wolfriders—a band of elfin hunters who ride wolves and live according to the rules of nature.

the general direction for the series as a team, then Wendy created the artwork while Richard handled the business end of publication. In 1977, after seeking a publisher for *Elfquest* for some time, they decided to start their own publishing company, which they called WaRP Graphics from a combination of their names (Wendy *and* Richard *Pini*). "We started out with a loan from my parents, not knowing how to publish, not knowing where to go, going to the Yellow Pages and looking for a printer because there was not the network of information that there is today," Richard remarked to Weber. "We printed up ten thousand copies of *Elfquest*, and then went to Bud Plant and Phil Seuling and said, 'Will you take our print run?' They said yes, and the rest is history."

Elfquest made its debut in *Fantasy Quarterly #1* in 1978. The series focuses on a band of elves known as the Wolfriders on the World of Two Moons, which resembles Earth in the Pleistocene era, and examines their complex interactions with other tribes of elves, trolls, humans, and nature. From the outset, the Pinis' fantasy world appealed to a wide audience because of its distinctive blend of adventure, romance, humor, and spirituality. It also influenced comics that followed, as Richard Meyers stated in *The Elfquest Gatherum, Volume 2*. "Elfquest has changed the comic world," he proclaimed. "Without it, there might have been no *American Flagg!*, no *Love and Rockets*, no *Concrete*, no *Elektra*, maybe not even a *Dark Knight* or *Watchmen*. Because the Pinis proved there was a market for something other than just full figures in action. There was a market for words, for deep emotions, for something other than 'comic book' art." The world of Elfquest also "has the unity of vision that could only be born from the dynamic of a creative partnership which has seen the idea through from the first hazy concepts batted across the dinner table," James Gurney noted in his introduction to *Elfquest: Kings of the Broken Wheel*. "It succeeds in the peculiar alchemy of all good fantasy, allowing each of us as a reader to conjure a world beyond what is printed on the pages."

The Pinis were able to mold their early success into an entire universe of Elfquest material that continues to evolve today. "*Elfquest* has done everything it's possible to do with a comic book," Wendy related to Weber. "We started out as an innovative, independent series, black and white, self published. We gained a huge readership—by the time we finished the twenty issue series, we were up to a circulation of 100,000. We were the

first independent series to be licensed and reprinted by a mainstream comic company, Marvel Comics. We were the first graphic novel series produced in America to be marketed through Waldenbooks and B. Dalton's." *Elfquest* has also been used in schools to encourage young people to read and has served as the subject of university courses in contemporary mythology. In addition, WaRP Graphics expanded to include a book-publishing division, Father Tree Press.

Wendy and Richard's Early Influences

Wendy Pini grew up in Gilroy, California, near San Francisco. She always enjoyed drawing and has said that she produced her first elf at the age of two. Her imagination was fueled by books she encountered in the library of her grandmother, Helen Fletcher, who was an elementary school teacher. As Wendy recalled in the introduction to *Law and Chaos: The Stormbringer Art of Wendy Pini*, "After her retirement her personal library became a treasure trove of the books she had taught from, books that would probably intimidate today's underread college freshmen. By the age of five I had been exposed to Shakespeare, Kipling, Milton and all the colors of Lang's fairy books. Although the words didn't always make sense, their music thrilled and painted mind pictures. Many of those early editions contained the romantic pre-Raphaelite and Art Nouveau illustrations that introduced me to the concepts of line and composition." Although in *Law and Chaos* Wendy discussed her childhood drawings with some disdain, she admitted that they demonstrate "a strong sense of personal direction. I wanted to be a cartoonist, to have my drawings move, come to life, like Bugs Bunny and Snow White."

As a teenager, Wendy discovered comic books. She practiced cartooning and fantasy illustration in her high school art classes—despite her teacher's protests—and frequented the local magazine racks during her lunch hour. "I read science fiction and comics—superhero comics—which was not the usual fare of a girlish go-go booter in 1967," Wendy remembered in *Law and Chaos*. "Moreover I liked to draw those trashy, rock-muscled heroes and villains, those male power fetishes." During this period she also encountered Japanese comic books and studied them in the original Japanese. She indicated to Weber that Sanpei Shirato's artwork in the *Kamui* series, in particular, had a pronounced influence on her later style.

The event which determined the course of Wendy's next several years occurred when she first spotted Michael Moorcock's novel *Stealer of Souls* on a magazine rack. She recognized the melancholy face of Elric of Melnibone from her own imagination and was immediately captivated by the character to the point of obsession. "Michael Moorcock's high-wrought, gloomful prose," Wendy admitted in *Law and Chaos*, "filled me with the reverence and fierce delight of a disciple. For the first time in my awareness, someone had portrayed 'the Haunter' as a glorified adolescent archetype, with all its insecurities, self hatred and fatalism spread like literary acne across page after page.... I had found a guru in Michael Moorcock and was overwhelmed by his kind responses to my fan letters."

In 1970 Wendy enrolled at Pitzer College in Claremont, California, largely because it featured an experimental program in which students could design their own curricula. "My chief joy came in gearing all my classes around one major project—*Stormbringer: The Film*—which Moorcock had given me permission to attempt," Wendy recalled in *Law and Chaos*. "I had literally dedicated my life to this project," she told Weber. "You know, that was way back in the flower child era, and my mind was expanded, and I just thought this was great. And so, everything that I did was built around getting this film done." Wendy majored in liberal arts but spent most of her time drawing scenes from the novel that she eventually planned to turn into an animated film. She also consulted with professional writers and artists and visited animation studios. After pursuing this goal for five years, Wendy realized the project was too extensive to conquer single handedly and reluctantly gave it up. The book *Law and Chaos*, however, includes about 120 of the color illustrations she created for the project and stands as a tribute to her efforts.

In 1972 Wendy left Pitzer and moved east to marry Richard Pini. Over the next few years, she embarked upon a career as a professional artist, providing cover illustrations and interior art for Marvel and DC Comics, as well as for science fiction magazines such as *Galaxy, Galileo,* and *Worlds of If.* She continued on this course until 1977, when she worked with Richard to realize her personal vision in *Elfquest.*

Richard Pini grew up on the opposite coast in New Haven, Connecticut, but like Wendy he developed an early fascination with comics and science fiction. In his early teens, he became an avid comic

Blood of Ten Chiefs

This illustration from the 1988 work, *The Elfquest Gatherum, Volume 2*, depicts some of the characters who inhabit the Elfquest universe.

collector. Eventually this interest in other worlds led him to study astronomy at MIT, where he obtained his degree in 1972. After graduation Richard worked at the Hayden Planetarium of the Boston Museum of Science, "writing and presenting star shows, nurturing a talent for both writing and public speaking," he noted in a WaRP Graphics biographical sketch. In 1977 he joined Wendy in developing and marketing *Elfquest* and assumed multiple roles as president, licensing manager, and editor in their new company. Richard described his position in an interview with Peter Sanderson for *The Elfquest Gatherum, Volume Two:* "The concept of finding the right market, or finding the right person to talk to, or finding the glue that holds two pieces of something together, of making it work— the phrase that is put in quotation marks is 'wheeling and dealing.' That's what I like doing, and I think I'll be doing it for a long, long time." As Richard noted in his biographical sketch, the Pinis cannot help but be pleased that "what began as a teenage hobby has grown into a multi-million dollar business."

The Troll King and his henchman plot to fool Cutter, the leader of the Wolfriders, and his followers in this series of panels from the 1988 work, *The Complete Elfquest, Book One.*

Evolution of the *Elfquest* Series

As *Elfquest* grew in popularity and readership over the years, the Pinis allowed their vision to evolve and change with the times. The original stories were published in many forms throughout the 1980s, while the series also continued and expanded. In his introduction to *The Elfquest Gatherum, Volume Two,* Richard conceded that "the title and its connected stories have been through sufficient permutations that, without a scorecard, the unwary may get confused." The original twenty issues of *Elfquest,* which are out of print and difficult to find, were produced independently in black and white. In the early 1980s, the Donning Company compiled these comics and published them in color as a four-volume set. In 1985, Marvel Comics began reissuing the original *Elfquest* stories, along with some new material, in thirty-two color issues. Finally, in the late 1980s the Donning volumes were revised and published by Father Tree Press, a division of WaRP Graphics. Also during this time, a novelization of the original *Elfquest* stories, a series of *Elfquest*-related shared-universe anthologies, and a series of graphic novels continuing the *Elfquest* saga became available.

The Pinis developed much of the story line for the *Elfquest* series even before they published the first of the original comics. "Our formula for doing *Elfquest* was initially to plot the whole thing out," Wendy told Sanderson. "Even before we did our first promo package back in 1977, we knew how it was going to end." However, Richard admitted in *The Elfquest Gatherum, Volume Two* that not every change was anticipated: "As it turned out, the story, the world, the characters grew in complexity and fascination beyond our original expectations. Plot threads twisted and turned in new directions. Personalities that started out simple 'got bent' and became convoluted. More and more an element of autobiography entered the picture, adding another dimension onto the structure of the tale. Elfquest evolved into a multi-layered experience that could be read as a simple fairy tale, an adventure story, or a psychological parable. The elves turned out to be a lot more versatile than we thought!"

In 1984, at the height of *Elfquest*'s early popularity, the Pinis decided—against conventional wisdom and the wishes of fans—to take a break from the series after twenty issues. "Here we've got the best selling independent comic going at the moment, and we're cutting it off," Richard stated in the interview with Sanderson. "After eight years of doing the same thing under very intense conditions, it was absolutely necessary that we take a break." The couple was determined to maintain control of their creation and keep a sense of balance in their lives. At this crucial point in the series, Wendy explained to Weber, "I was literally working around the clock. My health was failing. I was so involved with the characters and what was happening to them, because that's a very violent part of the story where we lose some favorite characters and so forth that, emotionally, I was pretty much of a wreck. I really was not thinking logically, and I don't know if I couldn't have done things in better proportion. That's how it happened." The Marvel Comics reprints filled in during the two-year absence of new Pini material.

In the meantime, Richard and Wendy began working with well-known science fiction and fantasy authors—such as C. J. Cherryh and Piers Anthony—on a series of shared-universe anthologies that began with *Elfquest: Blood of Ten Chiefs.* The stories provide other writers' interpretations of events in the Wolfriders' past, prior to the time of the original *Elfquest* series. "We're very excited about it because it represents an infusion of imagination beyond what we two are able to come up with on our own," Richard informed Sanderson. "It's easy at this point to feel burned out about the characters. But somebody who hasn't been living cheek by jowl with the story for the last eight years can manage to come up with all sorts of new things." Although the series expanded to include other voices, the Pinis still managed its direction carefully. For example, for several years the Pinis explored the possibility of producing an animated film or television version of *Elfquest,* but repeatedly found it too difficult to maintain creative control. "*Elfquest* does have a life of its own. It does now exist in the great 'out there' apart from us, in some ways. It continues to be carried along by its own momentum," Wendy told Weber. "We just feel that we are the guiding spirits behind *Elfquest* now. The vision is ours, and whoever handles it, whether it be in animation or when we start up a juvenile line of *Elfquest* stories aimed specifically at a younger audience . . ., we will still be where the buck stops. And that's how the story will maintain its integrity and how the characters will not go afield."

Characters and Themes in *Elfquest*

The *Elfquest* series centers primarily on the Wolfriders—a group of hunters who ride wolves, live in harmony with nature, and trust their instincts. Their leader is Cutter, whose exploits provide the focus of many of the early stories. The Wolfriders differ from humans in a few basic ways, as Wendy described in *The Elfquest Gatherum, Volume Two*: "Ultimately, the key to understanding elf-think (particularly Wolfrider-think) is an awareness of how three factors would affect life as humans know it: a sense of immortality (or lack of a sense of time pressure), an ability to live in the perpetual present, and the ability to communicate intimately with another mind/soul."

The series explores the Wolfriders' interactions with hostile humans and trolls, as well as with several other elfin tribes—particularly the Sun Folk, a group of farmers who live in the desert and depend on their mental powers. "Wolfriders and Sun Folk compliment each other," Deborah Dunn remarked in an article which appeared in *The Elfquest Gatherum, Volume Two*. "Each group alone has fine qualities that are nonetheless sharply limited in expression. The Wolfriders are strong and vigorous, but for the most part lack the use of magical powers. The Sun Folk possess much ancient wisdom, but are far from being full participants in the life of the physical. The encounters between the two tribes continues to be an enriching and horizon expanding experience for all." Other elfin tribes appearing in the series include the Go-Backs, an intolerant group of fighters who ride elks, and the Gliders, a sterile group of intellectuals whose members claim to be the "High Ones"—revered descendants of all the other elves. The quest in the title refers to Cutter's search for his tribe's origins.

Despite the complex cast of characters, readers of the *Elfquest* series encounter distinct personalities, meaningful relationships, and universal themes. "That, I think, is why Elfquest has acquired such a devoted following, because it speaks to the basic truths that ultimately affect all of us," Len Wein asserted in his introduction to *Elfquest: Siege at Blue Mountain*. "Jealousy, loyalty, laughter, fear, the flickering flame of courage, the unquenchable spark of love. In our time, we have known all these things and more, and yet Richard and Wendy show them to us from a new perspective, an acute angle from which we have never seen them before, but which brings them into sharp, or at least new, focus. The Pinis seem to know instinctively the secrets we hold closest to our hearts."

The Pinis' attention to characterization and relevant social issues, combined with Wendy's innovative artistic style, has earned *Elfquest* a reaction among reviewers that is unusual for a comic series. For example, a writer for *Science Fiction Review*

declared *Elfquest* a "life work," adding that the drawing in *Elfquest: Quest's End* "is superb, the story line multi-leveled and many-stranded." One *Booklist* reviewer called the artwork in *Elfquest: Siege at Blue Mountain* "as beautiful and detailed as ever," noting that it "surpasses most other graphic novels by far," while another praised the "wit, intelligence, and depth of characterization" in *Elfquest: The Cry from Beyond*. And when a *Fantasy Review* writer labelled the quest "trivial," the editor responded by praising *Elfquest* as "certainly the freshest, most accomplished and most rewarding work the graphics subgenre can offer."

The next planned addition to the *Elfquest* universe is *Jink*, which features a female main character and takes place on the World of Two Moons thousands of years after the time of the original series. In an interview with Patrick Daniel O'Neill for *Wizard: The Guide to Comics*, Wendy admitted, "It's a challenge because, traditionally, action heroines

This 1993 work, a collection of five stories that each center on a different Elfquest character, deals with such topics as prejudice, loyalty, and decision-making.

haven't been able to carry their own series very long; we're hoping Jink is going to break some prejudices and some preconceptions about what an action heroine should be. I hope guys can identify with her as easily as women do." The Pinis also introduced *Elfquest: The Hidden Years* in 1993, which is a collection of five stories, each centering on a different well-known series character. A WaRP Graphics press release explained that each "story also focuses on issues important to today's young readers—growing up, loyalty to friends, making difficult choices, and learning to live without prejudice."

The Pinis' Message

While many of the themes in *Elfquest* have particular relevance to young readers, they occasionally concern parents because the Pinis address social issues frankly. Richard explained in the interview with Sanderson that readers "have been forced all through *Elfquest* to accept the reality of the various and sundry things we've put in there. The reality of death. The reality of . . . sex. The reality of love as an emotion and what it means. The reality that you can think differently from the way I think, but that doesn't make you wrong and me right, or vise versa; and we can still get along. I hope it's been a subtle manipulation, but not an unkind one." The Pinis expect young readers to learn from *Elfquest*, and to use events in the series as a basis for honest communication about issues that affect their lives. "We give our younger readers some difficult things to deal with sometimes. For instance, one of the major themes in *Siege at Blue Mountain* right now, in a very subtle way, is child abuse," Wendy told Weber. "And what we are hoping is that this sparks discussion among people who trust each other, whether it's parents and children, friends and friends, teenagers among themselves, whatever. We don't feel that children should be protected from controversy, we don't feel that children should be protected from thinking."

Far from feeling intimidated by the more explicit themes in *Elfquest*, many young readers identify strongly with the characters and situations. Wendy remarked to Weber that "kids write to us, they write to other comics creators, and tell people what they like. They like the feeling of family and belonging. They like the feeling of a value system. They like the feeling of a direction. They like the feeling that a character might grow and learn after making a mistake, and that there isn't a punishment for all time. They really do relate to that."

While they appreciate the fact that young people become attached to the series, the Pinis also caution readers against letting *Elfquest* become an obsession. "You go to a convention, you know who they are, the 'moonshots,' the ones that drift around with that look in their eyes. You can spot them a mile away. They are the ones who live through fantasy because life is simply too unbearable for them. They get addicted to it. It's like a drug," Wendy recalled in the interview with Weber. "I feel very sorry that this is their only source of feeling that they belong to something, that they live in fandom because they don't have family at home, or an ability to talk to friends." But in proportion, the Pinis enjoy it when readers use their imaginations and produce *Elfquest* stories and drawings of their own. Wendy explained to Weber that "the fact that they're using all of that creative energy for something besides shooting up dope or bashing each other's brains in, I think, is fabulous. I would do anything to encourage that. And possibly, out of that, can grow some people who can actually and truly contribute to the *Elfquest* mythos someday."

■ Works Cited

Dunn, Deborah, "The Woman Wolfriders," *The Elfquest Gatherum: Volume Two*, Father Tree Press, 1988, pp. 109-119.

Review of *Elfquest: Siege at Blue Mountain*, *Booklist*, April 1, 1989, p. 1372.

Review of *Elfquest: The Cry from Beyond*, *Booklist*, September 1, 1991, p. 45.

Fantasy Review, July, 1985, p. 21.

Gurney, James, "Introduction," *Elfquest: Kings of the Broken Wheel*, WaRP Graphics, 1992.

Meyers, Richard, "Introduction," *The Elfquest Gatherum: Volume Two*, Father Tree Press, 1988.

O'Neill, Patrick Daniel, "Elfquest: The Wendy and Richard Pini Interview," *Wizard: The Guide to Comics*, February, 1993, pp. 50-54.

Pini, Richard, "Introduction: A Kind of Primer," *The Elfquest Gatherum: Volume Two*, Father Tree Press, 1988, pp. 4-5.

Pini, Wendy, "Getting Bent; or, Thinking Like an Elf," *The Elfquest Gatherum: Volume Two*, Father Tree Press, 1988, pp. 32-37.

Pini, Wendy, *Law and Chaos: The Stormbringer Art of Wendy Pini*, Father Tree Press, 1987.

Sanderson, Peter, "Further Conversations with WaRP," *The Elfquest Gatherum: Volume Two*, Father Tree Press, 1988, pp. 45-56.

Science Fiction Review, summer, 1985, p. 52.

WaRP Graphics, press releases and promotional materials, 1993.

Weber, John, "The Conversation Continues—Three Years Later," *The Elfquest Gatherum: Volume Two,* Father Tree Press, 1988, pp. 57-74.

Wein, Len, "Introduction," *Elfquest: Siege at Blue Mountain,* WaRP Graphics, 1988.

■ **For More Information See**

BOOKS

Contemporary Graphic Artists, Volume 1, Gale, 1986, pp. 216-218.

PERIODICALS

Comics Journal, May, 1984, pp. 87-96.

—Sketch by Laurie Collier Hillstrom

John Steinbeck

during World War II. Foreign correspondent in North Africa and Italy for *New York Herald Tribune,* 1943; correspondent in Vietnam for *Newsday,* 1966-67.

■ Awards, Honors

General Literature Gold Medal, Commonwealth Club of California, 1936, for *Tortilla Flat,* 1937, for novel *Of Mice and Men,* and 1940, for *The Grapes of Wrath;* New York Drama Critics Circle Award, 1938, for play *Of Mice and Men;* Academy Award nomination for best original story, Academy of Motion Picture Arts and Sciences, 1944, for "Lifeboat," and 1945, for "A Medal for Benny"; Nobel Prize for literature, 1962; Paperback of the Year Award, *Marketing Bestsellers,* 1964, for *Travels with Charley: In Search of America.*

■ Writings

NOVELS

Cup of Gold: A Life of Henry Morgan, Buccaneer, Robert McBride, 1929.
The Pastures of Heaven, Brewer, Warren & Putnam, 1932.
To a God Unknown (also see below), Ballou, 1933.
Tortilla Flat (also see below), Covici, Friede, 1935.
In Dubious Battle, Covici, Friede, 1936.
Of Mice and Men (also see below), Covici, Friede, 1937.
The Red Pony (also see below), Covici, Friede, 1937.

■ Personal

Full name John Ernst Steinbeck; also wrote under the pseudonym Amnesia Glasscock; born February 27, 1902, in Salinas, CA; died of heart disease, December 20, 1968, in New York, NY; son of John Ernst (a county treasurer) and Olive (a schoolteacher; maiden name, Hamilton) Steinbeck; married Carol Henning, 1930 (divorced, 1943); married Gwyndolyn Conger (a writer, singer, and composer), March 29, 1943 (divorced, 1948); married Elaine Scott, December 29, 1950; children: (second marriage) Tom, John. *Education:* Attended Stanford University as a special student, 1919-25.

■ Addresses

Agent—McIntosh & Otis, Inc., 310 Madison Ave., New York, NY 10017.

■ Career

Writer. Had been variously employed as a hod carrier, fruit picker, ranch hand, apprentice painter, laboratory assistant, caretaker, surveyor, and reporter. Special writer for the United States Army

The Grapes of Wrath (also see below), Viking, 1939, published with an introduction by Carl Van Doren, World Publishing, 1947, revised edition edited by Peter Lisca, 1972.

The Forgotten Village (also see below), Viking, 1941.

The Moon Is Down (also see below), Viking, 1942.

Cannery Row (also see below), Viking, 1945, published with manuscript, corrected typescript, corrected galleys, and first edition, Stanford Publications Service, 1975.

The Wayward Bus (also see below), Viking, 1947.

The Pearl (also see below), Viking, 1947.

Burning Bright: A Play in Story Form (based on Steinbeck's play; also see below), Viking, 1950.

East of Eden (also see below), Viking, 1952.

Sweet Thursday (also see below), Viking, 1954.

The Short Reign of Pippin IV: A Fabrication, Viking, 1957.

The Winter of Our Discontent, Viking, 1961.

SHORT STORIES

Saint Katy the Virgin (also see below), Covici, Friede, 1936.

Nothing So Monstrous, Pynson Printers, 1936.

The Long Valley (includes "The Red Pony," "Saint Katy the Virgin," "Johnny Bear" and "The Harness"), Viking, 1938, published as *Thirteen Great Short Stories from the Long Valley*, Avon, 1943, published as *Fourteen Great Short Stories from the Long Valley*, Avon, 1947.

How Edith McGillicuddy Met R. L. S., Rowfant Club (Cleveland), 1943.

The Crapshooter, Mercury Publications, 1957.

Steinbeck's short stories and short novels have appeared in numerous anthologies. Contributor of short stories to periodicals.

PLAYS

(With George S. Kaufman) *Of Mice and Men: A Play in Three Acts* (based on Steinbeck's novel; first produced on Broadway at The Music Box Theatre, November 23, 1937), Viking, 1937.

The Moon Is Down: Play in Two Parts (based on Steinbeck's novel; first produced on Broadway at Martin Beck Theater, April 7, 1942), Dramatist's Play Service, 1942.

Burning Bright: Play in Three Acts (first produced on Broadway at Broadhurst Theatre, October 18, 1950), Dramatist's Play Service, 1951.

NONFICTION

Their Blood Is Strong, Simon J. Lubin Society of California, 1938.

(With Edward F. Ricketts) *Sea of Cortez*, Viking, 1941, published as *Sea of Cortez: A Leisurely Journal of Travel*, Appel, 1971, revised edition published as *The Log from the "Sea of Cortez": The Narrative Portion of the Book, "Sea of Cortez,"* Viking, 1951.

Bombs Away: The Story of a Bomber Team, Viking, 1942.

A Russian Journal (travelogue), photographs by Robert Capa, Viking, 1948.

Once There Was a War, Viking, 1958.

Travels with Charley: In Search of America (travelogue), Viking, 1962.

America and Americans (travelogue), Viking, 1966.

Also author of *Letters to Alicia*, a collection of newspaper columns written as a correspondent in Vietnam. Contributor of "The Harvest Gypsies," a series of reports on migrant farm workers in California, San Francisco *News*, October 5-12, 1936. Author of syndicated column written during a tour of Vietnam, 1966-67. Contributor of essays and articles to periodicals.

SCREENPLAYS

The Forgotten Village (based on Steinbeck's novel), independently produced, 1939.

Lifeboat, Twentieth Century-Fox, 1944.

A Medal for Benny, Paramount, 1945, published in *Best Film Plays—1945*, edited by John Gassner and Dudley Nichols, Crown, 1946.

The Pearl (based on Steinbeck's novel), RKO, 1948.

The Red Pony (based on Steinbeck's novel), Republic, 1949.

Viva Zapata!, Twentieth Century-Fox, 1952, published version edited by Robert E. Morsberger, Viking, 1975.

OMNIBUS VOLUMES

Steinbeck, edited by Pascal Covici, Viking, 1943, enlarged edition published as *The Portable Steinbeck*, 1946, revised edition, 1971.

Short Novels: Tortilla Flat, The Red Pony, Of Mice and Men, The Moon is Down, Cannery Row, The Pearl, Viking, 1953.

The Red Pony, Part I: The Gift [and] *The Pearl*, Viking, 1953.

East of Eden [and] *The Wayward Bus*, Viking, 1962.

The Pearl [and] *The Red Pony*, Viking, 1967.

Cannery Row [and] *Sweet Thursday*, Heron Books, 1971.

To a God Unknown [and] *The Pearl*, Heron Books, 1971.

Of Mice and Men [and] *Cannery Row,* Penguin, 1973.

The Grapes of Wrath [and] *The Moon is Down* [and] *Cannery Row* [and] *East of Eden* [and] *Of Mice and Men,* Heinemann, 1976.

John Steinbeck, 1902-1968 (contains *Tortilla Flat, Of Mice and Men,* and *Cannery Row*) Franklin Library, 1977.

The Short Novels of John Steinbeck (contains *Tortilla Flat, The Red Pony, Of Mice and Men, The Moon is Down, Cannery Row,* and *The Pearl*), introduction by Joseph Henry Jackson, Viking, 1981.

OTHER

A Letter to the Friends of Democracy, Overbrook Press, 1940.

Journal of a Novel: The "East of Eden" Letters, Viking, 1969.

Steinbeck: A Life in Letters (collection of correspondence), edited by wife, Elaine Steinbeck, and Robert Wallsten, Viking, 1975.

The Acts of King Arthur and His Nobel Knights: From the Winchester Manuscripts of Thomas Malory and Other Sources, edited by Chase Horton, Farrar, Straus, 1976.

(Under pseudonym Amnesia Glasscock) *The Collected Poems of Amnesia Glasscock,* Manroot Books, 1976.

Letters to Elizabeth: A Selection of Letters from John Steinbeck to Elizabeth Otis, edited by Florian J. Shasky and Susan F. Kiggs, Book Club of California, 1978.

The Harvest Gypsies: On the Road to "The Grapes of Wrath," Heyday, 1988.

Working Days: The Journals of "The Grapes of Wrath," edited by Robert DeMott, Penguin, 1989.

Steinbeck's writing has been translated into numerous languages.

■ Adaptations

Of Mice and Men was first adapted for film by Eugene Solow and released by United Artists, 1939; a second film version was released in 1992; the novel was also adapted as an opera by Carlisle Floyd, premiering at the Seattle Opera House, 1970, and adapted as a teleplay by E. Nick Alexander. *The Grapes of Wrath* was adapted for film by Nunnally Johnson and released by Twentieth Century-Fox, 1940; *Tortilla Flat* was adapted for film by John Lee Mahin and Benjamin Glaser, Metro-Goldwyn-Mayer, 1942; *The Moon Is Down* was adapted for film by Johnson, Twentieth Centu-

ry-Fox, 1943. *East of Eden* was adapted for film by Paul Osborn, Twentieth Century-Fox, 1954; the novel was also adapted as a television miniseries and as a musical, *Here's Where I Belong,* opening at the Billy Rose Theatre, 1968. *Sweet Thursday* was adapted into a musical, *Pipe Dream,* by Oscar Hammerstein II, with music by Richard Rogers, 1955; *The Wayward Bus* was adapted for film by Ivan Moffat and released by Twentieth Century-Fox, 1957; *America and Americans,* 1967, and *Travels with Charley,* 1968, were adapted for television and broadcast by NBC; "The Harness" was adapted for television and broadcast in 1971; *The Red Pony* was adapted for television and broadcast in 1973; *Cannery Row* and *Sweet Thursday* were both adapted by David S. Ward for the film *Cannery Row,* Metro-Goldwyn-Mayer, 1982; *The Winter of Our Discontent* was adapted for television by Michael de Guzman and broadcast in 1983.

■ Sidelights

"I hold that a writer who does not passionately believe in the perfectibility of man has no dedication nor any membership in literature." With this declaration, John Steinbeck accepted the Nobel Prize for Literature in 1962, becoming only the fifth American to receive one of the most prestigious awards in writing. In announcing the award, Nobel committee chair Anders Osterling, quoted in the *Dictionary of Literary Biography Documentary Series,* described Steinbeck as "an independent expounder of the truth with an unbiased instinct for what is genuinely American, be it good or ill." This was a reputation the author had earned in a long and distinguished career that produced some of the twentieth century's most acclaimed and popular novels. Steinbeck's Nobel acceptance speech, also quoted in the *Dictionary of Literary Biography Documentary Series,* spoke not of his accomplishments, however, but of a writer's duty to his fellow man. "The ancient commission of the writer has not changed," Steinbeck said. "He is charged with exposing our many grievous faults and failures, with dredging up to the light our dark and dangerous dreams, for the purpose of improvement." Steinbeck believed that those services were in high demand in 1962. "Humanity," he said, "has been passing through a gray and desolate time of confusion."

Some twenty-four years earlier, the author had faced another desolate time. In the winter of 1938, the rains were falling in California, and Steinbeck was a worried and angry man. Since the mid-

1930s, Steinbeck's home state had seen the arrival of hundreds of thousands of poor farmers, refugees from the "dust bowl"—the farmlands of Oklahoma and other parts of the Midwest that had been devastated by drought. Steinbeck had been interested in these migrant farmers for several years, concerned about their lack of food and sanitary housing as they searched for work in California's farmlands. He had visited migrant camps throughout the state and written newspaper articles that documented the hardships he found there. Despite these efforts, conditions had grown worse for the farm workers. By 1938 Steinbeck was convinced that the state's large produce growers were harming the migrants by refusing to pay them satisfactory wages.

When the rains came, the migrants were soon threatened by flood waters in several parts of the state. Observing these events, Steinbeck's anger reached the boiling point, and he told his literary agent, Elizabeth Otis, that it was time to take further action. "I must go over to the interior valleys," Steinbeck wrote in his letter that was later published in *Steinbeck: A Life in Letters.* "There are about five thousand families starving to death over there, not just hungry but actually starving. The government is trying to feed them and get medical attention to them with the fascist group of utilities and banks and huge growers sabotaging the thing all along the line.... I must get down there and see it and see if I can't do something to help knock these murderers on the heads."

At the flooded encampment in Visalia, California, Steinbeck came face to face with the tragedy of the migrants. "I saw people starve to death," Steinbeck later told an interviewer for the London *Daily Mail.* "That's not just a resounding phrase. They starved to death. They dropped dead." Finding himself in the midst of the suffering, the author's first effort to "do something" about the situation was direct and immediate. "Steinbeck worked day and night for nearly two weeks (sometimes dropping to sleep in the mud from exhaustion) to help relieve the misery," wrote Robert DeMott in his introduction to *Working Days.* Steinbeck's second effort to aid the migrants was somewhat delayed, but its impact would prove more lasting. Four months after his visit to the migrant camps, Steinbeck began a novel that would not only publicize the plight of the dust bowl migrants, but also become one of the hallmarks of American literature in the twentieth century: *The Grapes of Wrath.*

Steinbeck's compassion for the downtrodden was exemplified throughout his literary career. As critics have noted, he perceived a materialistic trend in America, an unhealthy increase in greed and a corresponding lack of traditional values. As a result, he concentrated on the victims of this change, ordinary men and women struggling against destructive social and economic conditions. While his characters were sometimes faced by seemingly inhuman forces—technology, progress, natural disasters—Steinbeck also paid great attention to people and human relationships. His work analyzed the way people behave as part of a larger group, and he also featured characters who struggled with personal conflicts, attempting to overcome the destructive elements of their own personalities.

In the Beginning

The third of four children, Steinbeck was born in Salinas, California, in 1902. Steinbeck explored the surrounding area thoroughly as he grew up, and his later work often incorporated this landscape. *Of Mice and Men* and *The Grapes of Wrath* were set in farmlands much like those that surrounded Salinas, and the books *Tortilla Flat* and *Cannery Row* take place in the coastal town of Monterey, a favorite location of Steinbeck's boyhood rambles. After graduating from Salinas High School in 1919, Steinbeck attended college at nearby Stanford University. He remained at Stanford until 1925, but his attendance was frequently interrupted because of illness and indecision regarding a field of study. When not enrolled at the university, Steinbeck took temporary jobs in order to earn money.

His occupations in these years were varied, including store clerk, surveyor, and painter. He also held several positions that provided background material for his writing. Working as a ranch hand near King City, California, Steinbeck experienced the characters and surroundings later featured in *Of Mice and Men.* Likewise, his job with Spreckels Sugar Company introduced him to labor disputes, a topic that would figure in both *The Grapes of Wrath* and *In Dubious Battle.* Steinbeck's sporadic studies were also preparing him for his future as a writer. A summer course in marine biology laid the foundation for his later explorations into the biological nature of man's behavior, a theme that pervades much of his work. And finally, Steinbeck's college years allowed him to develop the craft of writing. He began by producing short fiction, and in 1924 two Steinbeck stories appeared in the Stanford *Spectator,* a newspaper at the college.

After leaving Stanford for good in 1925, Steinbeck thought that his prospects of becoming a successful writer might improve if he relocated to New York City, the publishing capital of the United States. After working his way to the city as a hand on a freighter, he took a job as a laborer. He later became a newspaper reporter for the *New York American,* but his journalism career proved as temporary as his other occupations. After being fired from the paper, he signed onto another freighter and returned to California. Throughout this time, Steinbeck worked on short stories and on his first novel, *Cup of Gold: A Life of Henry Morgan, Buccaneer,* which he completed in 1928. A second novel was soon underway, but Steinbeck still had no publisher for his work. As a result, he was writing books that no one was reading, and he had yet to earn his first dollar by writing fiction. On a personal level, however, his life was changing. He met Carol Henning, his future wife, in the summer of 1928, and their romance continued after he moved to San Francisco later that year. Steinbeck continued to work on his fiction after arriving in the city, and he hoped that his status as an unpublished author would soon change. In January, 1929, he got his wish.

The good news came from Amassa Miller, a friend of Steinbeck's who had been attempting to sell *Cup of Gold* to publishers in New York City. Miller finally convinced Robert M. McBride and Company that the book was worthwhile, and the first Steinbeck novel was published. The contract awarded a degree of financial security that the author hadn't known in his years of travel and temporary jobs. In a letter to his friend A. Grove Day, later published in *Steinbeck: A Life in Letters,* the author noted that the money he received from Robert M. McBride and Company allowed him "to live quietly and with a good deal of comfort." The only problem with the book's publication was that Steinbeck was no longer pleased with *Cup of Gold.* In a later letter to Day written shortly after the novel's debut, the author described *Cup of Gold* as "an immature experiment," suggesting that the book he had finished more than a year earlier now seemed inferior to his present work. His uncertainty about the quality of his first novel would grow with the passing years. In 1932 Steinbeck dismissed *Cup of Gold* by saying, "I've outgrown it and it embarrasses me."

As several critics have noted, *Cup of Gold* is quite different from Steinbeck's later work. A large reason for the disparity is that the book is a historical novel, creating a fictionalized story about Henry Morgan, an infamous English pirate of the 1600s. In creating this type of historical saga, Steinbeck was influenced by several authors whom he had once admired: James Stephens, James Branch Cabell, and Donn Byrne, who had all specialized in a similar type of adventure novel featuring historical figures. By 1929, however, Steinbeck felt that his literary abilities had surpassed those of his mentors. "I seem to have outgrown Cabell," Steinbeck wrote in his letter to Grove, also noting that "I have not the slightest desire to step into Donn Byrne's shoes." Steinbeck further realized that his future work was going to move in a different direction, proclaiming that "I have swept the Cabellyo-Byrneish preciousness out for good."

Two weeks after *Cup of Gold* was released, the stock market plummeted, and the Great Depression had begun. As the 1920s came to a close, Steinbeck had become a published author, but he had yet to achieve a literary voice that pleased him. As he grappled with his direction as a writer, he also paid increasing attention to the explosion of unemployment and misery caused by the Depression. In the following ten years these social concerns would become a vital source of material and inspiration for his work.

Looking Homeward

Seeking a more original means of literary expression, Steinbeck turned his attention away from the distant history in *Cup of Gold* and began to focus on material that was more familiar. One result of this shift in material was that Steinbeck began to utilize the landscape of his native state. His second novel, *To a God Unknown,* concerns a farmer who leaves Vermont and comes to California, eventually establishing a farm with his three brothers. *The Pastures of Heaven,* Steinbeck's next book, also drew on his western locale, relating various loosely connected tales about the inhabitants of a single California community. Steinbeck's model for the town was Corral de Tierra, a community between Monterey and Salinas that he had known since his childhood. Along with these familiar settings, Steinbeck began to feature characters who were also drawn from his own experience. The two books focus on farmers, schoolteachers, prostitutes—a cast of common people far removed from the swashbuckling pirates in *Cup of Gold.*

As *New Yorker* critic Robert M. Coates noted in his review of *The Pastures of Heaven,* Steinbeck's everyday characters gave the book "an effect as of real life." Other authorities on Steinbeck have commented on the simple, middle-class existence of the characters, but as Richard Astro pointed out in the *Dictionary of Literary Biography,* a great deal of frustration and failure is found in the author's common folks. "Steinbeck shows compassion, even affection for the plight of ordinary people who strive but cannot achieve happiness," Astro wrote. The reason for their failure, the critic maintained, is their inability to escape from the larger society. In *The Pastures of Heaven* they have withdrawn to the idyllic valley community, but this refuge proves short-lived. The characters soon face further dissatisfaction as a result of their shortcomings. "Steinbeck never condemns their innocence," Astro wrote, "but he portrays their self-destructive tendencies toward illusion and self-deception."

This 1936 novel depicts a violent labor strike in a California apple orchard.

By the time *To a God Unknown* appeared in 1933, Steinbeck's work was receiving increased critical attention. The novel failed to sell any better than his previous works had, however, and Steinbeck's agents were forced to search for yet another publishing contract. Throughout his early years, Steinbeck's tenure with publishing companies tended to be short. Each of his first three books was issued by a different press, and after *To a God Unknown* failed to sell Steinbeck was in danger of having no publisher at all. He was rescued by Pascal Covici of the Covici, Friede publishing house, a man who would continue to work with Steinbeck throughout his career.

The author's first novel for Covici, Friede was *Tortilla Flat,* which again illustrated his fascination with the simple inhabitants of central California. In this case, Steinbeck depicted the slums of Monterey and a group of good-natured idlers of mixed Mexican and American heritage—the *paisanos.* Led by Danny, in whose house they all live, the *paisanos* are Steinbeck's version of King Arthur and the Knights of the Round Table. The knights' primary quest, in this case, is to acquire a regular supply of red wine and to avoid any responsibilities that might come their way. While the book extended several of Steinbeck's familiar themes and settings, its gentle humor was a departure for the author. "Mr. Steinbeck knows the humorous side of his *Paisanos,*" wrote *New Republic* reviewer Jerre Mangione, adding that the author "rarely fails to be amusing." Whether it was due to Steinbeck's humorous treatment or some other aspect of the book, *Tortilla Flat* soon found an audience that his previous novels had missed. The book became a bestseller, and Steinbeck had to contend with an unfamiliar role: he was a popular author.

Despite the success of *Tortilla Flat,* Steinbeck quickly moved on to new material. His next novel, *In Dubious Battle,* avoided the humor of *Tortilla Flat* and instead presented a study of a serious subject—a labor strike in a California apple orchard. One reason for Steinbeck's varied writing styles during this period, according to Astro, was that the ideas that drove the author's fiction were still evolving. In 1930 he had become a friend of Ed Ricketts, a man Steinbeck would later characterize as "the greatest man I have known and the best teacher," as quoted by Thomas Kiernan in *The Intricate Music: A Biography of John Steinbeck.* Ricketts was a marine biologist who lived in Monterey, and Steinbeck, who had been interested in the study of sea life since his days as a student, was intrigued by Ricketts's biological analysis of ocean creatures. Ricketts's studies went beyond sea life, however. He had evolved a theory of nature that saw all creatures—including humans—belonging to a single, interconnected system. This idea supported and fleshed out some of Steinbeck's own beliefs, and it was soon reflected in the author's work. As critics have noted, Steinbeck's writings after 1930 often emphasize the biological aspects of his character's behavior—how, for instance, they must adapt to changing conditions in order to survive. He also began to consider the individual's role in a larger group and the ways that people gain power by organizing with others. These ideas, when applied to some of the prominent social issues of the Depression years, gave Steinbeck a source of fresh fictional material. He soon used it to create the acclaimed novels he published between 1936 and 1939.

The Hot Streak

In Dubious Battle was Steinbeck's first exploration of the labor unrest that marked the 1930s. The book got its start when the author had the opportunity to interview two farm-labor organizers who were active in the movement to unionize migrant workers. Drawing on their accounts, Steinbeck's novel follows two members of the Communist party as they organize a strike against a wealthy California apple grower who has drastically cut wages. The two men, Mac, a longtime party organizer, and Jim, a committed newcomer, successfully recruit the help of a local farmer and establish a camp for the strikers on his property. Doc Burton, who looks after the sanitary conditions in the strikers camp, is another outsider sympathetic to the fruit pickers' cause. He can do little to help them, however, when the walkout turns violent. In the end, Jim is killed but Mac struggles on, attempting to use Jim's death as a means of rallying the strikers.

In approaching the volatile topic of radical labor movements, *In Dubious Battle* roused controversy. Some, claiming that Steinbeck had sided too heavily with the strikers, labeled the book pro-communist. In assessing the book's literary merits, however, many critics praised Steinbeck's realistic portrayal of class conflict. William Rose Benet, reviewing the novel in *Saturday Review*, stated that "this is a book one respects. Mr. Steinbeck writes most graphic prose and conveys the thought and speech of ordinary laborers with great ability." Benet also found the book an even-handed account of the dispute, with both sides sharing responsibili-

ty for the conflict and the resulting violence. "The battle between those in authority and the strikers has plenty of bloody moments," Benet wrote. "In that desperate fight there is cruelty on both sides, there is the terrible side of the roused mass animal."

In his next work, *Of Mice and Men*, Steinbeck produced one of his most popular novels, and its sudden success—the book sold over one hundred thousand copies in its first month—made him a celebrity. The story is set in the rough-hewn surroundings of a California ranch and focuses on two hired hands, Lennie, immensely strong but mentally retarded, and George, an older hand who takes care of Lennie. The two men dream of gaining their own house and land and giving up their roving life. These plans are frustrated, however, through the cruelty of Curley, the son of the ranch boss, and finally, through the flirtations of Curley's wife. When the woman cuddles up to Lennie, he is unable to control his strength and inadvertently breaks her neck. Lennie then turns to his friend for help, and George must find a way to save Lennie from a hostile mob that seeks revenge for the murder.

Coming between *In Dubious Battle* and *The Grapes of Wrath*, *Of Mice and Men* steps away from the farm labor politics of the other two novels. As Astro pointed out, however, *Of Mice and Men* remains "a memorable parable about man's voluntary acceptance of responsibility for his fellow man." As such, the book continues to illustrate Steinbeck's concern for the weak and unfortunate. Critically, the novel received numerous enthusiastic reviews upon its release. Henry Seidel Canby, writing in *Saturday Review*, judged the novel "superb in its understatements. . . . Its style is right for its subject matter, and that subject matter is deeply felt, richly conceived, and perfectly ordered." This warm reception was soon echoed by theatre critics after Steinbeck adapted the novel into a play with the help of George S. Kaufman. The play had a successful run on Broadway and later played throughout the United States on a national tour. The appeal of the story would be illustrated for years after its release; the play has been repeatedly performed, and the novel has also been adapted into an opera, a television drama, and two major motion pictures.

Steinbeck's progressive success in the 1930s was measured by a change in residences. He and his wife, Carol, had lived in a small house in Pacific Grove, California, early in his career, moving to a larger residence in Los Gatos after the success of

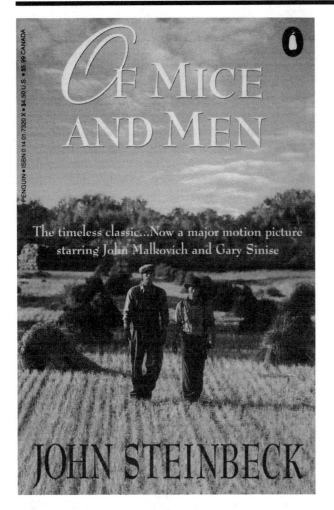

Steinbeck's concern for the weak and oppressed was the focus of this 1937 novel, the story of two drifters, Lenny and George, whose dreams of prosperity end in tragedy.

Tortilla Flat. The income from *Of Mice and Men* allowed them to build a house on a large tract of land in Los Gatos known as the Biddle Ranch, into which they moved in 1939. Steinbeck's fame also introduced him to the company of other celebrities, and he soon became friends with movie stars Charlie Chaplin and Wallace Ford. The trappings of success were not always welcome, however. The increased demands on Steinbeck's time frequently interrupted his writing schedule, and he made reference to these problems in the journal he kept while writing *The Grapes of Wrath,* later published in *Working Days.* "The wants, the demands, the dissatisfactions. They're breaking me down," Steinbeck confessed, speculating that "this success will ruin me as sure as hell."

One of the largest demands Steinbeck had to deal with during this time came from groups who requested his support for various causes. Since the

publication of *In Dubious Battle* and the appearance of his newspaper articles on the dust bowl refugees, many looked to Steinbeck as an influential authority on migrant living conditions. There was even talk in 1938 that he would consult with President Franklin Roosevelt in regard to California's farm workers. Though this meeting never developed, Steinbeck did, on occasion, lend his name in aid of certain causes and organizations. His real interest was literature, however, and Steinbeck was committed to documenting the migrant's plight in a work of fiction. It was a project that proved far from easy.

His first attempt, a novel entitled *The Oklahomans,* was abandoned after several months of work. His next effort was *L'Affaire Lettuceburg,* which he took up immediately after his experiences at the flooded migrant camp at Visalia. The book was intended to be a satirical jab at those Steinbeck saw as responsible for the migrant's problems, but his anger threatened to overwhelm the novel. Writing to his agent, Annie Laurie Williams, Steinbeck confessed the problems that he was having with *L'Affaire Lettuceburg.* "It is a vicious book," De-Mott quoted Steinbeck in the introduction to *Working Days,* "a mean book. I don't know whether it will be any good at all." After three months of work, Steinbeck decided the novel wasn't good enough. He destroyed the nearly-completed manuscript, declaring in a letter to Elizabeth Otis, quoted by Lewis Gannett in the introduction to *The Portable Steinbeck,* that *L'Affaire* "is a bad book and I must get rid of it. It can't be printed. It is bad because it isn't honest." Within days Steinbeck began a much different book about the migrants. This time he had better luck.

The Grapes of Wrath

In his third attempt to write about migrants, Steinbeck turned away from the broad satire he had attempted in *L'Affaire Lettuceburg,* centering instead on the intimate story of the Joads, a family of sharecroppers in Oklahoma. When drought makes the Joad farm unprofitable, they are forced off the land they have worked for generations but do not own. They then depart for California like thousands of similar families, expecting to find a promised land of fruit orchards and steady employment. Among the eleven members of the family are Tom, a grown son who has just served a prison term for killing a man in self-defense, and Ma, whose resilient spirit helps keep the family together during their travels. They are also accompanied by a former preacher, Jim Casy, who is intent on getting to the West Coast to observe the migration of families from Oklahoma.

After a troubled journey in which the grandparents die, the Joads find more trouble in California. They are frequently harassed by vigilantes and policemen and are often forced to live in unsanitary camps. Most importantly, the promise of steady, well-paid work proves empty. With so many people desperate for jobs, the farm owners are able to pay very low wages to the migrants, and the Joads barely make enough to survive. Beset by hunger, sickness, and floods, the family responds in two ways. Casy and Tom take up the cause of organized labor, promoting strikes against the growers. Their philosophy is voiced by Tom, who states that "a fella ain't got a soul of his own, but on'y a piece of a big one." By uniting in mass action, he reasons, the workers will be able to "throw out the cops that ain't our people. All work together for our own thing—all farm our own land." The family's other response is to adopt Ma's determination to carry on despite the disasters that confront them. "We're the people that live," Ma says. "They ain't gonna wipe us out. Why—we're the people. We go on."

In addition to the narrative incidents concerning the Joads, *The Grapes of Wrath* features alternate chapters that render a broader view of the migrants' situation. These chapters sometimes focus on nameless individuals, sometimes on the mechanics of economic or natural forces, sometimes on small, symbolic incidents such as a turtle's determination to get to its destination. Paul McCarthy, in his book *John Steinbeck*, noted that "craftsmanship in *The Grapes of Wrath* is generally excellent," and he emphasized the book's use of varying points of view and varying levels of language. "The most characteristic qualities of the written language," McCarthy wrote, "are precision, natural and sometimes biblical rhythms, and imagery customarily based on elements of the land or daily life." Comparing Steinbeck to other literary innovators of the 1930s, including William Faulkner and John Dos Passos, McCarthy judged *The Grapes of Wrath* as "one of the period's brilliant innovative works." Steinbeck also commented on the multileveled structure he created in the novel, writing in a letter to Pascal Covici quoted in the *Dictionary of Literary Biography Documentary Series* that "there are five layers in this book, a reader will find as many as he can and he won't find more than he has in himself."

Creating such a complex and lengthy work proved a difficult undertaking for the author. Though the book was written in only a five-month period, Steinbeck's journal in *Working Days* records his many difficulties and the physical exhaustion that resulted from the work. "If I am not careful, I will crash," he wrote at one point. "I feel the weariness creeping up on me again as it did that day when I was really in danger of collapse. But I can't now. Must finish this book." Even as he drove himself onward, Steinbeck often feared that he wasn't up to the task. "I'm not a writer," he wrote at a particularly low moment in the process. "I've been fooling myself and other people. I wish I were." When he completed the final page of the book on October 26, 1938, Steinbeck was indeed close to collapse, being "so dizzy I can hardly see the page." After finishing the final sentence of the novel, he recorded his thoughts in the journal. "Finished this day—and I hope to God it's good."

John Malkovich portrayed the gentle, mentally retarded Lenny in the 1992 film version of Steinbeck's *Of Mice and Men.*

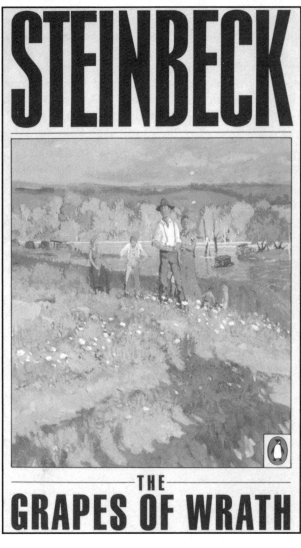

This 1939 novel, Steinbeck's most successful, describes the plight of the Joads, a family of dust bowl migrants, and the hardships they encounter while traveling from Oklahoma to California.

"*The Grapes of Wrath* is, without question, Steinbeck's most ambitious as well as his most successful novel," according to Astro. This lavish praise has been echoed by other critics in the years since the novel's release. A reviewer in *Time* considered *The Grapes of Wrath* the author's "strongest and most durable novel," and called it "a concentration of Steinbeck's artistic and moral vision." In summing up what this vision entails, Joseph Warren Beach, writing in *American Fiction: 1920-1940*, found that *The Grapes of Wrath* made two strident points about the American economy: "that our system of production and finance involves innumerable instances of cruel hardship and injustice; that it needs constant adjustment and control by people in authority." This dire warning, as critics such as Alfred Kazin have noted, is balanced by Stein-

beck's "refreshing belief in human fellowship and courage." As Beach put it, *The Grapes of Wrath* marked Steinbeck as "one who feels strongly on the subject of man's essential dignity of spirit and his unexhausted possibilities for modification and improvement."

Popular reaction to *The Grapes of Wrath* was overwhelmingly positive, with sales far surpassing any of Steinbeck's previous works, including *Of Mice and Men*. The book topped bestseller lists through most of 1939 and continued to sell steadily thereafter. After receiving an early royalty payment for the novel, Steinbeck wrote in a letter—later published in *Steinbeck: A Life in Letters*—that it was "an awful lot of money. . . . I don't think I've ever seen so much in one place before." Success had its drawbacks, however. A backlash of negative publicity was directed at Steinbeck, stemming largely from the agriculture industry that *The Grapes of Wrath* had criticized. Daniel Aaron, quoted in *World Literature Criticism*, noted that these groups "accused Steinbeck of writing a brief for Communism." Other groups in the United States also found the book objectionable. *The Grapes of Wrath* was criticized on the floor of the U.S. Congress and banned from some school libraries.

As the novel became a national sensation, Steinbeck's fame grew far beyond its previous boundaries, and he soon came to regret the hysteria and hoopla that surrounded him. Besieged by requests for money and public appearances, the calm privacy Steinbeck craved became harder and harder to achieve. In the journal he had kept while writing *The Grapes of Wrath*, Steinbeck had a premonition of the changes that would ensue after he completed the novel. "When this is finished," he wrote, "a goodly part of my life will be finished with it. A part I will never get back to." By 1940 these words had come true. *The Grapes of Wrath* had established him as both a major writer and a celebrity, and Steinbeck found that both his life and his work were going to be very different in the coming years.

Falling from Grace

One of the changes Steinbeck underwent was a personal one. In 1941 he and his wife, Carol, separated. They were later divorced and Steinbeck married Gwyndolyn Conger, a woman he had met shortly after the completion of *The Grapes of Wrath*. The United States's involvement in World War II also changed the author's work habits. He

The 1940 film *The Grapes of Wrath*, starring Henry Fonda, received two Academy Awards and was nominated for five others, including Best Picture.

undertook a writing project, *Bombs Away: The Story of a Bomber Team*, for the U.S. Army Air Force and later covered the war in North Africa and Italy as a journalist. These writing projects demonstrated Steinbeck's increasing devotion to genres other than fiction. One of his most highly acclaimed books of the 1940s was, in fact, not a novel but an account of a research expedition that he cowrote with Ed Ricketts. The book, *Sea of Cortez*, contained a catalog of their research findings and also incorporated geography, history, and philosophy into one diverse book. With these nonfiction projects consuming his time, Steinbeck's productivity as a novelist slowed in the early 1940s. When he did return to fiction with *The Moon is Down* in 1943, the critical response was far cooler than that which had greeted *The Grapes of Wrath* four years earlier.

Published in the midst of World War II, *The Moon is Down* concerns the invasion of an unidentified European town by an unidentified enemy, a situa-tion that was very similar to the Nazi occupation of Norway during the war. Initial assessments of the novel sometimes criticized Steinbeck's balanced portrayal of the German invaders, insisting that Steinbeck was "soft toward Nazis," as Warren French recalled in *John Steinbeck*. Once the war with Germany concluded, such patriotic criticism was given less emphasis, but other faults in *The Moon is Down* have been noted. "It is a failure as art not because Steinbeck failed to write a polemic against the horrors of Nazism," Astro wrote, "but rather because he was unable to relate abstract philosophical visions to concrete reality." One reason for this failure, Astro maintained, is that a novel about wartime Europe is too far removed from Steinbeck's personal experience, from the "feelings and insights" that had given substance to his California-based novels.

On a personal level, Steinbeck *had* moved farther away from California. After his second marriage, he resided in New York City for a period of time, returning to California on occasion to work on specific writing projects. This practice continued through the birth of his two sons and through the breakup of his second marriage in 1948. After marrying for a third time, Steinbeck became a more or less permanent resident of New York City, though he departed frequently for extended trips around the world. His literary home, however, was firmly established in California, and he continued to make the region a foundation of his writing.

For his novel *Cannery Row*, Steinbeck returned to the waterfront locale of Monterey, a setting he had first portrayed in *Tortilla Flat*. Like its predecessor, *Cannery Row* tells a seemingly lighthearted tale, focusing on the adventures of Doc, a marine biologist who is Steinbeck's fictional recreation of his friend Ed Ricketts. And like *Tortilla Flat*, *Cannery Row* proved popular with readers, becoming another best seller. F. W. Watt, quoted in *World Literature Criticism*, found that beneath the humorous surface of the novel Steinbeck had created a satire on contemporary American life, criticizing "its commercialized values, its ruthless creed of property and status, and its relentlessly accelerated pace." Other reviews were less kind, however. Astro, in *Dictionary of Literary Biography*, reported that "many critics, disturbed by the suddenness with which Steinbeck cut himself off from social and political concerns, attacked *Cannery Row*, charging that Steinbeck's plot ... is sentimental and its philosophy trivial." In describing his novel, Steinbeck, quoted in *Dictionary of Literary Biography Documentary Series*, admitted that *Cannery Row* was "a kind of nostalgic thing," written to entertain soldiers returning from World War II. This explanation did little to satisfy those reviewers who criticized the lack of serious content in Steinbeck's more recent work.

In attempting to explain the sudden change in Steinbeck's novels after *The Grapes of Wrath*, several critics maintained that Steinbeck's theories of human behavior had been profoundly altered. While his earlier novels had championed the goodness of the common man and the positive effects of group action, his work in the 1940s and afterward didn't seem as sure of these ideas. According to Astro's essay, John Ditsky found an early indication of this change in *Bombs Away*. Ditsky said the book's inability to muster enthusiasm for the combined efforts of the bomber squadron contains evidence of Steinbeck's "collapsing theory" regarding group efforts. Without a clear-cut theory to guide them, the critic suggests, Steinbeck's novels became less forceful. A similar

view was expressed by DeMott in *Working Days*. "With the publication of *In Dubious Battle, Of Mice and Men*, and *The Grapes of Wrath*," DeMott wrote, "Steinbeck concluded an integrated body of work about his native California, a trilogy of desire and illusion based on a notion of relatively fixed social reality." The key difference, according to DeMott, is that after *The Grapes of Wrath* Steinbeck "no longer believed" in this reality.

Whatever the reason for the change, the final novels of Steinbeck's career avoid the broad social issues that had been at the center of his earlier works. As Joseph Fontenrose noted in his study of Steinbeck, these later works show the author "clearly turning his principal interest from biology and sociology to individual ethics." One of the books that focuses on moral issues is *East of Eden*,

Steinbeck drew on the biblical story of Cain and Abel for this 1952 novel, the tale of three generations of brothers in the embittered Trask family.

published in 1952. The novel was viewed by Steinbeck as one of his most important books, and it is certainly his longest, an epic tale that follows the fortunes of two families over three generations. In a letter to Pascal Covici quoted in *Steinbeck: A Life in Letters*, the author declared that the novel contains "everything I have been able to learn about my art or craft or profession in all these years." Steinbeck also described *East of Eden* as "a book about morality." In order to tell this story of good and evil, he drew heavily on the biblical tale of Cain and Abel. Like the siblings in the book of Genesis, each generation of the Trask family has two brothers who come into conflict. And like the Bible story, the antagonism for each generation begins when the father favors one son over the other. In playing out this archetypal story, the novel also presents a history of the Salinas valley where both the Trasks and the Hamiltons—the second family in the novel—settle after the Civil War. The novel then traces the families' histories through 1918, concluding after one of the Trask brothers is killed in World War I.

Despite the author's high hopes for *East of Eden*, critical reaction to the novel was mixed. Critic Joseph Wood Krutch wrote a generally apprecia-

James Dean starred as a tortured adolescent yearning for his father's love and acceptance in the 1954 film version of *East of Eden*.

tive assessment of the book in the *New York Herald Tribune Book Review*. "Here is one of those occasions," Krutch asserted, "when a writer has aimed high and then summoned every ounce of energy, talent, seriousness and passion of which he was capable." This acclaim, however, did not prevent Krutch from questioning the book's use of symbolic characters who seem less than realistic. "What is most likely to disturb a reader," Krutch said, "at least during the first third of the book, is the tendency of the characters to turn suddenly at certain moments into obviously symbolic figures as abstract almost as the dramatis personae in a morality play." The critic also found a distinctive difference between the morality put forth in novels such as *The Grapes of Wrath* and that which is espoused in *East of Eden*. In *The Grapes of Wrath*, Casy states that "there ain't no sin and there ain't no virtue. There's just stuff people do." *East of Eden*, in contrast, shows Steinbeck as a "moralist," according to Krutch, who believed that "Good and Evil are absolute and not relative."

Fontenrose, in his analysis of the novel, also emphasized Steinbeck's treatment of morality. "For a novel on good and evil," Fontenrose noted, "*East of Eden* strangely lacks ethical insight." Due to this lack of insight, the critic found the characterization of a key character, Adam Trask, to be inadequate. "If Steinbeck had delved further into a father's ambivalent feelings for his sons," Fontenrose wrote, "then *East of Eden* might have been a great novel. As it is, we do not understand Adam's actions." In summarizing his opinion of *East of Eden*, Fontenrose declared that "few Steinbeck readers will place it higher than *The Grapes of Wrath*; the majority may see it as a second peak in his career, but not nearly so high as the first." The negative reviews of *East of Eden* were discouraging for Steinbeck, and according to Kiernan the author never recovered from the blow. "Although not his last book," Kiernan noted, "*East of Eden* was the climax of Steinbeck's artistic life, and a sad climax it was indeed."

Final Acclaim

Steinbeck published three more books of fiction after *East of Eden*, concluding his career as a novelist with *The Winter of Our Discontent* in 1961. As with most of his later novels, these books sold well but fared poorly in reviews. When he was awarded the Nobel Prize in 1962, some, such as one London *Times* obituary writer, contended that the award "had been earned by his earlier work," but the prize still represented a crowning achievement in Steinbeck's long career. Thereafter the author concentrated on nonfiction works, convinced, according to Kiernan, that "he was finished with fiction." The author continued to contribute articles to magazines and newspapers in the 1960s, and he also produced the popular *Travels with Charley* and *America and Americans,* two books about his travels in the United States.

After completing a 1967 trip to cover the Vietnam War, Steinbeck, with his health suffering, felt he had little left to write about. "I have nothing I can or want to communicate," he wrote Elizabeth Otis in a letter published in *Steinbeck: A Life in Letters,* "—a dry-as-dust, worked-out feeling." He was hospitalized later that year and again in 1968, surviving a series of heart attacks but never regaining his health. He died of heart disease on December 20, 1968, at the age of sixty-six. In assessing Steinbeck's status in American literature, critics have had to judge a large and widely varying body of work. Despite the disappointments of his later novels, many authorities believe Steinbeck has had a significant impact not only on American literature, but on the American society as a whole. Astro stressed the importance of Steinbeck's "great novels of the American Depression," stating that the caliber of these works "affirm that he is among the most important writers of our time." McCarthy also proclaimed the value of Steinbeck's books, pointing out the most significant qualities in the author's work: "Steinbeck's strongest convictions and passions appear in his fundamental belief in humanity in his expectation that man will endure, and that the creative forces of the human spirit will prevail."

■ Works Cited

Astro, Richard, "John Steinbeck," *Dictionary of Literary Biography,* Volume 9: *American Novelists, 1910-l945,* Gale, 1981, pp. 43-68.

Beach, Joseph Warren, *American Fiction: 1920-1940,* Macmillan, 1941, pp. 339-41, 345-46.

Benet, William Rose, "Apple Pickers' Strike," *Saturday Review,* February 1, 1936.

Canby, Henry Seidel, review of *Of Mice and Men, Saturday Review,* February 27, 1937, p. 7.

Coates, Robert M., review of *The Pastures of Heaven, New Yorker,* October 22, 1932.

DeMott, Robert, introduction and commentary in *Working Days: The Journal of "The Grapes of Wrath" 1938-1941,* Viking, 1989, pp. xxxix, xlii, 104.

Dictionary of Literary Biography Documentary Series, Volume 2, Gale, 1982, pp. 297, 314, 325.

Fontenrose, Joseph, *John Steinbeck: An Introduction and Interpretation,* Barnes & Noble, 1964, pp. 118-19, 123-26.

French, Warren, *John Steinbeck,* Twayne, 1961.

Gannett, Lewis, introduction to *The Portable Steinbeck,* edited by Pascal Covici, Viking, 1946.

Review of *The Grapes of Wrath, Time,* December 27, 1968.

Kazin, Alfred, *On Native Grounds: An Interpretation of Modern American Prose Literature,* Harcourt, 1942.

Kiernan, Thomas, *The Intricate Music: A Biography of John Steinbeck,* Little, Brown, 1979, p. 285, 300, 313.

Krutch, Joseph Wood, review of *East of Eden, New York Herald Tribune Book Review,* September 21, 1952.

Mangione, Jerre, "Under the Round Table," *New Republic,* July 17, 1935.

McCarthy, Paul, *John Steinbeck,* Ungar, 1980, pp. 67-70, 143.

Steinbeck, John, *The Grapes of Wrath,* Viking, 1939.

Steinbeck, John, *Steinbeck: A Life in Letters,* edited by Elaine Steinbeck and Robert Wallsten, Viking, 1975, pp. 15, 17-18, 158, 182, 429, 847.

Steinbeck, John, *Working Days: The Journals of "The Grapes of Wrath" 1938-1941,* edited by Robert DeMott, Viking, 1989, pp. 38, 56, 68, 93.

Times (London), December 21, 1968.

World Literature Criticism, Volume 5, Gale, 1992, pp. 3373, 3374.

"The Wrath *Hasn't* left Steinbeck," *Daily Mail* (London), September 18, 1961, p. 8.

■ For More Information See

BOOKS

Allen, Walter, *The Modern Novel,* Dutton, 1965.

Benson, Jackson J., *The True Adventures of John Steinbeck, Writer,* Viking, 1984.

Benson, Jackson J., editor, *The Short Novels of John Steinbeck: Critical Essays with a Checklist to Steinbeck Criticism,* Duke University Press, 1990.

Bode, Carl, editor, *The Young Rebel in American Literature,* Heinemann, 1959.

Concise Dictionary of American Literary Biography: The Age of Maturity, 1929-1941, Gale, 1989.

Contemporary Literary Criticism, Gale, Volume 1, 1973; Volume 5, 1976; Volume 9, 1978; Volume 13, 1980; Volume 21, 1982; Volume 34, 1985; Volume 45, 1987.

Davis, Robert Murray, editor, *Steinbeck: A Collection of Critical Essays*, Prentice-Hall, 1972.

Dictionary of Literary Biography, Volume 7: *Twentieth-Century American Dramatists*, Gale, 1981.

Frohock, W. M., *The Novel of Violence in America*, revised edition, Southern Methodist University Press, 1957.

Gardiner, Harold C., editor, *Fifty Years of the American Novel*, Scribner, 1951.

Geismar, Maxwell, *Writers in Crisis*, Houghton, 1942.

Hayashi, Tetsumaro, editor, *John Steinbeck: A Dictionary of His Fictional Characters*, Scarecrow, 1976.

Hedgpeth, Joel W., editor, *The Outer Shores*, Mad River Press, 1978.

Levant, Howard, *The Novels of John Steinbeck: A Critical Study*, University of Missouri Press, 1975.

Lisca, Peter, *The Wide World of John Steinbeck*, Rutgers University Press, 1958.

Lisca, Peter, *Steinbeck: The Man and His Work*, Oregon State University Press, 1971.

Moore, Harry T., *The Novels of John Steinbeck*, Kennikat Press, 1968.

Snell, George, *The Shapers of American Fiction: 1798-1947*, Dutton, 1947.

Tedlock, E. W., Jr., and C. V. Wicker, editors, *Steinbeck and His Critics: A Record of Twenty-five Years*, University of New Mexico Press, 1957.

Timmerman, John H., *John Steinbeck's Fiction: The Aesthetic of the Road Taken*, University of Oklahoma Press, 1986.

Timmerman, John H., *The Dramatic Landscape of John Steinbeck's Short Stories*, University of Oklahoma Press, 1990.

Watt, F. W., *John Steinbeck*, Grove, 1962.

Westbrook, Max, editor, *The Modern American Novel: Essays in Criticism*, Random House, 1966.

William Faulkner, Eugene O'Neill, John Steinbeck (Nobel Prize presentations and acceptance speeches), Gregory, 1971.

Wilson, Edmund, *The Boys in the Back Room*, Colt Press, 1941.

Wilson, Edmund, *Classics and Commercials: A Literary Chronicle of the Forties*, Noonday Press, 1950.

PERIODICALS

American Spectator, August, 1989, p. 41.
Antioch Review, spring, 1967.
Chicago Tribune, April 21, 1989; August 6, 1989; August 10, 1990.
Commonweal, May 9, 1969.
Detroit Free Press, January 9, 1967.
Esquire, November, 1969.
Globe & Mail (Toronto), December 20, 1986; April 22, 1989.
Horn Book, November, 1942, p. 397; March, 1948, p. 143; October, 1977, p. 56.
Life, November 2, 1962.
Los Angeles Times, December 6, 1987; May 1, 1989.
Nation, May 1, 1989, p. 577.
New Republic, October 6, 1952; August 21, 1961.
New Statesman and Society, June 30, 1961; June 30, 1989, p. 28.
Newsweek, November 5, 1962; January 30, 1967; May 1, 1989, p. 72.
New Yorker, October 5, 1987, p. 47.
New York Herald Tribune Book Review, February 28, 1937.
New York Times, June 2, 1969; August 11, 1989; March 23, 1990; May 9, 1990.
New York Times Book Review, February 16, 1947; September 21, 1952; April 14, 1957; November 16, 1958; June 25, 1961; July 29, 1962; October 24, 1976; April 9, 1989, p. 1.
Observer, December 22, 1968.
Saturday Review, September 20, 1952; November 1, 1958; September 28, 1968; February 8, 1969.
Time, December 27, 1968; April 24, 1989, p. 88.
Times Literary Supplement, July 7, 1961.
Washington Post, December 21, 1968; December 23, 1969.
Washington Post Book World, April 16, 1989, p. 3.
Yale Review, December, 1961.

OBITUARIES

Antiquarian Bookman, January 6-8, 1969.
Books Abroad, spring, 1969.
Newsweek, December 30, 1968.
New York Times, December 21, 1968.
Publishers Weekly, December 30, 1968.
Time, December 27, 1968.°

—*Sketch by Jeff Hill*

Joyce Carol Thomas

■ Personal

Born May 25, 1938, in Ponca City, OK; daughter of Floyd David (a bricklayer) and Leona (a house-keeper and hair stylist; maiden name, Thompson) Haynes; married Gettis L. Withers (a chemist), May 31, 1959 (divorced, 1968); married Roy T. Thomas, Jr. (a professor), September 7, 1968 (divorced, 1979); children: Monica Pecot, Gregory Withers, Michael Withers, Roy T. Thomas III. *Education:* Attended San Francisco City College, 1957-58, and University of San Francisco, 1957-58; College of San Mateo, A.A., 1964; San Jose State College (now University), B.A., 1966; Stanford University, M.A., 1967.

■ Addresses

Home—Caryville, TN. *Agent*—Mitch Douglas, International Creative Management, 40 West 57th St., New York, NY 10019.

■ Career

Worked as a telephone operator in San Francisco, CA, 1957-58; Ravenwood School District, East Palo Alto, CA, teacher of French and Spanish,

1968-70; San Jose State College (now University), San Jose, CA, assistant professor of black studies, 1969-72; Contra Costa College, San Pablo, CA, teacher of drama and English, 1973-75; St. Mary's College, Moraga, CA, professor of English, 1975-77; San Jose State University, San Jose, reading program director, 1979-82, professor of English, 1982-83; University of Tennessee, Knoxville, currently professor of English; writer, 1982—. Visiting associate professor of English at Purdue University, spring, 1983. *Member:* Authors Guild, Dramatists Guild, Authors League of America, Sigma Delta Pi.

■ Awards, Honors

Danforth Graduate Fellow at University of California at Berkeley, 1973-75; Stanford University scholar, 1979-80, and Djerassi Fellow, 1982 and 1983; *New York Times* outstanding book of the year, 1982, American Library Association best book, 1982, Before Columbus American Book Award from Before Columbus Foundation (Berkeley, CA), 1982, and the American Book Award (now National Book Award) for children's fiction from the Association of American Publishers, 1983, all for *Marked by Fire;* Coretta Scott King Award from the American Library Association, 1984, for *Bright Shadow;* named an Outstanding Woman of the Twentieth Century by Sigma Gamma Rho, 1986; *A Gathering of Flowers* was a National Conference of Christians and Jews recommended title for children and young adults, 1991.

■ Writings

YOUNG ADULT NOVELS

Marked by Fire, Avon, 1982.
Bright Shadow (sequel to *Marked by Fire*), Avon, 1983.
Water Girl, Avon, 1986.
The Golden Pasture, Scholastic Books, 1986.
Journey, Scholastic Books, 1990.
When the Nightingale Sings, (also see below), HarperCollins, 1992.

POETRY

Bittersweet, Firesign Press, 1973.
Crystal Breezes, Firesign Press, 1974.
Blessing, Jocato Press, 1975.
Black Child, illustrated by Tom Feelings, Zamani Productions, 1981.
Inside the Rainbow, Zikawana Press, 1982.
Brown Honey in Broomwheat Tea, HarperCollins, 1993.

PLAYS

(And producer) *A Song in the Sky* (two-act), first produced in San Francisco, CA, at Montgomery Theater, 1976.
Look! What a Wonder! (two-act), first produced in Berkeley, CA, at Berkeley Community Theatre, 1976.
(And producer) *Magnolia* (two-act), first produced in San Francisco at Old San Francisco Opera House, 1977.
(And producer) *Ambrosia* (two-act), first produced in San Francisco at the Little Fox Theatre, 1978.
Gospel Roots (two-act), first produced in Carson, CA, at California State University, 1981.
When the Nightingale Sings (musical based on Thomas's novel), first produced at the University of Tennessee at the Clarence Brown Theatre, 1991.

OTHER

(Editor) *A Gathering of Flowers: Stories about Being Young in America*, HarperCollins, 1990.

Contributor to periodicals, including *American Poetry Review, Black Scholar, Calafia, Drum Voices, Giant Talk*, and *Yardbird Reader*. Editor of *Ambrosia* (women's newsletter), 1980.

■ Adaptations

Marked by Fire was adapted by James Racheff and Ted Kociolek for the stage musical *Abyssinia*, first produced in New York City at the CSC Repertory Theater in 1987.

■ Sidelights

Landscaped with the rural Oklahoma scenery that enlivened her youth, Joyce Carol Thomas's young adult novels have virtually become overnight classics. Growing up as a migrant farm worker in Oklahoma and California has given Thomas a fertile stock of characters and situations with which to fill her novels. Her chronicling of the African-American experience in the West has caused her to be compared to such well-known authors as Maya Angelou, Alice Walker, and Toni Morrison. As a testament to her abilities as a writer, despite the fact that *Marked By Fire* was her first novel it has become standard reading in many high schools and colleges.

Ponca City, Oklahoma, was a poor, rural, agricultural town when Thomas was born there in 1938. Since then, it has found a permanent home in Thomas's consciousness. Her early memories of the town inform nearly all of her work—from her books of poetry to her plays and novels. Three of her novels are set there: *Marked by Fire, Bright Shadow*, and *The Golden Pasture*. "Although now I live half a continent away from my hometown," Thomas related in her *Something about the Author Autobiography Series (SAAS)* entry, "when it comes to my writing I find that I am still there." Thomas cited the influence of the small, close-knit community, the beauty of the fields, and the many varieties of plants and animals as being key images that helped in her development as a writer.

"I must have fallen in love with words when I was still in the womb," Thomas wrote in *SAAS*. "Probably because my mother fairly lived in the church house while she was pregnant with me." The ambiance of the church and the beautiful gospel singing crept into Thomas's soul and stayed there. Also, her father was a singer, which helped the young Thomas to appreciate music. "He sang with an *a cappella* choir at radio station WBBZ on the Sunday morning broadcast. I remember sitting with one ear glued to the cloth-covered speaker at the bottom of the Emerson radio, hugging the long thin mahogany legs of the floor model trying to listen to every bend of the liquid notes that curled and turned this way and that as they flooded the room. It seemed to me that even the plainest lyric sounded sweet when sung in four-part harmony," she related.

Her mother, who was the town's hairdresser as well as a homemaker and mother of eight children and an adopted nephew, was an avid churchgoer. It was a family joke that her mother was hanging

In this 1982 novel, Abyssinia Jackson, scarred slightly at birth during a brush fire, is nursed back to health by the town's elders after being raped.

around the church one day when their house burned down and she didn't realize it until she got home. Thomas herself spent plenty of time at church. It became a strong formative influence both on her life and her development as a writer. She was inspired by the lyricism of the singing and worked to make her prose equally melodic. "In that little wooden chapel on an Oklahoma hillside even the spoken words were sung with a kind of lilting sweetness, measured in breaths that rose and fell; words, chanted back and forth from the preacher, the deacon, and the female missionaries. In my writing I try to recreate this music on the printed page. Sing the way those people used to speak," she mused.

After awhile, the constant churchgoing became a burden to Thomas. "We went to church so often

that by the time I was sixteen or seventeen years old, I decided I would be happy never to see the inside of a church again," She once told Jean W. Ross in *Contemporary Authors*. Yet she admitted that her early experience was important: "It made a mark: No matter what I do, somehow that religious training is present. Even when I think I'm getting away from the ten commandments, my life is really quite steeped in them." Religion and spiritually were to become strong themes in her future novels.

The Rural Life

"At a little place outside of Ponca City, a place called Red Rock, my family and I picked and chopped cotton," Thomas remembered in *SAAS*. "To keep us from being economically exploited too much, my mother kept the books." The author has talked fondly of the beauty of the cotton fields, from the dew glistening in the morning to the sounds of crickets and the sparkle of fireflies. Many of these images have found their way into Thomas's novels. "My character Abyssinia Jackson was born in the cotton patch," Thomas related. "Telling her story lets me go there once again. Not only to the hard work but to the place where ghost stories were told, to the place where night was so dark my favorite brother ran into a tree and gashed his forehead wide open."

Life in the country not only brought crickets and fireflies into Thomas's childhood, but less pleasant insects as well. Her mother was once bitten by a black widow spider while picking cotton. The wound was serious, and it was feared for awhile that her leg might have to be amputated. Later, Thomas found that a nest of these same spiders was under her mattress. She also had a terrifying experience with wasps when her brother locked her in a closet containing a nest of the stinging pests. These brushes with insects piqued Thomas's imagination. In her novel *Journey,* spiders have a central role, but most of them are good spiders; and *Marked by Fire* also contains some scary scenes with wasps. Frightening events are one thing that Thomas likes to explore in her novels. "A book is a safe place to experience fear," she wrote.

Education played an important role in the author's life, too. Thomas lived right across the street from her school. She loved school as a child and became anxious whenever she thought she might be late because she didn't want to miss anything. She usually missed the first month of school anyway because she had to help her family finish the farm work for the season. The young Thomas also didn't want to be overlooked at school the way she felt she was in a family full of siblings. "My mother had all these other children to attend to, my younger sister's hair to braid, for instance," the author recalled. "And there I was impatiently hopping from one foot to the other, waiting my turn to bow down, ducking and cringing under Mama's exacting comb as I watched the clock inch up relentlessly to bell time." Some days the spirited girl would simply brush down the stray hairs and slip out the door without her mother noticing.

In such a large family, Thomas often found it difficult to find the time alone that she needed to develop her writing instincts. Yet that need to be alone was very strong, and the creative Thomas found just the place where privacy was possible. Because of the threat of floods, her family's house was built on stilts to keep it a few feet off the ground. She hid in the space under the house, where she could be away from the prying eyes of the siblings, as well as the seemingly endless chores. "I would go there and find some solitude," she wrote. "I made up songs in my head in the rare quiet. And sang them there, clothed them with melodies. Nobody bothered me or asked me questions or commanded me to do anything in my special hideaway."

Of Comfort Food and Spanish

Besides church, family life also revolved around the kitchen table. Food has significance for Thomas, and images of food often make their way into her novels. Although times were lean, Thomas's mother found a way to make healthy, tasty meals for the large group. Cereal and pet milk for breakfast, and cornbread and beans for lunch were staples. But for Sunday dinners the tone changed, and more elaborate meals were planned. Thomas's memories of huge spreads being laid out for Sunday dinners are nothing less than poetic. Roast chicken, yams, string beans, delicious coconut cake, sweet-potato pie and pear cobbler were just a few of the sumptuous treats. These scenes of food stuck with Thomas. "Because in such a home food was another language for love, my books are redolent of sugar and spice, kale and collards," Thomas commented in *SAAS*.

Whenever Thomas was sick, her mother had one sure-fire recipe: broomwheat tea that was hand-picked in the nearby weed fields. It was good for whatever ailed her, from the pain of an accidental scalding to a cold or chicken pox. Somehow, this elixir finds its way into the cups of many of Thomas's characters. For example, her 1993 book of poetry, *Brown Honey in Broomwheat Tea,* which explores her African-American identity, has its roots in this and other traditions she experienced while growing up.

Thomas had to leave the beloved landscape of Ponca City when she was ten years old. The family moved to another rural area: Tracy, California. The landscape there was decidedly different, yet it was just as rich to the author as her old home had been. In Tracy, Thomas got to milk cows, fish for minnows, and slop hogs. Also, she continued harvesting crops during the long summers. Tomatoes were the primary crop she picked, but she also spent time working with yellow onions and black grapes. The grapes were a favorite because she could sample them as she worked.

In California she spent time working with many Mexicans. She became impressed with the Maria-chi singers who played in the field. The rhythms and character of the Spanish language washed over her and she began a long-lasting love affair with the language. "When the Spanish speakers talked they seemed to sing," Thomas commented in *SAAS*. In high school, she pursued courses in Spanish and Latin and became very fluent, coupling her learning with the memories of the spoken words as she had heard them in the fields.

The importance of foreign languages in Thomas's life began to combine with the importance of music and religion. "I found foreign languages the language of the church, and that of the Ponca and Tracy people to be a fitting foundation for writing," she said. "The music of the word is what I wanted to be able to master in my study of languages. The music of the word is what I want to create in my writing of books." Thomas never took a class in creative writing. "From this base of languages I taught myself all I know about writing," she remarked.

Entering the Professional World

In 1959, shortly after she had finished high school and attended various colleges for a brief time, she married a chemist named Gettis L. Withers. Almost immediately, the couple started a family. But Thomas wanted an education, too, so while raising her children she began working full-time as a telephone operator to earn tuition money. She received an associate's degree from College of San Mateo in 1964, followed in 1966 by a bachelor's degree with distinction in Spanish and French from

California State University, San Jose. She then went on to earn a master's degree in education and Spanish from Stanford University. Her first job after graduation was as a middle school foreign language teacher.

In 1969, Thomas began teaching at San Jose State College. She then went to Contra Costa College in 1973 and St. Mary's College in 1975. During this time, Thomas began turning the images gathered in her youth into poems. From 1973 to 1981, Thomas wrote several books of poetry as well as many plays for adults. *Bittersweet, Crystal Breezes,* and *Blessing* are some of her notable early poetry collections. All three books were later combined and new poems were added to make *Inside the Rainbow.* Of these efforts, Charles P. Toombs wrote in the *Dictionary of Literary Biography:* "In her poetry Thomas refuses to make simple, general statements regarding her subject matter. Instead she presents real portraits of specific families, recreates Afro-American rituals, and establishes a 'once' communion with such natural objects as raindrops, fireflies, and the red dirt of Oklahoma cornfields to frame her themes."

Thomas's poems offer glimpses into her life in Ponca City and Tracy. She deals with a wide variety of themes and images, including birth and death, church and spirituality, African-American rituals and racism, and hope and suffering. Although sometimes Thomas's images are haunting and sorrowful, Toombs found that her verses are "for the most part, affirmative songs, seeing in some of life's most vicious atrocities some new fruit for the continuation of the human species." Thomas also published a booklet of poetry entitled *Black Child* in 1981. The poems in this collection are dedicated to the schoolchildren who lost their lives in the Atlanta murders. She found affirmation in this, too, writing in the foreword that "we can pay no greater tribute to those remaining than this: that we recommit our lives to the salvation of our youth."

Moves to Another Genre

"For as long as I can remember, even before I started grade school, I was creating poems," Thomas told Ross. In 1982, the author found another outlet for her creative energy: novels. However, poetry remained close to her heart. "When I began to write novels, I still continued to write poems. Poems are never far from me. Poems come to me between chapters of fiction. Verses wake me up at midnight. What I do—at first I was

doing it unconsciously—is bring a dimension of poetry—simile, metaphor—to my fiction." Thereafter, the two genres seemed to meld in her mind, work in each area strengthening the work she did in the other. "Then I decided to make a conscious effort to bring poetry to my fiction," she added. "So I do include it, using symbols and allusions to tell the story more faithfully, I hope."

The poetic images and scenes of her youth in Oklahoma find their way into *Marked by Fire,* a novel for young adults. Steeped in the traditions of her home town, the novel focused on Abyssinia Jackson. The name Abyssinia has poetic ramifications for Thomas because it comes from the old name for Ethiopia and many black churches also bear the name. "I wanted my character to have a name that nobody else had used," she related in *SAAS.* "It had to be distinctive, arresting, fresh, with a meaning I could embellish. I wanted the original meaning to be shaped by the personality of the character."

Abyssinia is born in a cotton field during harvest time, attended by the other women of the community. However, during her birth there is a brush fire and the tiny infant receives a mark on her face that inspires the name of the book. This leaves her "marked for unbearable pain and unspeakable joy" according to the local healer. The townspeople of Ponca City believe that this scar means she is marked spiritually as well as physically, and they watch her closely as she grows up. She becomes the darling of the community and develops a beautiful singing voice and a remarkable ability to tell stories.

Tragically, Abyssinia is raped by an elder in the church when she is ten. Abby becomes mute after the violent act and is nursed back to health through the strength of the local women as well as her family. Abby's mother is named Patience in honor of Thomas's mother, who was a very patient parent. Strong, the father, has left the family in their time of need, but returns to them later—ironically—because he is not strong enough to face a crisis in his life. When Abby eventually regains her voice, she is able to tell her friend Lily Norene that after the rape she "felt dirty. Dirtier than playing in mud. The kind of dirt you can't ever wash off. . . . But the worst part was I felt like I was being spit on by God." It is the seeming abandonment by God that strikes Abby to the core—she must work through the horror before she can recover completely. Mother Barker, the town's midwife and healer, has a special role in the rehabilitation of Abby. In a more macabre way, so

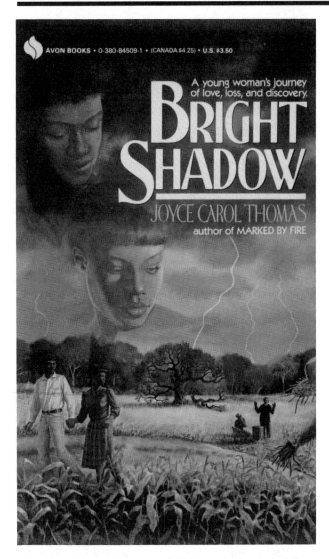

In this 1983 sequel to *Marked by Fire*, Abyssinia falls in love and, with the support of her boyfriend Carl Lee, learns to deal with her grief over her aunt's murder.

does Trembling Sally, a frightening, crazy woman who assaults the young girl with strange trials of fire, water, and insects. Eventually, Abby recovers with Mother Barker's help.

Enthusiastic Reception

Marked by Fire has been well received by critics. Wendell Wray wrote in *Best Sellers* that Thomas "captures the flavor of black folk life in Oklahoma. . . . [She] has set for herself a very challenging task. . . . [But] Thomas' book works." Critic Dorothy Randall-Tsuruta commented in the *Black Scholar* that Thomas's "poetic tone gives this work what scents give the roses already so pleasing in color. In fact often as not the lyrical here carries the reader beyond concerns for fast action. There too Tho-

mas's short lived interest in playwrighting figures in her fine regard and control of dialog." Hazel Rochman, writing in *School Library Journal*, admitted that "the lack of a fast-paced narrative line and the mythical overtones may present obstacles to some readers," but she says that "many will be moved" by Abby's story.

Some reviewers have commented on Thomas's ability to show how terrible circumstances in people's lives can have a positive effect. Rochman observed that Thomas's writing can show that "violence can lead to rebirth and to revelation; and that the fierceness of a tornado is as beautiful and necessary as Abby's own singing gift." The author once revealed in *Something about the Author* (*SATA*) that "as a writer I work to create books filled with conflict. . . . I address this quest in part by matching the pitiful absurdities and heady contradictions of life itself, in part by leading the heroine to twin fountains of magic and the macabre, and evoking the holy and the horrible in the same breath."

Both *Marked by Fire* and its sequel, *Bright Shadow*, have become required reading in high schools and universities around the country. Even Thomas's own children have been assigned their mother's books to read for class assignments. "My fourteen-year-old came home one day with a copy of *Marked by Fire* in his backpack," the author told Ross. "His class was reading it. I'm not anybody special to him, and that's the way it should be; I'm just his mother. I think he was kind of astonished when his classmates selected his mother's novel to read for an English assignment. That it was special to them amazed him."

Another Abyssinian Adventure

Bright Shadow was published in 1983. In this work, Abyssinia goes to college and ends up falling in love with Carl Lee Jefferson. Abby is a young woman now, searching for what she wants as she completes her pre-medical studies. For reasons she can't figure out, Abby's father disapproves of Carl Lee. She suspects, however, that it is because of Carl Lee's alcoholic father. At the same time, the psychically sensitive Abby begins to have forebodings about her Aunt's new husband. These feelings are validated when Aunt Serena is found brutally murdered.

Carl Lee begins to show his true colors when he is there to support Abby through her grief. Soon he has a revelation of his own when he finds out that the mysterious Cherokee woman that has been lurking around town is actually his mother. Despite these difficult hurdles, nothing is able to disrupt the young couple's love and support for one another. It is because of Carl Lee that Abby finds the light when all she can see are the dark shadows of her Aunt's death. *Bright Shadow* concludes when Abby has a dream in which her Aunt revisits her and gives her a lesson: "We are all taken from the same source: pain and beauty. One is the chrysalis that gives to the other some gift that even in death creates a new dimension in life."

Critical reaction to *Bright Shadow* was generally more mixed than for *Marked by Fire*. Carolyn Caywood, writing in *School Library Journal*, found the plot of *Bright Shadow* touched with melodrama and lacking in credibility, but admitted that Thomas's "story is readable and her sensuously descriptive passages celebrating the physical beauty of the black characters are a nice touch." In the *Bulletin of the Center for Children's Books*, Zena Sutherland said that *Bright Shadow* as "a love story . . . is appealing, and the characterization is strong." However, she felt that "the often-ornate phraseology" sometimes weakens the story.

Water Girl, Thomas's next novel, is the story of a remarkable teenager named Amber Westbrook. Amber is a sensitive girl who is strongly attuned to the world around her, a gift that makes her stand out from the others in her family. Her life becomes much more complicated when the disruption from a California earthquake causes Amber to find an old letter that reveals she was adopted. Amber is really the biological daughter of her cousin, Abyssinia Jackson. Shocked, Amber takes a backpack and heads into the wilderness, having a spiritual experience during the days she is away. By the story's end, she discovers that a "mother is the one who loves you."

Water Girl has inspired different reactions from reviewers. Although *Booklist* contributor Sally Estes is confused by the fact that readers never find out why Abyssinia gave up Amber for adoption, the critic concluded that "teens who liked the first two books won't be disappointed." A reviewer in *Bulletin of the Center for Children's Books* was less positive, indicating that "this plot is padded by irrelevancies, gushy passages . . . and interruptions" that bog down the action. However, citing a writing style that includes flashbacks and a terse, intense style, Ruth Fitzgerald concluded in *School Library Journal* that readers who enjoyed the first novel "will want to read this story."

Back to Ponca City

Thomas's next novel, *The Golden Pasture*, takes the reader to Carl Lee's adolescence and the "Golden Pasture" near Ponca City, Oklahoma, where he spent his summers on his grandfather's ranch. During his twelfth summer with Grandfather Gray Jefferson, an ex-rodeo star who always has colorful stories to tell, Carl Lee is told that he can enter the Boley rodeo if he can get ready for it in time. Much to his grandfather's surprise, Carl Lee gets a horse by capturing an injured, wild Appaloosa and learning how to ride him. The rodeo in the story serves not only as an important part of Carl Lee's voyage to manhood, but also as an opportunity for him, his father, and his grandfather to settle long-standing differences. *The Golden Pasture* ends with all three generations realizing that they "can't build a fence around our feelings or the people we love."

Combining elements of folklore, fantasy, and mystery, this 1990 work tells how a girl who has been blessed at birth by a magical spider becomes the kidnapping victim of a band of murderous adults.

The Golden Pasture was met with generally favorable reviews. Several critics cited the beauty of the language and Thomas's interesting characters. A *Publishers Weekly* review called the book "a spirited, lyrical tale with a memorable cast of characters." Janet Hickman, writing in *Language Arts*, commented that the author's style and characterization "raise this book well above the level of most conventional horse stories." David A. Lindsey wrote in the *School Library Journal* that the book's conclusion seems "somewhat contrived," but he conceded that "the story's tinges of realism and excellent characterization make the book a delight to read."

Trials, Tribulations, and Tarantulas

Tracy, California is the setting for Thomas's next novel, *Journey,* which combines folklore, fantasy, and mystery. It focuses on a girl named Meggie Alexander who is blessed at birth by a tarantula.

The orphaned Marigold finds solace from her foster mother's abusive ways by joining the gospel choir at church in this 1992 novel.

The spider makes many return visits to the girl's cradle to spin tales and deliver wisdom. As she grows up, Meggie has only dim memories of the spider, yet somehow she retains its mystical wisdom.

Trouble begins when Meggie reaches adolescence. When some of her friends begin disappearing in their favorite woods area, and a few have been found murdered, she decides to investigate. She ends up being kidnapped by the three adults—one a former high-school teacher—who are behind the horrible kidnappings. Some reviewers of *Journey* have felt that Thomas had not combined the elements of the story satisfactorily. "This discordant mixture of fantasy and mystery . . . never blend successfully," wrote Starr LaTronica in *School Library Journal.* Kimberly Olson Fakih and Diane Roback had a similar opinion of the book, writing in *Publishers Weekly* that not only does the mixture of genres not work, but "the variations in point of view are often confusing." However, a *Kirkus Reviews* overview of the book was more favorable, asserting that "Thomas dramatically juxtaposes her story's horror with the joy of existence."

In 1992 Thomas came out with *When the Nightingale Sings,* a young adult novel about the orphaned Marigold. The fourteen-year-old girl is living with a foster mother whose verbal abuse and bad temper make her less than an ideal parent. Marigold, however, resists believing in her foster mother's insults and instead turns to the Rose of Sharon Baptist Church, where the search to find a new lead gospel singer fills her heart with a song.

Sources of Inspiration

Thomas has been a full-time writer since the publication of *Marked by Fire.* She keeps a daily writing schedule from 8 a.m. to 2 p.m., which is usually preceded by a long walk around her home in Berkeley, California. However, she wrote in *SAAS* that "the characters who wake me up out of sound sleep, I must tell you, are no respecters of office hours. . . . They come and go when they choose. I am at their mercy and I have been known to write well past my two o'clock closing time." In addition to her short morning walking trips, the author has drawn inspiration from such idiosyncratic journeys as taking her son to the barbershop. "Even today, I love to accompany my fourteen-year-old son to the barbershop. I'm always asking him, 'Are you ready to go to the barbershop? And he often says, 'Listen, I just got a haircut. It's not time yet.'" This kind of 'research' helps her get the dialog in her scenes just right.

But Thomas's excursions haven't been limited to her own neighborhood. She has travelled widely to such places as Mexico, Nigeria, Hong Kong, Saipan, Rome, and Haiti. She uses her experiences to bring new dimensions to her writing, just as she uses the landscapes of her youth. "Often I travel to relax, although I'm always writing," she told Ross. "So if I'm in Rome I'm looking at Michelangelo's Florentine *Pieta* or his sculpture of David and my eye follows the lines of marbled muscles and bones he's sculpted and my mind translates them into lines of words on the page, using the simple curve of a hand in describing some male character. So when I'm traveling I'm looking at landscapes or works of art and jotting down settings and descriptions."

A major source of inspiration for the author, however, remains her own past. As she once commented in *SATA*, she knows she's succeeded "if [my writing] interests a reader who hasn't walked the dusty Oklahoma roads I've walked, who has not heard the storytellers I used to hear." "I work for authenticity of voice, fidelity to detail, and naturalness of developments," she also remarked. With several book awards and much reader acclaim, Thomas has gained wide acceptance for her efforts. In all her work, Thomas has tried to cross the boundaries of race, sex, and upbringing and to touch people with her timeless characters. She adds that "I treasure and value the experiences that include us all as people. I don't pay any attention to boundaries. What I look for too in my readers is people who won't feel, 'Well, I'm not black or I don't come from a rural setting so therefore I can't read Joyce Carol Thomas,' but who will read my work and say, 'I felt that experience, I'm right there next to her on that rough-boarded bench, feeling the splinters and the cobwebs when the ghost touched my hand.'"

■ Works Cited

Caywood, Carolyn, review of *Bright Shadow*, *School Library Journal*, January, 1984, pp. 89-90.

Estes, Sally, review of *Water Girl*, *Booklist*, February 15, 1986, pp. 861-62.

Fakih, Kimberly Olson, and Diane Roback, review of *Journey*, *Publishers Weekly*, September 9, 1988, p. 140.

Fitzgerald, Ruth, review of *Water Girl*, *School Library Journal*, April, 1986, p. 100.

Review of *The Golden Pasture*, *Publishers Weekly*, July 25, 1986, p. 191.

Hickman, Janet, review of *The Golden Pasture*, *Language Arts*, November, 1986, p. 733.

Review of *Journey*, *Kirkus Reviews*, September 15, 1988, p. 1410.

LaTronica, Starr, review of *Journey*, *School Library Journal*, October, 1988, p. 165.

Lindsey, David A., review of *The Golden Pasture*, *School Library Journal*, August, 1986, p. 107.

Randall-Tsuruta, Dorothy, review of *Marked by Fire*, *The Black Scholar*, summer, 1982, p. 48.

Rochman, Hazel, review of *Marked by Fire*, *School Library Journal*, March, 1982, p. 162.

Something about the Author, Volume 40, Gale, pp. 208-9.

Sutherland, Zena, review of *Bright Shadow*, *Bulletin of the Center for Children's Books*, February, 1984, p. 119.

Thomas, Joyce Carol, foreword to *Black Child*, Zamani Productions, 1981.

Thomas, Joyce Carol, *Marked by Fire*, Avon, 1982.

Thomas, Joyce Carol, *Bright Shadow*, Avon, 1983.

Thomas, Joyce Carol, *Water Girl*, Avon, 1986.

Thomas, Joyce Carol, *The Golden Pasture*, Scholastic Books, 1986.

Thomas, Joyce Carol, in an interview with Jean W. Ross, *Contemporary Authors*, Volume 116, Gale, 1986, pp. 462-65.

Thomas, Joyce Carol, essay in *Something about the Author Autobiography Series*, Volume 7, Gale, 1989, pp. 299-311.

Toombs, Charles P., "Joyce Carol Thomas," *Dictionary of Literary Biography*, Volume 33: *Afro-American Fiction Writers after 1955*, Gale, 1984, pp. 245-50.

Review of *Water Girl*, *Bulletin of the Center for Children's Books*, April, 1986, p. 160.

Wray, Wendell, review of *Marked by Fire*, *Best Sellers*, June, 1982, pp. 123-24.

■ For More Information See

BOOKS

Children's Literature Review, Volume 19, Gale, 1990.

Yalom, Margaret, editor, *Women Writers of the West*, Capra Press, 1982.

PERIODICALS

Bakersfield Californian, February 9, 1983.

Berkeley Gazette, July 21, 1983.

New Directions, January/February, 1984.

San Francisco Chronicle, April 12, 1982.

San Jose Mercury News, January 31, 1993.

Voice of Youth Advocates, June, 1993, p. 96.

   —Sketch by Nancy E. Rampson

Andy Warhol

■ Personal

Full name, Andrew Warhola; born August 6 (one source says August 8), 1928 (some sources say 1926, 1927, 1930, or 1931), in Pittsburgh (some sources say Philadelphia; one source says McKeesport), PA (one source says Cleveland, OH); died of heart failure following gallbladder surgery, February 22, 1987, in New York, NY; buried at St. John the Baptist Byzantine Catholic Cemetery in Pittsburgh, PA; son of Ondrej (a laborer) and Julia (Zavacky) Warhola. *Education:* Carnegie Institute of Technology (now Carnegie-Mellon University), A.B., 1949. *Religion:* Roman Catholic.

■ Addresses

Home—New York, NY.

■ Career

Artist, filmmaker, and writer. Worked as a commercial artist in New York City in the early to mid-1950s. Created the films *Sleep; Kiss; Andy Warhol Films Jack Smith Filming Normal Love; Tarzan and Jane, Regained . . . Sort Of; Dance Movie; Haircut; Eat;* and *Salome and Delilah,* all in 1963; *Blow Job;*

Batman Dracula; Empire; Henry Geldzahler; Drunk; Couch; Shoulder; Mario Banana; Soap Opera; Taylor Mead's Ass; 13 Most Beautiful Women; 13 Most Beautiful Boys; 50 Fantastics and 50 Personalities; Harlot; The End of Dawn; Messy Lives; Naomi Kisses Rufus; Apple; Pause; and *Lips,* all in 1964; *Ivy and John; Screen Test #1; Screen Test #2; The Life of Juanita Castro; Horse; Vinyl; Suicide; Poor Little Rich Girl; Bitch; Restaurant; Kitchen; Prison; Face; Afternoon; Beauty #2; Outer and Inner Space; Space; My Hustler; Camp; Paul Swan;* and *Lupe,* all in 1965; *Hedy; More Milk Yvette; The Velvet Underground and Nico; The Closet; Bufferin; Eating Too Fast; The Chelsea Girls;* and *Whips,* all in 1966; *24 Hour Movie* (also known as °°°° or *Four Stars*); *The Loves of Ondine; The Imitation of Christ* (suggested by the writings of Thomas a Kempis); *I, a Man; Bikeboy; Nude Restaurant; Withering Sighs;* and *Construction—Destruction,* all in 1967; *Lonesome Cowboys; San Diego Surf; Blue Movie;* and *Flesh,* all in 1968; *Trash,* 1969; *Heat* and *Women in Revolt* (filmed through 1972), 1970; *L'Amour,* 1971; *Andy Warhol's Frankenstein* and *Andy Warhol's Dracula,* 1973; *Bad,* 1976; and *Vibrations* and *Wee Love of Life.* Produced the album *The Velvet Underground with Nico,* Metro-Goldwyn-Mayer, 1967. Hosted the cable television show "Andy Warhol's TV," beginning in 1980. *Exhibitions:* Warhol's art has been displayed in exhibitions all over the world, including the Hugo Gallery, New York City, 1952; the Bodley Gallery, New York City, 1956, 1957, 1958, and 1959; the Leo Castelli Gallery, New York City, 1965; Moderna Museet, Stockholm, Sweden, 1968; the Museum of Contemporary Art, Chicago,

IL, 1970; the Institute of Contemporary Arts, London, England, 1971; and the Musee d'Art Moderne, Paris, France, 1971; collections of his art are held in many museums, including the Museum of Modern Art, New York City, the Tate Gallery, London, and the Museum of Contemporary Art, Chicago. *Member:* Film Cooperative.

■ Awards, Honors

Art Director's Club Medal for design, 1957, for creating a giant shoe; Independent Film Award, *Film Culture,* 1964, for *Eat, Haircut, Sleep, Kiss,* and *Empire;* award from Los Angeles Film Festival, 1964; Warsaw Poster Biennale Prize, 1968.

■ Writings

(With Stephen Shore, David Paul, and others) *Andy Warhol's Index Book,* Random House, 1967.

(With Gerard Malanga) *Screen Test: A Diary* (poems and drawings), Kulchur Press, 1967.

(With Malanga) *Intransit: The Andy Warhol-Gerard Malanga Monster Issue,* Toad Press, 1968.

a: A Novel, Grove, 1968.

Blue Movie: A Film (screenplay), Grove, 1970.

Pork, (two-act comedy), produced in London at the Roundhouse, August 2, 1971, produced Off-Off-Broadway at La Mama Theatre, 1971.

The Philosophy of Andy Warhol (From A to B and Back Again), Harcourt, 1975.

(Author of text with Bob Colacello) *Andy Warhol's Exposures* (photographs), Grosset & Dunlop, 1979.

Andy Warhol: Portraits of the '70s, essay by Robert Rosenblum, edited by David Whitney, Random House, 1979.

(With Pat Hackett) *POPism: The Warhol '60s,* Harcourt, 1980.

America (photographs), Harper, 1985.

Vanishing Animals, text by Kurt Benirschke, Springer-Verlag, 1986.

Holy Cats by Andy Warhol's Mother, Panache Press, 1987.

25 Cats Name Sam and One Blue Pussy, Panache Press, 1987.

(With Hackett, and photographer with Hackett, Paige Powell, and others) *Andy Warhol's Party Book* (also known as *Party Book*), Crown, 1988.

The Andy Warhol Diaries, edited by Hackett, Warner Books, 1989.

(Illustrator) Margarita Madrigal, *Madrigal's Magic Key to Spanish,* Doubleday, 1989.

A Coloring Book, Simon & Schuster, 1990.

Ten Lizes, Abrams, 1991.

(Illustrator with Joseph Johns and Mary Cassatt) *Art What Thou Eat: Images of Food in American Art,* Mayer Bell, 1991.

Polaroids, Pace/MacGill Gallery, 1992.

Also illustrator of *Andy Warhol's Children's Book.* Contributor to *New York in Photographien* by Reinhard Wolf, Gruner und Jahr, 1980, published as *New York in Photographs,* Vendome Press, 1981; contributor to *Artists' Portraits* by Alex Kayser, Abrams, 1981. Publisher, cofounder, and contributor to *Andy Warhol's Interview* magazine (now titled *Interview*).

ART COLLECTIONS AND CATALOGUES

Raid the Icebox with Andy Warhol: An Exhibition Selected from the Vaults of the Museum of Art, Rhode Island School of Design, catalogue by Stephen E. Ostrow, Rhode Island School of Design, 1969.

Andy Warhol, Buechergilde Gutenberg, 1971.

Ladies and Gentlemen/Andy Warhol: Presentazione di Janus, G. Mazzotta, 1975.

Jesse Kornbluth, *Pre-Pop Warhol: 1949-61,* Panache Press, 1988.

Rainer Crone, *Andy Warhol: The Early Work, 1952-1962,* Rizzoli International, 1988.

The Andy Warhol Collection: Sold for the Benefit of the Andy Warhol Foundation for the Visual Arts (six volumes), Sotheby's, 1988.

■ Sidelights

Andy Warhol was worried about a pimple he had found that morning. B, on the other end of the telephone line, told him to cover it up. Warhol got some makeup and did so. "Okay, B, okay. So now the pimple's covered. But am I covered? I have to look into the mirror for some more clues. Nothing is missing. It's all there. . . . The childlike, gum-chewing naivete, the glamour rooted in despair, the self-admiring carelessness, the perfected otherness, the wispiness, the shadowy, voyeuristic, vaguely sinister aura, the pale, soft-spoken magical presence, the skin and bones. . . . The albino-chalk skin. Parchmentlike. Reptilian. Almost blue. . . . The roadmap of scars. . . . The shaggy silver-white hair, soft and metallic. . . . It's all there, B. Nothing is missing. I'm everything my scrapbook says I am."

This obsessive self-description appears in the late American artist Andy Warhol's 1975 book, *The Philosophy of Andy Warhol (From A to B and Back Again),* and the detail it provides stands in odd contrast to the secrecy in which Warhol cloaked other aspects of himself. An interviewer asking Warhol where he had been brought up would likely have gotten the response, "I come from nowhere," as Victor Bockris quoted in his biography *Warhol*, and Warhol did keep people guessing about his origins throughout his life. As soon as interest in his childhood arose, he simply made up stories about his past and upbringing. His birth date was never verified because he continually changed it: sometimes it was 1925, then 1928, then 1931. Occasionally he had been born in McKeesport (south of Pittsburgh), sometimes Philadelphia, once or twice in Hawaii. His mythologized history included being raised by a family devastated by the Great Depression—only able to afford soup made from ketchup for meals—and being roughed up by his older brothers Paul and John. He also admitted to never having any friends and said that, by the time he had reached the age of twelve, he had lost all his hair and skin pigmentation. Slivers of truth are embedded in all of these statements. To answer questions about his past, Warhol would select an actual experience from his life and then build on it, often implying that something that might have happened only once was a common occurrence. Regardless of where Andy Warhol came from, where he ended up is more obvious: many people regard him as the most famous American artist of the twentieth century, a reputation he achieved by painting the particular details of everyday reality—a coffee can, a pop bottle—in such a passionless, objective way that his admirers claim the unconventional approach itself is enough to merit Warhol attention.

Andrew Warhola

Despite Warhol's attempts to mask the biographical details of his life, many biographers agree that he was born to immigrant parents on August 6, 1928, in Pittsburgh and was given the name Andrew Warhola. His father was a working man who had brought his family to the United States from a Ruthenian village in the Carpathian Mountains, near the border of Poland and Russia. Warhol's mother could not speak English, and at home the Warhola boys spoke the Ruthenian language—a combination of Hungarian and Ukrainian—*Po nasemu* ("in our own manner"). The family was devoutly Byzantine Catholic, and their faith served as the center of both their religious and social lives. Being surrounded by a population of Roman Catholics who spoke different languages also compelled the Warholas to become a tightly knit family. The family's finances were often dire, and they did have to eat tomato soup made from ketchup on occasion.

When Warhol was four, Paul, who often assumed the role of man of the house when his father was away working, decided that his younger brother should start going to school even though, at that time, children didn't usually begin classes until they had reached the age of six. Picking Warhol up after the first day, however, Paul found his little brother crying, and the tears continued to stream down his face until the boys reached home. Later, Warhol told his family that a girl had slapped him during the day and he refused to go back to school, an idea his mother supported. So Warhol spent most of his time between the ages of four and six drawing pictures with his mother. Their subjects were usually either each other or the family cat. Warhol developed a dependence on his mother, often clinging to her, and he frequently spoke of her later in his life. He rarely mentioned his father, though, claiming he hadn't seen him often because he was usually away working. These comments have confused Warhola family members, who have said that, though his work did keep him from the family, Mr. Warhola was an honest, supportive, hard-working family man who struggled in order to send his children (especially young Andy, whose intelligence he recognized) to school.

When Warhol successfully entered school at the more common age of six, he went straight into the second grade because the single, traumatic day he had spent in class when he was four had been counted as a full year. He began to speak English. Every day he went home for a bowl of Campbell's Soup at lunchtime and, after doing his homework in the evening, he entertained himself by drawing. A major setback to his schooling occurred in the autumn of 1936 when he fell ill with rheumatic fever, which then developed into St. Vitus's Dance, an affliction of the central nervous system. As a result, Warhol slurred his words, his hands shook, and he was often disoriented. St. Vitus's Dance is more a psychologically than physically dangerous disease, however, because the afflicted often think that they are losing their sanity. Warhol was bedridden, and his mother kept him occupied with coloring books and movie magazines, which gave Warhol his first look at the dream world of Hollywood. In *The Philosophy of Andy Warhol*, Warhol related that he spent his time "listening to the radio and lying in bed with my Charlie McCarthy doll and my un-cut-out cut-out paper dolls all over the spread and under the pillow." He drew and listened to the radio for a month, and then his mother and brothers thought it was time for him to return to school. Warhol disagreed: not truly back to his full health, he threw a tantrum on the front porch and a neighbor, who assumed a fatherly role for the family when Mr. Warhola was away, tried to physically force Warhol to go to school. The trauma put Warhol back in bed for four more weeks and instilled in the boy a lifelong fear of violence. His relapse was spent as idyllically as the first spell, drawing and reading magazines, but left him with a blotchy red skin condition that lasted throughout his life.

As a child, Warhol exhibited an almost two-sided personality: with his girlfriends he was charming, but at home he acted very pompous, superior, and occasionally aggressive. His interest in girls led him to write to the Shirley Temple fan club. The dime membership fee earned him a picture with the inscription, 'To Andy Warhola from Shirley Temple,' an item that became his prized possession. A devoted fan, he watched all Temple's movies and tried to model his gestures after hers. Only one thing bothered Warhol about the films, as Bockris quoted in *Warhol:* "I was so disappointed whenever Shirley Temple found her father. It ruined everything. She had been having such a good time, tap dancing with the local Kiwanis Club or the newspaper men in the city room. I don't want to know who the father is."

Warhol's own father passed away in 1942. He had been confined to the house for three years, not bedridden but unable to work after drinking contaminated water at a job site. The traditional funeral service called for his body to be laid out in the house for three days, during which Warhol refused to see his father, finally staying with his aunt because of his fear of sleeping in the same house with the coffin. Though he did attend the funeral, Warhol's fear of death throughout the rest of his life drove him to keep distant from anything that concerned or suggested it. Warhol seemed to have the opposite response to his father's death than one might expect, though. "In a series of photographs taken outside [the Warhola's] house after the funeral," Bockris wrote, "Andy appears to be bursting forth as if both relieved of some inner burden and fuelled by new energy that will take him through his teens." And Warhol's brother John told Bockris, "If there was any outstanding thing that affected Andy during his childhood more than anything else I think it was when my dad passed away." His father's death left Warhol with a lifelong fear of hospitals because his father had

been handled roughly there during his illness. His mother's colostomy, performed two years after her husband's death, added to this phobia. Though medically successful, the operation, which replaces most of the colon, had an emotionally devastating effect on Warhol's mother. Warhol's resulting fear of hospitals oddly foreshadowed his own early death.

The 1940s Teenager

Warhol spent his high school years at Schenley High School. He became seriously interested in his art, and in art class he would go immediately to his desk and draw, never moving from his pictures and never discussing them. Drawings accumulated in his bedroom and his mother once threw away a number of them because they took up so much space. Family members related that his interest in his work, and the seriousness with which he approached it, became a sort of monomania. Art was all he talked about and all he did—a sketchbook never left his hands. But despite this earnestness, Warhol was a relatively typical teenager. He wore traditional clothes and, though he didn't wear his hair in the crewcut style the other boys did, he was popular with girls and noted for his ability to talk with them when other boys fumbled. In his senior yearbook, the caption next to his picture, according to Bockris, read: "As genuine as a fingerprint."

The 1940s witnessed the press's obsession with disaster—plane crashes, suicides, earthquakes, flu epidemics, World War II—beheld a revolution in animation spurred by Warner Brothers and Walt Disney, and teemed with excellent, high quality films populated by larger-than-life movie stars. All of this cultural material influenced the teenaged Warhol. Elizabeth Taylor replaced Shirley Temple as his child star idol, and the Shadow, who knew "what evil lurks in the hearts of men," was his favorite radio character. Animation and comic books would inform much of the work of Roy Lichtenstein, a pop art contemporary of Warhol's, and the stress the media placed on disasters later inspired some of Warhol's own paintings. At the time, Warhol clipped many of the pictures from newspapers and used them in collages.

After high school, Warhol attended Carnegie Institute of Technology (now Carnegie-Mellon University), which he chose over the University of Pittsburgh because he preferred its art department. He managed to have trouble with most of his classes because of his accent and the difficulty he had writing proper English. The other members of his class tended to watch over him because of his slight build and quiet manner. His untraditional art made many of the faculty question his artistic ability, and he was constantly threatened with expulsion. But other teachers immediately recognized his talent, and he was able to continue his studies. After his first year, however, he was temporarily suspended and had to make up the work over the summer—a rejection that so affected Warhol that he later would deny he had ever gone to college. By the end of his four years at Carnegie, he had become something of an art hero. Seen around campus in oversized jeans, loose work shirts, and work boots, Warhol paid tribute to his family history by adopting a "working class" look and evoking a lifestyle that would soon be manifested in the works of such Beat generation writers as Jack Kerouac and Allen Ginsberg. He was enchanted by the writer Truman Capote, whose lifestyle—living in an apartment in New York, hosting parties attended by the rich and famous, and receiving respect for his artistry—Warhol dreamed of.

While still in school, Warhol discovered a method of drawing that would help him get his first job. He would draw on one piece of paper and, before the ink could dry, blot it onto another sheet, producing a smudged line—or "blotted line," as the technique is called. Warhol particularly liked this process because it distanced him from the final product. Since he hadn't actually made the lines on the final drawing but had blotted them, he was personally removed from the drawing, an aesthetic idea that also inspired the factory-production method Warhol later used to create his paintings. Warhol also learned something in his senior year that would inform the way he sought publicity throughout his life. A regional institution held an exhibition of local work each year, and in 1949 Warhol submitted a painting depicting a young boy with one of his fingers up his nose, called *The Broad Gave Me My Face, but I Can Pick My Own Nose* (also known as *Nosepicker*). The resulting stir—some jurors felt the painting inappropriate and wanted to have it removed while others championed its importance—merely made the painting more notable than it may have been without any controversy. This lesson in how the perceived scandalousness of an artwork can make it popular wasn't lost on Warhol.

Aside from questioning the preconceived, "acceptable" subjects of art, Warhol also played with his name—both first and last—in his final year at

The sterile, repetitious quality of this 1962 silkscreen, *One Hundred Campbell Soup Cans*, illustrates familiar Warhol themes of mass production and consumerism.

Carnegie. He signed his name Andre on Christmas cards, was listed as Andrew Warhol in an exhibition, and was known to his friends as Andy. As graduation approached, he worried about what he would do after school. He considered a career as a high school art teacher, going so far as to send his portfolio to a school in the Midwest. But when he was unable to find a teaching position he decided, with the encouragement of his friends, to leave Pittsburgh and move to New York.

Though his mother didn't want Warhol to leave home, she also didn't want to hinder his career. So when Warhol secured a sublet apartment and planned his trip, his mother let him go even though she had become as attached to him as he had been to her when he was a boy. Warhol arrived in New York City with two hundred dollars and his portfolio—which Philip Pearlstein, Warhol's traveling companion at the time and roommate-to-be, called "simply dazzling" in *Warhol*. His second day there, Warhol got a break at an appointment with the art director of *Glamour* magazine. Impressed with his drawings (and buying one for her own collection), Tina Fredericks asked if Warhol could bring some pictures of shoes before 10 a.m. the next day. Warhol drew the shoes, but surprised Fredericks with their worn in, sexual look. She asked him to draw shoes that looked new and would be able to serve as advertisements. Warhol brought new drawings the following morning and sold them. He did more work for *Glamour*, and began to establish himself as a commercial artist. Later that summer, his first illustration (for an article) was published in the magazine, and the credit listed his name as Andy Warhol, which Warhol claimed was a misspelling and then claimed as his own forever after.

"I'm Starting Pop Art"

Professionally, Warhol grew comfortable in New York. He became the highest-paid fashion illustrator working in the city and was also the best known. Aside from the drawings he made for advertisements, he was selling illustrations and even did the cover art for several record albums. Every day, he wrote his mother a postcard and spent long hours blotting, completing at night the drawings that he had been assigned during the day. Personally, Warhol's life wasn't as successful. He met Truman Capote after having drinks with Capote's mother and began to call the writer every day, much to Capote's annoyance. Warhol, Bockris quoted Capote as saying, "seemed one of those helpless people that you just know nothing's ever going to happen to. Just a hopeless born loser, the loneliest, most friendless person I'd ever seen in my life."

After living with several different roommates, Warhol moved into an apartment by himself. But then he found a new, unexpected living companion. "My mother had shown up one night at the apartment where I was living with a few suitcases and shopping bags," he wrote in his 1980 autobiographical book *POPism: The Warhol '60s,* "and she announced that she'd left Pennsylvania for good 'to come live with my Andy.'" Warhol thought his mother would get tired of the city, but when she didn't they got a house uptown. He described the home situation in *POPism:* "My house was on four floors, including a living area in the basement where the kitchen was and where my mother lived with a lot of cats, all named Sam."

By the early 1960s, Warhol was painting when he wasn't doing his commercial drawings. One day, a friend from Carnegie Tech, Leonard Kessler, met with Warhol—loaded down with paints and can-

vases—as he came out of an art supply store. As Bockris told the story, Kessler asked Warhol what he was doing. "I'm starting pop art," Warhol replied. Kessler asked him why. "Because I hate abstract expressionism. I hate it!" Abstract expressionism, a method of painting that emphasizes the manner in which paint is actually applied to the canvas instead of the image that results, was a popular movement at the time. Abstract expressionist paintings—covered with hectic splatters, heavy blobs and streaks, and erratic color combinations—often look like a painter's palette rather than the painting's subject. Sometimes the artists would set their canvases on the floor and walk or roll over them. The American artist Jackson Pollack was one of the most influential of the abstract expressionists. Warhol wasn't taken with the movement, however. Bockris explained what exactly Warhol did in response: "He decided to paint a series of big black and white pictures of what artists were supposed to hate most, advertisements for wigs, nose jobs, television sets and cans of food. He took the simplest, crummiest, cheapest ads from the backs of magazines, made them into slides and projected them on to blank canvas. Then he painted a fractured section of the ad in black paint, letting drips and splashes accidentally splatter. The paintings were ugly and banal but reverberated with anger and contempt."

Along with trying to initiate a movement that would change the art scene, Warhol altered his own image. He wore white and blond wigs that he would arrange wildly. He began to talk differently, speaking in a way that was intentionally difficult to understand. Art collectors came to see his paintings and a few of the pictures sold. His artistic vision demanded that he make his mind as vacant as he possibly could while he painted so that the work would be devoid of any emotion or passion. To do this, he surrounded himself with loud music, sometimes from a radio and a phonograph at the same time, and left the television on, too. His oddball appearance and behavior worked negatively for him in the art world, as did his homosexuality. The new art movement was taking hold, but Warhol was having problems finding a gallery that would show his work. He was also having difficulties with money and his nerves. Desperate to have a new idea, knowing that the new pop-movement that was developing in the United States as it had in other countries would pass him by if he didn't paint something that would jolt the art world, he paid gallery owner Muriel Latow fifty dollars for an idea. As Bockris related the story, once Latow had

A pioneer of the Pop Art movement, Warhol exploited the medium of silk screening by creating series of bold, colorful prints, like this 1967 work, *Marilyn*.

A Can of Campbell's Soup

the check in her hand, she asked Warhol, "'What do you like most in the whole world?'" Warhol didn't know. "'Money,' she replied. 'You should paint pictures of money.'" Latow also told Warhol that he should paint things that everyone would recognize—like soup cans.

Warhol was inspired by Latow's ideas. He was hit with the realization that he had always wished to paint the contents of his mother's kitchen. He had his mother buy each of the varieties of Campbell's Soup—thirty-two cans—so he could prepare to paint them. He experimented with the design that he wanted and finally decided he would do an entire series of paintings with each can on a separate canvas, a white background intensifying the effect of the color. Bockris quoted what Warhol told an interviewer about his subject matter and intention: "I've never been touched by a painting. I don't want to think. The world outside would be easier to live in if we were all machines. It's nothing in the end anyway. It doesn't matter what anyone does." Despite these negative comments from the artist himself, Warhol's art was being noticed. His studio was filled with visitors every night and his own appearance and manner finally became accepted in art circles. A gallery owner from Los Angeles paid him a visit and agreed to show the Campbell's Soup can paintings the next summer, in 1962, by which time Warhol would have them all completed.

In what would become typical Warholian fashion, the paintings became news even before they were shown. The mass media had started to take an interest in the pop art movement and Warhol received publicity. When the Campbell's Soup can paintings opened, the gallery displayed them in a very low-key fashion, merely lining them up on shelves without an official opening—Warhol didn't even travel to the West Coast to serve as host. The press made jokes about the paintings, questioning their status as works of art because of their untraditional subjects. But Warhol charged on. He painted Coke bottles, coffee cans, and more Campbell's Soup cans in different sizes and in different formats—in essence, modern folk art. Warhol himself, in *POPism*, described the new art movement in this way: "By 1960, when Pop Art first came out in New York, the art scene here had so much going for it that even all the stiff European types had to finally admit we [the pop artists] were a part of world culture. Abstract Expressionism had already become an institution, and then, in the last part of the fifties, Jasper Johns and [Robert] Rauschenberg and others had begun to bring art back from abstraction and introspective stuff. Then Pop Art took the inside and put it outside, took the outside and put it inside." "The Pop artists," Warhol continued, "did images that anybody walking down Broadway would recognize in a split second—comics, picnic tables, men's trousers, celebrities, shower curtains, refrigerators, Coke bottles—all the great modern things that the Abstract Expressionists tried so hard not to notice at all." One motif he explored was repetition. What happens when fifty Campbell's Soup cans are stacked on the same canvas? A hundred? Bert Greene told Bockris that when he asked Warhol why he had chosen to paint Campbell's Soup cans, the artist replied, "I wanted to paint nothing. I was looking for something that was the essence of nothing, and [the soup can] was it."

Warhol often manipulated images of cultural icons to reflect society's distortions of its celebrities, as in this 1964 work, *Elvis I and II.*

Warhol also capitalized on the duplication motif when he learned the silk-screening process. "In August '62 I started doing silkscreens," he wrote in *POPism*. "The rubber-stamp method I'd been using to repeat images suddenly seemed too homemade; I wanted something stronger that gave more of an assembly-line effect." Silk-screening is a technique used to copy a picture. First, a screen is designed so that its holes form the photographic image desired. Then, the screen is set on top of a canvas and painted over, leaving behind a copy of the image. This can produce a nearly identical picture over and over again; using the same screen, you merely move from canvas to canvas, reapplying paint over the screen. Warhol's first experiments with this process were of stars like Elvis Presley, Warren Beatty, and Natalie Wood. His big idea came when he heard that Marilyn Monroe had committed suicide on August 4, 1962. Warhol embarked on a series of twenty-three Marilyns, but the monumental canvas turned out to be one with a hundred copies of Monroe's face in bold and vibrant colors. By repeating the same image, the painting questioned what happens when mass production can endlessly repeat the same object, or what happens when a human being is so often seen in pictures that she becomes an object. Can originality exist in such an environment? "The more you look at the same exact thing," Warhol related in *POPism*, "the more the meaning goes away, and the better and emptier you feel."

After the Marilyn Monroe paintings, Warhol's output suddenly increased exponentially. He painted many pictures—a hundred in just three months—silk-screening the soup can and pop bottle paintings he had made at the beginning of the year. Critical acclaim and respect started coming his way. Pop art was taking off. A show at the Sidney Janis Gallery in New York on Halloween Day, 1962, announced its coming, and Warhol had three of his works in the show. A week later, Warhol's private show at the Stable, another New York gallery, revealed many of his now-classic paintings. Criticism as well as success poured in. Some people bought his paintings but others attacked the method Warhol used, commenting that anyone could produce his pictures, a fact that they felt made them unoriginal and worthless. Warhol was an easy target for anyone who wanted to attack the new movement—especially those abstract expressionists whose work was being replaced in the galleries by the new art—because his appearance made him stick out and his visibility made him more reproachable. Warhol's response

to the criticism was as untraditional as his art: he agreed with it. He liked the idea that anyone could paint his paintings or come up with his ideas—after all, he had paid for an idea himself. Much as he liked to falsify his own history and leave it up to others to decide what was true or not, Warhol left the critics to decide the artfulness of his work for themselves and, while they decided, painted more for them to consider.

Personally, Warhol had become a socialite and began to show up at parties with small groups centered around him. He went out every night. Artistically, during 1963 Warhol turned from the creation of paintings that have been variously called his "disaster" or "car crash" paintings. After renting a run-down studio—his art was making his home uninhabitable—and hiring an assistant, Gerard Malanga, Warhol focused on scenes of violence or death taken directly from photographs. Using the silk-screening process, Warhol and Malanga worked quickly; and Warhol celebrated the blurred images and splashes of paint that resulted from their haste. Some of the paintings were of famous people who had passed away, and others were merely of people who had killed themselves or had been victimized in such a way that their tragedies were publicized. One painting simply depicted an electric chair with a small "Silence" sign in the corner. Most of the paintings had colors in their names like *Vertical Orange Car Crash* and *Lavender Disaster*. One painting, *Optical Car Crash*, repeated the image of a dead person in a car thirty-five times. In *New Statesman and Society*, Kathy Acker wrote, "In *Optical Car Crash*, Andy Warhol both represented death and, through the use of repetition and the lack of painterliness, by turning death into an advertisement, devalued death." Some of his most famous paintings, the "death and disaster" canvases were cited by critics for their political impact and importance, but Warhol himself merely said that the paintings were meaningless and that the overall mood was one of indifference, his way of pointing to the human tendency to look past the horrors of the day because they are so commonplace.

The Factory

Warhol's fame as an artist would never surpass the attention he experienced in the years from 1962 to 1964. He enjoyed his new status as a rich and famous idol, something he had dreamed of since being charmed by Shirley Temple as a boy. His party-going and hosting abilities became legendary. He moved his studio to a new location, a former hat factory which he dubbed "The Factory." Warhol began working with sculpture and wanted to make wooden reproductions of common grocery store items, such as boxes of Kellogg's cornflakes and Brillo soap pads, that would look exactly like the originals. More and more people began gathering at the Factory, especially troubled, reckless drug addicts who would hang around the studio for days on end.

Warhol also became interested in film at this time. His movie *Sleep,* a six-hour portrayal of a man sleeping run at a slightly slower speed than it was filmed (Warhol was using a camera that only held three minutes worth of film and, since he had to stop and reload every three minutes, he had to make up the time somehow), was being noticed by independent filmmakers. "Seeing everybody so up all the time made me think that sleep was becoming pretty obsolete, so I decided I'd better quickly do a movie of a person sleeping," he wrote in *POPism.* Other films that explored similarly simple subjects include *Haircut* and *Eat.*

Warhol again changed his image in this new Factory environment. His wigs turned silver, his glasses darkened, he wore a black leather jacket over T-shirts, his paint-splashed blue jeans were swapped for tight, black jeans under which he wore panty hose, and his boots had high heels. Occasionally he wore makeup. His public demeanor was distant and quiet. He told one commentator, according to Bockris, "If you want to know all about Andy Warhol, just look at the surface of my paintings and my films, and there I am. There's nothing behind it." Warhol became rougher and ruder in public and at parties, and his entourage of openly gay men distanced him from the friends he had had before his image change. But his fame had made Warhol *the* name of pop art. His celebrity was so huge it pulled him out of the community of underground pop artists and into his own world, surrounded by his own art and by people of his own association. His paintings and sculptures, however, weren't selling.

Meanwhile the Factory had become something of a film studio. Warhol made scriptless, random films with more characters in them than his earlier movies, calling the actors his "superstars" (the most famous superstar was Edie Sedgwick, whom Warhol met in 1965). The tinfoil-covered walls and windows, the boxes of Brillo pads, and the number of social dropouts that filled the Factory created an atmosphere that Warhol thrived on. Poetry readings and films proliferated in the creative atmosphere, as did parties, which were often attended by celebrities. Warhol became known for his ability and tendency to manipulate people. He made people compete for his attention. Critics have accused him of unfairly feeding off the drug-induced frenzy and general pandemonium created by the superstars, who worked for free. The filming of *Empire,* an eight-hour visualization of the Empire State Building as night falls and its lights come on, was almost entirely done by his assistants. Warhol didn't want to touch the camera because he wanted it to make the art for him. Something about Warhol's procedures worked, however. Jonas Mekas wrote in the *Village Voice* that if everyone in the world could have the patience to sit and watch *Empire* in its entirety, "there would be no more wars, no hate, no terror—there would be a happiness regained upon earth." Despite this critical recognition, other underground filmmakers were disturbed by how little Warhol knew about film from an academic standpoint and how little actually went into making his movies. After Warhol won an award from *Film Culture* in 1964, his filmmaking peers complained that he should not be the one to receive recognition and fame while they slaved in obscurity. And Warhol's tendency to let the cameras roll while people actually performed personally destructive or harmful actions caused a stir among his followers and the art world in general. Police officers began to visit the Factory with some regularity.

The Chelsea Girls, one of Warhol's most daring films, was made from twelve reels of footage that had not been intended to be shown together but which, when Warhol sat down to review them, seemed to connect. He spliced them together and called the result *Chelsea Girls.* Because the film was so long—six and a half hours—Warhol decided to cut the overall length by showing one half of the film simultaneously with the other on adjacent screens and leaving the sound of only one side on at a time. This original presentation resulted in a vibrant visual effect as well as a somewhat disturbing overtone. "More than a randomly artistic, at times unconsciously brilliant and beautiful expose of perversion and display of underground pop, hip and drug culture," Pamela Crawford wrote in *Cineaste,* "Andy Warhol's *Chelsea Girls* is a violent reflection of 'our times,' a roundabout comment on middle class society." The movie was also a near documentary of what was going on in the Factory in 1966: drug taking, crying, stripping, sex, self-destruction. The Factory group was distraught and the atmosphere was tense. The wildness and craziness were intensified because no one thought that anything unusual was going on. When a former boyfriend of Warhol's, Danny Williams, killed himself by swimming out into the ocean, the general feeling in the Factory was, according to Bockris, "If that's what he wants to do, that's cool." Life at the Factory was fine as long as no one showed that they were weak or, therefore, human.

A Visit from SCUM

Warhol would not live off the Factory's wildness without incident, however. In 1967, he made the movie *I, a Man*, which Bockris called "not a particularly good or funny film." The movie eventually became notable because Valerie Solanas, a lesbian and leader of the Society for Cutting up Men (SCUM), acted in it. Solanas had dropped a script off to Warhol hoping he would film it, but

Warhol holds a portrait of Queen Elizabeth II, part of his 1985 series, *Reigning Queens* (photograph by Derek Hudson).

when he didn't she started calling him at the Factory, asking for money. Often described as someone who could never say no, Warhol told her he would give her twenty-five dollars if she came and acted in *I, a Man,* and she did. This didn't pacify her for long, though, and soon after she was calling Warhol a thief. On Monday, June 3, 1968, Solanas showed up at the Factory (which had been moved into a building more like an office building by this time) looking for Warhol. After being told that he wasn't around, she walked down the street and waited. When he did show up later that afternoon, she walked into the Factory with him and Jed Johnson, his boyfriend. As they rode the elevator up, Warhol noticed something strange about Solanas: she had combed her hair and had lipstick on, two unusual things for her to do. When they got off the elevator, Warhol sat at a desk and began talking to Viva, one of his superstars, on the telephone. The rest of the people in the room, including Mario Amaya, an art critic and curator who had stopped by to speak with Warhol, continued on with their usual business, not ignoring Solanas but not paying her much attention. Solanas pulled a handgun out of a paper bag she was carrying, still without anyone noticing. She aimed at Warhol, who was just leaning forward to hang up the phone, and fired. "At the other end of the telephone," related Bockris, "Viva thought someone was cracking a whip.... In that frozen second only Andy saw what was really happening. Surprised, he dropped the phone, jumped from the desk and started to move, looking directly into the woman's pinched face. 'No! No! Valerie!' he screamed. 'Don't do it!'" Solanas shot two more times, the final time from short range as Warhol tried to crawl under the desk. Solanas then shot twice at Amaya, first missing and then hitting him near the hip. Amaya scrambled out of the room as Solanas took aim at the last person still standing in the room, Fred Hughes, one of Warhol's employees. As he pleaded for her to leave, Solanas aimed at his head and shot. Luckily, the gun misfired, and as Solanas dug in the paper bag for the other gun she had brought, the elevator came. Hughes begged her to leave, and Solanas walked onto the elevator and disappeared.

At 4:51 p.m., not quite half an hour after he had been shot, the doctors pronounced Warhol clinically dead. Amaya, pleading with the doctors to do something, got them to operate. But even after a nearly six-hour surgery, Warhol's chances of surviving were only fifty-fifty; his lung, esophagus, gall bladder, liver, spleen, and intestines had all been damaged. Paul and John Warhola arrived at the hospital soon after Warhol's weeping mother was taken home. Solanas had walked up to a policeman and handed him the guns, telling him that she had shot Warhol because he had too much control over her. The police and newspapers tried to find a motive in Solanas's actions. She continued to tell them he had control of her life and to cite her SCUM activities. Later, Warhol wrote in *POPism:* "I couldn't figure out why, of all the people Valerie must have known, I had to be the one to get shot. I guess it was just being in the wrong place at the right time. That's what assassination is all about." Warhol's struggle for life was documented in papers all over the country, and was only bumped off the headlines by another assassination: a few days later, presidential candidate Robert Kennedy was shot after he won the California primary.

Warhol was able to return to his home on July 28. He stayed there until he went out to dinner in September, his first public appearance after the shooting. Bockris reported that in an interview with Leticia Kent, with whom he dined, Warhol said: "Before I was shot, I always suspected I was watching TV instead of living life. Right when I was being shot I knew I was watching television. Since I was shot everything is such a dream to me. I don't know whether or not I'm really alive—whether I died. It's sad. Like I can't say hello or goodbye to people. Life is like a dream." Kent then asked Warhol if he was afraid. "I wasn't afraid before," he responded. "And having died once, I shouldn't feel fear. But I'm afraid. I don't understand why. I am afraid of God alone, and I wasn't before."

The New Andy Warhol

Valerie Solanas's attempt to assassinate Andy Warhol had many repercussions on the artist's life. Much as the perceived scandalousness of his *Nosepicker* painting had caused a fervor in Warhol's college years, the shooting created an even greater demand for his artworks. His 1968 movie *Flesh* received solid reviews and enjoyed a popularity that rivaled that of his other, more experimental films. The shooting also made Warhol very nervous. Back at the Factory for several hours a day, he would twitch every time the elevator doors opened. The Factory was closed off, and the days when anyone was allowed in were over. "Before, I'd always loved being with people who looked weird and seemed crazy—I'd thrived on it, really—but now I was terrified that they'd take out a gun and shoot me," Warhol wrote in *POPism.* But,

he continued, this new atmosphere at the Factory produced even more problems for him creatively: "I was afraid that without the crazy, druggy people around jabbering away and doing their insane things, I would lose my creativity. After all, they'd been my total inspiration since '64, and I didn't know if I could make it without them." As for the new people hanging around the Factory, Warhol described them at the end of *POPism:* "All the morality and restriction that the early superstars had rebelled against seemed so far away—as unreal as the Victorian era seems to everybody today. Pop wasn't an issue or an option for this new wave: it was all they'd ever known."

The end of the sixties ushered in the end of part of Warhol's life. He explained in *The Philosophy of Andy Warhol:* "During the 60s, I think, people forgot what emotions were supposed to be. And I don't think they've ever remembered. I think that once you see emotions from a certain angle you can never think of them as real again. That's what more or less happened to me." The last twenty years of Andy Warhol's life were not as driven or packed as the years that preceded them. The man whose party-going tendencies had become legend suddenly was going home by eight o'clock, getting up early, and calling people to find out what had happened the night before. He began to tape record everything, and most of the people who entered the Factory were asked if they could transcribe tapes or if they knew anyone who would. The chattering of typewriters filled the air. The idea that everyone else was also taping their conversations inspired Warhol to publish a magazine entirely made up of interviews. *Andy Warhol's Interview,* later renamed *Interview,* was the result. Of his tape recorder, Warhol wrote in *The Philosophy of Andy Warhol,* "The acquisition of my tape recorder really finished whatever emotional life I might have had, but I was glad to see it go. Nothing was ever a problem again, because a problem just meant a good tape, and when a problem transforms itself into a good tape it's not a problem anymore. An interesting problem was an interesting tape."

During the 1970s, Warhol's influence as an artist became less newsworthy than the fact that he was Andy Warhol. He gave creative control of his films to Paul Morrisey, who had been assisting Warhol with his filmmaking. Most of the art Warhol produced was commissioned, silk-screened portraits of celebrities. He gave less and less of his time to *Interview.* He didn't entirely give up his art, still producing collages, art for children, and experimental silk screens, but the rapidity and fever with which he had produced his early paintings were gone. Polaroid pictures became the art form he was most interested in and he carried the camera on his visits to celebrity parties. By the end of the 1970s, he was using more complicated camera equipment to make his portraits. Two volumes of these pictures, *Andy Warhol's Exposures* and *Andy Warhol: Portraits of the '70s*, were published.

Aside from his portraits, Warhol also produced writings during the 1970s. He filled his 1975 book *The Philosophy of Andy Warhol (From A to B and Back Again)* with pages of short takes from his thought process. "Beauty doesn't have anything to do with sex." He also commented, "Beauty has to do with beauty and sex has to do with sex." And: "I can never get over when you're on the beach how beautiful the sand looks and the water washes it away and straightens it up and the trees and the grass all look great. I think having land and not ruining it is the most beautiful art that anybody could ever want to own." Warhol even turned his eye on America: "What's great about this country is that America started the tradition where the richest consumers buy essentially the same things as the poorest. You can be watching TV and see Coca-Cola, and you can know that the President drinks Coke, Liz Taylor drinks Coke, and just think, you can drink Coke, too. A Coke is a Coke and no amount of money can get you a better Coke.... All the Cokes are the same and all the Cokes are good.... The idea of America is so wonderful because the more equal it is, the more American it is."

The Diaries of Andy Warhol

Continuing Warhol's interest in photography, his 1985 photographic essay *America* is a collage of often humorous, often sad pictures. Warhol, known for taking pictures and tapes of anything, included many different subjects in the book—bag ladies, folk artists—but still seemed focused on celebrity portraits. His approach to picture-taking, as well as to painting, was often paradoxical. In an interview with Michelle Bogre published in *American Photographer*, Warhol said, "All photography is pop, and all photographers are crazy.... Because they feel guilty since they don't have to do very much—just push a button.... Most of them don't even look." Asked what the difference between a picture and a photograph is, Warhol answered, "A picture just means I know where I was every minute. That's why I take pictures. It's a visual diary."

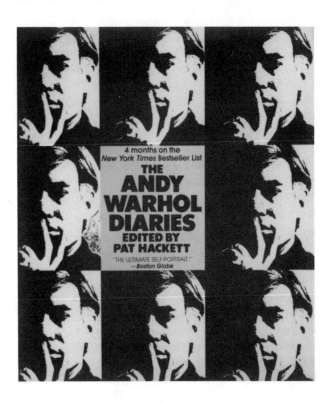

The entries from this 1989 work, transcribed from more than a decade's worth of Warhol's daily phone updates to his secretary, reveal the author's thoughts on his health, his contemporaries, and his art.

Warhol also kept a verbal diary from 1976 to 1987. Each morning he would call Pat Hackett, his secretary, and tell her what he had done the day before. Hackett taped the "diary entries"—which in the end totalled over ten thousand pages and were originally intended as a way for Warhol to keep track of business expenses—and the transcriptions were published as *The Andy Warhol Diaries*. The book's rambling, unedited pages chronicle his successively graver and more desperate hypochondria, his thoughts on celebrities, and pure gossip. Some of the habits uncovered, such as his generosity, his volunteer work at soup kitchens on holidays, and his faithful attendance of Sunday Mass, undermined the picture many people had of the artist. In the *Washington Post Book World*, William McPherson called *The Andy Warhol Diaries* "sometimes ... fascinating." "Despite their virtuoso triviality, their naive snobbery, and their incredible length," wrote Martin Amis in the *New York Times Book Review*, "the diaries of Andy Warhol are not without a certain charm."

Aside from the changes the shooting spawned in Warhol's personal life—behaviors more and more distant from those that characterized the 1960s—

the paintings he made also changed. They leaned away from the earlier, passionless pictures and took on more religious and human themes. His series of Last Supper paintings, inspired by the Leonardo da Vinci masterpiece, had done well upon opening in Milan. Bockris recorded John Richardson's observations about the paintings: "Andy's use of a pop conceit to energize sacred subjects constituted a major breakthrough in religious art. Andy even managed to give a slogan like Jesus Saves an uncanny ring of urgency." And in Warhol's last series of self-portraits, completed in the summer of 1986, he made his hair into a halo.

Warhol's health soon quelled the creative energy he was finally building after the shooting. His gallstones were causing him enough pain to slow him down, but his fear of hospitals was overwhelmingly strong at the time: he wouldn't even look at the building if he happened to pass one by. Eventually, however, the pain wouldn't go away unattended, and Warhol went into the hospital on Friday, February 20, 1987, cloaked in secrecy. On Saturday, the gallbladder surgery over, Warhol was recovering in his hospital room. He watched a bit of television, and doctors noted that nothing was unusual. Bockris wrote that, before the operation, Warhol had told his doctors, "I'm not going to make it," and his words became an eerie prophesy. For reasons not fully understood, early in the morning of the twenty-second the nurse watching Warhol noticed that he had turned blue and attempts to resuscitate him failed. As the news broke the next day, people wondered if it was true or merely a rumor or publicity stunt. Once Warhol's death was verified, the hospital was criticized and allegations that the nurse hadn't stayed with Warhol or properly monitored his fluid intake arose. Whatever the reasons or mistakes, one of the most famous artists of the twentieth century, rivaling even the popularity of Pablo Picasso, was dead before his sixtieth birthday, perhaps the victim of the hospital that he had always feared.

The Auction

Warhol's will stipulated that all his possessions be sold and the money, outside of some given to his brothers, be used to found the Andy Warhol Foundation for the Visual Arts. Warhol himself wrote in *The Philosophy of Andy Warhol*, "Buying is more American than thinking and I'm as American as they come.... I would rather watch somebody buy their underwear than read a book they wrote." He probably would have loved the auction his horde of possessions created: it was one of the biggest estate sales ever. Beginning on April 23, 1988, the sale spanned a ten-day period. The collection was so large that just the catalogue of the ten thousand items to be sold required six volumes and cost ninety-five dollars (the catalogue even described one lot that consisted of four hundred of Warhol's own, scribbled-in auction catalogues). "For some," Margot Hornblower noted in *Time*, "Warhol's vast collection was a monument to the materialism that the artist enshrined in his Campbell Soup can and Brillo pad artworks." In accumulating all the items to be sold at the auction—cookie jars, furniture, paintings, photographs, rugs, baskets, art—the sum total of Warhol's years of obsessive acquisitiveness was on display. Some speculated that all the possessions together formed Warhol's largest artistic statement, the objects pulled from every facet of life emphasizing his democratic thinking. In his purchase-filled home, the auction house Sotheby's found bags full of items that Warhol had never even bothered to unpack. Though none of Warhol's own paintings were hanging in the house, Sotheby's did locate a painting by Picasso in a closet. A crucifix was on Warhol's nightstand.

Sotheby's estimated that the sale would bring in $15 million, but that figure quickly rose when bidders, hoping to take a piece from Warhol's life home with them, pushed the prices up. A Fred Flintstone watch, with two other similar watches, had been estimated to be worth fifty to sixty dollars in the catalogue; they sold for $2,640. A pair of console tables by Pierre Legrain, a French artisan, were expected to sell for $40,000 to $60,000 each; together, they brought $418,000. 136 cookie jars went for a total of $198,605. Surprisingly, the art that the king of pop himself had collected was something less than what might have been expected. Except for a few pictures, the paintings he owned were unexceptional. In all, the auction collected more than $25 million.

Warhol typically criticized those things he sought and reveled in. The man desperate for wealth and fame wrote in *The Philosophy of Andy Warhol:* "Being famous isn't all that important. If I weren't famous, I wouldn't have been shot for being Andy Warhol. Maybe I would have been shot for being in the Army. Or maybe I would be a fat schoolteacher. How do you ever know?" Finally respected as the artist that he had aspired to be, Warhol asked later in the book: "Why do people think artists are special? It's just another job." Regardless of his comments, Warhol was both an artist and famous, and his legacy continues. In November, 1992, his painting *Marilyn X 100* sold at Sotheby's for $3.74 million, just short of the record $4 million another Warhol silk screen of Monroe sold for in 1990. And many of the doubts critics leveled against him while he was alive have been replaced with appreciation. Warhol's influence as a chronicler of the common moments of everyday life and the objects that come to represent those moments has been felt throughout the world, apparently discrediting Warhol's own self-assessment: "My work won't last," Bockris quoted him as once saying. "I was using cheap paint."

■ Works Cited

Acker, Kathy, "The Last Supper," *New Statesman and Society*, September 22, 1989, p. 44.

Amis, Martin, review of *The Andy Warhol Diaries*, *New York Times Book Review*, June 25, 1989, p. 9.

Bockris, Victor, *Warhol*, Muller, 1989.

Bogre, Michelle, "Andy Warhol," *American Photographer*, October, 1985, pp. 76-81.

Crawford, Pamela, "Andy Warhol's *Chelsea Girls*," *Cineaste*, winter, 1967-68, pp. 20-1.

Hornblower, Margot, "Garage Sale of the Century," *Time*, May 9, 1988, p. 90.

McPherson, William, review of *The Andy Warhol Diaries*, *Washington Post Book World*, August 13, 1989, p. 4.

Mekas, Jonas, "Movie Journal," *Village Voice*, August 13, 1964, p. 13.

Warhol, Andy, *The Philosophy of Andy Warhol (From A to B and Back Again)*, Harcourt, 1975.

Warhol, Andy, and Pat Hackett, *POPism: The Warhol '60s*, Harcourt, 1980.

■ For More Information See

BOOKS

American Artists on Art, Harper, 1982.

Andy Warhol: A Picture Show by the Artist, edited by Rainer Crone, translated by Martin Scutt, Rizzoli, 1987.

Brown, Andreas, *Andy Warhol, His Early Works, 1947-1959*, Gotham Book Mart, 1971.

Colacello, Bob, *Holy Terror: Andy Warhol Close Up*, HarperCollins, 1990.

Contemporary Artists, St. James Press, 1989, pp. 1011-14.

Contemporary Literary Criticism, Volume 20, Gale, 1982, pp. 414-23.

Contemporary Photographers, St. James Press, 1988, pp. 1090-91.

Coplans, John, Jonas Mekas, and Calvin Tomkins, *Andy Warhol*, New York Graphic Society, 1970.

Crone, Rainer, *Andy Warhol*, translated by John William Gabriel, Thames & Hudson, 1970.

Feldman, Frayda, and Jorg Schellmann, editors, *Andy Warhol Prints: A Catalogue Raisonne*, R. Feldman Fine Arts, 1985.

Finkelstein, Nat, *The Factory Years, 1964-1967*, St. Martin's, 1989.

Gidal, Peter, *Andy Warhol: Films and Painting*, Studio Vista Dutton Paperback, 1971.

Koch, Stephen, *Stargazer: Andy Warhol and His Films*, Praeger, 1973.

Makos, Christopher, *Warhol: A Personal Photographic Memoir*, Virgin, 1989.

Ratcliff, Carter, *Andy Warhol*, Abbeville Press, 1983.

Schickel, Richard, *Second Sight: Notes on Some Movies, 1965-1970*, Simon & Schuster, 1972, pp. 229-32.

Shanes, Eric, *Warhol, The Masterworks*, Portland House, 1991.

Smith, Patrick S., *Andy Warhol's Art and Films*, UMI Research Press, 1986.

Smith, Patrick S., *Warhol: Conversations about the Artist*, UMI Research Press, 1988.

Stein, Jean, and George Plimpton, editors, *Edie, An American Biography*, Knopf, 1982.

Taylor, John Russell, *Directors and Directions: Cinema for the Seventies*, Hill & Wang, 1975, pp. 136-64.

Tomkins, Calvin, *The Scene*, Viking, 1976.

Ultra Violet, *Famous for 15 Minutes: My Years with Andy Warhol*, Harcourt, 1988.

Viva, *Superstar*, Putnam, 1970.

Wilcock, John, *The Autobiography and Sex Life of Andy Warhol*, Other Scenes Inc., 1971.

PERIODICALS

Art in America, May, 1987; March, 1989.

Atlantic, August, 1989.

Chicago Tribune, November 17, 1985; April 24, 1988.

Chicago Tribune Book World, May 18, 1980.

Cineaste, winter, 1967-68, pp. 9-13.

Cosmopolitan, March, 1989.

Cue, November 14, 1970.

Detroit News, November 18, 1992, p. 8A.

Esquire, March, 1974.

Evergreen Review, April, 1967, pp. 28-31, 87-88.

Film Culture, spring, 1964, p. 13; summer, 1965, pp. 20-21; fall, 1965, pp. 62-63.

Film Quarterly, winter, 1967-68, p. 60; summer, 1968, p. 59; fall, 1969, pp. 41-44.

Films and Filming, June, 1971, pp. 72, 74.

Globe and Mail (Toronto), June 27, 1987; July 29, 1989.

House and Garden, December, 1987.

Interview, February, 1989; November, 1989.

Life, June 13, 1969; December, 1989.

Los Angeles Times, March 1, 1987; March 8, 1987; April 26, 1988; May 5, 1988; May 8, 1988, January 19, 1990.

Los Angeles Times Book Review, August 13, 1989, p. 4.

Nation, April 3, 1989.

National Observer, October 28, 1968.

New Republic, April 26, 1969; May 18, 1987.

Newsweek, December 2, 1968; April 22, 1974; September 15, 1975; December 3, 1979; March 24, 1980; February 22, 1988; April 18, 1988, pp. 60-64.

New York, March 9, 1987; March 7, 1988; October 31, 1988; May 29, 1989; January 27, 1992.

New Yorker, January 6, 1968, p. 74; October 27, 1975; April 27, 1987; April 10, 1989.

New York Times, December 17, 1967; May 18, 1969; September 17, 1969; November 9, 1969; February 26, 1987; February 28, 1987; April 2, 1987; December 10, 1987; April 11, 1988; April 15, 1988; April 25, 1988; June 14, 1989; August 22, 1989; October 3, 1989; October 8, 1989; November 26, 1989.

New York Times Book Review, January 12, 1969; October 7, 1973; September 14, 1975; November 20, 1988; June 25, 1989, p. 9.

New York Times Magazine, November 10, 1968.

Observer, June 18, 1989.

People, November 7, 1988; May 8, 1989; May 15, 1989.

Record (Hackensack, NJ), February 23, 1987.

Saturday Night, February, 1970.

Take One, May 10, 1970, p. 28.

Time, September 17, 1969; August 4, 1975; May 9, 1988, p. 90.

Times (London), February 24, 1987; May 13, 1989; June 24, 1989.

Times Literary Supplement, April 17, 1981.

Village Voice, February 21, 1967; June 6, 1968; January 16, 1969; February 20, 1969; May 8, 1969; July 2, 1970.

Vogue, March 1, 1970; February, 1989.

Washington Post, April 2, 1987; March 13, 1988; April 22, 1988; May 2, 1988; May 3, 1988.

Washington Post Book World, March 9, 1980; March 2, 1987.

World Monitor: The Christian Science Monitor Monthly, January, 1990.

Yale Literary Magazine, May, 1967, pp. 6-7.

Yale Review, autumn, 1989.

OBITUARIES

Chicago Tribune, February 23, 1987.

Los Angeles Times, February 23, 1987.

Newsweek, March 9, 1987.

New York Times, February 23, 1987.

People, March 9, 1987.

Rolling Stone, April 9, 1987.

Time, March 9, 1987.

Times (London), February 23, 1987.

Washington Post, February 23, 1987.°

—*Sketch by Roger M. Valade III*

Robert Westall

Personal

Full name, Robert Atkinson Westall; born October 7, 1929, in Tynemouth, Northumberland, England; died April 15, 1993, in London, England; son of Robert (a foreman and fitter at the local gas works) and Maggie Alexandra (Leggett) Westall; married Jean Underhill (an administrator), July 26, 1958 (divorced, 1990); children: Christopher (deceased). *Education:* University of Durham, B.A. (fine arts; with first class honors), 1953; Slade School, University of London, D.F.A., 1957. *Politics:* "Left-wing Conservative." *Religion:* Church of England. *Hobbies and other interests:* Designing, building, and sailing model yachts; Gothic architecture; local history; film; sculpting; religion and the supernatural; "cats (you have to earn their friendship), old clocks, Buddhist statues, bird-watching and people-watching, other people's gardens, ruins, and the sea."

Addresses

Home—1 Woodland Ave., Lymm, Cheshire WA13 0BT, England; and c/o Macmillan Publishers, 4 Little Essex St., London WC2R 3LF, England.

Career

Erdington Hall Secondary Modern School, Birmingham, England, art master, 1957-58; Keighley Boy's Grammar School, Yorkshire, England, art master, 1958-60; Sir John Deane's College, Northwich, England, art master and head of department, 1960-85, head of careers guidance, 1970-85; antiques dealer in Davenham, Cheshire, England, 1985-87; full-time writer, 1987-93. Director of Telephone Samaritans of Mid-Cheshire, 1965-75. *Military service:* British Army, Royal Signals, 1953-55; became lance corporal.

Awards, Honors

Carnegie Medal from Library Association of Great Britain, 1976, for *The Machine-Gunners,* and 1982, for *The Scarecrows;* Guardian Award commendation, 1976, for *The Machine Gunners; Boston Globe-Horn Book* awards, 1978, for *The Machine-Gunners,* 1982, for *Scarecrows,* and 1983, for *Break of Dark;* Carnegie Medal nomination and American Library Association selection as a Best Book for Young Adults, both 1979, for *The Devil on the Road;* Leseratten Prize (Germany), 1988, for *The Machine-Gunners,* 1990, for *Futuretrack Five,* and 1991, for *The Promise;* Children's Book Prize nomination, 1988, for *Urn Burial;* Senior Smarties Prize, 1989, and Children's Book Award commendation, both for *Blitzcat;* Carnegie Award commendation and Sheffield Children's Book Prize, both 1991, for *The Promise;* Guardian Award and Carnegie Award runner-up, both 1992, for *The Kingdom by the Sea.*

■ Writings

FICTION FOR YOUNG ADULTS

The Machine Gunners (also see below), Macmillan (London), 1975, Greenwillow, 1976.
The Wind Eye, Greenwillow, 1976.
The Watch House, Greenwillow, 1977.
The Devil on the Road, Macmillan, 1978, Greenwillow, 1979.
Fathom Five, Macmillan, 1979, Greenwillow, 1980.
The Scarecrows, Chatto & Windus, 1980, Greenwillow, 1981.
Break of Dark, Chatto & Windus, 1980, Greenwillow, 1982.
The Haunting of Chas McGill and Other Stories, Greenwillow, 1983.
Futuretrack Five, Greenwillow, 1983.
The Cats of Seroster, Greenwillow, 1984.
The Other: A Christmas Story, Macmillan, 1985.
The Witness, Macmillan, 1985.
Rachel and the Angel and Other Stories, Greenwillow, 1986.
Rosalie, Macmillan, 1987.
Urn Burial, Viking Kestral, 1987, Greenwillow, 1988.
The Creature in the Dark, illustrated by Liz Roberts, Blackie, 1988.
Ghosts and Journeys, Macmillan, 1988.
Ghost Abbey, Scholastic, 1988.
Blitzcat, Scholastic, 1989.
Old Man on a Horse, Blackie, 1989.
A Walk on the Wild Side, Methuen, 1989.
The Call and Other Stories, Viking Kestral, 1989.
Echoes of War, Viking Kestral, 1989, Farrar, Straus, 1991.
Cat!, Methuen, 1989.
The Kingdom by the Sea, Methuen, 1990, Farrar, Straus, 1991.
Stormsearch, Blackie, 1990, Farrar, Straus, 1992.
If Cats Could Fly, Methuen, 1990.
The Promise, Scholastic, 1991.
The Christmas Cat, Methuen, 1991.
The Stones of Muncaster Cathedral, Kestral, 1991, Farrar, Straus, 1993.
Yaxley's Cat, Scholastic, 1992.
The Fearful Lovers, Macmillan, 1992.
Size Twelve, Heinemann, 1992.
The Ghost in the Tower, Methuen, 1992.
In Camera and Other Stories, Scholastic, 1992.
A Place for Me, Macmillan, 1993.
A Trick of Light: Five Unnerving Stories, Scholastic, 1993.
Demons and Shadows, Farrar, Straus, 1993.

OTHER

(Editor) *Children of the Blitz: Memories of Wartime Childhood*, Viking, 1985.
The Machine Gunners (play; adapted from Westall's book of the same title), Macmillan, 1986.
(Editor) *Ghost Stories* (for children), illustrated by Sean Eckett, Kingfisher Books, 1988.
Antique Dust: Ghost Stories (for adults), Viking Kestral, 1989.

Staff writer for *Cheshire Life*, 1968-71. Art and architecture critic for *Chester Chronicle*, 1962-73; art critic for *Guardian*, 1970, 1980.

■ Sidelights

"Perhaps all the best books," wrote Robert Westall in *Signal*, "start by being written for only one child, and that child very close to you. They start when the child-within-the-author turns to the real child and says, 'Come away with me and I will show you a place you otherwise will never see, because it is buried under thirty, or three hundred or three thousand years of time.'" Westall bases this opinion on personal experience: it was not until he attempted to recreate his childhood as fiction for his twelve-year-old son that he emerged as a successful writer. The careful recollection for his son of the tensions of a childhood spent in wartime England resulted in Westall's first novel, *The Machine Gunners*, and immediately made him a prominent figure in contemporary young adult literature.

Since the publication of *The Machine Gunners*, Westall has written many well-received novels. The most notable of these include *Futuretrack Five*, *Urn Burial*, *The Scarecrows*, and *The Kingdom by the Sea*. While Westall's fiction ranges from historical drama to time-travel fantasy, in all his works a quality in the rendering of character lends even the most fantastic tale an aspect of reality. Westall's adolescent characters often indulge in violence and profanity and are not always heroic—behavior that Westall believes is closer to children's lives than most librarians and critics would care to admit. This has caused some controversy, but neither his audience nor his critics have denied the emotional power of Westall's best writing.

Robert Atkinson Westall was born October 7, 1929, in Tynemouth, Northumberland, England. His father, to whom he attributes the variety and vigor of his writing, "was a foreman-fitter at the local gasworks," Westall wrote in his *Something about the Author Autobiography Series (SAAS)* entry, "but to me he was the Oily Wizard. When he came home from work, he smelt of strange and terrible magic—benzine and sulfur hung around his overalls and a cap, so filthy you could see no pattern on it." Westall continued, "But his wizardry lay in more than that. I would watch him looking at an ailing engine, with his finger held lightly against it, feeling for vibration and his head cocked on one side, listening for the one tiny sound that would mean trouble. I have never seen such concentration."

As a boy Westall eagerly looked forward to trips to the gasworks, an industrial otherworld that provided the perfect backdrop for his father's mechanical wizardry. After work, however, the perpetual grime of the gasworks clashed with his father's cultivated talents, which included drawing and toymaking. Westall's father taught him to draw, and this early instruction put Westall on course to pursue an education, and later a career, in fine arts. But in his youth Westall took his artistic advantages for granted. Before starting school and learning otherwise, he thought anyone could draw. He remembered in *SAAS* that his appreciation of his father's talents was directed elsewhere: "Best of all were the stupendous toys he made for me in his spare time at work, in the summer when things were slack in the gas business."

His father's nurturing served Westall well when he started school. By then he was already reading and possessed an unwavering self-confidence. It was this trait above all others that Westall felt prevented him from suffering too much at the hands of overly strict British schoolmasters.

First Writing Efforts

As an adolescent Westall began his first experiments as a writer. "I wrote my first novel in the summer holidays when I was twelve," he recalled in *SAAS*. "In the loneliness of the four summer holidays that followed, I wrote four novels of increasing length and increasingly comprised of hopeless cliches borrowed from bad war movies and my parents' cowboy-novels.... I had been entrapped by the two classical snares of the teenage novelist, total self-indulgent wish-fulfillment and the re-use of a mass of cliches already third-hand and third-rate. I never dreamt of writing about my own life and times, as I regarded these as being so insufferably dull and boring that no one would want to read of them."

Westall's interest in writing was diverted when he began high school. He fell in with a new bunch of

friends who both eased his loneliness and left him with little time for writing. He was not to write seriously again for another fourteen years. In the meantime, Westall studied art. Sculpture was his primary concentration and he was "too busy carving funny shapes in stone or plaster" to give much thought to writing.

There were, however, two memorable exceptions. As a first year college student, Westall juxtaposed the peaceful memories of a bicycle trip and the hustle of his first college days into a short piece titled "Two Roads to Otterburn." The piece was published in the "Old Students Section" of Westall's high school magazine. After reading the piece, Westall's high school English teacher said, "You'll make a writer—if you go on writing honestly about what you *know*." Westall took the advice to heart, and seven years later, in 1956, while he was a graduate student at the University of London, he was again compelled to communicate his experiences in writing. The Soviet Union had just invaded Hungary, and Westall joined a student protest of Soviet aggression. Nearly ten thousand students marched on the Soviet embassy, where they were met by British police. There was a brief struggle between the students and the authorities, which left Westall so inspired that he wrote a four-thousand word editorial on the encounter. The piece was published in Westall's hometown newspaper, the *Newcastle Journal*. Despite these successes as a journalist, Westall still hadn't given a second thought to writing fiction.

After completing graduate school, Westall took a job teaching art in a rough district in Birmingham. He then married and found a teaching job at a boy's grammar school in Yorkshire. In 1960, Westall was offered a position as head of the art department at a four-hundred-year-old grammar school in Cheshire. "Writing couldn't have been further from my mind," he recalled. "I spent the summer holiday of 1961 laying crazy paving paths all over the garden of my new house. Six weeks doing nothing but handling stones and mixing concrete!"

An opportunity to write came to Westall two years later, when, inspired by the work of an engineer-turned-painter, he walked into the offices of the local newspaper and asked that the artist be given some publicity. The editor in charge agreed to Westall's request, but insisted that Westall write the necessary review of the artist's paintings. The piece was well received, and the editor asked Westall to write a regular art review. As a journalist, Westall learned to edit his own writing, to cut away the excess, and discuss abstract art in common terms without flaunting his critical vocabulary. As his reputation increased, Westall began to write for larger newspapers and magazines, eventually contributing antiques articles to *Homes and Gardens*. "As a journalist," Westall wrote in *SAAS*, "I learnt to write crisply, interestingly, and even amusingly—I think as a journalist I became a real pro."

The Machine Gunners

It was around this time that Westall resumed his attempts at fiction. At first, the novels he began were as unsuccessful as those he had written as a teen. Westall was discouraged—he thought he "might have gone on writing trash forever, but for something that happened as [his son's] twelfth birthday approached." His son Christopher had taken to playing with a gang of boys in the neighborhood, and they were in possession of a secret clubhouse, the whereabouts of which was a very closely guarded secret. This clubhouse had a leaky roof, and the leader of this group apparently knew something of Westall's experience with architecture, so he invited him out to the club house to look at the roof. Westall went and managed to fix the leak. More importantly, his visit to the secret clubhouse inspired him. An enlightened vision of his son's adolescence overwhelmed him with the desire to share his own childhood with the boy. Westall began to communicate across generations by writing, a chapter at a time, the story that was to become Westall's first published novel, *The Machine Gunners*. The completed manuscript sat for two years before it was submitted for publication.

When the novel was finally published, it won Great Britain's prestigious Carnegie Medal for excellence in children's literature. Set in England during World War II, *The Machine Gunners* tells the tale of five adolescent boys struggling to survive the German Blitz. When a German plane crashes near the boys' town, the leader of the group, Chas McGill, scavenges a machine gun from the rear of the plane which he then hides. In para-military fashion, he organizes the other boys around the weapon, intending to secretly use the gun to bring down other enemy planes. Throughout, Chas keeps the gang silent and loyal with a violent ferocity that eventually proves his undoing.

As a tale of unsupervised youth, *The Machine Gunners* has often been compared to William Golding's *Lord of the Flies* and has generated

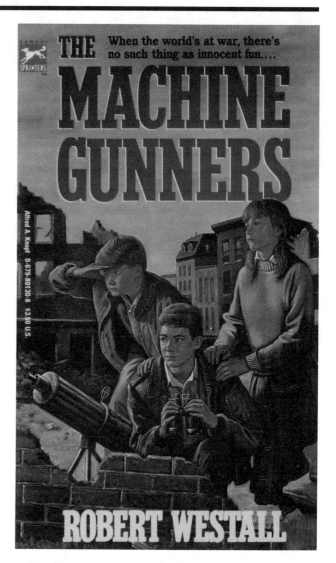

Five boys in wartime England recover a machine gun from a downed German plane in this 1975 work, a Carnegie Medal winner.

similar controversy. Some critics objected to Westall's graphic portrayal of the violence employed by Chas to keep the gang loyal, and many also questioned the common use of profanity in the dialogue. Westall answered the latter criticism in *Library Association Record*: "Swearing can be seen as part of the male adolescent's toughness ethic. Unlike shoplifting ..., it is not criminal. Unlike smoking, drinking and riding mopeds too fast it is not lethal either. So swearing only concerns me to the degree with which I want adolescents to empathize with my characters. . . . So I allowed the boys in my book *minimal* swearing." In the same article, Westall commented on the violence of *The Machine Gunners*: "The hero of the book, Chas, as a result of using violence loses his best friend, his gang, his most precious possession (the machine gun) and his good name. Was there anything else for him to lose? Surely my whole theme is violence does not pay?''

Critics who favored the book praised Westall for its uncompromisingly realistic depiction of life during wartime. Aidan Chambers found the book's characters and episodes to ''add up to a vivid three-dimensional picture of that time and place: the battered streets, the refugee families, the weary nights and days, the shortages, the acts of courage, love, and decent neighborliness, and the moments of desperation, cowardice, and stupidity too.'' Similar praise was offered by Margery Fisher, who wrote in *Growing Point*, ''I can think of few writers who have put on paper as successfully as Robert Westall has done in *The Machine Gunners* the sheer muddle of [World War II] and the day-to-day difficulty, for civilians at least, of deciding what was important.''

Although his first novel had achieved success, Westall found himself trying to win the approval of those critics who considered *The Machine Gunners* an unworthy recipient of the Carnegie Medal. In an article in Signal magazine, Westall later described the influence of negative criticism on his next several novels: ''To my shame, I tried [to please the critics]. Crawlingly and contemptibly, though unconsciously, I tried. The amount of swearing in my books dropped; the intellectual content, the scholarship and research grew. I began writing books for the children of publishers, librarians, and the literary gent of *The Times*. . . . Now that I am at last conscious of what I was doing, I look round and see so many 'good' children's books written for the same bloody audience. Books that gain splendid reviews, win prizes, make reputations and are all unreadable by the majority of the children.''

From Realistic to Supernatural Novels

Despite the fact that Westall felt he was writing more for adult critics and parents than children, he maintained a robust popularity with young people. He abandoned the strict realism of *The Machine Gunners* and turned to the supernatural plots of the popular books *The Wind Eye* and *The Devil on the Road*. ''I write two kinds of books,'' Westall stated in *SAAS*, ''realistic, earthy, comical books; and spooky books. And they really have no relationship to each other.'' *The Machine Gunners* certainly belongs to the former category, while Westall's second Carnegie Medal winner, *The Scarecrows*, written in 1980, belongs to the latter.

The Scarecrows relates the tale of Simon Brown, a young teenage boy whose father has recently died. When his mother remarries, Simon is filled with an almost uncontrollable rage, directed primarily at his step-father. In a supernatural twist, Simon's anger rouses the spirits of the past at an old mill near his home. These spirits are manifest in the forms of three lifelike scarecrows, which move daily through the fields toward the house. ''Simon identifies them as participants in a pre-war tragedy of passion that ended in murder and closed the mill forever,'' observed Sara Hayes in the *Times Literary Supplement*. ''The events of the past are going to be re-enacted unless Simon can break the power of the mill.''

In spite of the frightening presence of the scarecrows, Hayes found that how ''people talk and relate to each other, to their families and to themselves is what [Westall's] work is really about. And despite its earnest intent, his story is exciting, agonizing, tender and terrifying by turns, and

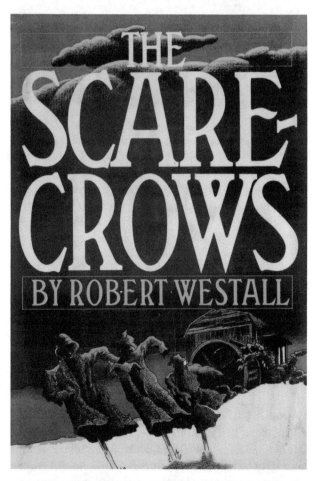

In this 1980 thriller, a boy's rage at his stepfather arouses murderous spirits, manifested in the form of three scarecrows who are intent on recreating their deadly past.

Believing his family killed in a Nazi bombing raid, young Harry travels across war-torn England in this award-winning 1990 novel.

never fails to grip." Neil Phillip, writing in the *Times Educational Supplement*, presented less positive criticism of the book: "Robert Westall is a writer with an obsession: violence.... [He] is a talented writer, capable of achieving powerful emotional effect, but in *The Scarecrows* he eschews the discipline which should harness the passion. The book has no emotional shape, it simply blasts the reader with a scream of pain and insecurity."

While characters like Simon Brown usually manage to overcome their inherently flawed personal situations, Westall's vision of society is somewhat bleak. "I cannot say I like the way the world is going," Westall remarked. "There have been advances; more prosperity in the West; a growth of conscience among the Western middle classes; the liberation, still incomplete, of women. But there has been a decay in the way people belonged together, looked after each other, and were proudly determined to stand on their own two feet."

Westall expresses this sentiment in literary fashion in his pessimistic novel about the future, *Futuretrack Five*. The novel is set in Great Britain in the early twenty-first century, where the entire social order is monitored and directed by Laura, a supercomputer with a deliberately disarming name. Society is sorted according to a nationally administered series of tests. Those who fail are sent to the ruined cities to scrape together a living in whatever manner possible. Higher test scores result in greater privilege, although even the pursuits of the leisure class (video games, sex, and motorcycle racing) are by nature suspect. Henry Kitson, the protagonist, uncovers a government plan to reduce the population through genetic control. Together, he and his companion Keri set out to undermine the government's sinister plot, resulting in a final confrontation with Laura.

Fisher commented on the book in *Growing Point:* "The sardonic ending, with its suggestion that human nature has done little to improve in two thousand years, should not in fact induce pessimism so much as argument and resolve in the young people who see reflected in this turbulent, incisive tale a challenge to their intelligence and goodwill, a metaphor of the kind of world which apathy could in fact bring about."

Kingdom by the Sea

In a later work, *Kingdom by the Sea*, Westall returned to realistic depictions of life in Great Britain during World War II. Westall recounts the fictional journey of Harry, who believes he is the sole surviving member of his family after a bomb raid by the Germans. Determined to avoid being handed over to an insufferable relative, Harry sets out to make his own way in war-torn England. Every experience of Harry's nomadic life becomes a trial, from the simple act of securing food to resisting the advances of a homosexual officer. Harry weathers this adversity well and manages to emerge more mature and ready to face future challenges. As his journey nears its end, Harry meets Mr. Murgatroyd, whose own son was lost at sea during the war. Mr. Murgatroyd takes Harry in as his adopted son. Harry finds his "kingdom by the sea" utterly blissful and feels the entire world opening before him as new worlds of learning and adventure are revealed to him. In the end, however, Harry's family is found to have survived, and he must return to the small town of his childhood, a place far too small to contain the worldly young man Harry has become.

"For the remainder of his adolescence, Harry will dream of his other life," explained Mary M. Burns in *Horn Book*, "biding time until he can once more journey to that country of the heart and mind which both sustained and changed him." In an article in *Books for Children*, N. Thomas reached a similar conclusion: "The twist in the tale is a poignant reminder that in war there are few truly happy endings."

Following *Kingdom by the Sea*, Westall published nearly another dozen books before his death in 1993. In addition to his novels for young adults, he adapted *The Machine Gunners* into a play and edited what would become a well-received collection of memoirs, *Children of the Blitz: Memories of Wartime Childhood*. Westall's books remain popular, and *The Machine Gunners* is so widely read in England that it has become a standard text in British classrooms. Westall's highly charged, and sometimes controversial, writing will generate interest for a long time to come, particularly because his characters so clearly depict the struggles of adolescence. His insight into the lives and minds of the youth of both his own and his son's generation continues to startle readers by appealing to what Westall, writing for *SAAS*, called "children's love of inevitable catastrophe."

■ Works Cited

Burns, Mary M., review of *The Kingdom by the Sea*, *Horn Book*, January/February, 1992, p. 76.

Chambers, Aidan, "War Efforts," *Times Literary Supplement*, September 19, 1975, p. 1056.

Fisher, Margery, review of *Futuretrack Five*, *Growing Point*, January, 1984, p. 4194.

Fisher, Margery, review of *The Machine Gunners*, *Growing Point*, October, 1975, pp. 2707-8.

Hayes, Sarah, "Threats from Within," *Times Literary Supplement*, March 27, 1981, p. 339.

Phillip, Neil, "Through a Film of Blood," *Times Educational Supplement*, May 8, 1981, p. 27.

Thomas, N., review of *The Kingdom by the Sea*, *Books for Children*, summer, 1992, p. 24.

Westall, Robert, "Defence of—and by—Author Robert Westall," *Library Association Record*, January, 1977, pp. 38-9.

Westall, Robert, "How Real Do You Want Your Realism?," *Signal*, January, 1979, pp. 34-46.

Westall, Robert, autobiographical entry in *Something about the Author Autobiography Series*, Volume 2, Gale, 1986, pp. 305-23.

■ For More Information See

BOOKS

Children's Literature Review, Volume 13, Gale, 1987.

Contemporary Literary Criticism, Volume 17, Gale, 1981.

PERIODICALS

Horn Book, August, 1976.

Junior Bookshelf, April, 1979.

New York Times Book Review, May 16, 1982.

School Librarian, June, 1979.

School Library Journal, April, 1993, p. 144.

Times Literary Supplement, December 10, 1975; December 14, 1979; March 27, 1981; July 23, 1982; November 30, 1984; October 11, 1985.

Voice of Youth Advocates, June, 1993, p. 96.

Washington Post Book World, November 7, 1976; November 11, 1979.

OBITUARIES

School Library Journal, June, 1993, p. 134.°

—*Sketch by Ronie-Richele Garcia-Johnson*

Acknowledgments

Acknowledgments

Grateful acknowledgment is made to the following publishers,
authors, and artists for their kind permission to reproduce copyrighted material.

MARGARET ATWOOD. Cover of *The Handmaid's Tale*, by Margaret Atwood. Reprinted by permission of Random House, Inc./ Cover of *The Edible Woman*, by Margaret Atwood. Bantam Books, 1991. Copyright © 1969 by Margaret Atwood. Reprinted by permission of Bantam Books, a division of Bantam Doubleday Dell Publishing Group, Inc./ Cover of *Cat's Eye*, by Margaret Atwood. Bantam Books, 1989. Copyright © 1988 by O.W. Toad, Ltd./ Cover art copyright © 1989 by Fred Marcellino. Reprinted by permission of Bantam Books, a division of Bantam Doubleday Dell Publishing Group, Inc./ Photograph © Jerry Bauer.

VERA CLEAVER. Illustration from *Ellen Grae*, by Vera Cleaver. Copyright © 1967 by Vera and William J. Cleaver. Illustrations by Ellen Raskin. Reprinted by permission of HarperCollins Publishers, Inc./ Cover of *Where the Lilies Bloom*, by Vera and Bill Cleaver. Copyright © 1969 by Vera and William J. Cleaver. Illustrations by Jim Spanfeller. Reprinted in the United States by permission of HarperCollins Publishers, Inc. Reprinted in the British Commonwealth by permission of Hamish Hamilton, a division of Penguin Books Ltd./ Cover of *The Kissimmee Kid*, by Vera and Bill Cleaver. Copyright © 1981 by Vera A. Cleaver and William J. Cleaver. Cover illustration copyright © 1991 by Daniel Mark Duffy. Reprinted by permission of Greenwillow Books, a division of William Morrow and Company, Inc./ Cover of *The Whys and Wherefores of Littabelle Lee*, by Vera and Bill Cleaver. Atheneum, 1973. Copyright © 1973 by Vera and Bill Cleaver. Reprinted by permission of Atheneum Publishers, an imprint of Macmillan Publishing Company./ Cover of *Belle Pruit*, by Vera Cleaver. Copyright © 1988 by Vera Cleaver. Cover art copyright © 1988 by Deborah Chabrian. Cover copyright © 1990 by Harper & Row, Publishers, Inc. Reprinted by permission of HarperCollins Publishers, Inc./ Movie still from *Where the Lilies Bloom*, courtesy of United Artists.

J. CALIFORNIA COOPER. Cover of *Family*, by J. California Cooper. Copyright © 1991 by J. California Cooper. Cover illustration by Vivienne Flesher. Reprinted by permission of Doubleday, a division of Bantam Doubleday Dell Publishing Group, Inc./ Cover of *Homemade Love*, by J. California Cooper. Copyright © 1986 by J. California Cooper. Cover design by Karen Katz. Reprinted by permission of St. Martin's Press, Incorporated./ Cover of *A Piece of Mine*, by J. California Cooper. Copyright © 1984 by Joan Cooper. Cover art: detail of a quilt, from *The Afro-American Tradition in Decorative Arts*, by John Michael Vlach. Copyright © 1978 by The Cleveland Museum of Art. Cover design by Sarah Levin. Reprinted by permission of The Cleveland Museum of Art./ Cover of *Some Soul to Keep*, by J. California Cooper. Copyright © 1987 by J. California Cooper. Jacket illustration copyright © 1988 by Sandra Dionisi. Reprinted by permission of St. Martin's Press, Incorporated./ Photograph by Robert Allen.

ANNE FRANK. Illustrations from *The Last Seven Months of Anne Frank*, by Willy Lindwer. English translation copyright © 1991 by Random House, Inc. Copyright © 1988 by Willy Lindwer. Reprinted by permission of Willy Lindwer./ Cover of *Anne Frank: The Diary of a Young Girl*, translated from the Dutch by B.M. Mooyaart-Doubleday. Copyright, 1952 by Otto H. Frank. Cover copyright © 1968 by Pocket Books. Reprinted by permission of Pocket Books, a division of Simon & Schuster, Inc./ Photograph of the secret annex entrance, courtesy of The Consulate General of The Netherlands./ Movie still from *Diary of Anne Frank*, courtesy of Twentieth Century Fox./ Photograph, The Granger Collection, NY.

WILLIAM GIBSON. Cover of *Count Zero*, by William Gibson. Copyright © 1986 by William Gibson. Cover art by Richard Berry. Reprinted by permission of The Berkley Publishing Group./ Cover of *Neuromancer*, by William Gibson. Copyright © 1984 by William Gibson. Cover art by Richard Berry. Reprinted by permission of The Berkley Publishing Group./ Cover of *Burning Chrome*, by William Gibson. Copyright © 1986 by William Gibson. Cover art by Richard Berry. Reprinted by permission of The Berkley Publishing Group./ Cover of *Mona Lisa Overdrive*, by William Gibson. Copyright © 1988 by William Gibson. Cover art copyright © 1989 by Will Cormier. Reprinted by permission of Bantam, a division of Bantam Doubleday Dell Publishing Group, Inc./ Photograph by Alex-Waterhouse Hayward.

JOANNE GREENBERG. Cover of *In This Sign*, by Joanne Greenberg. Copyright © 1970 by Joanne Greenberg. Reprinted by permission of Avon Books, New York./ Cover of *I Never Promised You a Rose Garden*, by Joanne Greenberg. Copyright © 1964 by Joanne Greenberg. Reprinted by permission of Dutton Signet, a division of Penguin Books USA Inc./ Cover of *Rites of Passage*, by Joanne Greenberg. Copyright © 1966, 1967, 1968, 1969, 1970, 1971, 1972 by Joanne Greenberg. Reprinted by permission of Avon Books, New York./ Jacket of *The Far Side of Victory*, by Joanne Greenberg. Copyright © 1983 by Joanne Greenberg. Jacket design by Paul Bacon. Reprinted by permission of Paul Bacon./ Photograph courtesy Joanne Greenberg.

GREG AND TIM HILDEBRANDT. Cover by Tim Hildebrandt from *Sweet Silver Blues*, by Glen Cook. Copyright © 1987 by Glen Cook. Reprinted by permission of Dutton Signet, a division of Penguin Books USA Inc./ Cover of *Pinocchio*, by Carlo Collodi. Cover and interior graphics © 1986 by The Unicorn Publishing House. Artwork © 1986 by Greg Hildebrandt. Reprinted by permission of The Unicorn Publishing House./ Illustrations by Greg and Tim Hildebrandt from *The Art of the Brothers Hildebrandt*, by Ian Summers. Text copyright © 1979 by Ian Summers. Artwork copyright © 1979 by Greg Hildebrandt and Tim Hildebrandt. Reprinted by permission of Ballantine Books, a division of Random House, Inc.

LANGSTON HUGHES. Cover of *Selected Poems of Langston Hughes*, by Langston Hughes. Copyright © 1959 by Langston Hughes, copyright renewed 1987 by George Houston Bass, Surviving Executor of the Estate of Langston Hughes, Deceased. Cover design by Pamela Scheier. Reprinted by permission of Random House, Inc./ Cover of *Not without Laughter*, by Langston Hughes. Copyright © 1985 by Macmillan Publishing Company. Cover design by Mario J. C. Pulice. Reprinted by permission of Macmillan Publishing Company./ Cover of *The Ways of White Folks*, by Langston Hughes. Copyright © 1933, 1934 by Alfred A. Knopf, Inc. Copyright renewed 1962 by Langston Hughes. Reprinted by permission of Random House, Inc./ Cover of *The Best of Simple*, by Langston Hughes. Copyright © 1961 by Langston Hughes, copyright © 1989 renewed by George Houston Ball. Cover illustration by Bernhard Nast. Reprinted by permission of Hill and Wang, a division of Farrar, Straus and Giroux, Inc./ Cover of *The First Book of Jazz*, by Langston Hughes. Copyright © 1955, 1976 by Franklin Watts, Inc. Cover design by Paul Gamarello. Reprinted by permission of Franklin Watts, Inc./ Photograph of Hughes with Gwendolyn Brooks, courtesy of the Beinecke Rare Book and Manuscript Library, Yale University./ Photograph, AP/Wide World Photos.

LYNN JOHNSTON. Illustrations by Lynn Johnston from her *If This Is a Lecture, How Long Will It Be?*. Copyright © 1990 by Lynn Johnston. *For Better or for Worse*, copyright Lynn Johnston Prod., Inc. Reprinted by permission of Universal Press Syndicate. All rights reserved./ Illustrations by Lynn Johnston from her *Just One More Hug*. Copyright © 1984 by Lynn Johnston. *For Better or for Worse*, copyright Lynn Johnston Prod., Inc. Reprinted by permission of Universal Press Syndicate. All rights reserved./ Cover of *Hi, Mom! Hi, Dad!*, by Lynn Johnston. Copyright © 1977, 1992 by Lynn Johnston Productions Inc., and Lynn Johnston. Reprinted by permission of the publisher, Meadowbrook Press./ Photographs courtesy Lynn Johnston.

NORMA JOHNSTON. Jacket of *A Nice Girl Like You*, by Norma Johnston. Atheneum, 1980. Copyright © 1980 by Norma Johnston. Jacket painting copyright © 1980 by Judith Gwyn Brown. Reprinted by permission of Judith Gwyn Brown./ Jacket of *The Crucible Year*, by Norma Johnston. Atheneum, 1979. Copyright © 1979 by Norma Johnston. Jacket painting by Kinuko Craft. Reprinted by permission of Kinuko Craft./ Jacket of *The Time of the Cranes*, by Norma Johnston. Copyright © 1990 by Dryden Harris S. John, Inc. Copyright © 1990 by Macmillan Publishing Company, a division of Macmillan, Inc. Copyright © 1990 by Wende Caporale. Reprinted by permission of Wende Caporale./ Jacket of *The Keeping Days*, by Norma Johnston. Atheneum, 1973. Copyright © 1973 by Norma Johnston. Jacket by Velma Ilsley. Reprinted by permission of Atheneum Publishers, an imprint of Macmillan Publishing Company./ Photograph by Pitcher.

DIANA WYNNE JONES. Jacket of *Aunt Maria*, by Diana Wynne Jones. Copyright © 1991 by Diana Wynne Jones. Jacket art copyright © 1991 by Jos. A. Smith. Reprinted by permission of Greenwillow Books, a division of William Morrow and Company, Inc./ Jacket of *The Ogre Downstairs*, by Diana Wynne Jones. Copyright © 1974 by Diana Wynne Jones. Jacket painting copyright © 1990 by Jos. A. Smith. Reprinted by permission of Greenwillow Books, a division of William Morrow and Company, Inc./ Jacket of *Howl's Moving Castle*, by Diana Wynne Jones. Copyright © 1986 by Diana Wynne Jones. Jacket painting by Jos. A. Smith. Reprinted by permission of Greenwillow Books, a division of William Morrow and Company, Inc./ Cover of *Dogsbody*, by Diana Wynne Jones. Copyright © 1975 by Diana Wynne Jones. Cover art copyright © 1990 by Pamela Patrick. Reprinted by permission of Alfred A. Knopf, Inc./ Photograph courtesy of Diana Wynne Jones.

RON KOERTGE. Cover of *Where the Kissing Never Stops*, by Ron Koertge. Copyright © 1986 by Ronald Koertge. Reprinted by permission of Avon Books, New York./ Jacket of *The Harmony Arms*, by Ron Koertge. Copyright © 1992 by Ron Koertge. Jacket collage by Amy L. Wasserman. Reprinted by permission of Little, Brown and Company./ Cover of *The Arizona Kid*, by Ron Koertge. Copyright © 1988 by Ron Koertge. Reprinted by permission of Avon Books, New York./ Photograph courtesy of Ron Koertge.

JULIUS LESTER. Cover of *The Knee-High Man and Other Tales*, by Julius Lester. Text copyright © 1972 by Julius Lester. Pictures copyright © 1972 by Ralph Pinto. Reprinted in the United States by permission of Dial Books for Young Readers, a division of Penguin Books USA Inc./ Cover of *This Strange New Feeling*, by Julius Lester. Copyright © 1981 by Julius Lester. Reprinted by permission of Scholastic Inc./ Cover of *Black Folktales*, by Julius Lester. Text copyright © 1969 by Julius Lester. Cover illustration by Ron Flemmings./ Cover of *To Be a Slave*, by Julius Lester. Text copyright © 1968 by Julius Lester. Illustrations copyright © 1968 by Tom Feelings. Reprinted by permission of Scholastic Inc./ Photograph from *Lovesong: Becoming a Jew*, by Julius Lester. Copyright © 1988 by Julius Lester. Reprinted by permission of Little, Brown and Company.

SHARON BELL MATHIS. Cover of *Teacup Full of Roses*, by Sharon Bell Mathis. Copyright © 1972 by Sharon Bell Mathis. Cover copyright © 1972 by Viking Penguin. Cover illustration by Reynold Ruffins. Reprinted by permission of Viking Penguin, a division of Penguin Books USA Inc./ Cover of *Listen for the Fig Tree*, by Sharon Bell Mathis. Copyright

Cumulative Index

Author/Artist Index

The following index gives the number of the volume
in which an author/artist's biographical sketch appears.